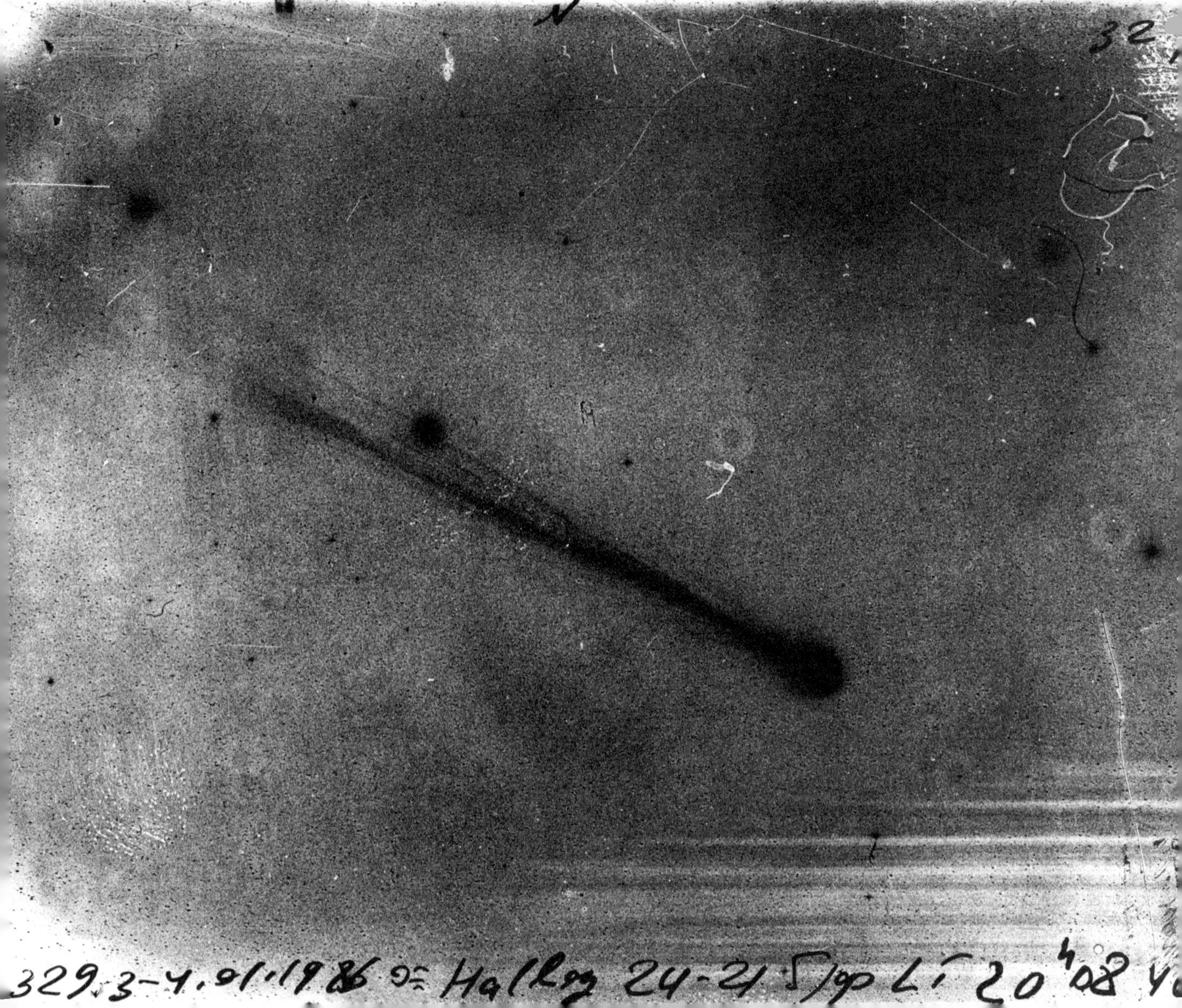
N
32
329.3-4.01.1986 Halley 24-21 Sep Li 20ʰ08

GREAT IS THE SCIENTIST'S PRIVILEGE
WHAT IS SOWN MUST GROW FROM IDEAS.

Borys Grinov
Director of the Institute for Scintillation Materials
Kharkiv, Ukraine

SOVIET SCIENTIFIC INSTITUTES

ERIC LUSITO

FUEL

A GLORIOUS AND AGING EXPERIMENT: SOCIALIST SCIENTIFIC INSTITUTION BUILDING

Paul Josephson

The Soviet Union, at its founding a country of illiterate peasants, woefully backward agriculture and barely nascent factory production, was transformed into a scientific and industrial superpower in 25 short years. Soviet leaders saw modern science and technology, freed of 'bourgeois' organisations and ideologies, as the key to rapid modernisation. Scientific specialists, if distrustful of Bolshevik intentions, welcomed the state's interest in supporting the scientific enterprise. Towards the utopian goal of building a vanguard workers' paradise, communist leaders endorsed the dreams of experts to expand the fragile tsarist system of universities and poorly equipped research centres into a vast network of institutes covering the entire spectrum of scientific disciplines. In the 1920s the number of research establishments increased manyfold. After World War II, with the Cold War impetus to meet and surpass Western advances in space exploration, atomic energy, and other strategic fields, the number of institutes and scientific workers expanded rapidly again, including within the union republics of the USSR. By the eve of the break-up of the USSR, the country had 1.3 million specialists amounting to one-third of the world's engineers and one-quarter of its physicists.

Eric Lusito's photographs of Soviet Scientific Institutes capture the constructivist verve, geographical reach and disciplinary breadth of these facilities. Scientific research institutes arose in all climates and situations, from the Arctic north to the Central Asian deserts; from the conquered countries of the Baltic to those of the East European Soviet bloc dominated by the USSR during the Cold War. They were established to harness science to the economy and to celebrate unlimited human potentiality. Every tile mural in the entryway of every institute claims inevitable

scientific progress: the taming of the power of the atom, the piercing of the secrets of the galaxies, the formulation of new chemicals. Control rooms with multitudinous dials indicate the command of specialists over each aspect of complex physical processes. The public embraced their early successes in space exploration and atomic energy, and more than any other group of scientists, Soviet physicists appeared on television shows and in newspapers and magazines. Just as significantly, they were often in positions of authority within the Communist Party. It seemed there was little that could go wrong.

Unfortunately, empty corridors and solitary researchers in many of the photos reveal another side to the story: a mere 35 years after the fall of communism, the rusty equipment and peeling paint hint at the fragility of socialist science. It was planned, funded and controlled from above, and this meant that scientists were denied the autonomy needed to adjust quickly to any crisis. Leaders insisted on immediate applications and thus weakened the foundations of basic research.

In the uncertain years after the collapse of the USSR, institutes lost both financial support and the ability to attract younger scholars. The sciences in Russia and the other nations of the former Soviet Union have fallen into disarray. Budgets have dried up, bills remain unpaid, workers are let go. The photographs capture the squalor of abandoned science: lonely instruments in otherwise empty rooms, tired walls adorned with messages and portraits from a past era – Soviet leader Vladimir Lenin (1870–1924) and scientist Igor Kurchatov (1903–1960), beloved hero of the Soviet atomic bomb project, dead since 1960 – and among it all the occasional, aging specialist. Obsolete experimental reactors, some of them no longer functioning, indicate the failed promise of nuclear power and the peaceful atom. Most of the former republics, now independent countries, have turned to the European Union, Japan and the United States to supplement meagre budgets, and have joined international research programmes that were closed to them when they were part of the Soviet bloc.

And yet the world of science has never experienced such determined institutional growth as that under Soviet rule. Socialist science pursued discovery in every imaginable branch of the economy. One institute focused exclusively on peat and coal tar products, another on reagents, another on medicines never before produced in Russia, another on motors and dynamos, another on radio technology, another on nascent hydraulics and aeronautics, another on metallurgy, another on heat engineering, on oil, on the fishing industry, on forestry, on ceramics, on ball bearings, on textiles, on locomotives, and so on and on. The photos here concern mainly the institutes of basic rather than applied science, and of those, primarily the physical sciences.

Lusito takes us through the corridors of institutes in countries unwillingly forced into the socialist orbit: the Baltic nations, Ukraine, Central Asia and East Central Europe, which was subjugated to the USSR from 1945 until the Berlin Wall fell in 1989, with the USSR collapsing two years later. The Bolsheviks vanquished such briefly independent countries as Ukraine, Georgia and Armenia during the Civil War (1918–1920). Under Joseph Stalin, who signed a non-aggression pact with Adolf Hitler to divide Eastern Europe between them in 1939, the USSR conquered the independent Baltic states. After the World War II the regime arrested and slaughtered their leaderships, condemned tens of thousands of citizens to slave labour camps in Siberia, incorporated the nations into its empire as republics, and eventually approved expansion of the scientific enterprise in each of them. A number of national academies of science opened in the 1940s and 1950s. The only republic without a new academy was Russia itself, though it was home to the prestigious

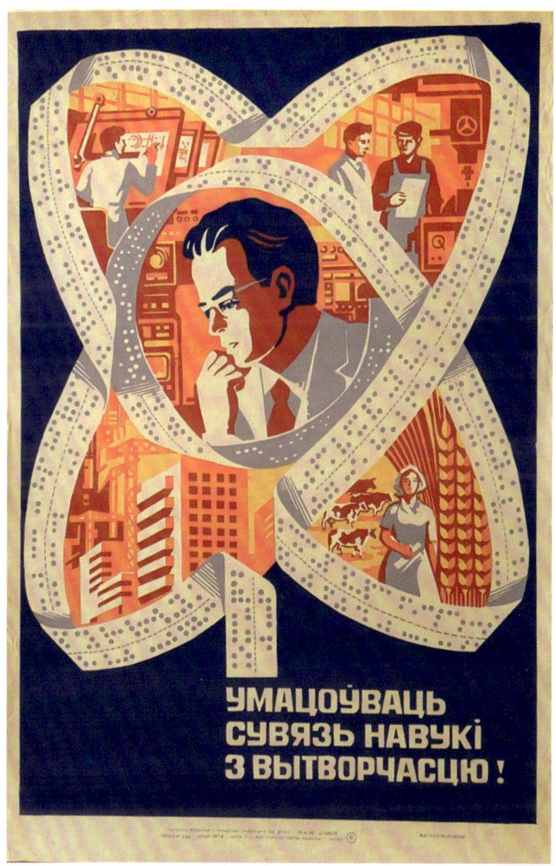

'Strengthen the Connection between Science and Agriculture!' (1982)
Silk screen poster by Roman Malinovsky.

Soviet Academy of Sciences founded by Peter the Great in 1725 – as many another 18th-century European king and queen did as a sign of their enlightened rule. In similar fashion, Hungary established its Academy in 1827, and the Czech Academy was founded in 1890. Under Soviet rule, the moribund Tsarist academy switched focus from the humanities to the sciences and increased the number of high-performing institutes and researchers.

Scientific research institutes were established in response to a series of pressures and trends: the search for and promise of modernity; the development of power, transport, production and other applications that would ensure the true path to the socialist wonderland; the use of science as a force of Soviet Russian colonialism over conquered territory; and, through its great and varied achievements, to demonstrate to the West, and particularly to the US, that socialism was superior to capitalism.

The Growth of the Soviet Scientific Enterprise
After the Russian Revolution in 1917 scientists and communist activists reached a difficult accommodation. Lenin protected scientists from blanket charges of being agents of the bourgeoisie; they were mistrusted by party administrators and radical workers, but the socialist reconstruction of the scientific enterprise required the transformation of so-called bourgeois specialists into loyal scientists. Many were won over by the huge increase in funding under the Bolsheviks. Between 1918 and 1919, 33 research institutes were founded. From 1928 to 1932 with the onset of the first five-year plan, the number of research institutes increased by another 50 per cent. By the mid-1930s Stalin had established a new scientific intelligentsia. Many scientists had been marshalled into the service of the state, others were drawn from the burgeoning working class, and still others – some of whom worked in the institutes captured in these photographs – were arrested, sent to labour camps and murdered, which treatment served to cow other specialists into silent allegiance.

During World War II the creation of scientific academies and institutes in the union republics accelerated, often triggered by the evacuation of entire facilities and their personnel to these distant places just before the Nazi Wehrmacht conquered the western territories. These then served as the foundations for new institutes, many of which are photographed here.

After the death of Stalin in 1953, physicists assumed an almost mythic presence in the Soviet Union, benefitting from a cult based on their success in nuclear weaponry, atomic-power engineering, space exploration and the applications of radioisotopes to industry and agriculture. The cult of science was part of the general environment of de-Stalinisation in which Soviet scientists became prominent actors in the political arena, reasserting control over the scientific enterprise. They demanded the right to embark on new research programmes, including those without immediate or obvious practical application. Physicists took advantage of the Communist Party belief that scientific success would contribute to the legitimacy of the Soviet regime.

The Cold War provided another impetus to institutional growth, especially under the leadership of Nikita Khrushchev (1953–1964). He initiated a series of reforms in Soviet society, abandoning some aspects of Stalinism, although maintaining one-party rule. The goal of scientific reform was to reinvigorate the Soviet economy. Leading specialists and party officials recognised that, for all of the quantitative indicators of scientific excellence, the quality of research results and the slow pace of innovation in industry left much to be desired. In spite of official pronouncements to the contrary – notwithstanding the example of Sputnik in 1957 – Soviet science lagged behind its European and American counterparts. Along with the Khrushchev reforms giving greater autonomy to scientists to define their foci of research, was the increase in the total number of scientists from 162,500 in 1950 to 665,000 in 1965. An entire city of science with 20 institutes, in Akademgorodok in Siberia, opened in the late 1950s.

As in the United States, the military enterprise expanded rapidly during the Cold War. Seemingly no expense was barred. The director of the Soviet atomic bomb project, Igor Kurchatov, presided over the creation of entire cities dedicated solely to military or scientific endeavour, built in short order, often by prisoners; in Russia today there remain 40 of these closed military research and development sites. Moscow subsequently approved the creation of nuclear research institutes in the republics and the socialist nations of East-Central Europe, and made available to them research reactors and enriched uranium, and training programmes to fill them. These include facilities in Romania and Hungary shown in this book. Between 1940 and 1985 the number of scientific research institutes in the USSR grew more than threefold from just under 800 to over 2,600.

Reactors to the Republics!

Advances in both civilian and military nuclear applications were a major stimulus to institutional growth. As part of a worldwide competition to demonstrate commitment to the 'peaceful atom', the US and the USSR supported this effort at home and among their allies with isotopes, enriched fuel, particle accelerators and several models of experimental reactor. Such reactors serve a variety of research purposes including materials science, biomedicine, genetics, and nuclear processes. From the 1950s, the Soviets' nuclear establishment installed Standard Research Reactors (IRT-2000) at facilities in Tomsk, Sverdlovsk, Salaspils in Latvia, Tbilisi in Georgia (page 56), and Dubna. They commissioned Water-cooled, Water-moderated Reactors (VVR) in Gatchina, Obninsk, Kyiv in Ukraine, Almaty in Kazakhstan, and several East European socialist nations.

Hungary, with its rich tradition in the physical sciences, acquired one such reactor (page 68) against a backdrop of political turmoil. With its domestic political freedoms destroyed in the Soviet invasion of 1956 – which led to 2,500 people killed and 200,000 sent into exile – Hungary's socialist leaders determined nonetheless to follow the Soviet path to the 'peaceful atom', partly to maintain contact with Western specialists. In 1950 the Hungarian Academy of Sciences in Budapest founded the Institute of Nuclear Techniques (KFKI). Its research foci included materials science, radiation studies and, later, solid-state physics, optics, and particle and reactor physics, using a Soviet-supplied unit.

Still in operation today, the experimental reactor serves Hungary's nuclear power industry with its four Soviet-designed reactors in operation at Paks 1 – and, to the consternation of the European Community, with construction underway on two new Rosatom 1,200 MW units at Paks 2, financed by the Putin government. In light of the Soviet Russian suppression of the Hungarian revolution in 1956 and the draining of resources from Eastern Europe to the Soviet economy, it is dismaying to see Viktor Orbán's government turning to Russian science and debt servicing in the 21st century.

Another nuclear colony of the USSR was Romania (page 106). The Horia Hulubei National Institute for Research and Development in Physics and Nuclear Engineering (IFIN-HH) dates to the late 1940s. Its researchers contributed to the successful embrace of nuclear power in Romania, ultimately based on two Canadian CANDU natural uranium reactors that provide one-fifth of the country's electrical energy. IFIN, Romania's largest research centre, acquired a VVR-S research reactor and a U-120 cyclotron from the USSR.

The Kremlin also promoted nuclear programmes in the republics. The decommissioned Georgian IRT-M reactor is located just 20 km outside the centre of Tbilisi, in the Andronikashvili Institute of Physics. Elephter Andronikashvili (1910–1989), the director of the institute and member of Moscow's scientific elite, secured the reactor from Moscow in 1957, and it came online in 1959.

Scientific Colonialism and Military Conquest

Lusito's photographs capture another important facet of socialist scientific institutional history. Leading researchers and party

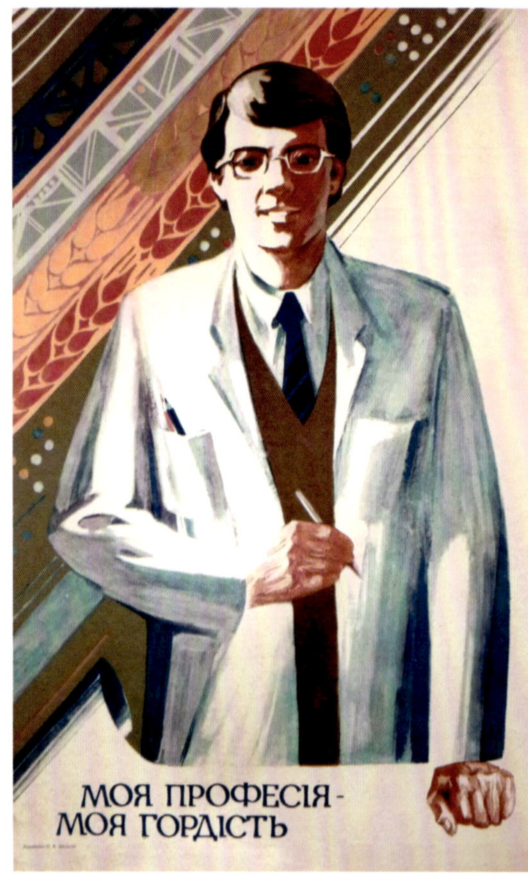

'My Profession – My Pride' (c.1980s)
Silk screen poster, artist unknown.

officials in the republics and Eastern Europe desired cutting edge laboratory facilities as signs of their entry into the world of scientific excellence. They lobbied their counterparts in Moscow for increased funding and new equipment. At the same time, Moscow intended expansion of research and development in the socialist periphery to serve primarily Soviet interests and directions of research. New institutes and equipment thus contributed to the colonial programme of tying the republics ever closer to the Kremlin's economic and strategic demands.

The construction of research facilities under these circumstances might reasonably be called scientific colonialism – using specialised knowledge and technologies to undergird empire building. Historically, when conquering nations established colonies, they typically built roads, impoundments, canals and power plants; surveyed and imposed arbitrary borders; and studied flora and fauna, all in the service of control of new lands and people. The tsars and the Bolsheviks followed these paths towards internal colonisation of the Russian empire, from the Northwest to the Arctic, the Far East, the Pacific Ocean and Central Asia.

The histories of scientific institutes are closely connected with Soviet colonialism. Research institutes in the Baltic countries grew on foundations of conquest and violence. The Academy of Sciences of the Latvian SSR was created at the end of World War II under the conditions of Soviet occupation. The Academy of Sciences of the Estonian SSR was established in April 1946, following an order by the Soviet occupiers. Tens of thousands of Estonian, Latvian and Lithuanian leaders, intellectuals and their families including thousands of children had already been arrested and deported to Siberia by 1941. A second wave of deportations followed in 1945–1946 as part of the creation of Soviet institutions in these countries.

The Academy of Sciences of Lithuania was established in January 1941 before the Nazi invasion. Its profile reflected typical Soviet focus on the exploitation of natural resources to serve the economy – in particular, Lithuania's fishing and forestry. In the 1980s the Soviets chose Lithuania as the place to build two units of the world's largest Chornobyl-style High-Power Channel-Type reactors (RBMK), both now shuttered. But the Lithuanian Academy of Sciences was also active in the restoration of the country's independence: the first public meeting of Sąjūdis (the National Reform Movement) was held in the Academy's conference hall in June 1988; a Green movement was also born in the Academy.

Having conquered the Baltic countries, the Soviets proceeded to build military facilities. They opened submarine bases in Estonia and Latvia; the Linksmakalnis strategic missile base in Lithuania; troop centres in Tallinn, Pärnu and Liepāja; and the Skrunda early-warning radar in Latvia. Estonian sites held rocket and missile launchers. Ventspils in Latvia gained 'Little Star', a top-secret radio telescope installation (page 88). Unlike Russia, which is rearming, many of the institutes in post-Soviet spaces have been re-committed to basic research.

Science in the Desert

Elites in Central Asia sought and welcomed Moscow's approval of the formation of their own academies that were often linked to domestic economic development. In the late 1940s and 1950s new academies of science and specialised research institutes specifically served oil and gas development, water resource management, and agriculture including cotton production. Scientific subjugation of Central Asia dates to the Imperial era when the tsars used military settlements to push Kazakhs, Uzbeks and Tajiks aside. The Red Army finished the task during the Civil War, especially in Kazakhstan. Slavic farmers flooded the country, disrupting nomadism in favour of collectivised agriculture. Stalin ordered the suppression of traditional culture to create a socialist landscape; at least 1.5 million Kazakhs died in the 1931–1933 famine. Russians came to dominate the nation demographically, reaching a peak of 40 per cent of the population.

Inevitably, World War II and the Cold War were the major spurs to the rapid expansion of Kazkah science. Wartime evacuation of scientists from the west triggered the growth of scientific institutions in Siberia, Central Asia and the Urals region. For its Cold War science, Kazakhstan paid high environmental and human costs. The Kremlin decided to locate nuclear weapons development and space launches in Kazakhstan at the Baikonur Cosmodrome and the Semipalatinsk Nuclear Test Site. The result of radioactive fallout from 456 bomb tests and toxic waste from rocket launches has caused long-term public health problems including cancers, birth defects and respiratory diseases. When the Russians left Kazakhstan at the break-up of the USSR, they plundered military, scientific and other strategic sites. As they had done in Nazi Germany in 1945, they confiscated equipment, instruments and data collections, leaving behind radioactive waste and toxic chemicals.

Institutes in post-Soviet spaces have re-entered world science, in part with support from the European Union, Japan and the US. A major contributor is the International Science and Technology Centre (ISTC, 1992–present) which was intended to provide employment for weapons scientists. In 2015, Putin's government, which had benefitted most from ISTC, unilaterally severed its connections and the headquarters were relocated from Moscow to Astana in Kazakhstan, contributing to the further evolution of Kazakh's former socialist scientific institutions into international ones. Photographs of the Fesenkov Astrophysical Institute (page 80) indicate the crucial place of basic research to Kazakh scientists.

Into the Galaxies

Successes in astronomy sadly occurred against the backdrop of a Stalinist purge. In the late 1930s, the entire Leningrad astronomical community was devastated by the arrest and murder of dozens of its leading scientists. Nevertheless, astronomy flourished in the republics, especially in the Caucasus. After a brief period of independence, Armenia was sovietised and forced to live through brutal Stalinist repressions of intellectuals, artists and religious figures. These attacks slowed the development of Armenian science into the 1940s, in spite of the Academy of Sciences of the USSR creating branches in Armenia, Azerbaijan and Georgia.

In 1943 an independent Armenian Academy was founded under the leadership of the Alikhanian brothers (page 14), Viktor Ambartsumian (1908–1996) and others. These scientists established the Aragats Cosmic Ray Research Station and contributed to the development of such fields as astrophysics, information technology, applied mathematics and mechanics. Artem and Abraham Alikhanian (1908–1996) were interested in the origins of the universe and the nature of high-energy particles, and laid the groundwork that eventually led to the discovery of dark matter. By 1950 the Armenian Academy had grown to over 30 institutions.

Today, as in other post-Soviet countries, Armenian research and development suffers from a lack of funding and an aging workforce. But its scientists hark back to a significant, long-term programme in astrophysical research centred on the Byurakan Astrophysical Observatory (1946), established by the beloved Viktor Ambartsumian. Ambartsumian pushed the boundaries of planetary, stellar and extragalactic astronomy. His science, teaching and public persona were closely linked. He was the scientific secretary of Pulkovo Observatory, south of Leningrad, but could not prevent the purge of Leningrad astronomers. During the collapse of the USSR Ambartsumian turned to national politics, participating in a hunger strike in 1989 to draw attention to the campaign for the Armenian enclave of Nagorno-Karabakh to rejoin Armenia. The Bolsheviks had promised Karabakh to Armenia, but to placate Turkey, which had carried out a genocide against Armenia, Stalin transferred the region, with its Armenian population, to Azerbaijan in 1923. In 1991 the Armenian population declared its independence from Azerbaijan, leading to a war between the two countries that continues to this day.

The Tragedy of Ukrainian Science

For over 100 years modern Ukraine has sought autonomy from Moscow. During the Civil War the Bolsheviks conquered the briefly independent nation. Stalin ordered the slaughter of Ukrainian intellectuals and forced the collectivisation of the peasantry that directly led to millions of people dying of famine. Putin has renewed murderously false claims of sovereignty over Ukraine through war. All along, even as the sciences suffered mightily, the Ukrainians established world-class institutes in Kharkiv, a mere 30 kilometres from the Russian border.

Ukrainian science was second only to Russia's in the USSR. Its Academy of Sciences was founded in 1918. Its nuclear power and rocketry programmes were crucial in achieving Cold War parity with the US. Now the entire enterprise is under attack from Russia, including the Chornobyl exclusion zone and the Zaporizhzhia nuclear power station, which was captured by hostile Russian forces in March 2022. The ghost of Stalin has hit Kharkiv hard; Russian attacks have caused millions of dollars' worth of damage to institutes including a laboratory holding a neutron source and dozens of kilogrammes of enriched uranium; a direct missile strike, of which there is a real risk, would cause widespread radioactive contamination.

The leading institute in Ukraine is the Kharkiv Institute of Physics and Technology (often referred to as UFTI). UFTI's glorious history of world-class scientific achievement commenced in the 1930s with discoveries in nuclear, theoretical and low temperature physics. Lusito visited a number of spinoffs of UFTI. One, the Verkin Institute for Low Temperature Physics (page 132), was founded in 1960, though built on the tradition of the cryogenic laboratory under Lev Shubnikov (1901–1937) who was murdered by the secret police for 'anti-state activities.'

UFTI's fifth director, Kyrylo Synelnykov (1901–1966) was related by marriage to Igor Kurchatov, the head of the atomic bomb programme (each married the other's sister). They worked closely in nuclear physics, including conducting postwar research on the atomic bomb and fusion. But they were not capable of saving the institute from Stalin's purges; dozens of specialists were arrested and killed for imagined crimes against the state. A final blow to the health of the institute was the invasion of the Nazis who reached Kharkiv, picked the facilities clean, and destroyed what they could not pilfer. In the 1950s, at Kurchatov's initiative, UFTI physicists created advanced equipment for fusion research centred on the 'Uragan' stellarator reactor and a series of particle accelerators. The work of these and other Kharkiv institutes shows the resilience of science in times of constant crisis.

Gigantic Institutes

A final feature of socialist science was its 'gigantomania'. Socialist science was large scale and centralised. Its institutes tended to be much bigger than their Western counterparts. Buildings were expansive, the number of employees much greater. Their scale reflected a nearly unbreakable faith in the power of scientific armies to march towards the communist future. Confident in their infallibility, physicists joined engineers on programmes that reflected growing technological hubris. The institutes acquired great ideological significance as symbols of the legitimacy of the state and in cementing public faith in scientists as defenders of the socialist motherland. The Uzbek Institute of Materials Science (page 196) is necessarily gigantic with a solar furnace at 1,906 m^2 made from over 10,700 mirror facets, second in size only to a French counterpart.

Of course, Eric Lusito could not include photographs of institutes in the authoritarian remnants of the USSR: Russia, Azerbaijan and Belarus remain closed polities. Because of their isolation from world science, they must plod along with fewer personnel and more constrained research programmes than in the socialist era.

Kremlin communist and scientific leaders exerted pressure on the republican and East European academies to conform to socialist economic desiderata and ideological precepts.

Nevertheless, researchers and their institutes maintained a great degree of autonomy and intellectual strength, and they founded leading institutes in a variety of fields: astrophysics in Armenia, low temperature and nuclear physics in Ukraine, solar physics in Uzbekistan, and so on. Today, a number of these institutes have garnered support from European programmes and agencies that provide a buffer to institutional uncertainty. The collapse of the USSR meant the collapse of the scientific apparatus. Institutes lost funding, their personnel aged, and research programmes fell on hard times. But Lusito's photographs capture the essence of scientific research: specialists who enthusiastically explore the microworld, distant galaxies, low and high temperatures, and so on, as active members of international scientific communities after political walls and barriers have been removed.

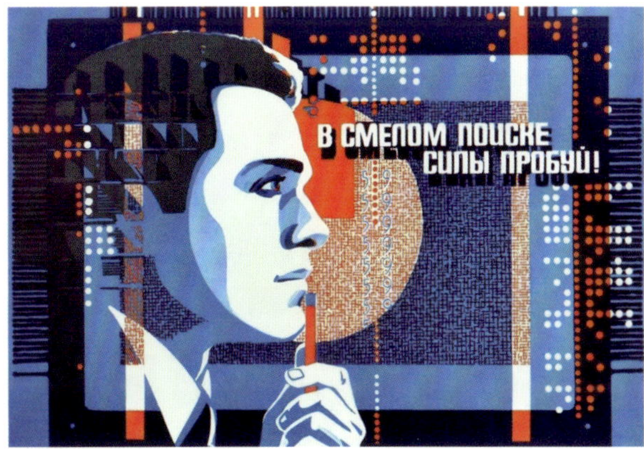

'Test your strength in bold exploration!' (1986)
Silk screen poster by V. Zhabskiy.

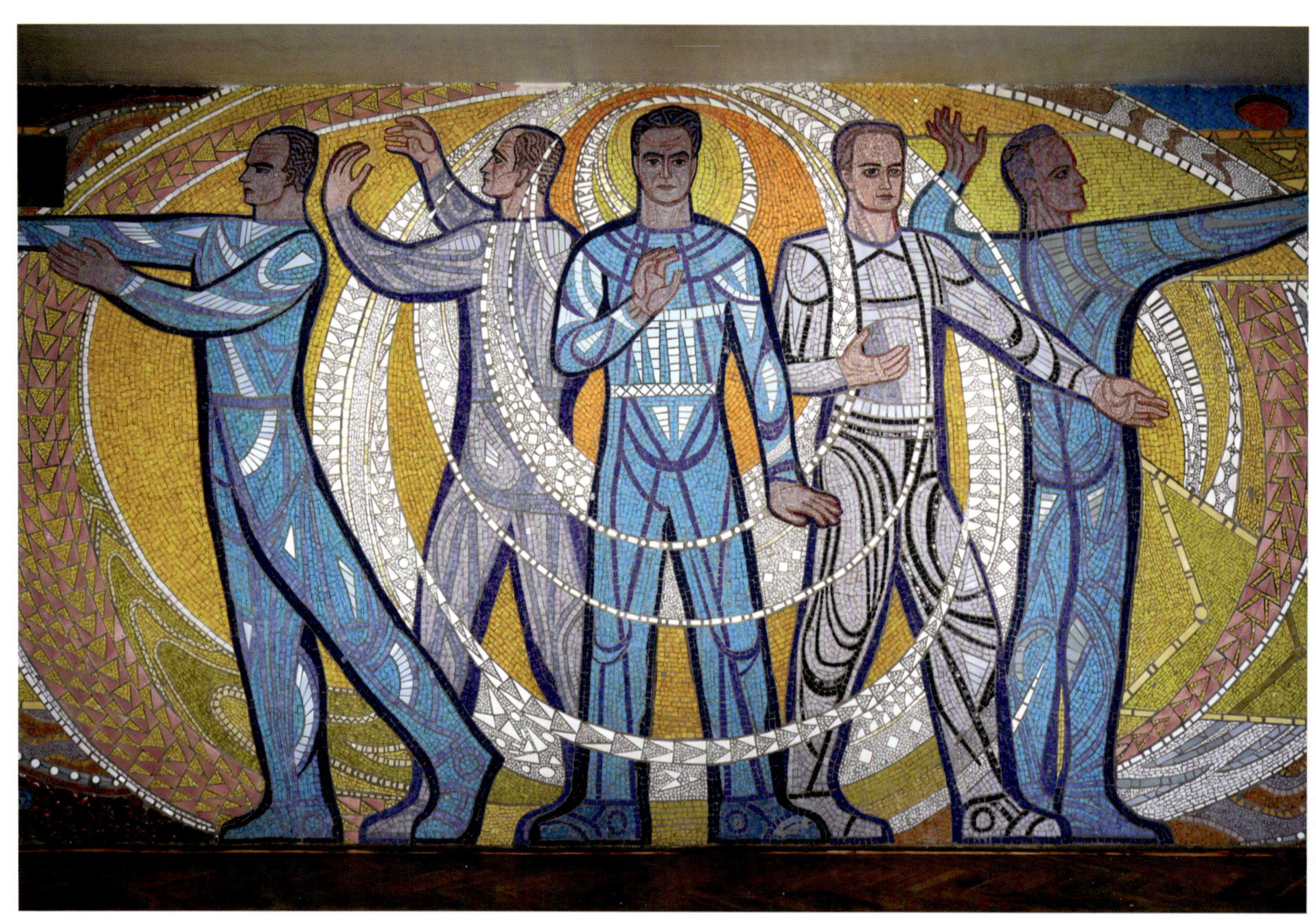

Above and right: *Masters of Time* (1975), mosaic by Halyna Zubchenko and Hryhoriy Prysheddko, Institute of Cybernetics, Ukraine.

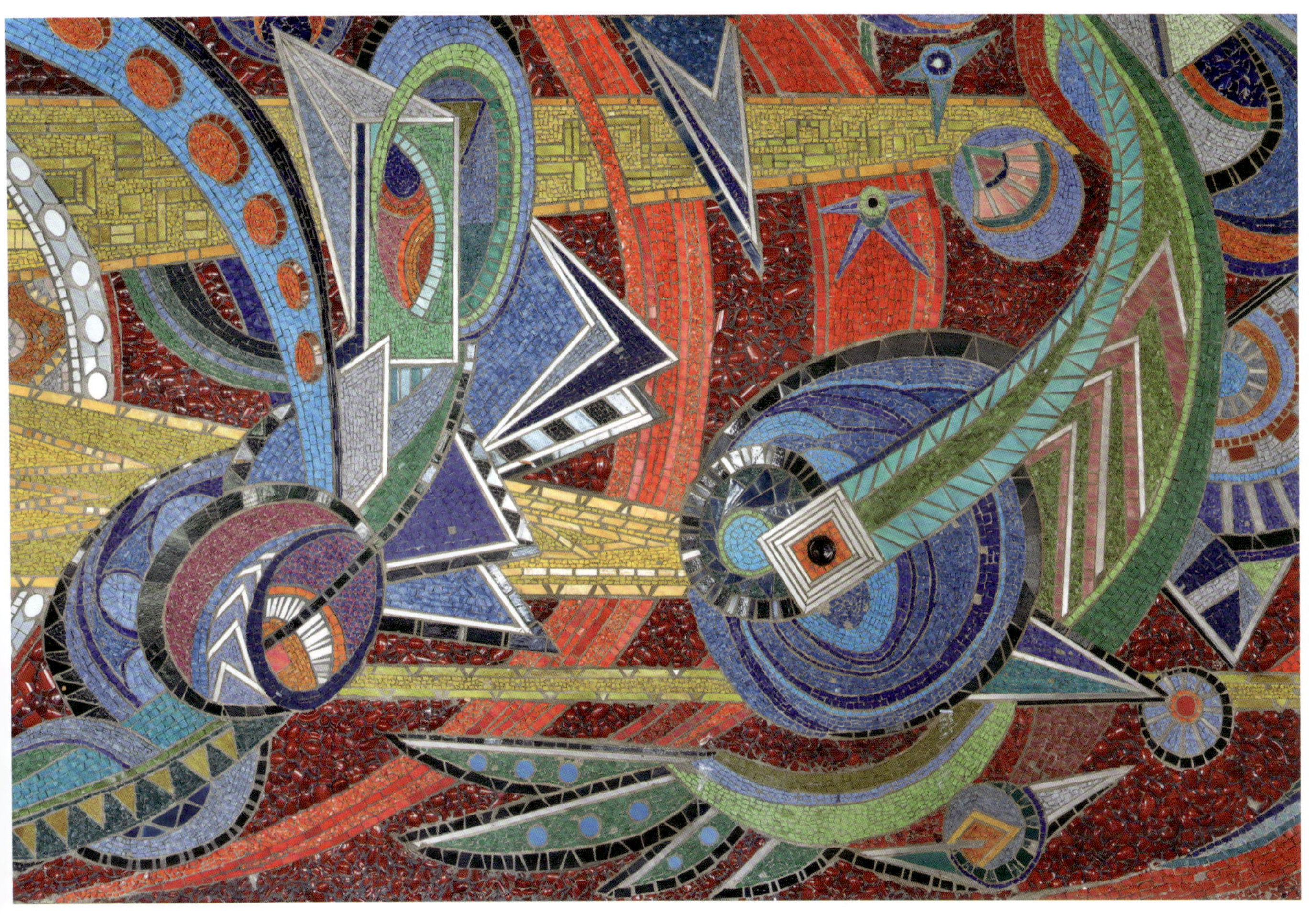

ARAGATS COSMIC RAY RESEARCH STATION

A.I. Alikhanyan National Science Laboratory

Mount Aragats, ARMENIA

Despite being the smallest of the Soviet republics, this mountainous country in the South Caucasus was ranked among the most scientifically advanced. Its vital role in the Soviet military-industrial complex and broader scientific landscape drew in a wealth of researchers and engineers who constructed remarkable facilities near the capital, Yerevan.

In 1943, as World War II raged across the globe, one of the largest high-altitude research stations was founded by the nuclear physicist brothers Abram Alikhanov (1904–1970) and Artem Alikhanian (1908–1978), who were among the first particle physicists in the Soviet Union. Situated on Mount Aragats, at 3,200 metres above sea level, the station was ideally placed for the study of cosmic rays.

At that time, before the era of particle accelerators, scientists focused on naturally occurring fluxes of particles born in violent solar and galactic explosions. When primary particles (mostly protons) collide with the Earth's atmosphere, the interaction produces showers of secondary particles (muons, electrons, positrons and others) that reach mountain altitudes in large numbers. Detector arrays record these particles and, with specialised analysis, information on their origins and energies can be retrieved. Years of observation reveal how high-energy particles are accelerated and how they interact in our atmosphere.

In the 1980s, construction began on the world's largest cosmic ray facility, the Hadron Ground-Based Research (Adronnye Nazemye Issledovaniya, or ANI) experiment. After the collapse of the USSR, the early years of Armenian independence were critical, with funding discontinued and construction being halted. With no electricity or heating, fuel scarce, and salaries falling to a few dollars a month, the station's survival seemed uncertain, but international grants and support from the Armenian diaspora bridged the gap, allowing Aragats to continue its work uninterrupted. From the unfinished ANI project, the scientists were able to successfully realise two experiments, MAKET-ANI, a prototype (maket) extensive air shower array and GAMMA, a surface and underground array.

Severe winters mean that for around half the year supplies can only be delivered by caterpillar-tracked vehicles, with scientists and technicians working month-long shifts, isolated and self-reliant. Today, high-speed internet connects the summit to Yerevan, which enables remote monitoring and real-time data sharing, reducing the need for on-site staffing.

In recent years, physicists from the Cosmic Ray Division have developed the Space Environmental Viewing and Analysis Network (SEVAN), adding new detectors on Aragats and other mountaintops across Eastern Europe and Germany. Current research spans galactic and solar cosmic rays, high-energy atmospheric physics, thundercloud electrification and space weather. Among the group's significant results are insights into particle-acceleration mechanisms during supernovae explosions, the measurement of exceptionally energetic solar protons, the discovery of atmospheric neutron production and the measurement and interpretation of intense particle bursts from thunderclouds.

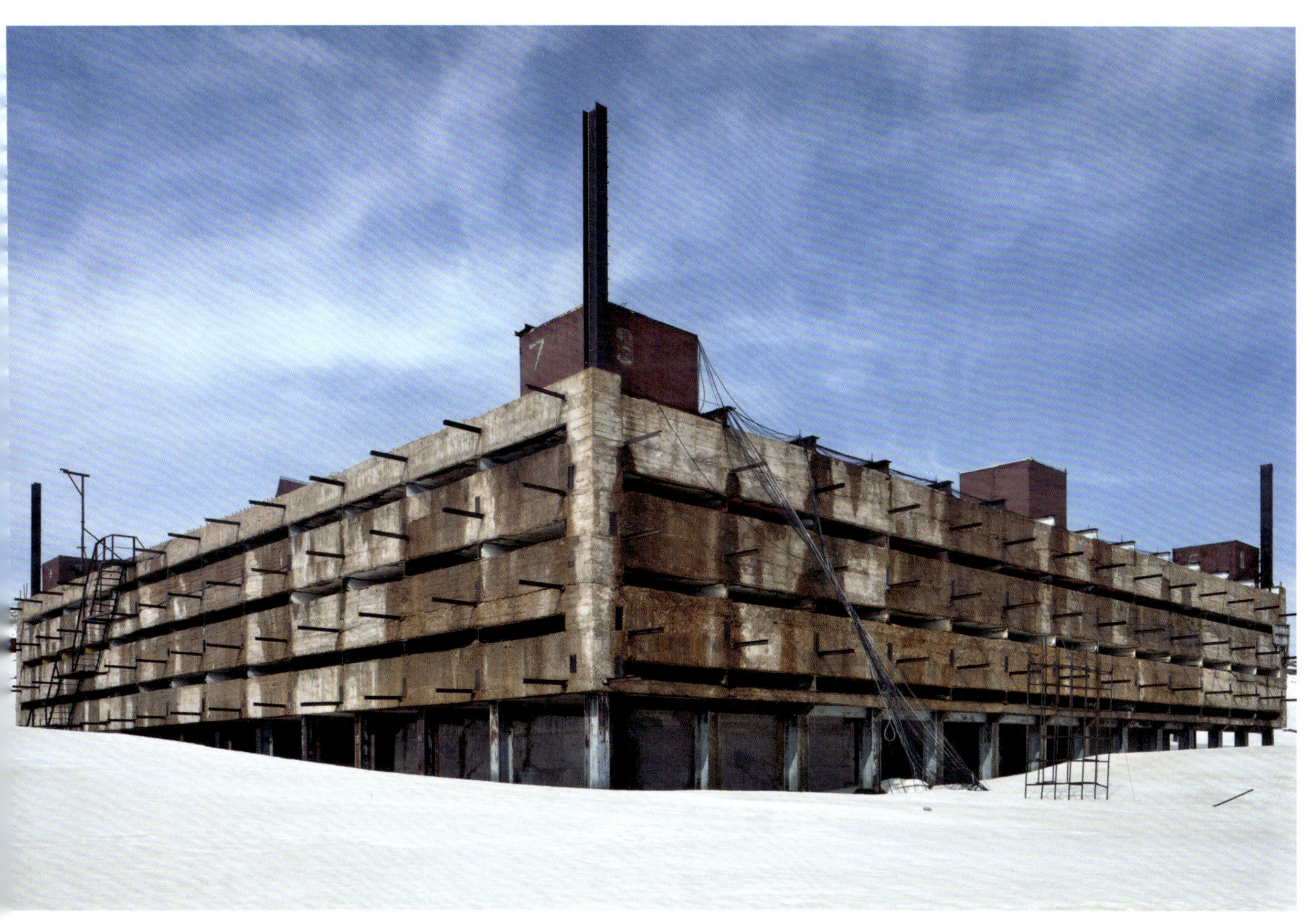

This absorber uses layers of concrete and air gaps to filter specific particles, allowing others to be measured using underground detectors. Built for the ANI experiment, which remained half completed after the dissolution of the Soviet Union, it was finally used for the GAMMA installation. Additional metal boxes housing cosmic ray surface detectors are arranged in concentric circles.

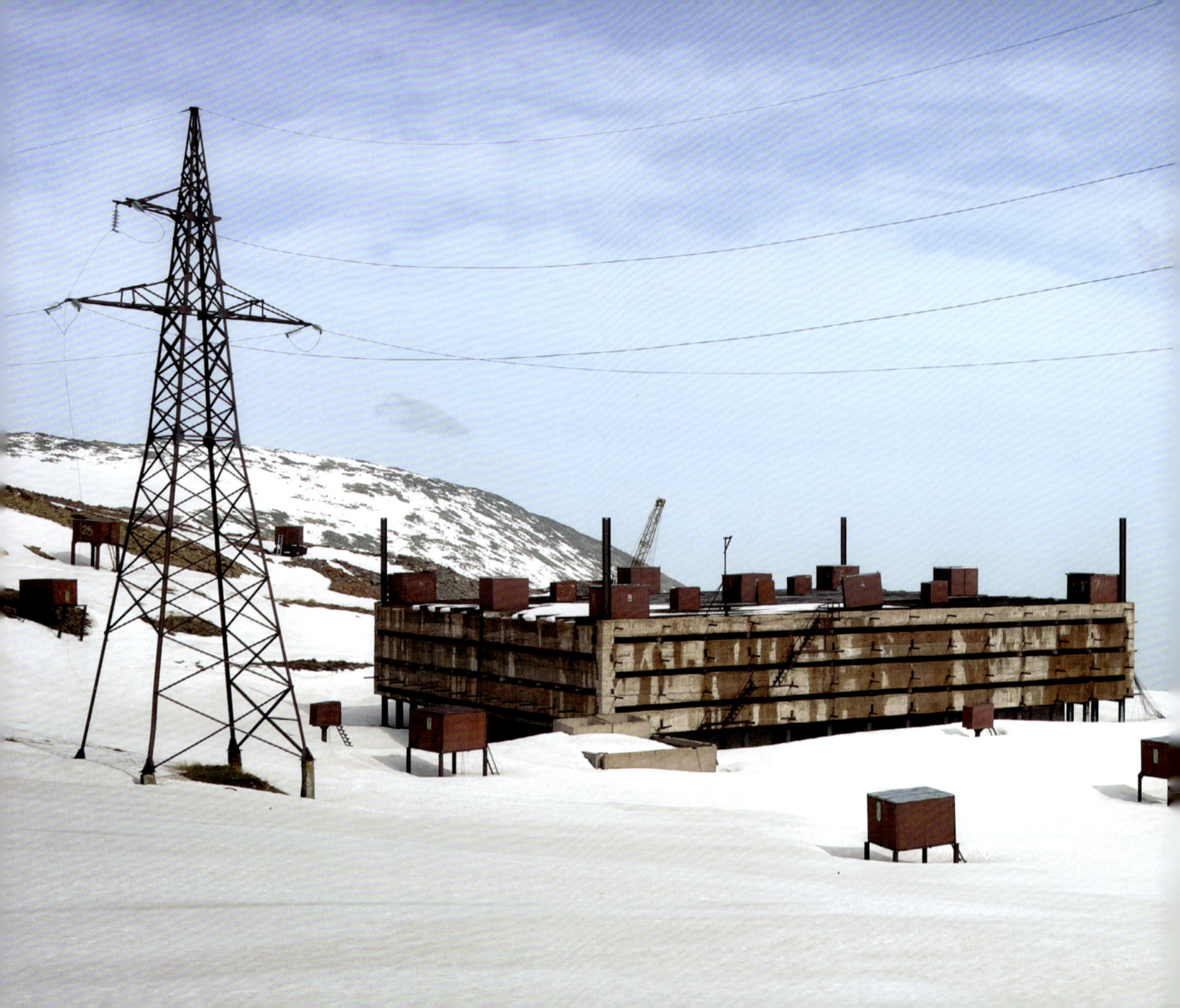

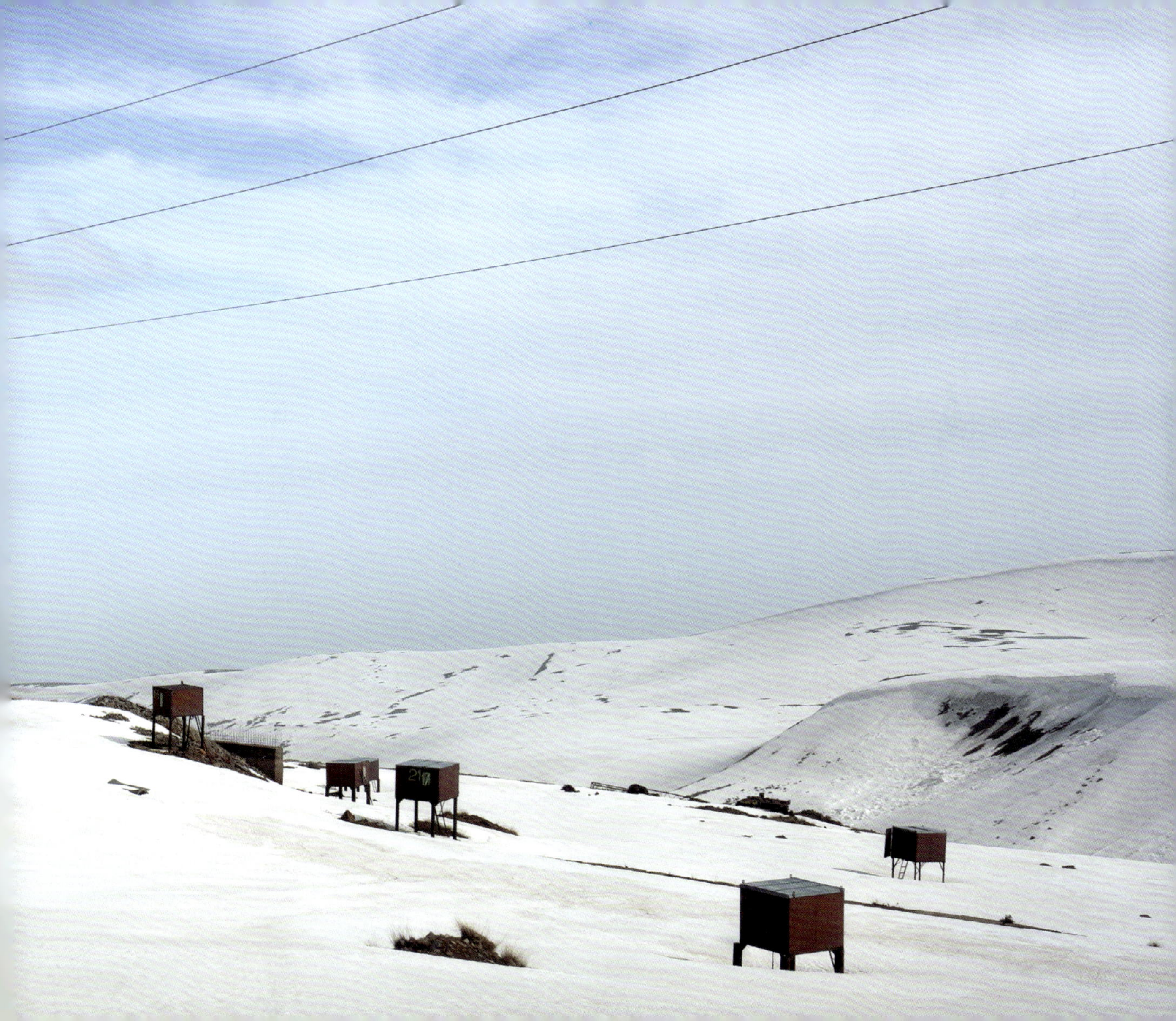

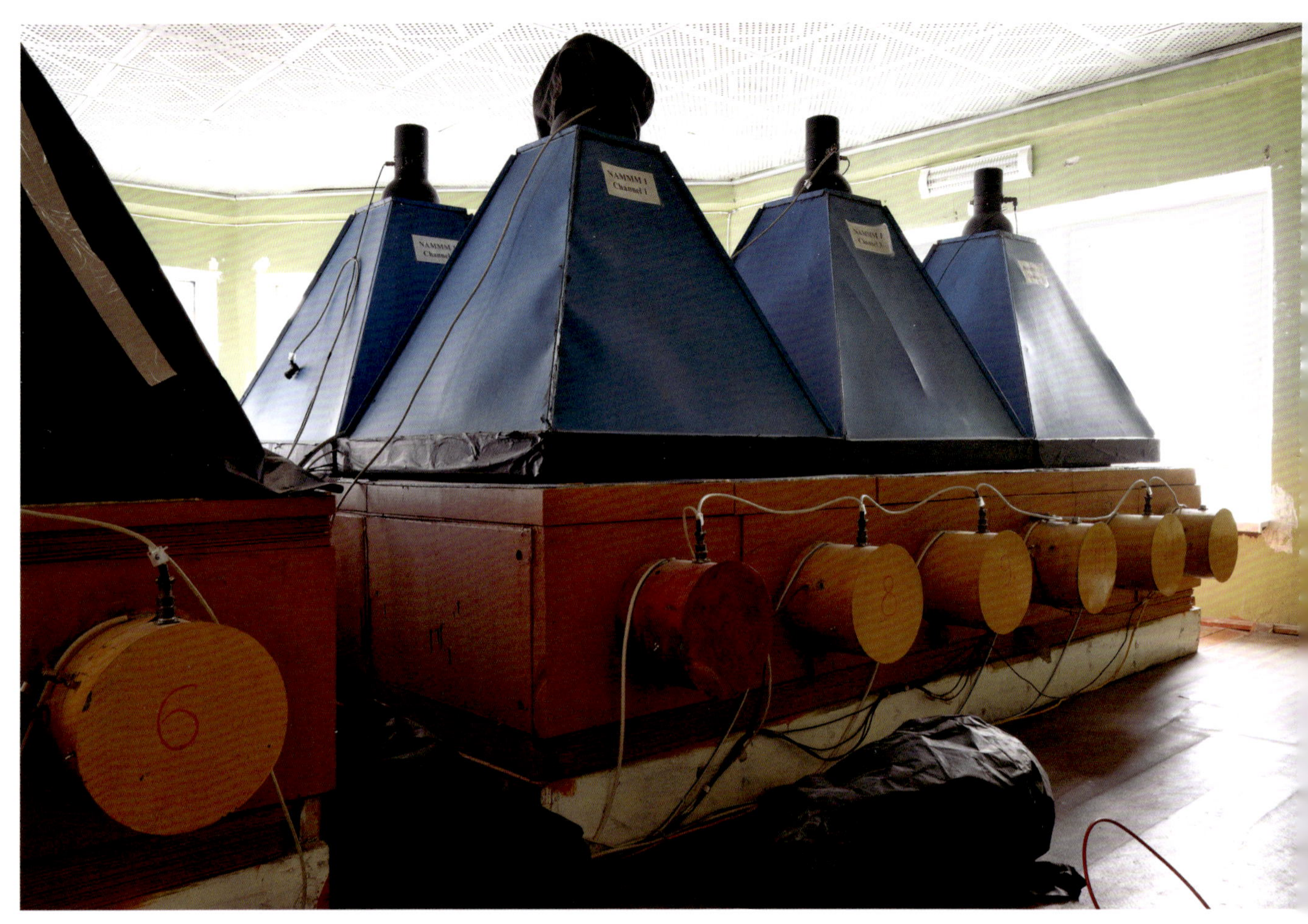

Built in 1960 at an altitude of 2,000 metres, the Nor-Amberd research station houses the Nor-Amberd Multidirectional Muon Monitor (NAMMM). The data obtained from this apparatus contributes to a global network studying violent solar events that cause of geomagnetic storms. This site also hosts scientific conferences and serves as a base for the Aragats station in winter.

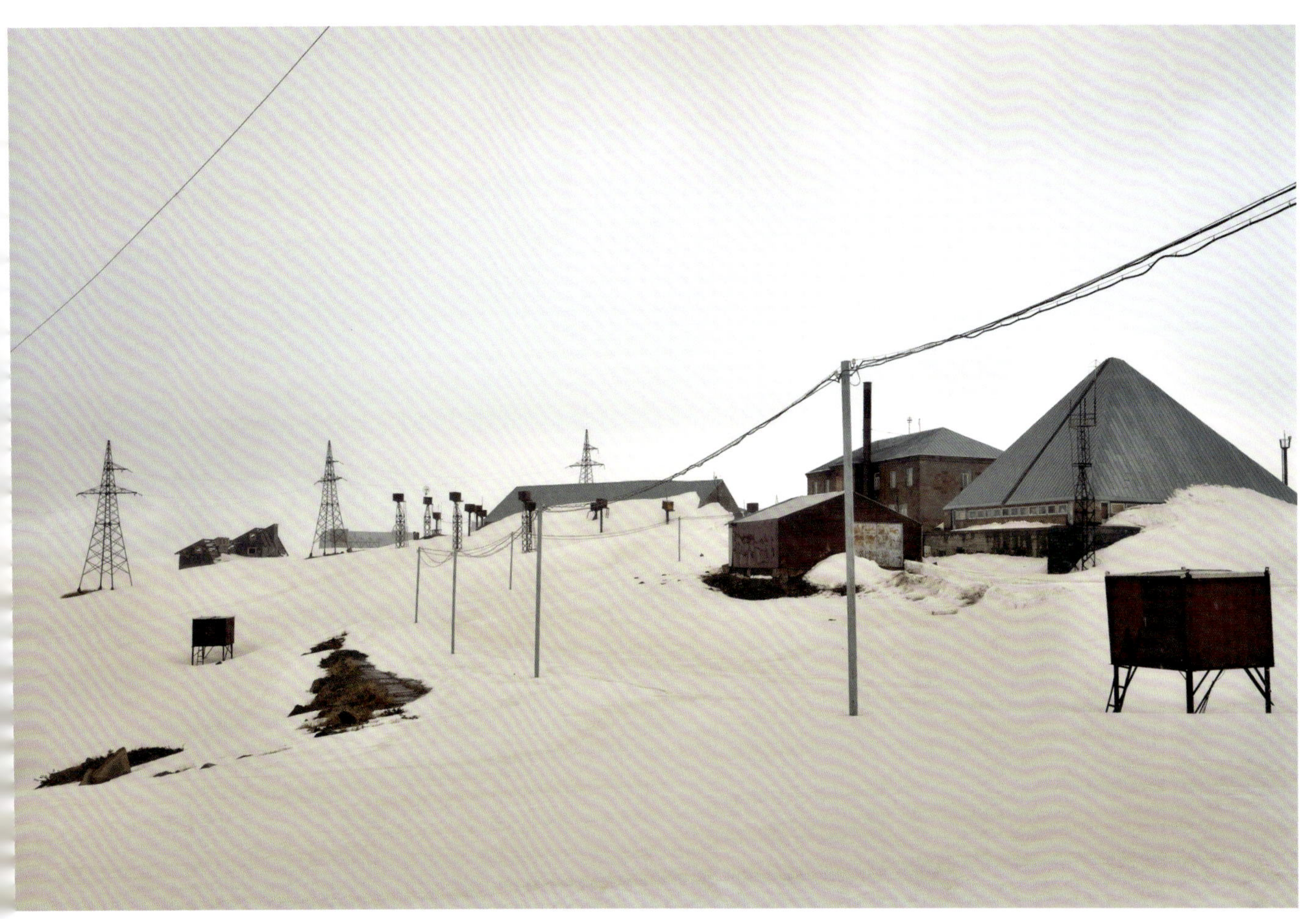

To conduct their experiments, the physicists have built a variety of detectors over the years, which are installed around the Aragats station. New facilities are constantly being added.

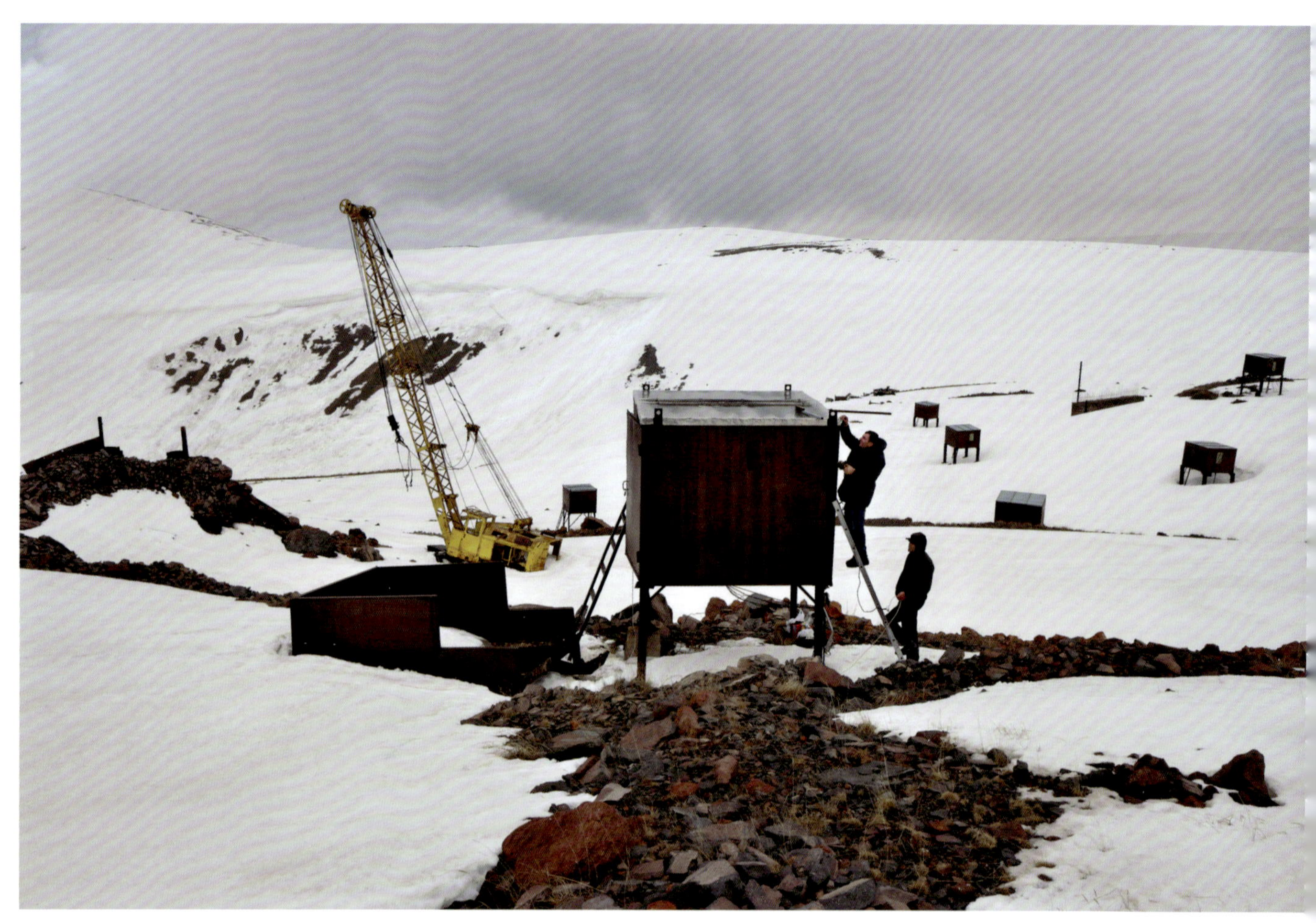

Dr Tigran Karapetyan and technician Gourgen Jabaryan perform maintenance on a surface station.

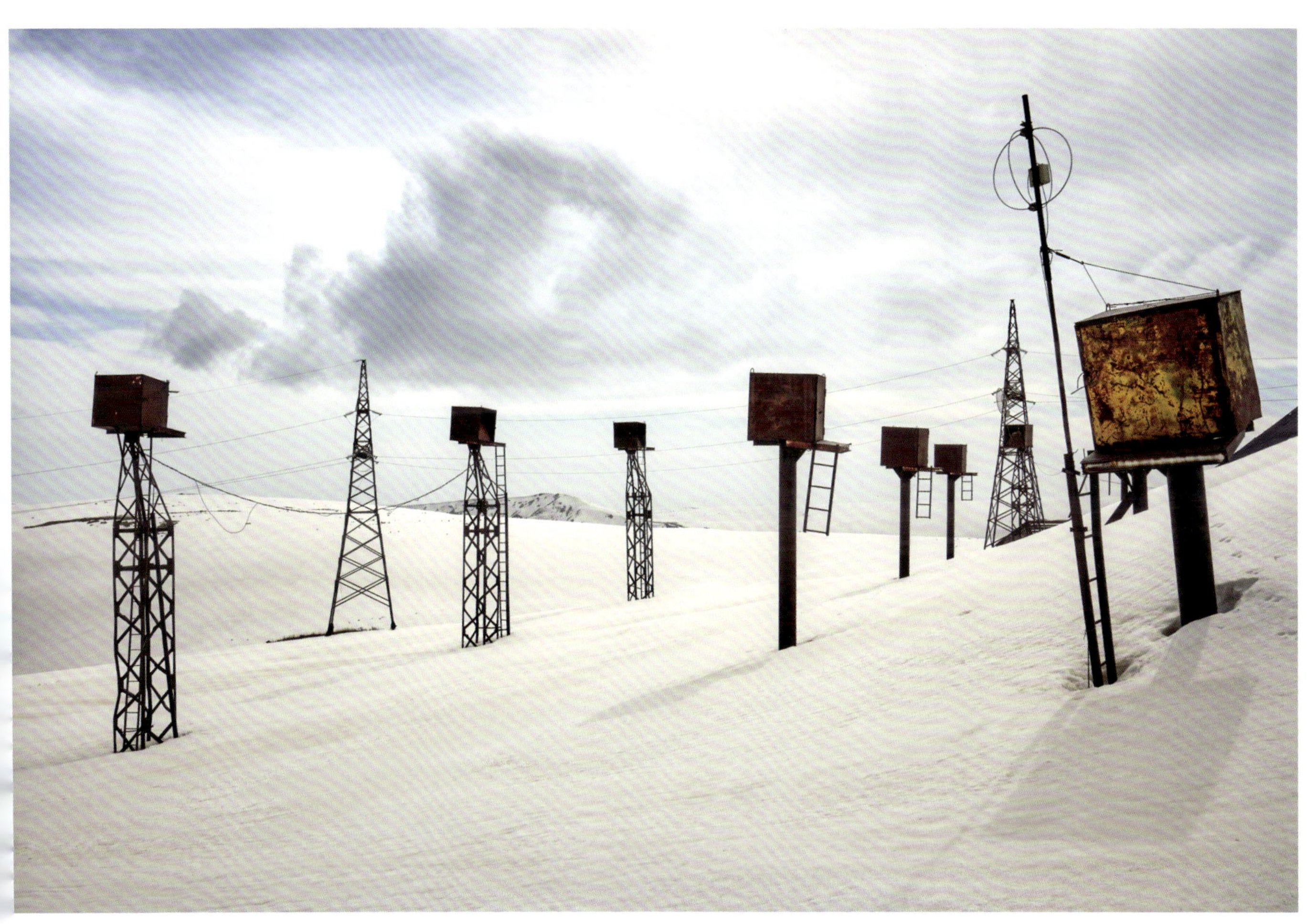

Surface stations forming part of the MAKET-ANI, an experiment array to study the flux in the 'knee' region of the primary cosmic ray spectrum. At this altitude it is possible to accurately reconstruct the size and shape of extensive air showers.

BYURAKAN ASTROPHYSICAL OBSERVATORY

Armenian National Academy of Sciences

Byurakan, ARMENIA

The Byurakan Astrophysical Observatory (BAO) was founded in 1946 by Viktor Ambartsumian (1908–1996). Aged 11, he became fascinated by a book on celestial bodies, delivering lectures to his classmates on the Solar System and the possibility of extraterrestrial life. He served as director of the BAO and president of the Armenian Academy of Sciences for 42 and 46 years respectively. In 1947 he discovered stellar associations – very loose clusters of about 10 to 1,000 stars. Observing these, he concluded that star formation is a continuous process, a concept that countered contemporary scientific ideas and powerfully influenced subsequent research in this field. Twice winner of the Stalin Prize (in 1946 and 1950), he was the second person to be awarded the title of National Hero of Armenia (1994). He received international recognition, serving as an honorary or foreign member of various scientific academies in more than 25 countries. Today he is regarded as one of the leading astronomers of the 20th century.

In 1960, a Schmidt telescope, reportedly offered by Hitler to Mussolini and transferred to the USSR as part of war reparations, was installed at the BAO. This was used by Beniamin Markarian (1913–1985) to study the spectra of hundreds of faint galaxies. His work, conducted from 1965 to 1980, comprises the First Byurakan Survey (FBS) which revealed 1,517 galaxies with ultraviolet-excess emissions, known today as the Markarian galaxies. The FBS remains the largest ever astronomical study of the near universe and is considered one of the most important achievements in modern astronomy.

In 1971, the observatory hosted the first international symposium on the search for extraterrestrial intelligence. Organised by the USSR Academy of Sciences alongside the US National Academy of Sciences, the conference gathered notable astronomers, physicists, radio physicists, geneticists, biologists, chemists, archaeologists, linguists, anthropologists, historians and sociologists, including three Nobel Prize winners.

In 1975 a ZTA-2.6 telescope was installed at BAO. Designed by Bagrat Ioannisian (1911–1985), constructor-in-chief of large Soviet astronomic apparatus, it was at that time the seventh largest telescope in the world. Experts from the observatory also designed and built space telescopes such as Orion-1 (which operated onboard the Soviet orbital station Salyut in 1971), Orion-2 (onboard spacecraft Soyuz-13 in 1973) and Glazar (onboard Mir space station in 1987). Over 40 cosmonauts, including Alexei Leonov (1934–2019), were secretly trained in simulated space conditions by BAO staff to use these telescopes.

The fall of the Soviet Union in 1991 proved difficult for the BAO both financially and scientifically. However, thanks to international collaborations, its telescopes have been modernised, greatly increasing the efficiency of observations and expanding opportunities for Armenian astronomers. It remains one of the most important astronomical centres in Eastern Europe.

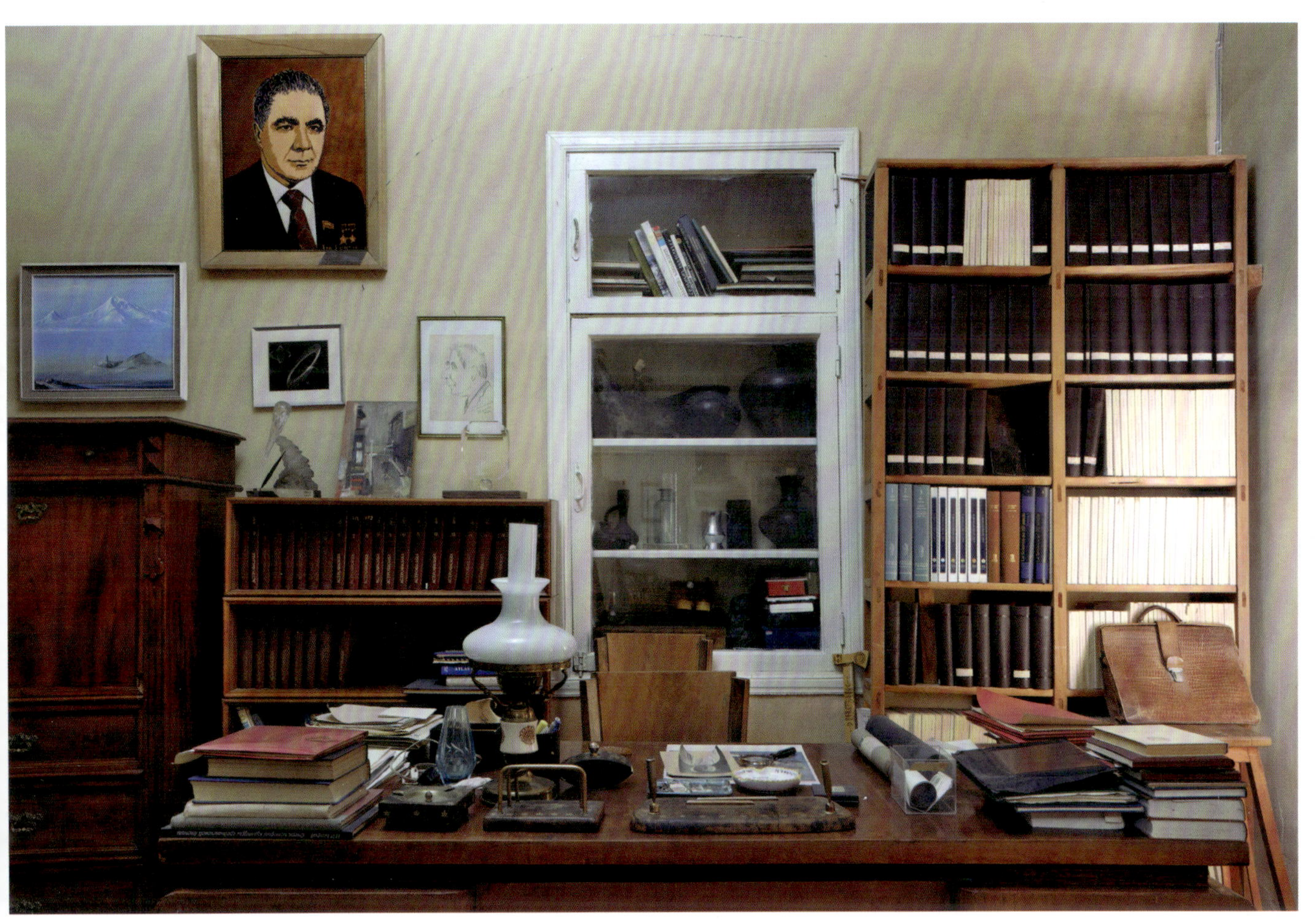

Viktor Ambartsumian's home office. His pioneering scientific work resulted in him being awarded the Stalin Prize twice – in 1946 and 1950. He used the prize money (100,000 Soviet rubles) from the last win to build this house for himself within the grounds of the observatory.

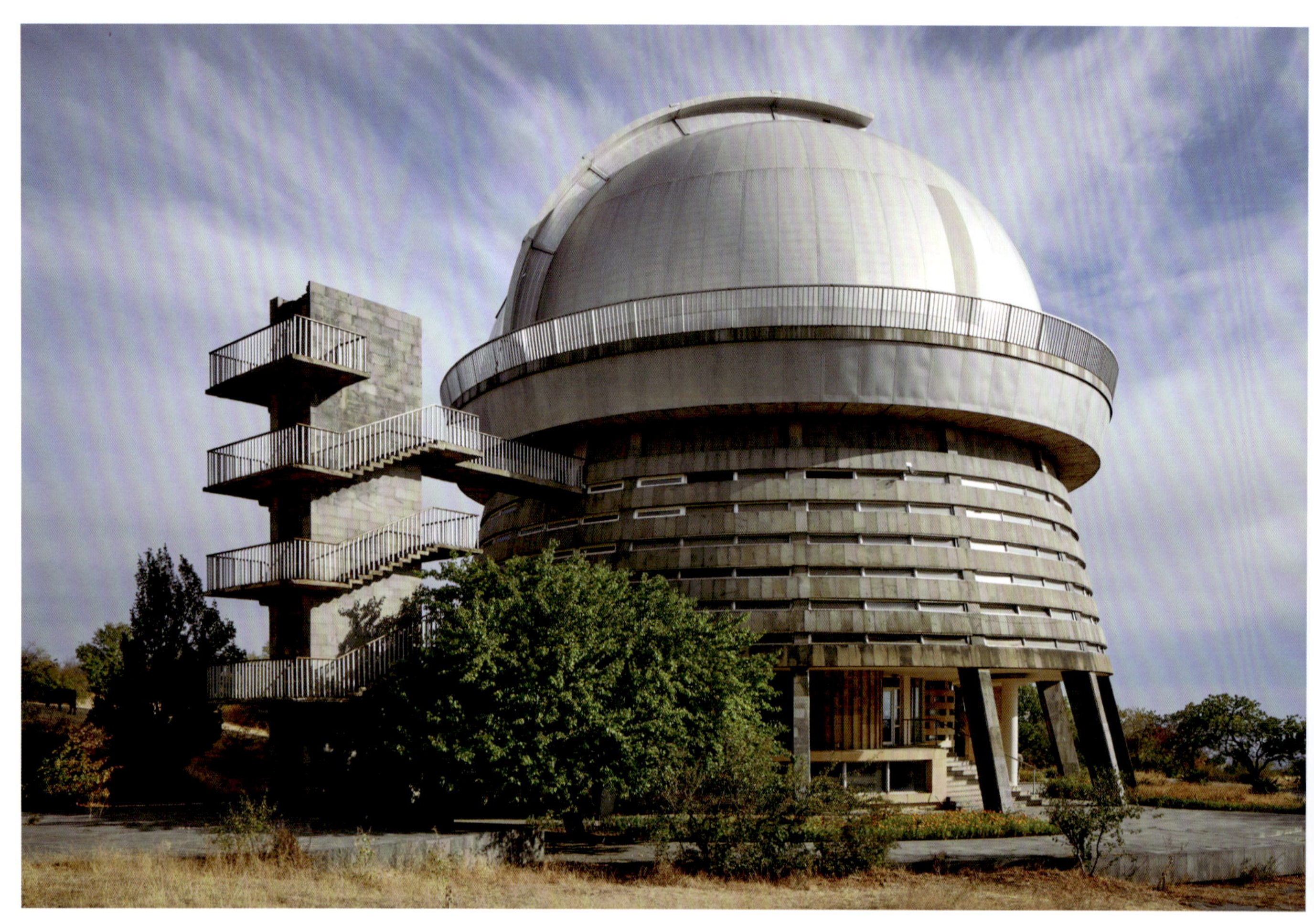

The tower housing the ZTA-2.6 telescope was designed by Sargis Gurzadyan (1929–2015), the observatory's principal architect, and completed in 1975. Its dome, weighing 60 tonnes, is constructed from a material called duraluminium, an aluminium-copper alloy that hardens over time.

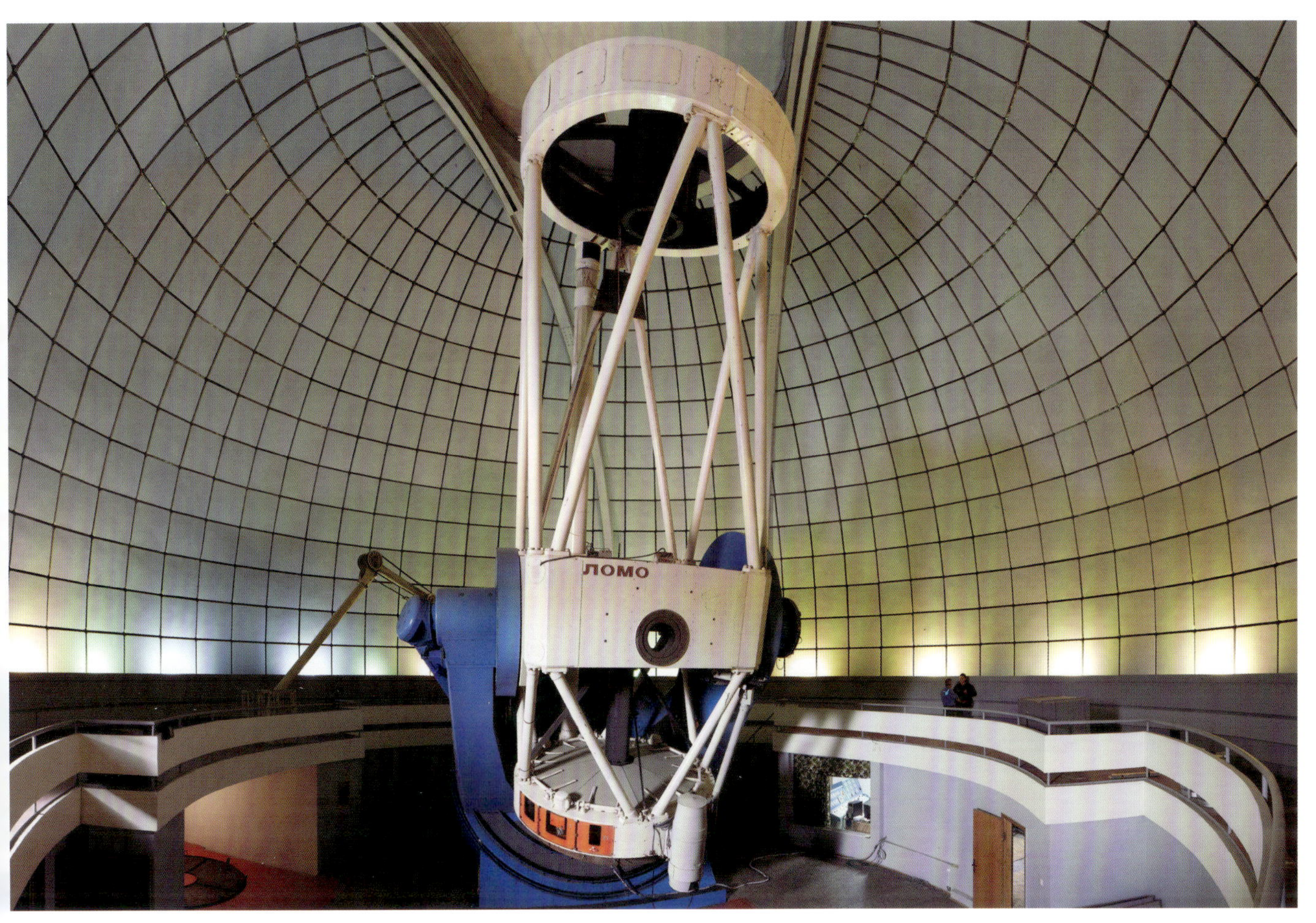

ZTA-2.6 refers to the Ambartsumian Reflecting Telescope with a 2.6-metre main mirror diameter. The largest instrument at the observatory, it was constructed at the Leningrad Optical-Mechanical Association (LOMO) and installed in 1976.

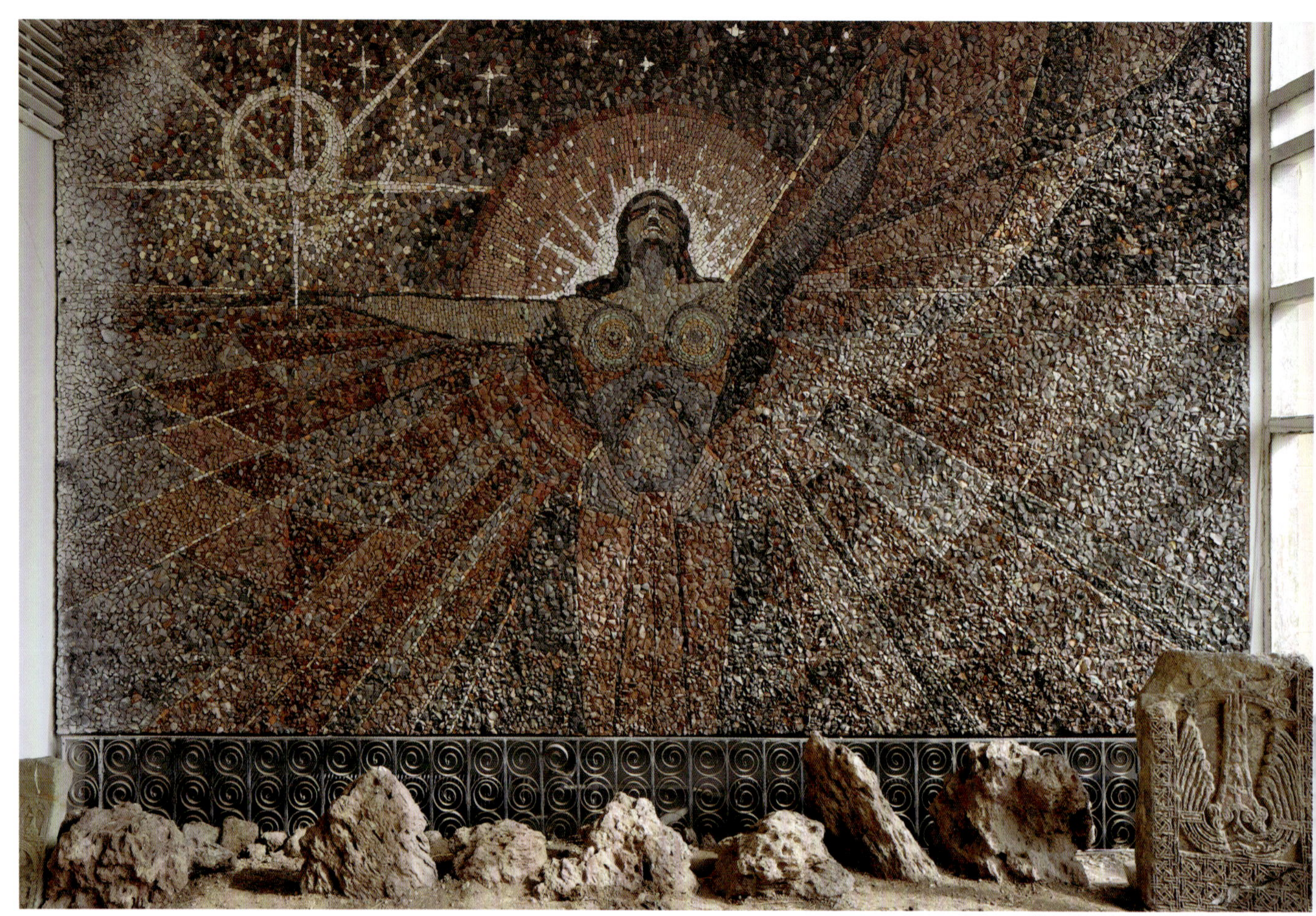

This mosaic, titled *To the Stars*, is situated inside the conference hall.

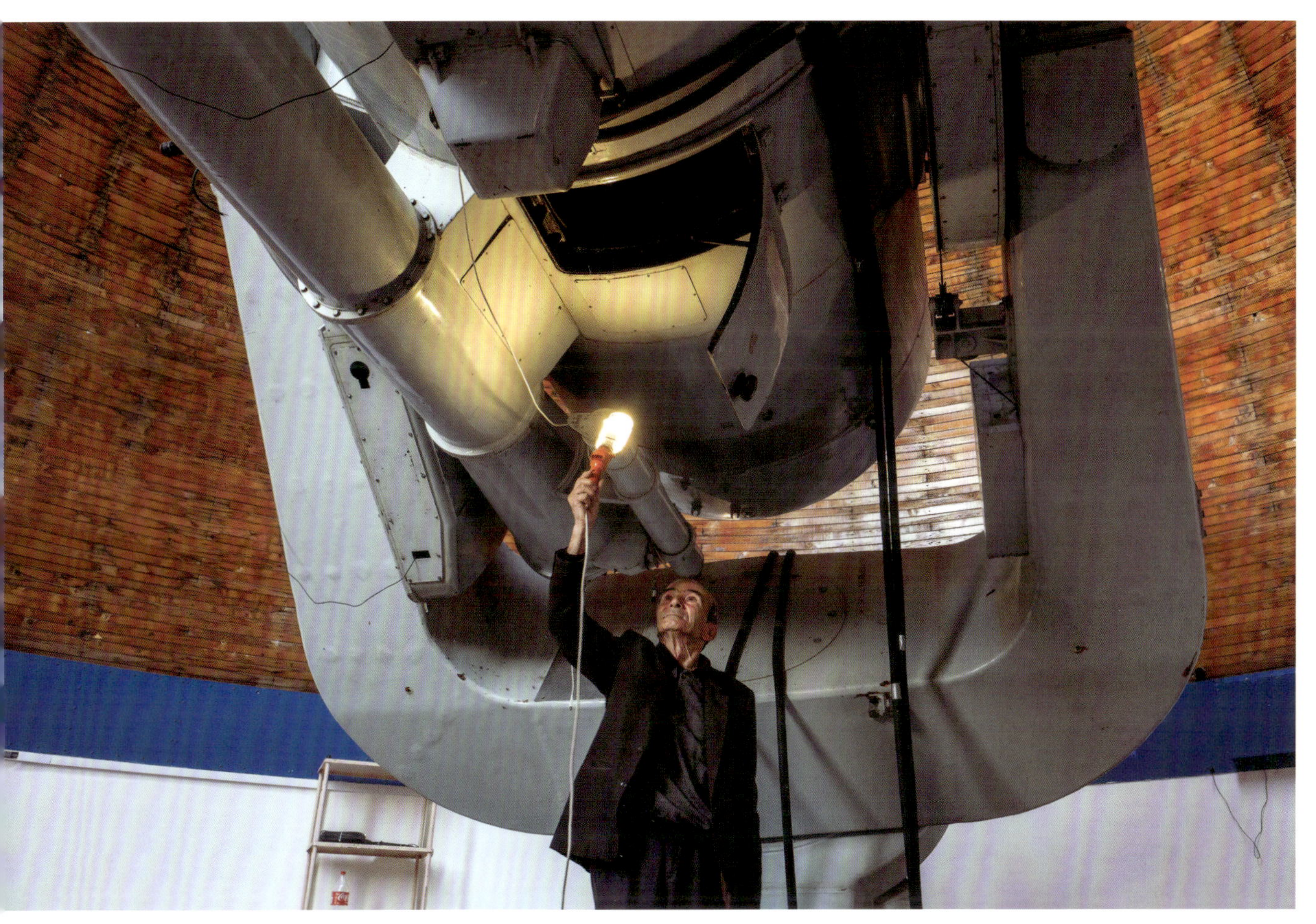

This 1-metre Schmidt telescope, installed in 1960, was instrumental in several significant discoveries, including Markarian galaxies. It ceased operating in 1991, but after modernisation in 2015, was brought back into use. Engineer Henrik Sargsyan, who has worked at the observatory since 1958, illuminates the hatch housing the new digital sensor.

RADIOPHYSICS RESEARCH INSTITUTE

National Body of Standardisation and Metrology

Orgov, ARMENIA

In 1957, while Paris Herouni (1933–2008) was working as a young radio engineer at the Byurakan Astrophysical Observatory, he happened upon an article titled 'A New Form for a Giant Radio Telescope' by A.K. Head, in the scientific journal *Nature*. Herouni decided to bring this idea to life and in 1962, after devoting his doctoral thesis to the subject, built a working 5-metre prototype. Having confirmed the system's viability, he proposed a 200-metre version to the Soviet authorities, and after 17 years of persistence on his part they agreed to construct one, though on a smaller scale than he had hoped.

Talented and ambitious, Herouni rapidly joined the ranks of the scientific elite. In 1971 he established the Radiophysics Research Institute which, with considerable state attention and funding, became responsible for the metrology and standardisation of antenna systems across the entire USSR, and employed at its peak in the 1980s 850 staff. To conduct full-scale tests, a 100-hectare testing ground called the State Reference Centre for Antenna Measurements was established in the Armenian mountains. The institute received many orders from the military-industrial complex, providing Herouni with the means to launch his Big Antenna project. The design process for this began in 1975, with construction taking place from 1981 to 1985. The resulting Radio Optical Telescope (ROT-54/2.6) is unique in combining both optical and radio capabilities in one instrument. The hemispherical primary reflector of the radio telescope – at 54 metres in diameter, one of the largest in the world – is embedded in the fabric of the mountain and covered with almost 4,000 metre-square aluminium alloy panels, each one hand-moulded and precision finished to an accuracy of within 70 microns in order to detect very weak radio signals from space. Rising from its centre on three supports is the 5-metre diameter secondary radio reflector which, being movable, gives it an effective diameter of about 32 metres. The 2.6-metre diameter optical telescope, also located here, is mounted coaxially with the main antenna.

During the first calibration test conducted in the summer of 1985, Herouni's team observed well-known sources of radiation signals, but was also the first to record a powerful radio-flare from a red giant star, in this case Eta Geminorum 380 light years away.

In 1988 a devastating earthquake hit the country, though the radio telescope fortunately escaped with only minor damage. However, the break-up of the USSR had a bigger impact and after losing substantial funding, operations were halted. Between 1995 and 2010, the telescope was modernised, allowing work to resume, but again, in 2012, it fell into disuse due to a lack of financial resources, and today this unique instrument stands inert awaiting a new era of interest and use.

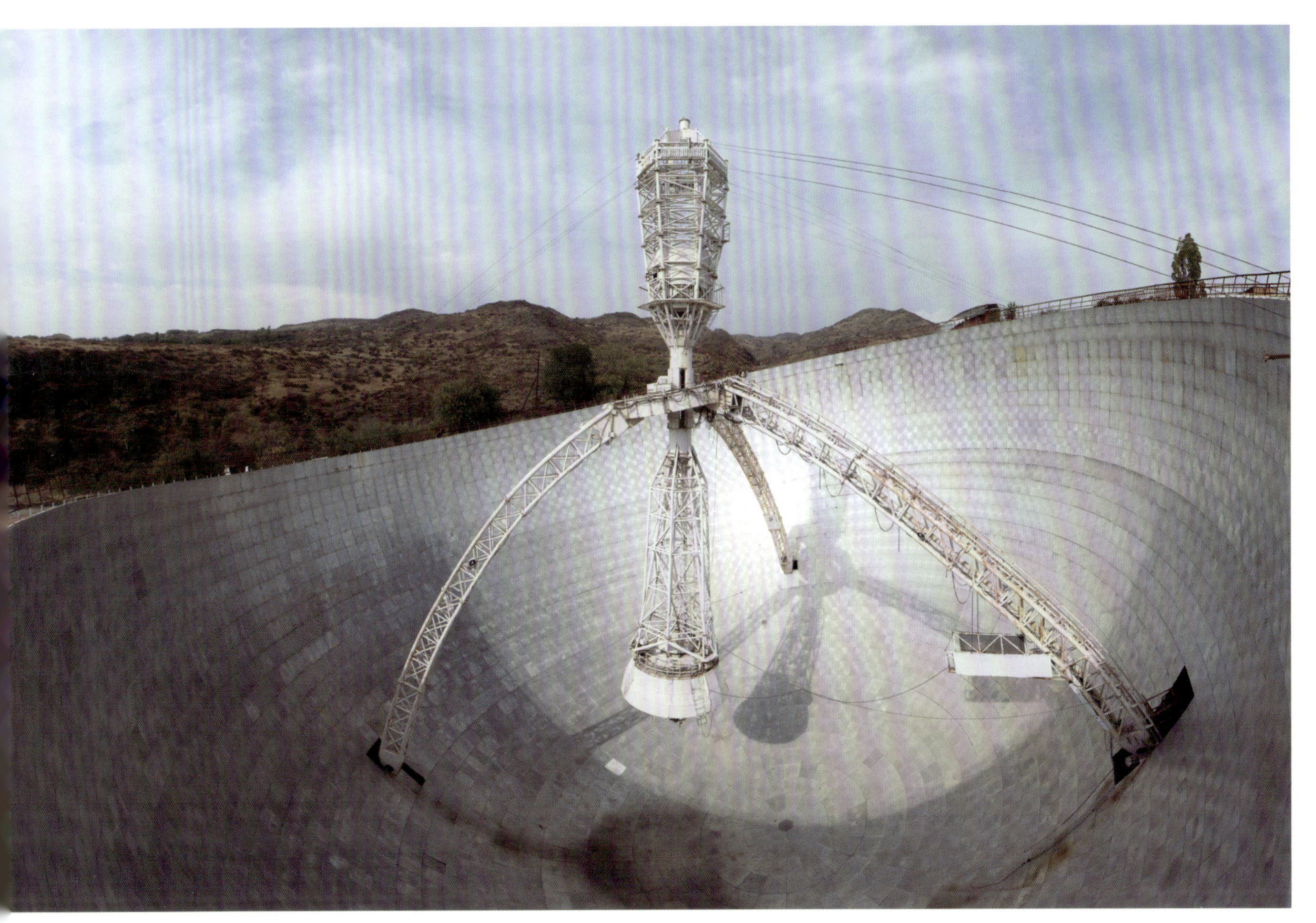

The ROT-54/2.6 primary reflector is covered with 4,000 aluminium alloy panels, each approximately 1 metre square and weighing around 55 kilogrammes.

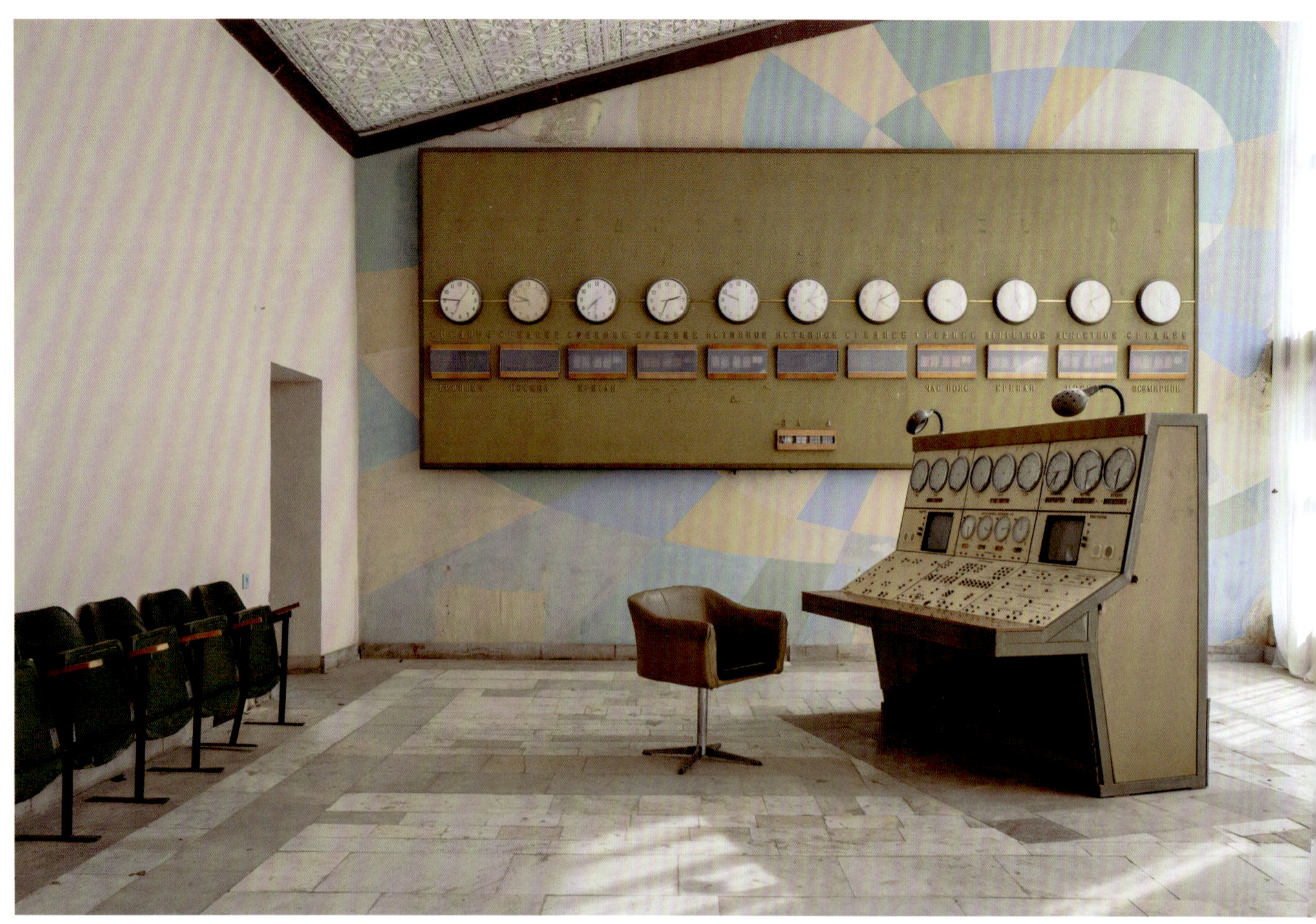

The control room for the ROT-54/2.6 with the radio control panel. The clocks display the time in Greenwich, Moscow and Yerevan, showing both solar time (a standard 24 hours, based on the position of the Sun) and sidereal time (based on Earth's rotation relative to the fixed stars, which is used by astronomers to track celestial objects).

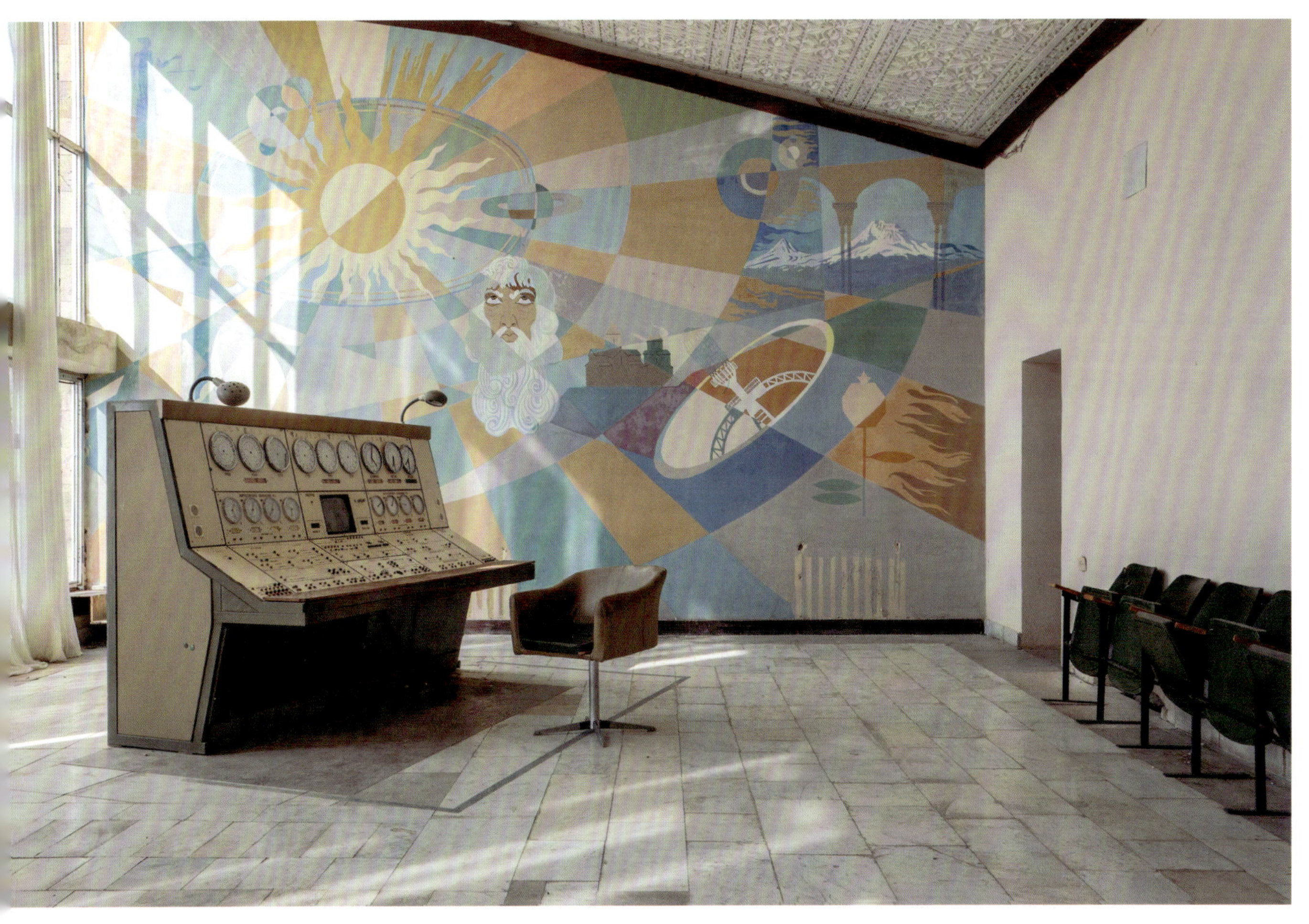

A view in the opposite direction, showing the optical control panel and its mural featuring the reflector itself alongside other symbols of Armenia.

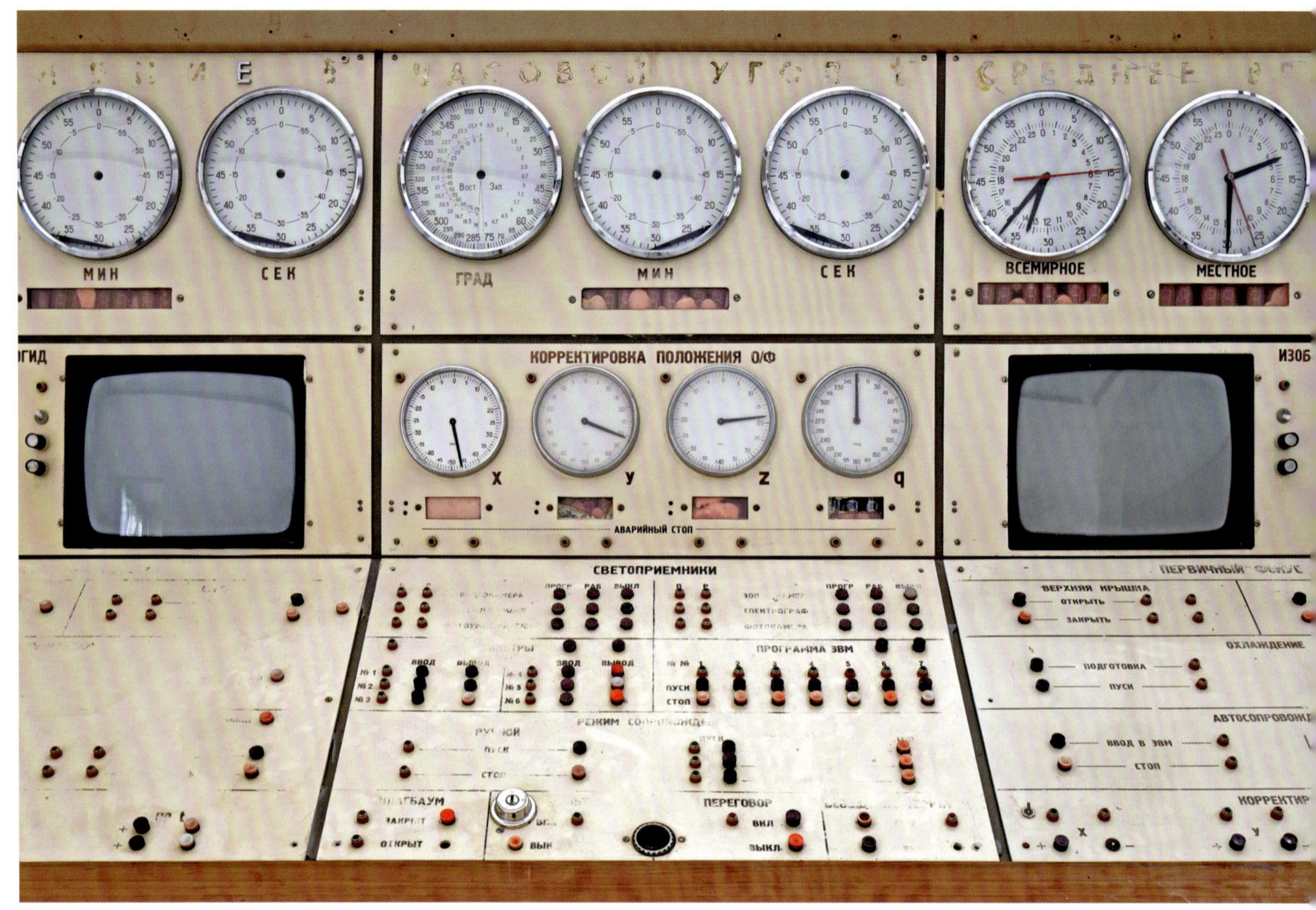

An operator's view of the radio control panel. On the top row: coordinate sensor dials for right ascension (measured in hours, minutes and seconds) and declination (measured in degrees, minutes and seconds); on the middle row: antenna beam position correction sensor (measuring any misalignment) and on the bottom row: the photo-receiver sensor (recording the optical signal).

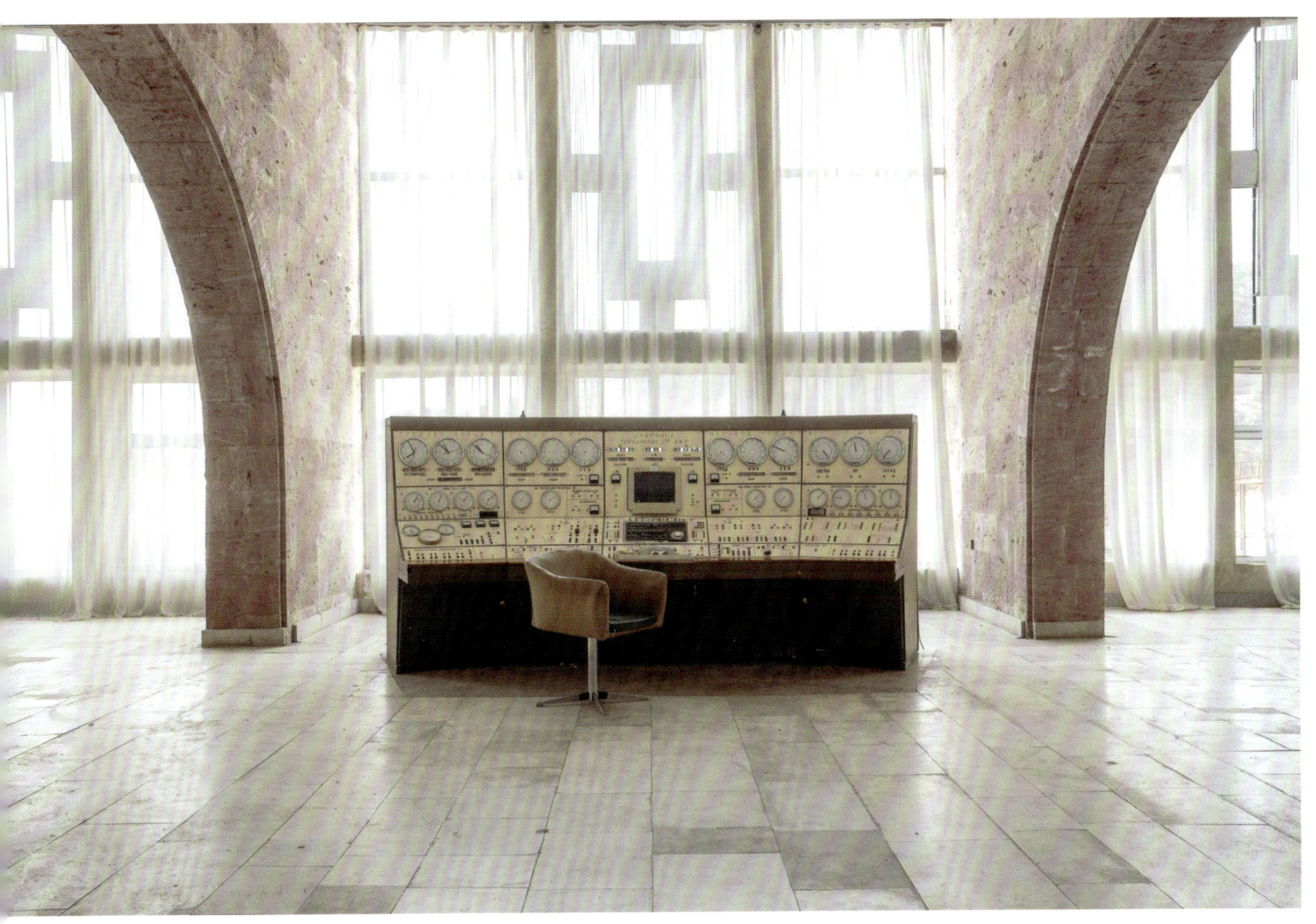

A frontal view of the central control panel. (The radio control panel stands to the left and the optical control panel to the right.)

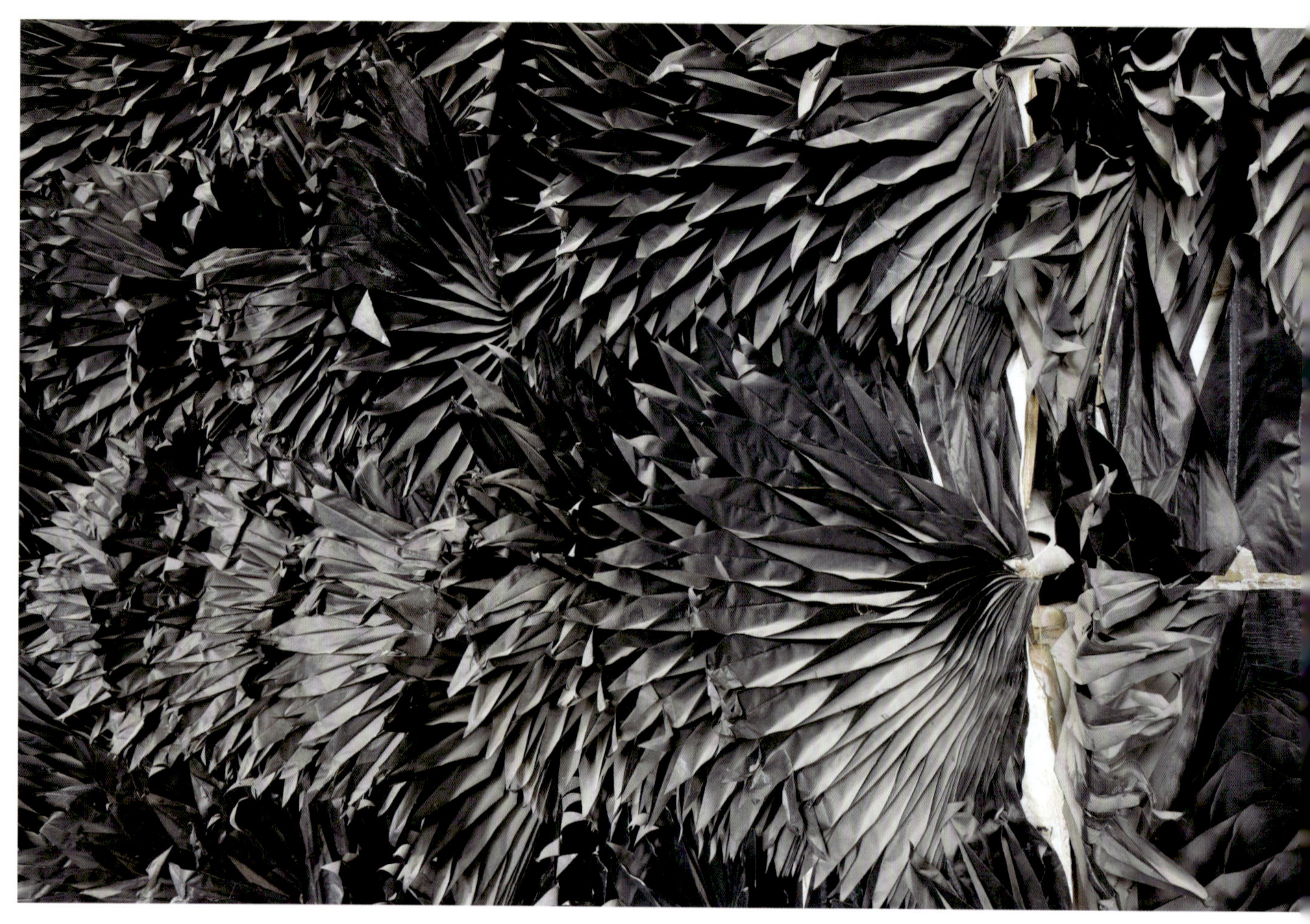

Inside the anechoic chamber. This space contains petal-like wave absorbers, designed to eliminate electromagnetic reflections, creating an echo-less environment for testing and measurement.

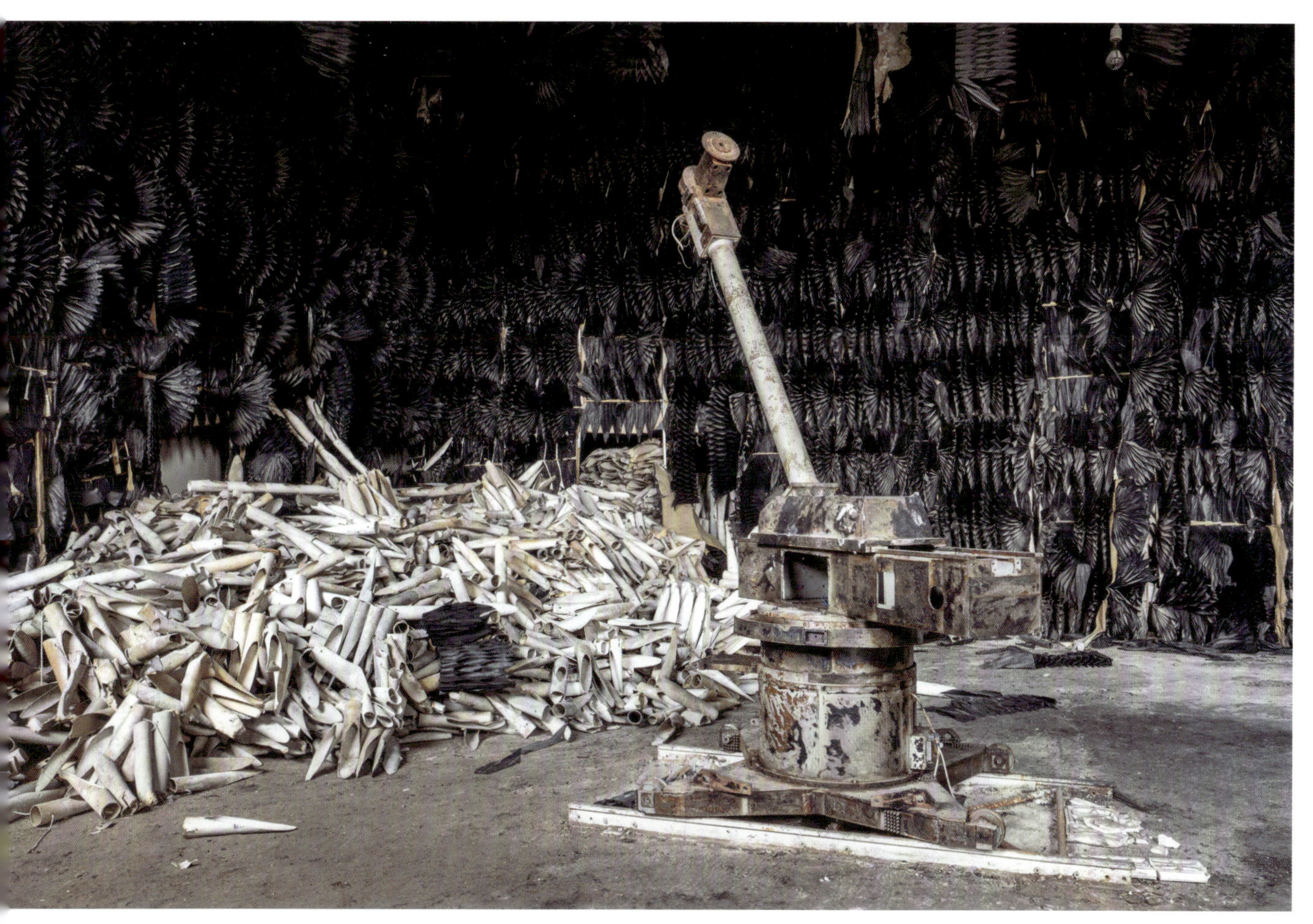

The anechoic chamber used the near-field method for antenna certification. With this method, both the measurement (probe) antenna and the antenna under test are moved over a predefined surface, allowing the comparison of near-field data. This information is then processed mathematically to determine the test antenna's far-field characteristics.

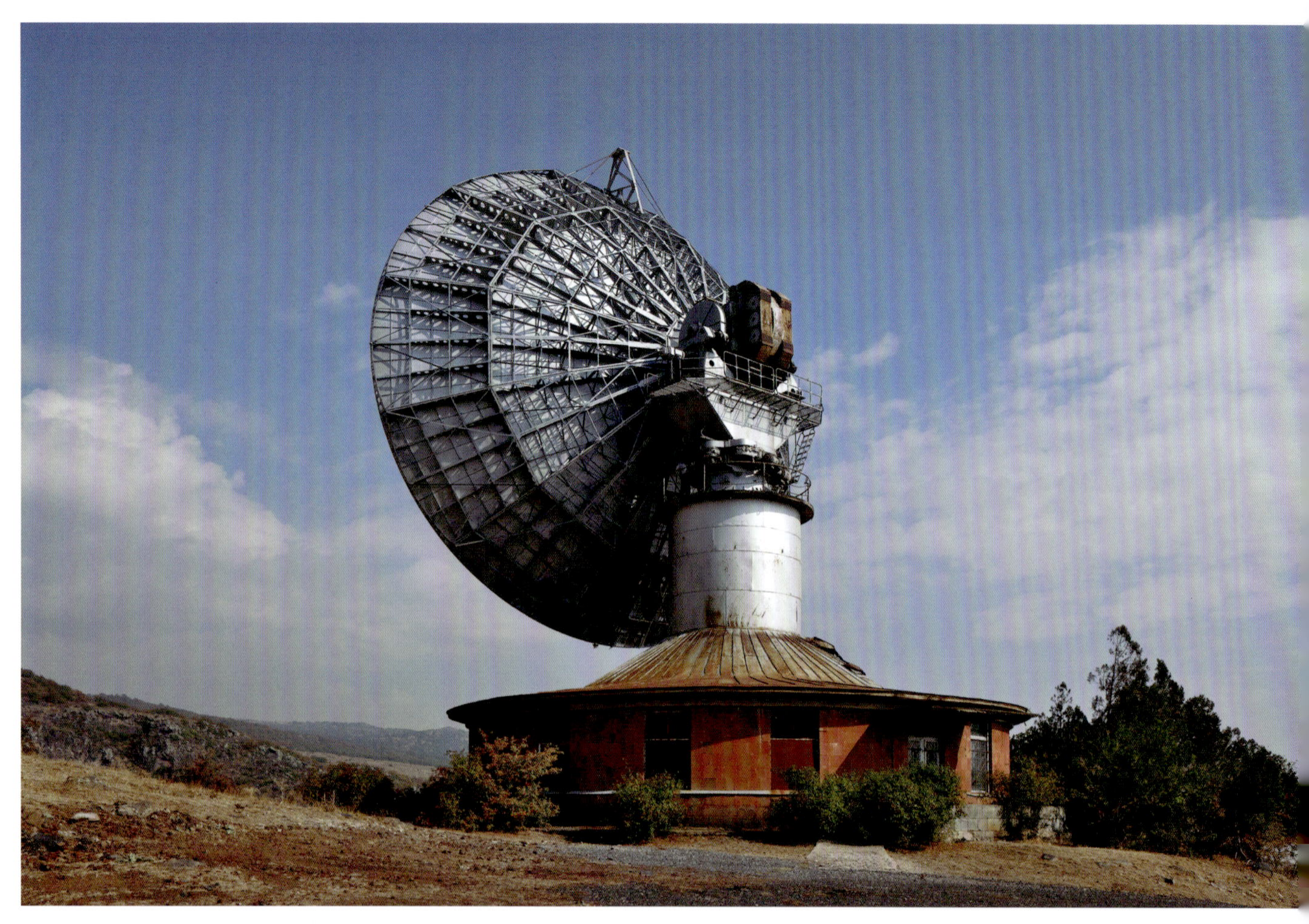

This radio telescope with its fully steerable 18-metre antenna was used as the state standard to measure radio waves for metrological purposes.

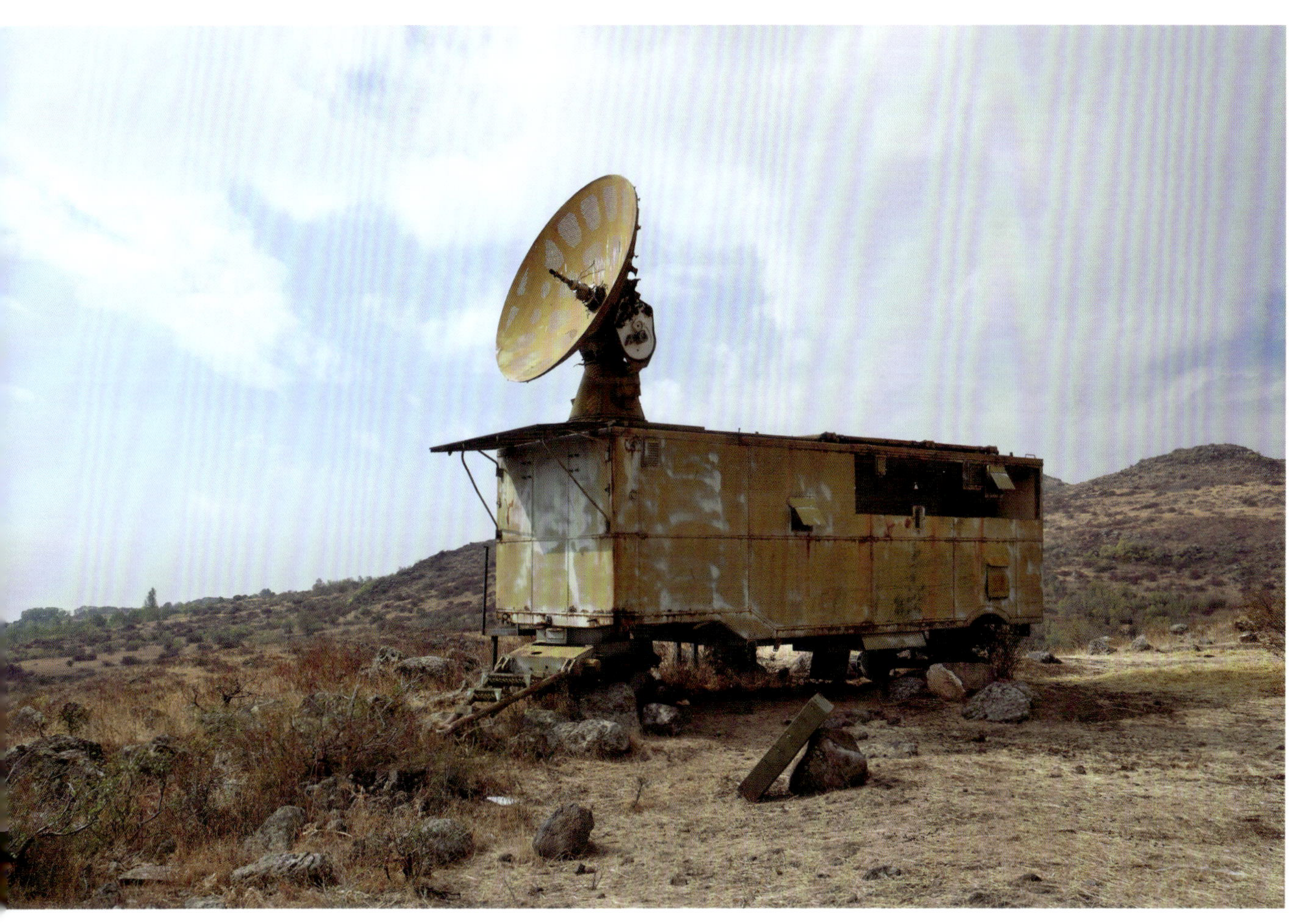

A SON-30 type Soviet-era mobile fire control radar intended for use with 130 mm KS-30 towed anti-aircraft guns. The antenna features a 3-metre-diameter parabolic reflector.

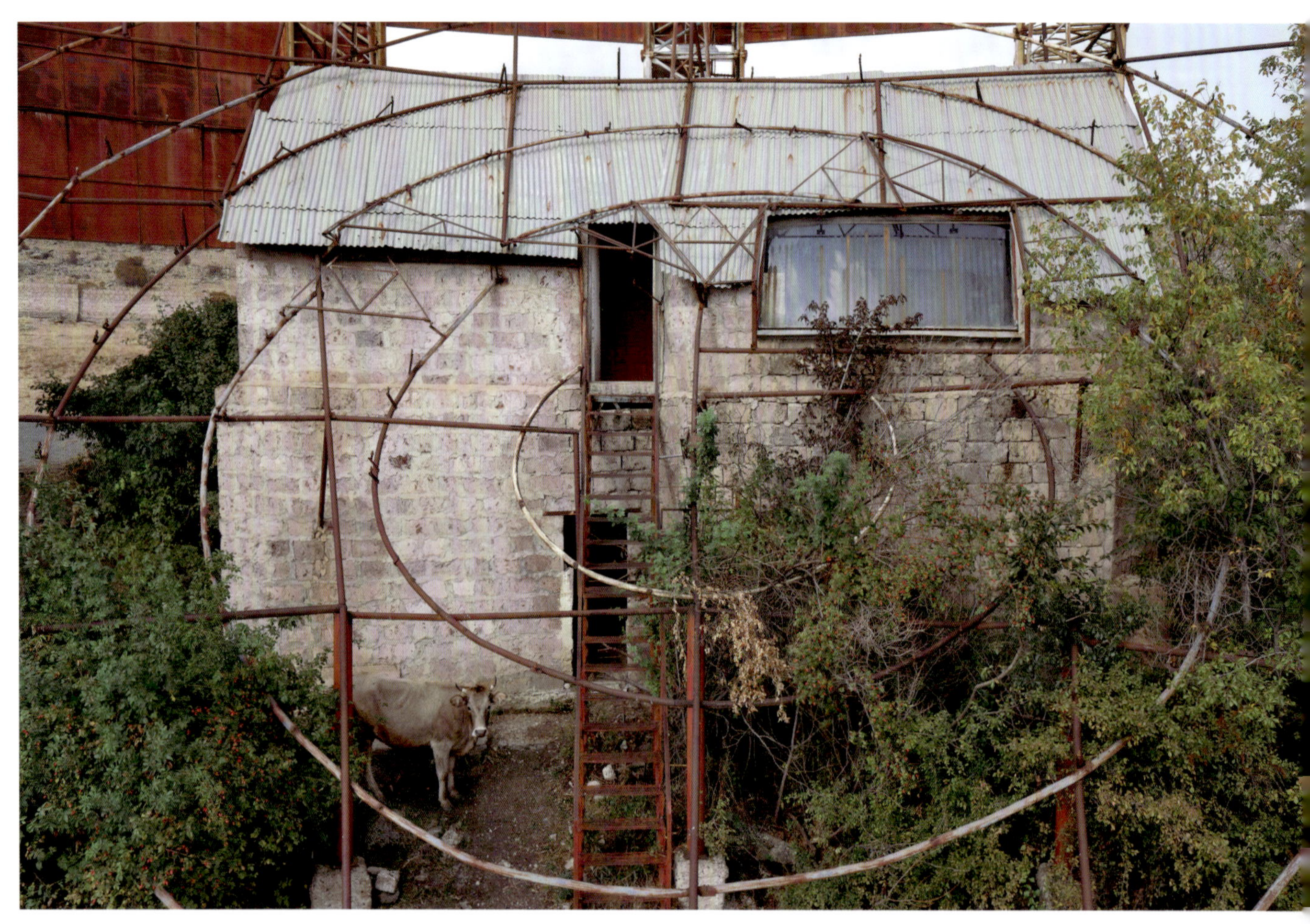

During the energy crisis of 1991–1995 in Armenia, inventor Herouni developed an idea for a new type of solar energy power plant that concentrated the Sun's rays to achieve high temperatures. Air was heated in a thermal exchanger and then directed to a turbine, which powered an electrical generator and a compressor.

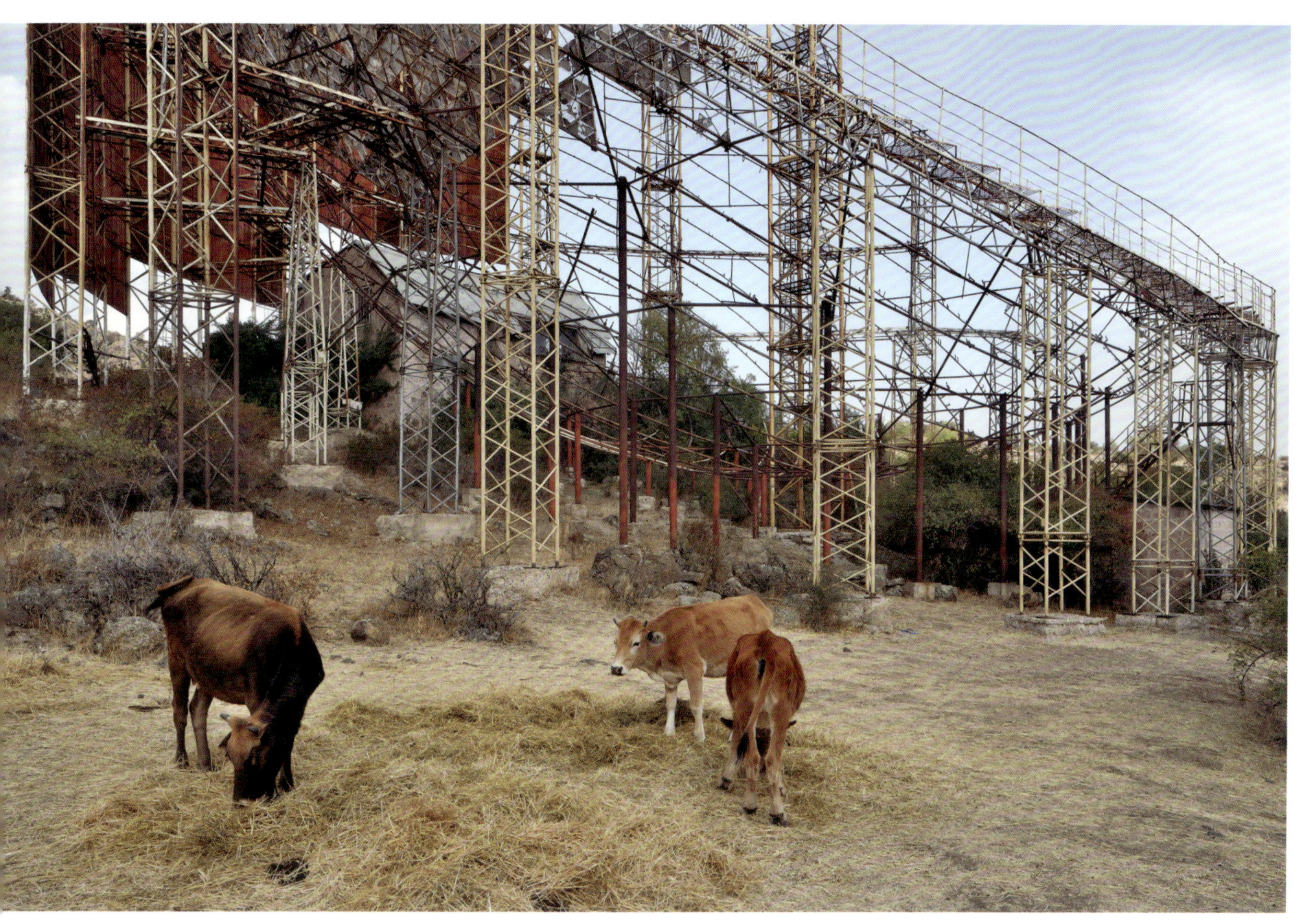

The pilot project named 'AREV' (meaning 'SUN' in Armenian), used a 36-metre diameter spherical mirror, fixed with props. Herouni planned for the next version to be more effective, with a mirror measuring 75-metres in diameter. However, the thermal power plant was eventually discontinued due to disagreements with foreign investors and a lack of state support.

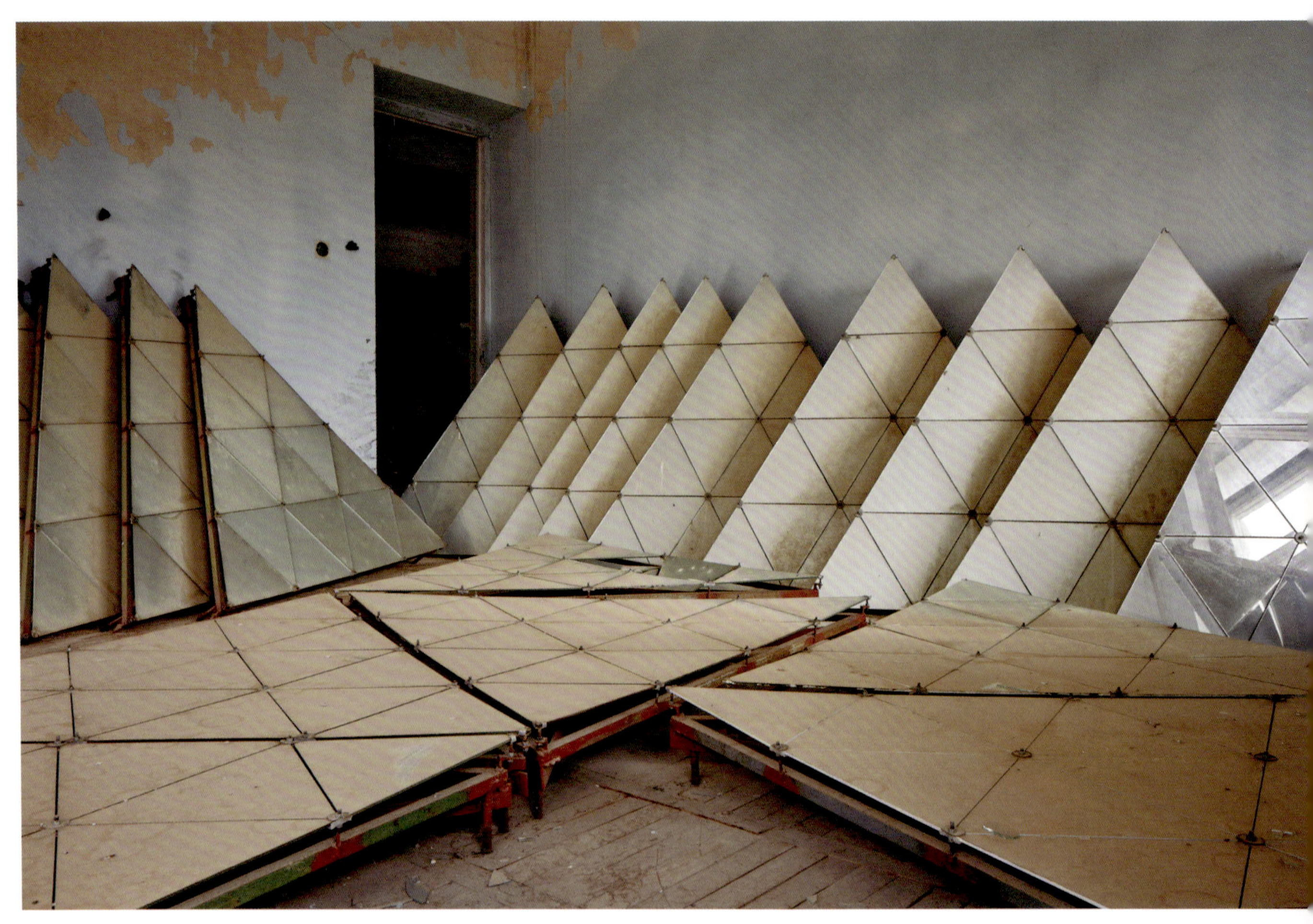

Blocks of mirrors for the AREV solar power plant in storage. Antenna reflectors no longer used for radio physics research have been modified as mirror concentrators.

Right: The partially constructed AREV solar thermal power station on Mount Aragats.

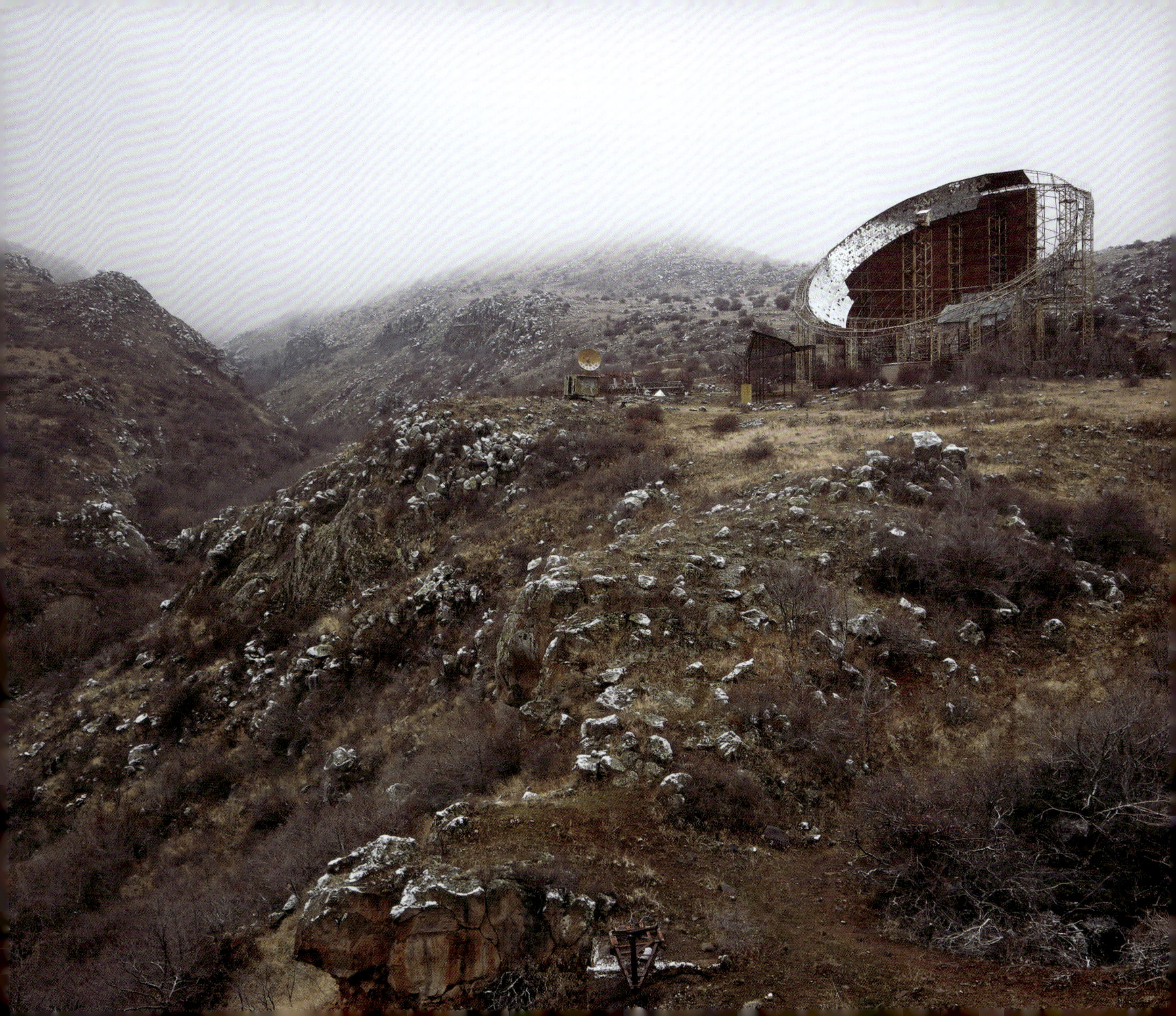

YEREVAN PHYSICS INSTITUTE

A.I. Alikhanyan National Science Laboratory
Yerevan, ARMENIA

In 1956, 13 years after co-founding and directing the Yerevan Physics Institute with his brother Abram Alikhanov (1904–1970), Artem Alikhanian (1908–1978) began the development of the Armenian Accelerator (known as ARUS, from the Russian *Armyanskii Uskoritel*). His aim was to construct the most powerful electron synchrotron in the world. Capable of accelerating particles to nearly the speed of light around a closed loop, these sophisticated machines are used to study the elementary building blocks of matter.

Following a detailed geological survey, a suitable area of basalt rock was found, providing a stable foundation that would minimise any risk from potential seismic activity. In order to procure the huge financial and logistical support needed for this project, as well as maintaining the facilities and the ongoing research in high-energy physics and related fields, Alikhanyan transferred control of the institute to the USSR State Committee for Atomic Energy. Between 1960 and 1966, construction of the accelerator was the biggest project in the country. The installation and subsequent modifications were completed by 18 separate organisations. Along with the creation of new departments, services and laboratories, a new town – nicknamed 'Physcity' – was built, incorporating employee housing, schools, kindergartens, shops, clinics, a cultural centre and a hotel. Alikhanian commented that 'The construction of the accelerator is first of all the construction of socialism,' though in fact the brothers were never members of the Communist Party. This was a rare exception within the Soviet elite, where key administrative positions could only be obtained with Party approval.

In 1956, the scientist and dissident Yuri Orlov (1924–2020) was expelled from the Party after being accused of anti-Soviet speech, and fired from his job at the Institute for Theoretical and Experimental Physics in Moscow. He was invited by the brothers to join them in Armenia, where his groundbreaking theoretical work pioneered the advance of particle accelerators. Designed to accelerate electrons to 6 gigaelectron volts (GeV), ARUS formally achieved a beam energy of 6.1 GeV when it was was officially launched on 25 October 1967 (coinciding with the 50th anniversary of the October Revolution). Between 1970 and 1991, the synchrotron regulary performed around 15 experiments a year on both military and civilian projects.

At its peak the institute employed around 4,500 staff. Today, the figure has fallen below 400. After gaining independence in 1991 Armenia suffered a severe energy crisis, bringing work to a standstill. After the synchrotron was brought back online in 1998, a small number of experiments were carried out, but in 2008, economic difficulties led to the suspension of operations. While it remains idle, this complex machine continues to deteriorate and the chances of its functioning again become increasingly remote.

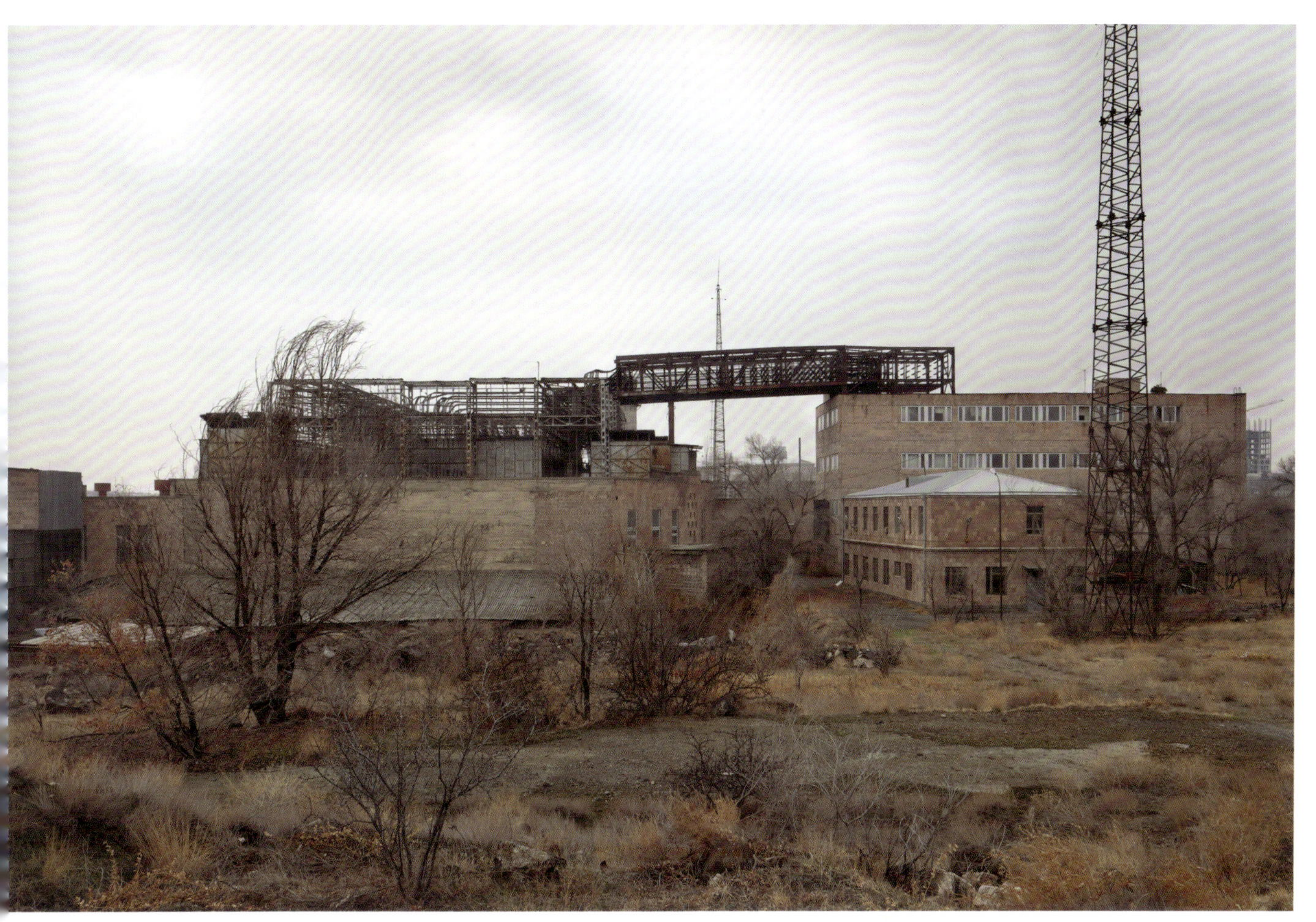

Buildings housing the ARUS synchrotron facility.

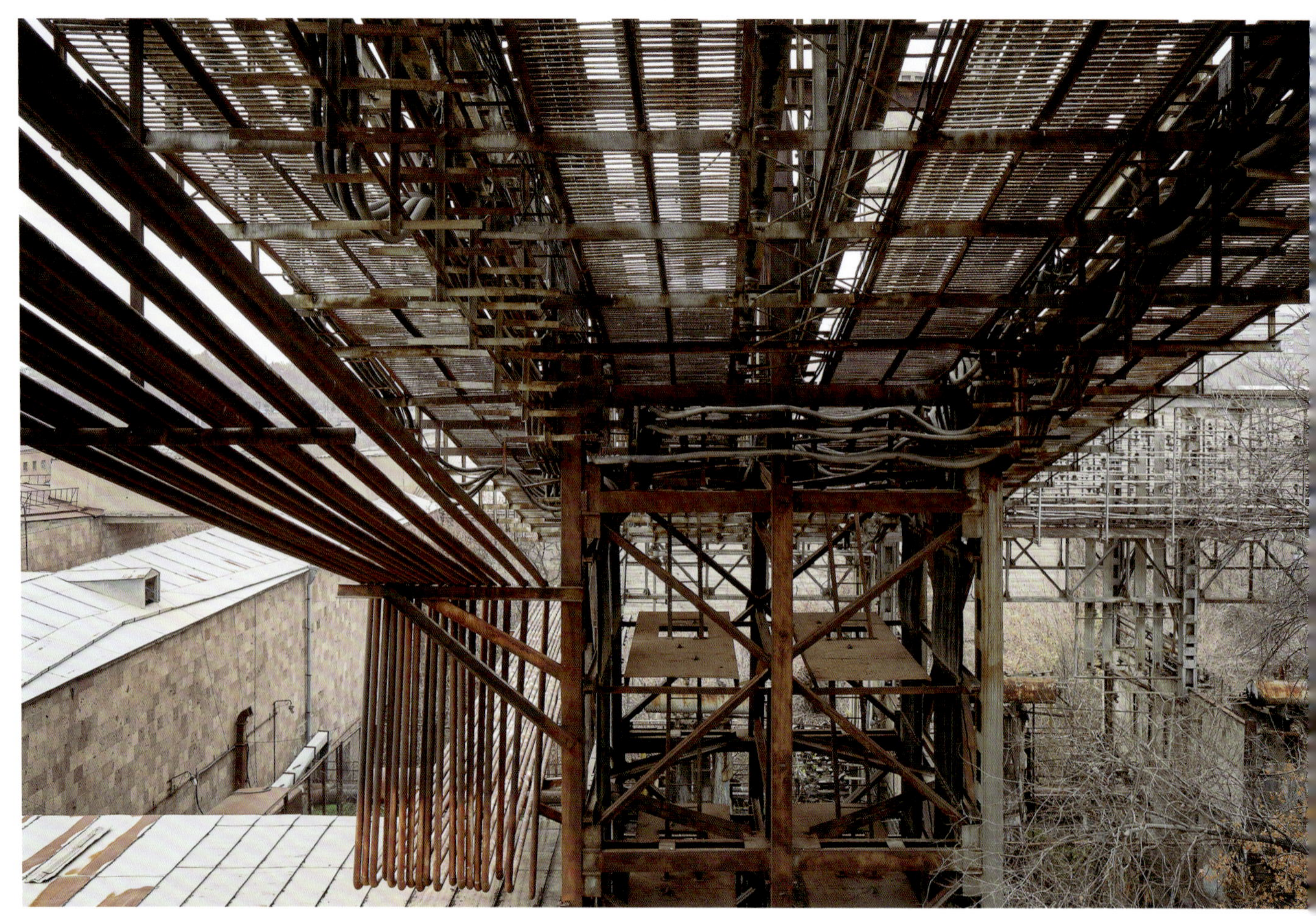

This exterior framework construction carries power supplies across the roof.

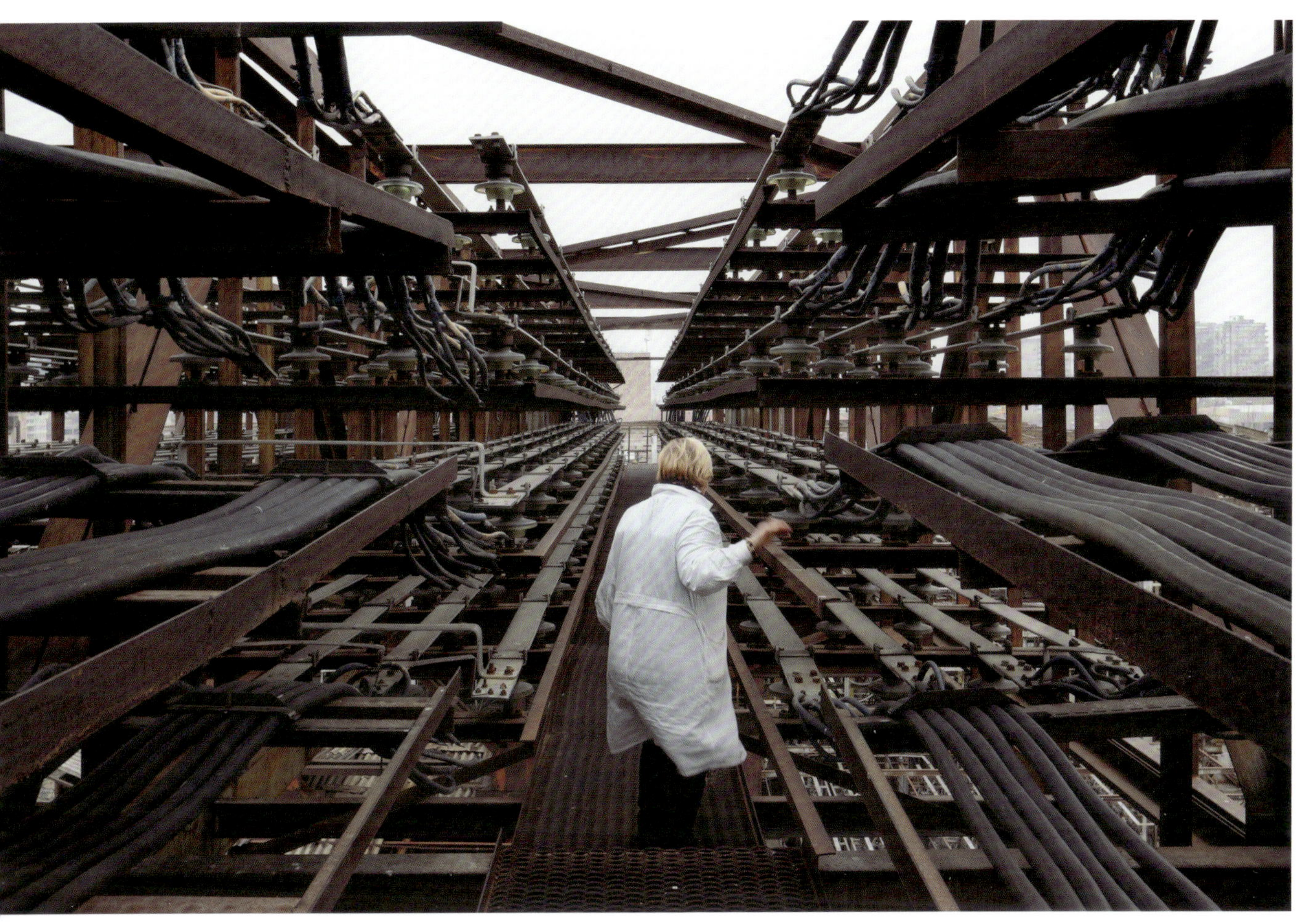

Stasia Khosrovyan specialises in electrical cables and their connections. She has worked at the institute since 1966.

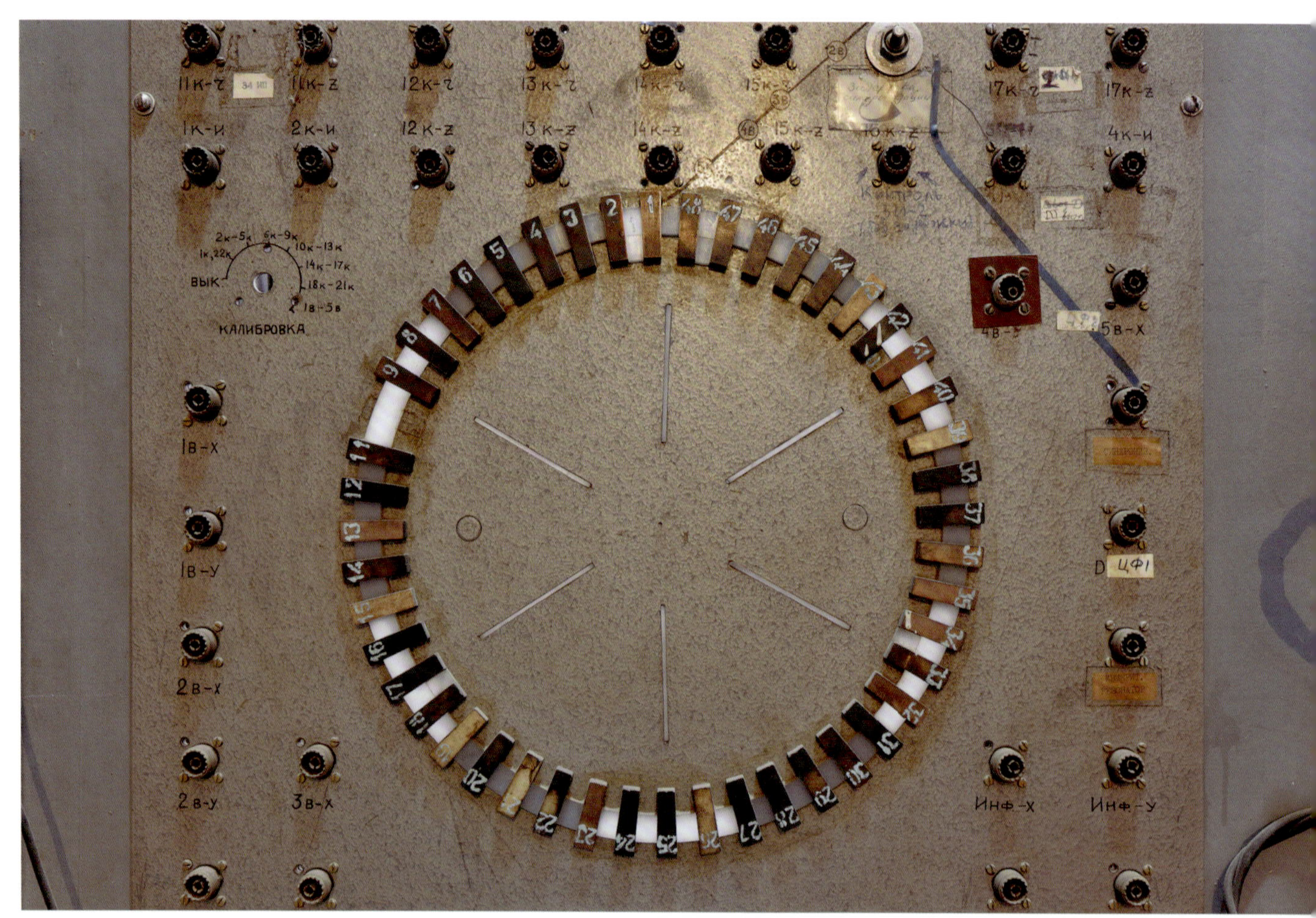

This panel displays a model of the accelerator, which was used to obtain information about the operation of its 48 magnets.

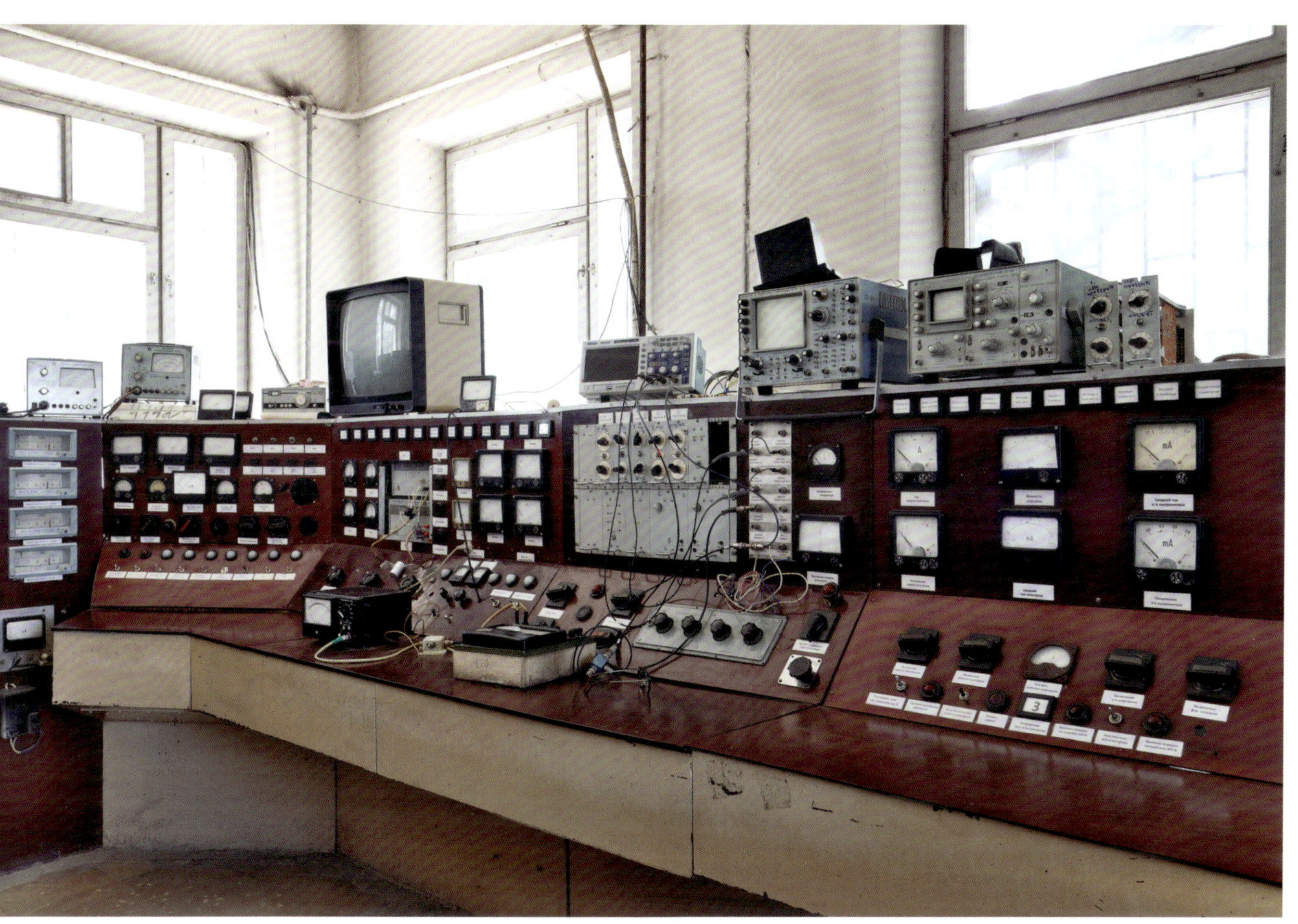

The control room of the LUE-75, a linear accelerator once used as the injector for the synchrotron. In this capacity, it would accelerate charged particles to a high enough energy and speed before injecting them into the main synchrotron ring. Today, it functions as an independent apparatus, enabling research into low-energy nuclear physics.

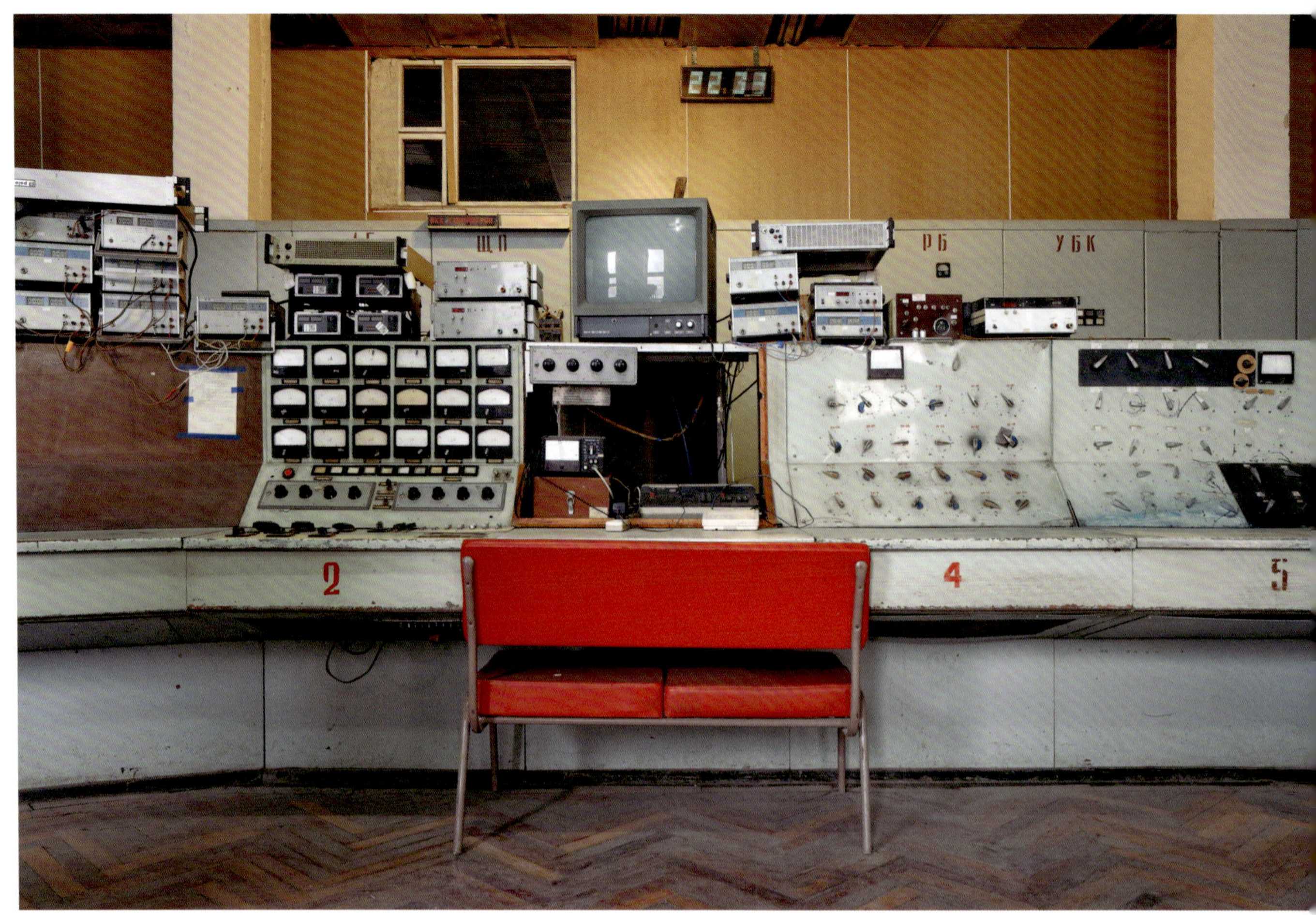

The synchrotron control room.

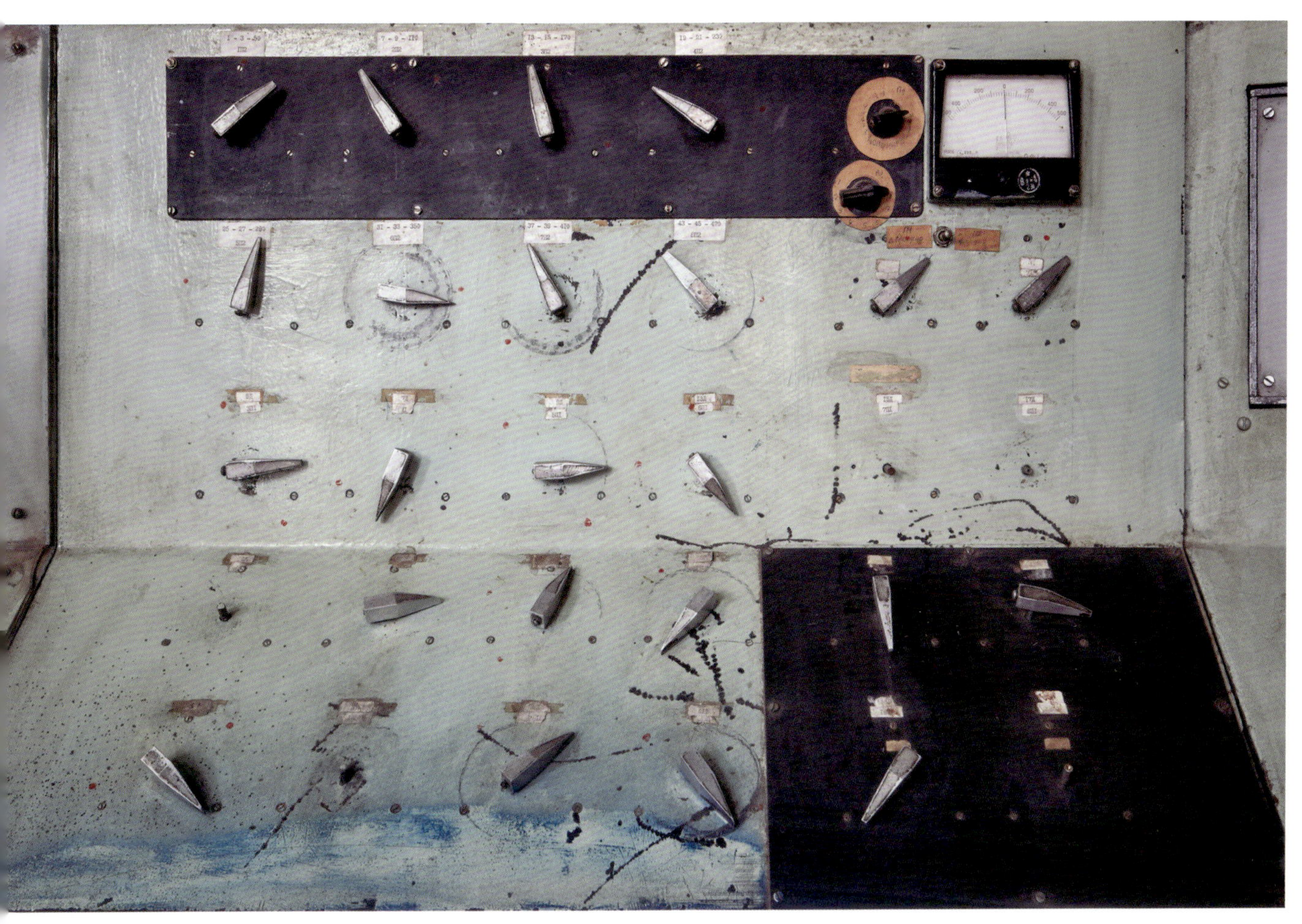

This control panel was used to adjust the 48 magnetic blocks of the synchrotron. Adjusting these powerful magnets allows the operator to accurately direct the circular path of the electron beam, maintaining a stable orbit.

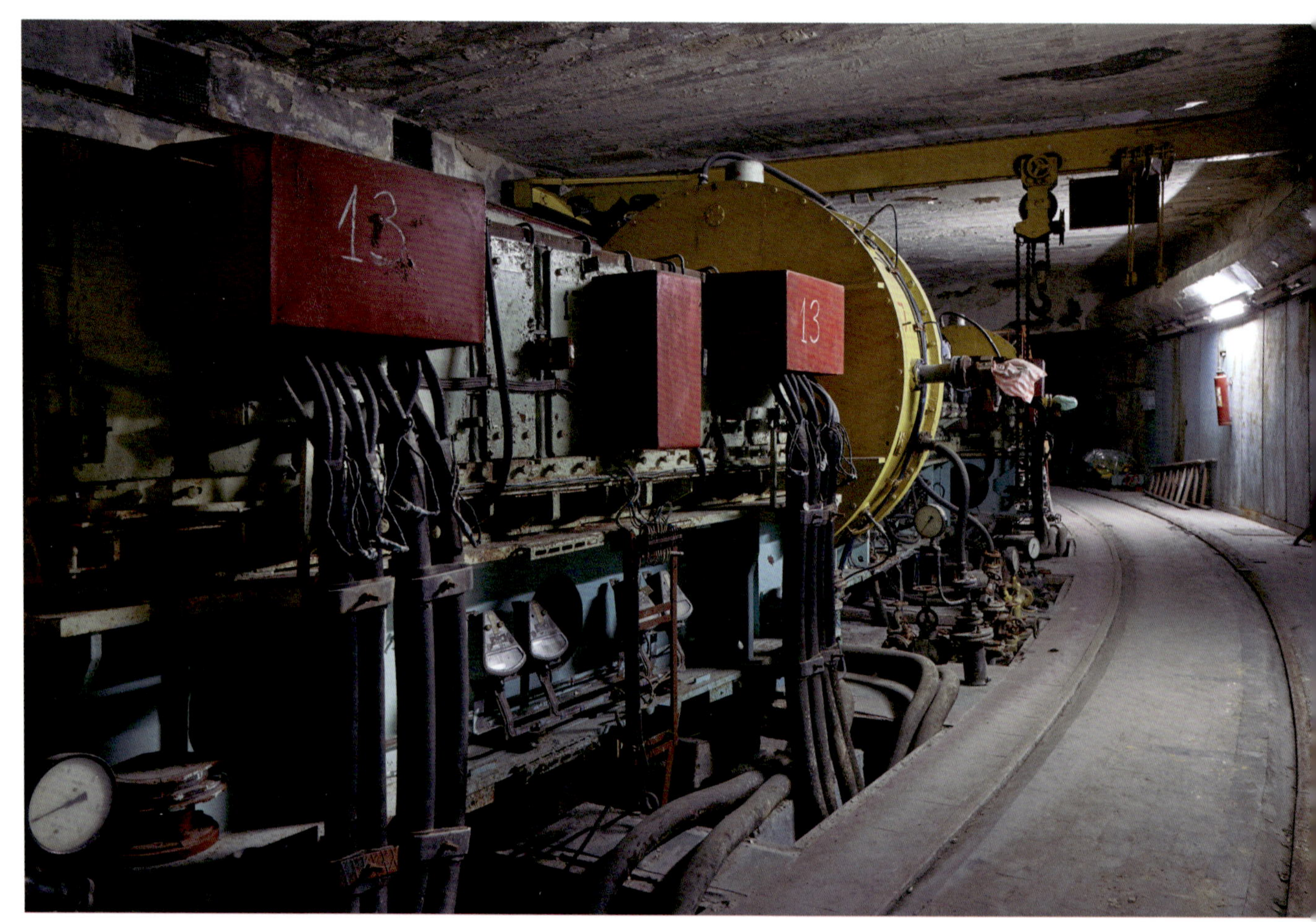

The 48 magnetic blocks of the synchrotron are evenly distributed around a 217-metre-long ring, three storeys below ground.

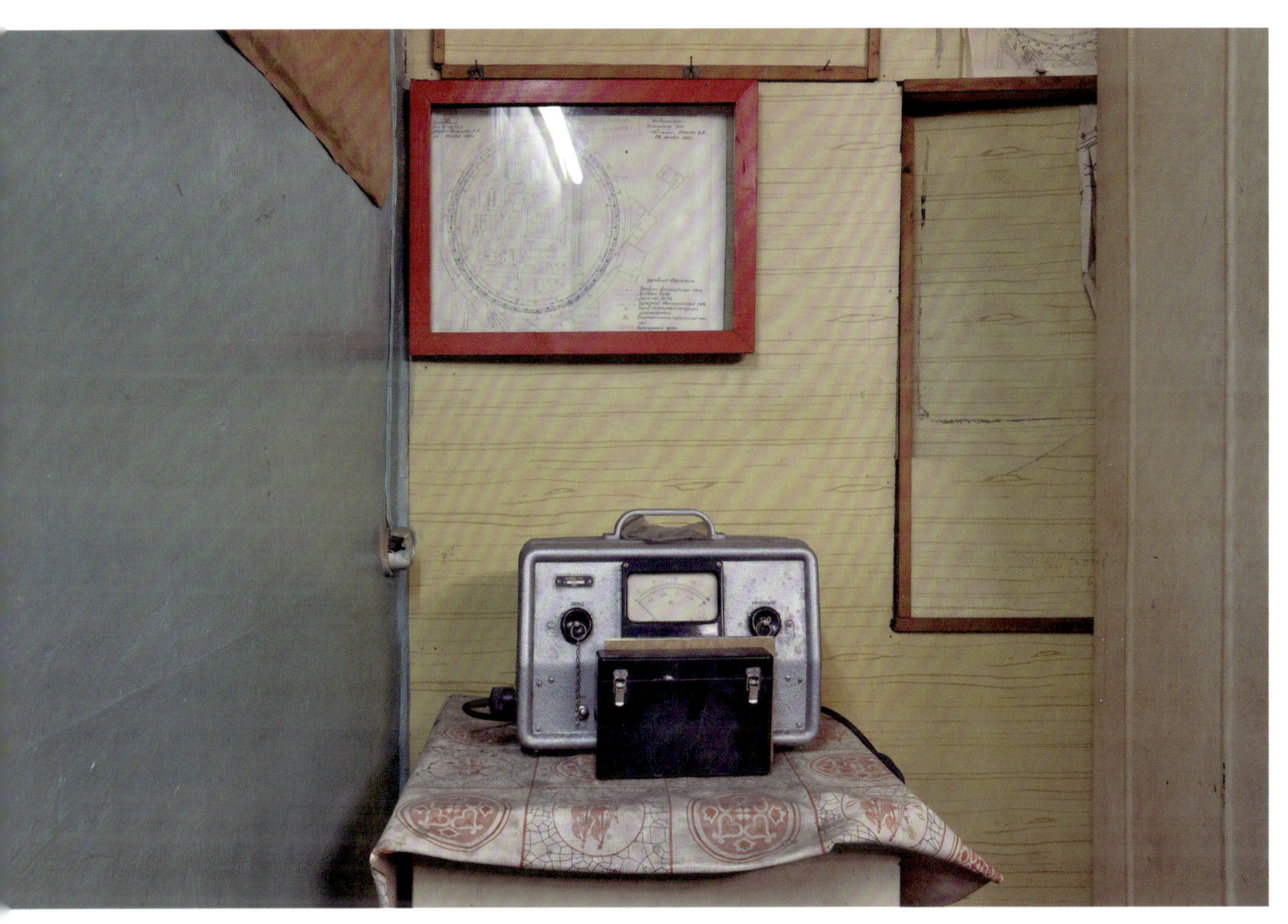

On the table is an Individual Dosimetric Kit KID-1 from 1965, designed to measure accumulated X-ray and gamma radiation doses. The red frame mounted on the wall above contains a plan of the synchrotron dated 28 December 1984.

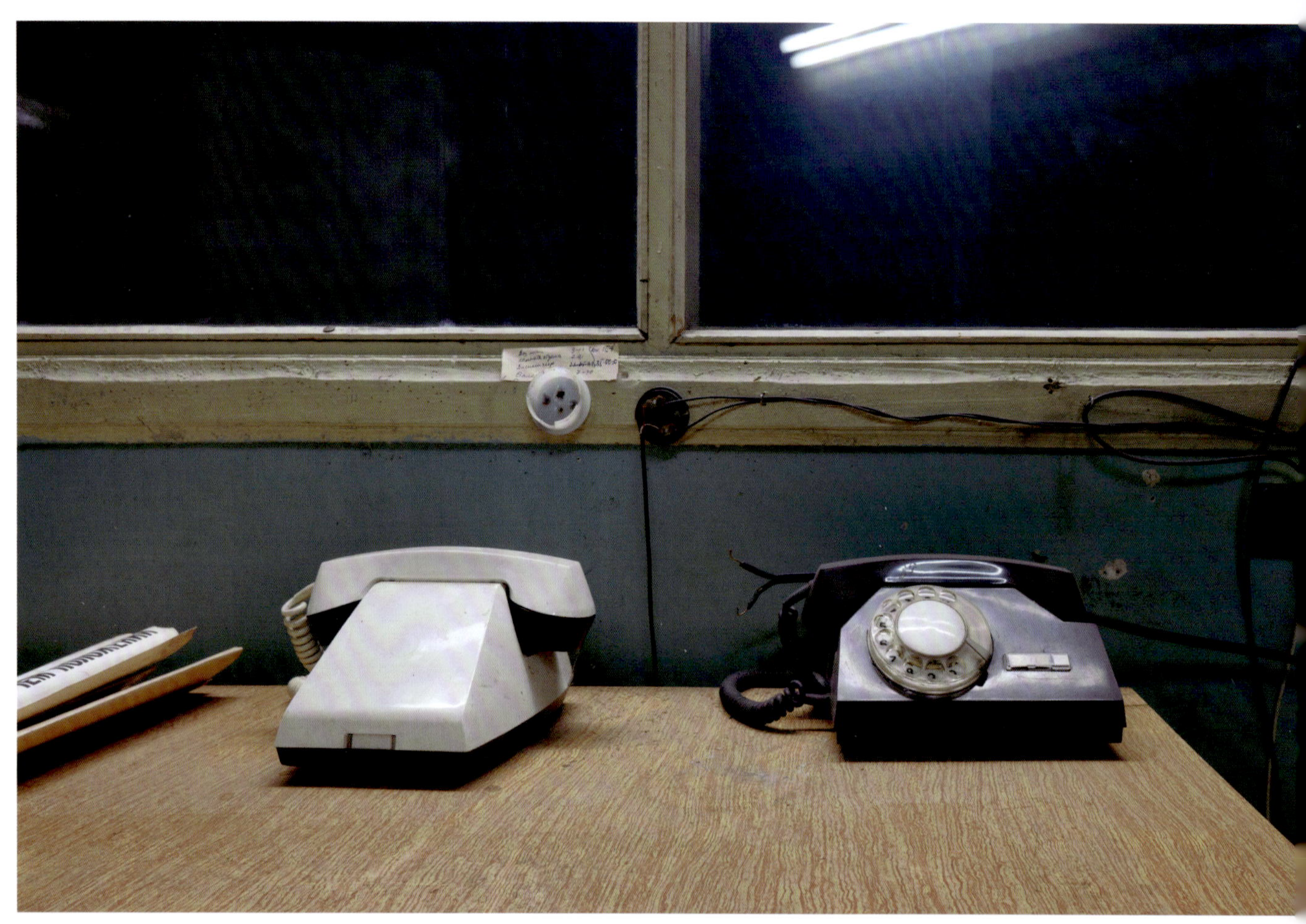

Soviet-era telephones in the machinery hall office.

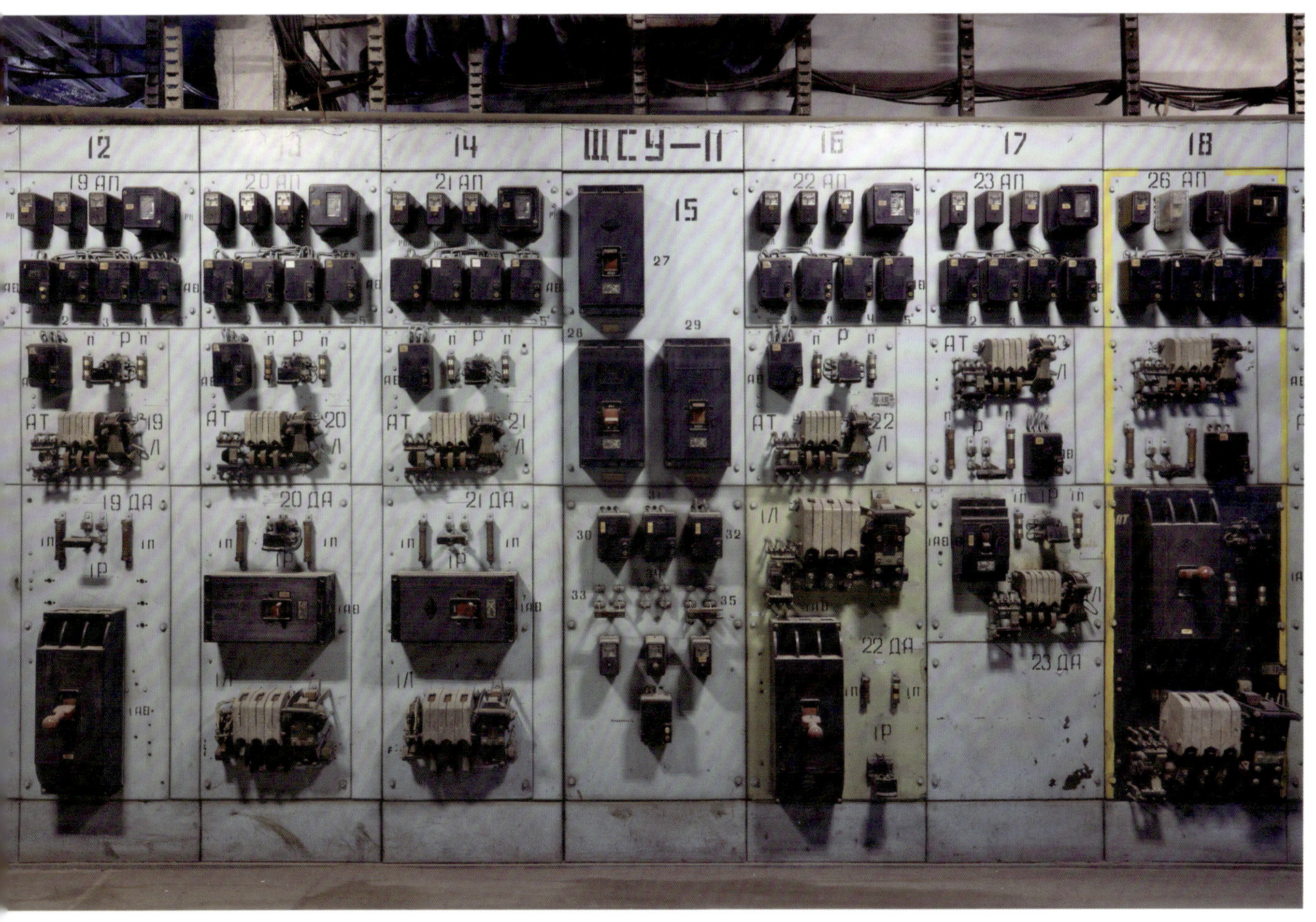

Electrical switchgear in the machinery hall.

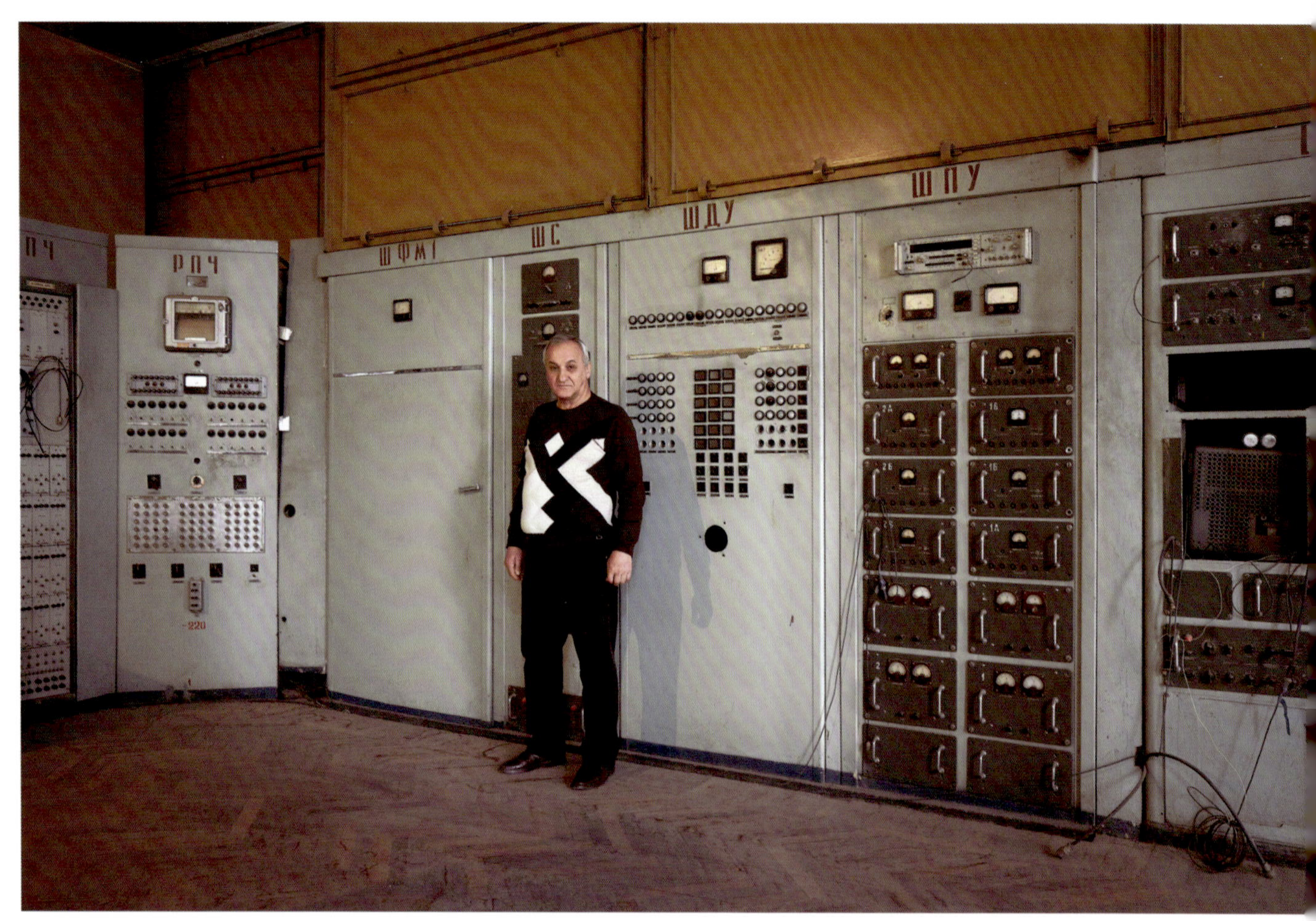

Aram Bayburdtsyan is one of the last employees still working with the synchrotron.

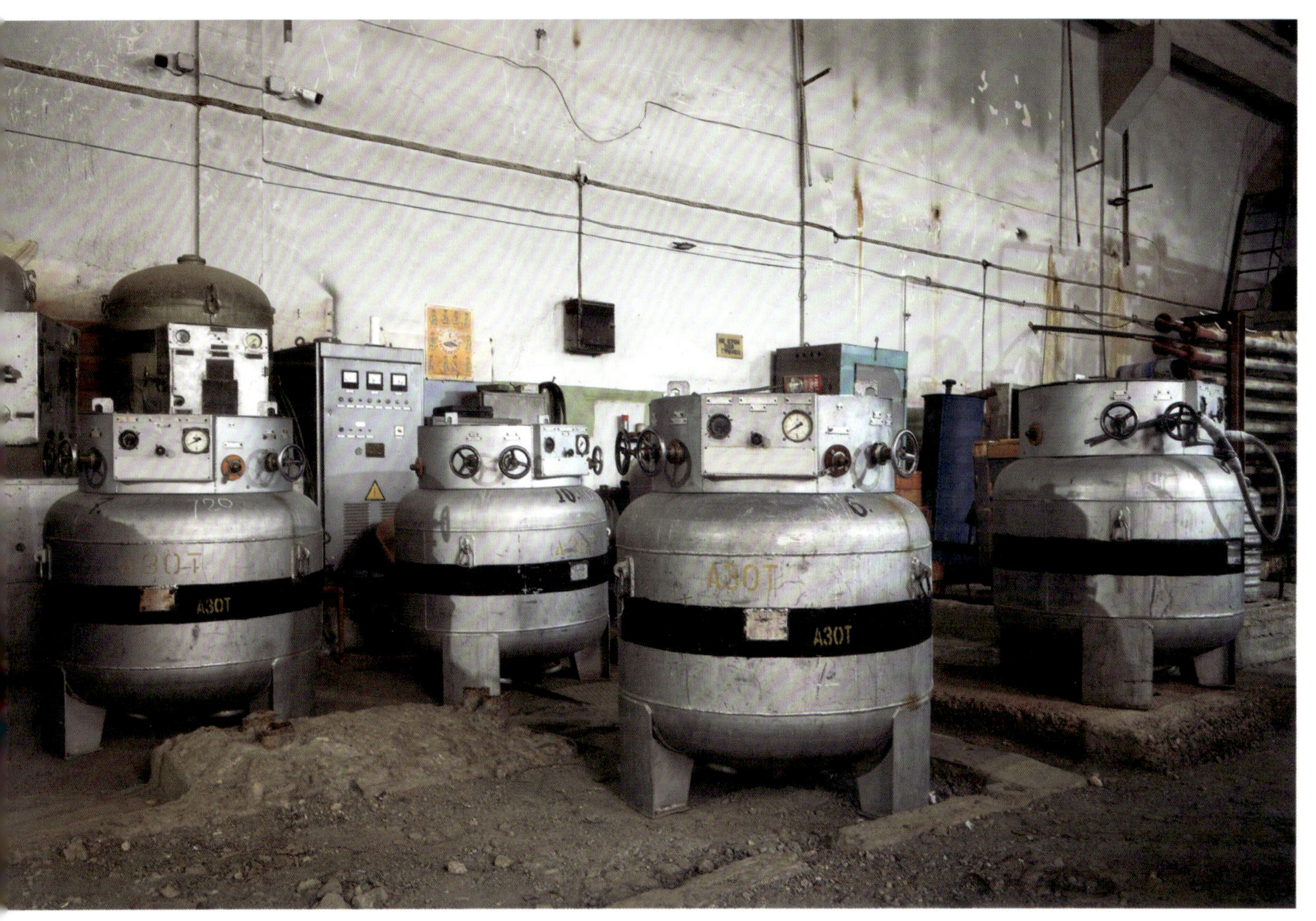

Containers of liquid nitrogen in the cryogenic laboratory.

ANDRONIKASHVILI INSTITUTE OF PHYSICS

Ivane Javakhishvili Tbilisi State University

Tbilisi, GEORGIA

Renowned physicist Igor Kurchatov (1903–1960) led the Soviet quest to develop nuclear capabilities in both weaponry and energy. As part of this programme, experimental prototype reactors were assembled that led to the construction of the Standard Research Reactor (IRT) and the Water-cooled, Water-moderated Reactor (VVR). These models were then reproduced throughout the country and abroad, with construction peaking in the late 1950s and early 1960s, when over 30 were built in the USSR alone.

One of the first of the IRT reactors was constructed near Tbilisi in Georgia, a project initiated in 1957 by Elephter Andronikashvili (1910–1989), founder and director of the Institute of Physics and renowned specialist in low-temperature physics. Scientists at the institute accurately modelled conditions found in space, allowing them to study the effects of low-temperature irradiation on various materials. At the height of the Space Race, this information provided valuable data to the military on how to protect electronic devices in such an extreme environment. All information concerning the scientists' identities and their research was highly classified.

During its lifespan the reactor had two major refurbishments, increasing its capacity from 2 to 8 megawatts. After the Chornobyl nuclear accident in 1986 all work at the facility was suspended as safety checks were carried out. Subsequently, control and emergency systems were upgraded and by the beginning of 1990 operations were ready to resume. However, with a limited lifespan, increasing political instability and continuous protests over the proximity of a nuclear facility to the capital, the decision was made to shut down the reactor completely.

In the early 1990s, following the break-up of the USSR, Georgian society experienced chaotic instability, the collapse of the rule of law and the rise of criminality. At this time the reactor was targeted by armed paramilitary groups attempting to seize valuable uranium. Employees remained on site around the clock in order to prevent such a catastrophe. To avoid the risk of future nuclear proliferation, discussions began with the US and UK as to how best deal with this sensitive material. In April 1998, Operation Auburn Endeavour secured and transported 4.3 kg of highly enriched uranium from the site to a safe storage facility in the UK.

A lack of financial resources meant that the standard decommissioning process of completely dismantling the reactor could not be realised. Instead, a new on-site disposal strategy was adopted, with the reactor core being 'entombed' using a special concrete containing barium. This process was effectively completed in 2016.

Today, the site is occasionally used by the International Atomic Energy Agency to run courses on nuclear safeguarding, while scientific research into radiobiology and radioecology utilises old sources of radiation found on the site.

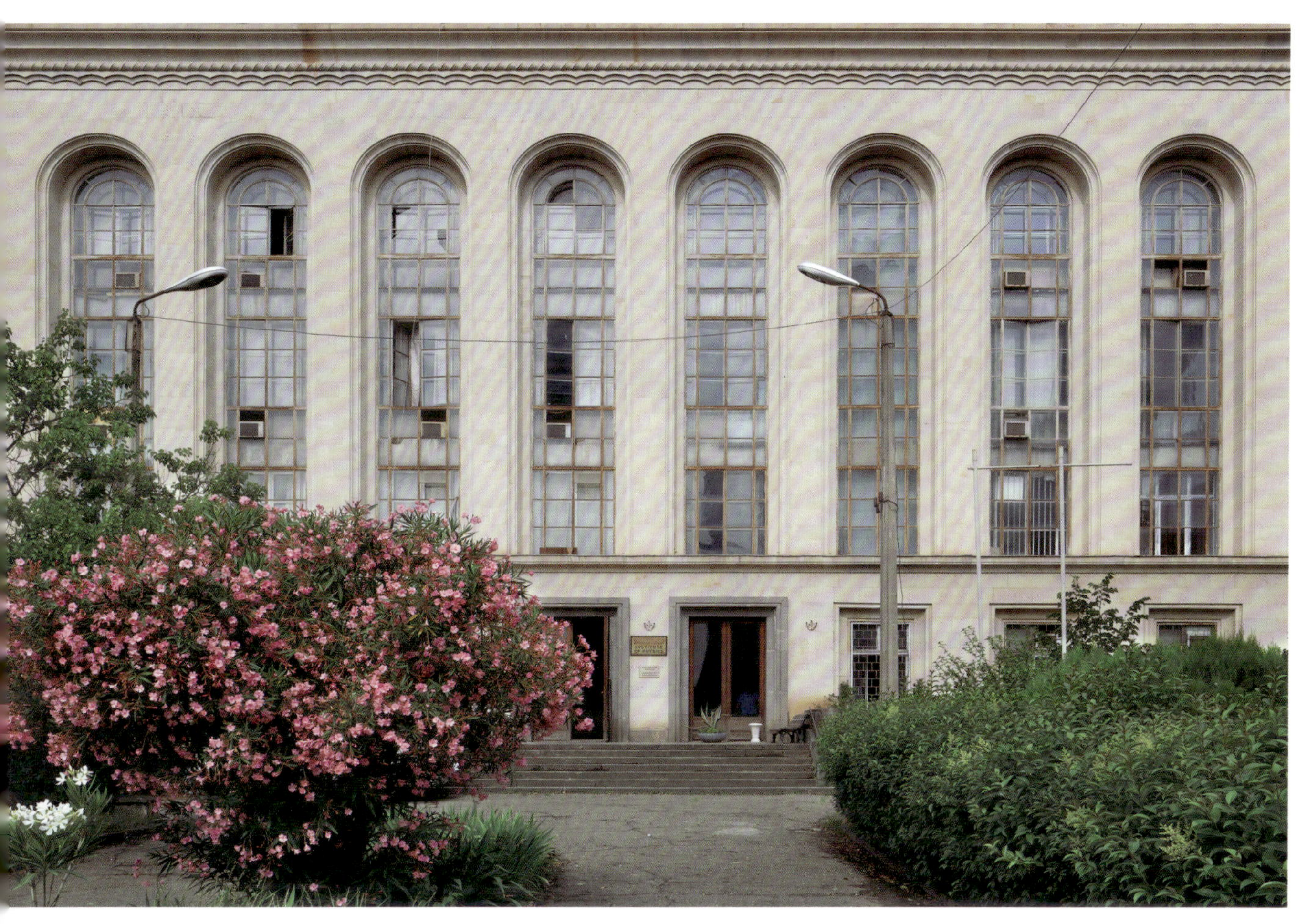

The Institute of Physics in Tbilisi was established in 1950 by Academician Elephter Andronikashvili (1910–1989). He was appointed director in 1951, a position he retained until 1988. The institute was named after him in 1999.

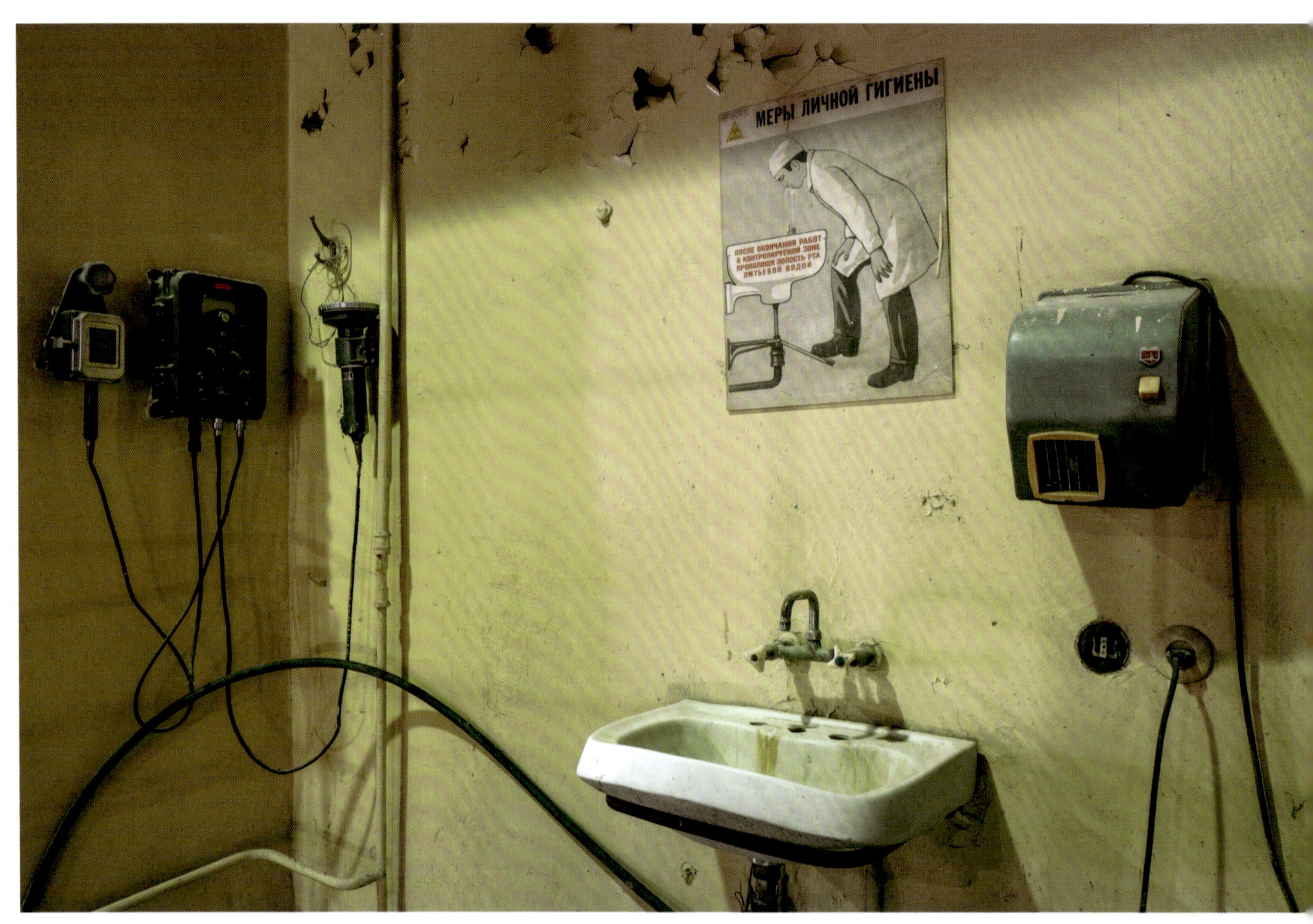

A device to measure radioactivity hangs on a wall next to a washbasin. The poster above the basin reads (in Russian) 'Personal hygiene measures – after finishing work in the controlled area, rinse your mouth with drinking water'.

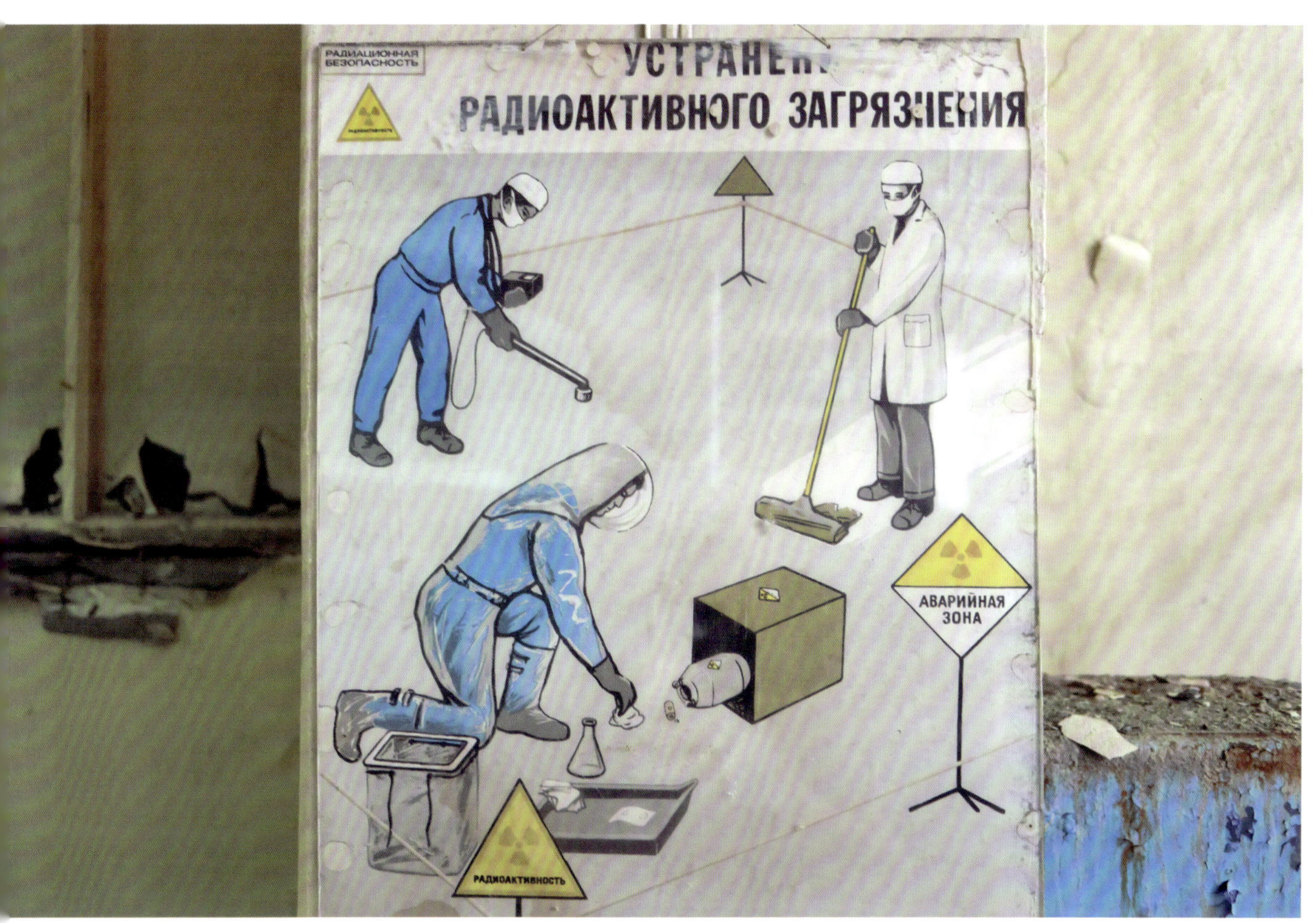

The poster reads (in Russian) 'Elimination of radioactive contamination'.

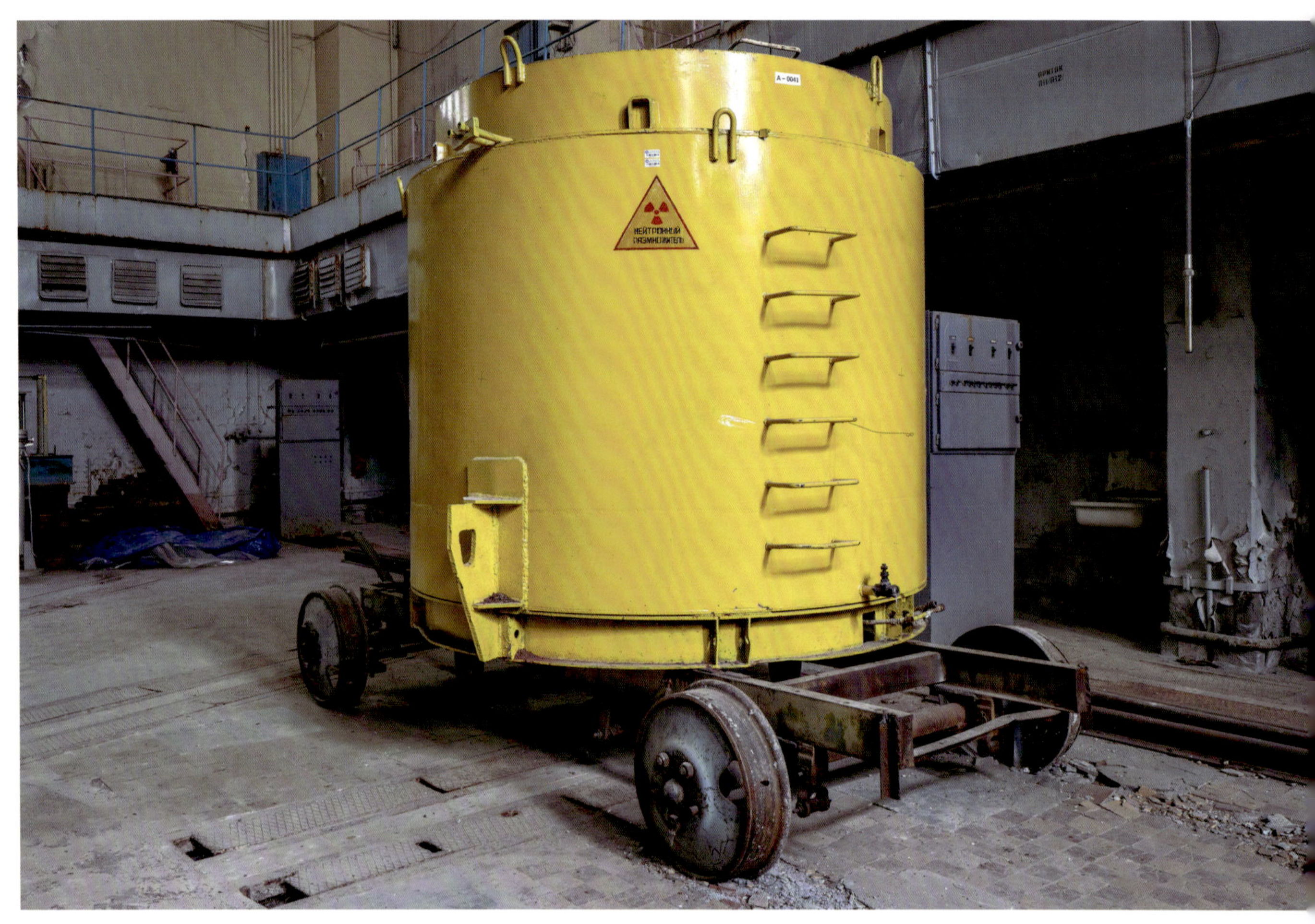

The Breeder-1 Neutron Source (Razmnozhitel-1) was utilised for non-destructive analyses in various fields, including mineral exploration, agricultural studies and criminal investigations. In 2015, 1.83 kg of highly enriched uranium was transported outside Georgia as part of a non-proliferation programme.

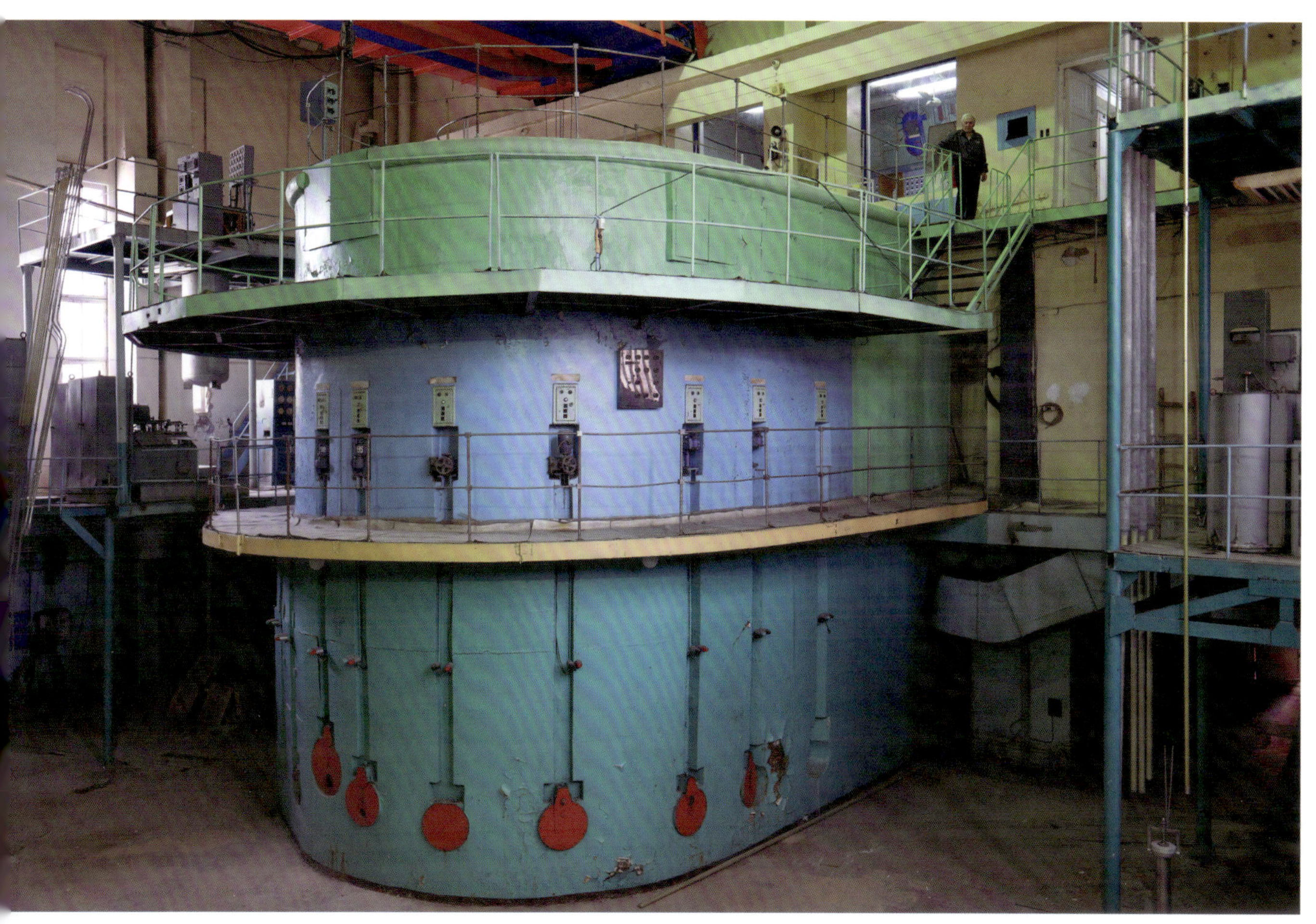

The Standard Research Reactor is a pool-type reactor using water as moderator, neutron reflector, coolant and as part of the biological shielding of the reactor. The channels spaced around the core served as outlets (via the apertures painted red) allowing neutron beams to be directed to external experimental devices for research purposes.

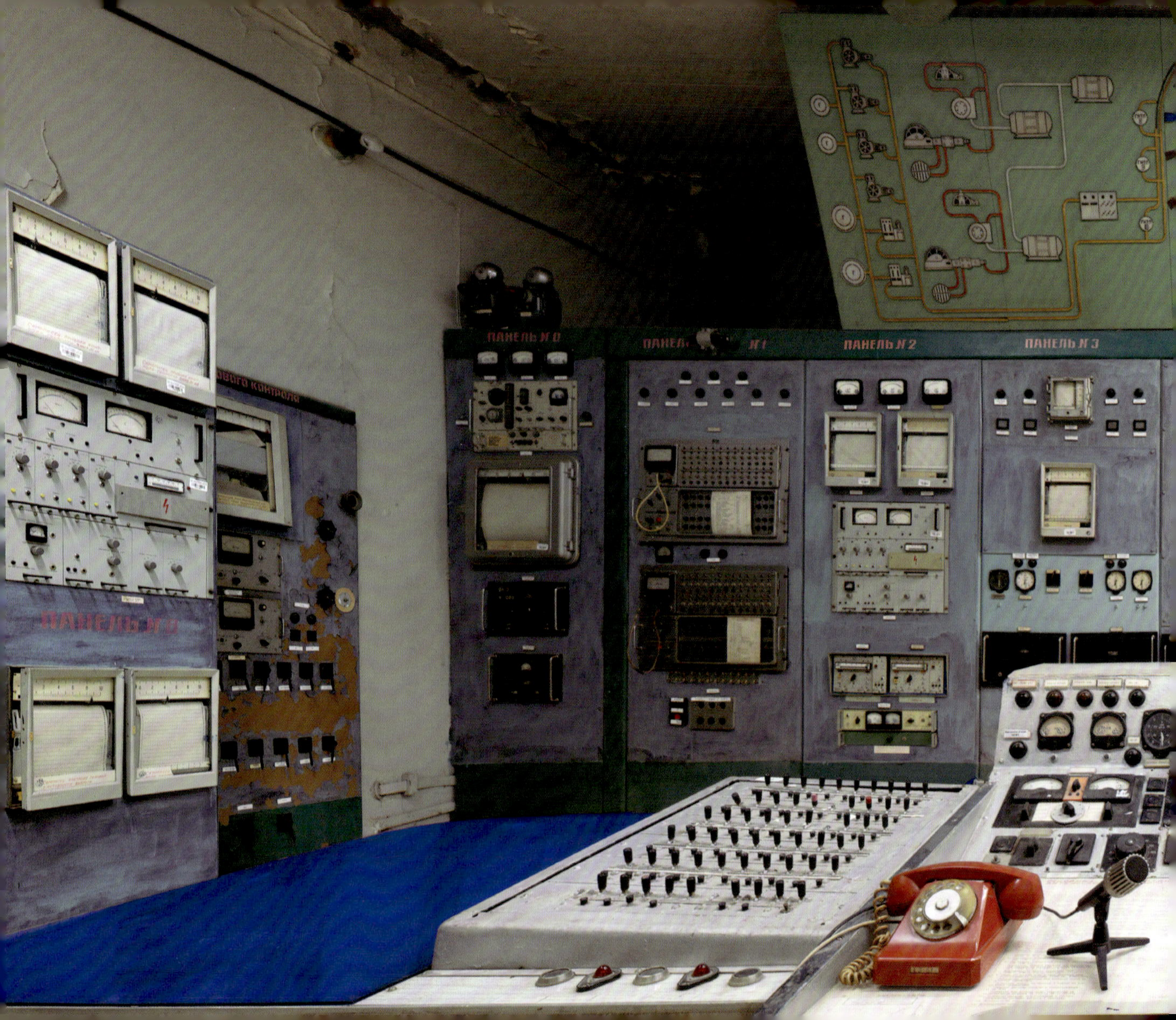
ПАНЕЛЬ №0
ПАНЕЛЬ №1
ПАНЕЛЬ №2
ПАНЕЛЬ №3
ПАНЕЛЬ №0

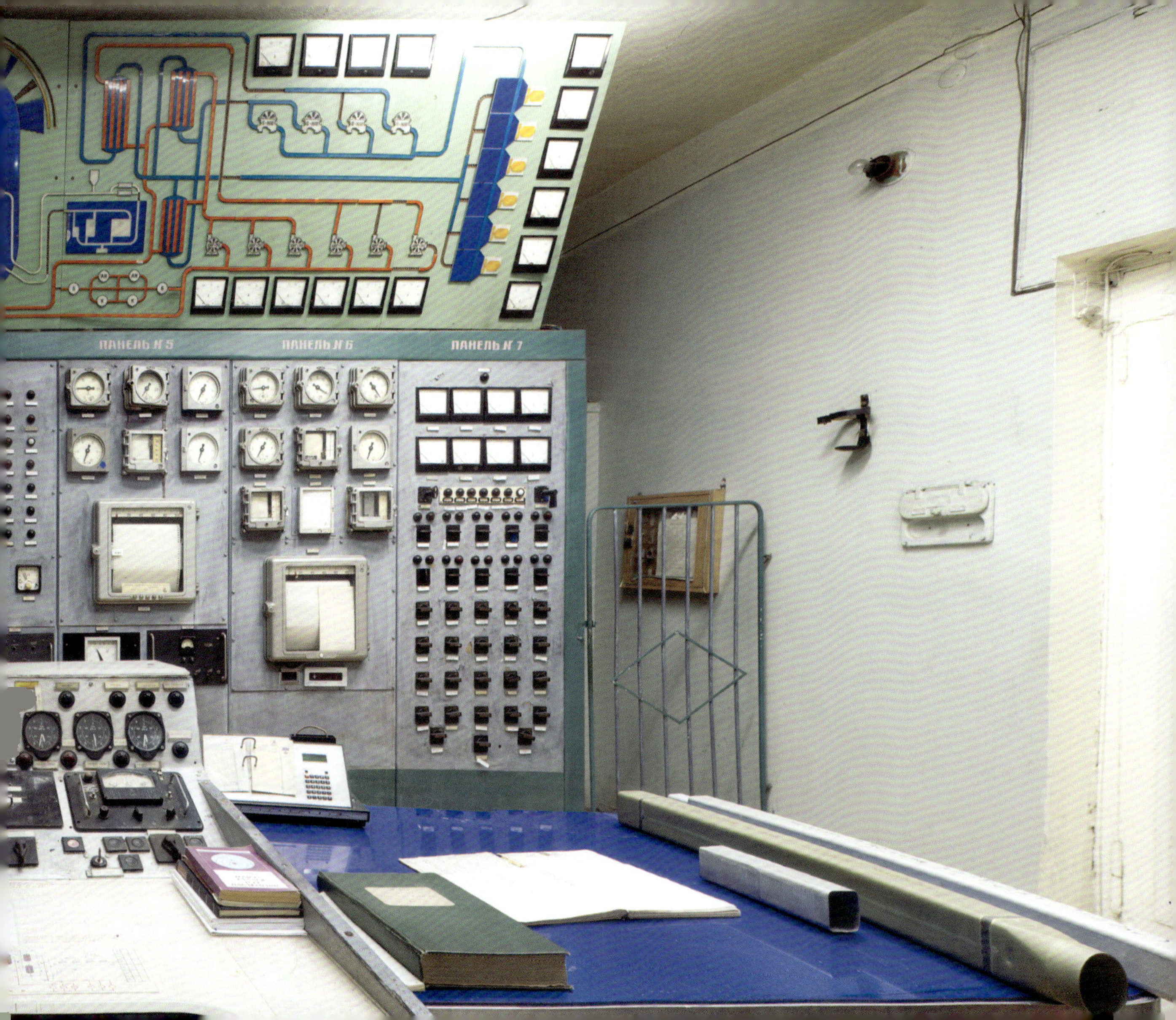
ПАНЕЛЬ № 5
ПАНЕЛЬ № 6
ПАНЕЛЬ № 7

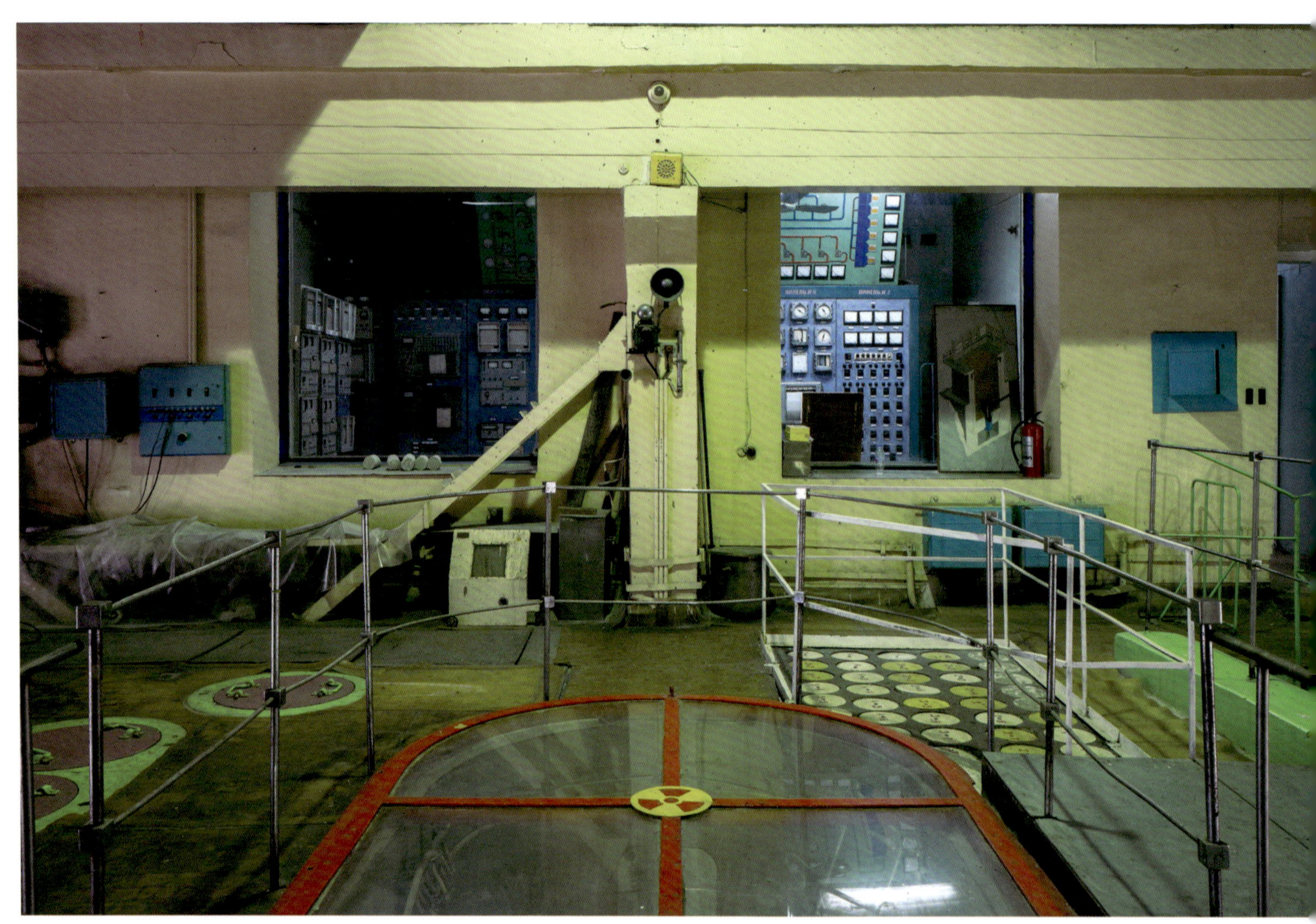

The area above the pool where the uranium fuel rods were immersed. The height of the pool was 7.6 metres and the volume about 60 cubic metres.

 Previous pages: The reactor control room.

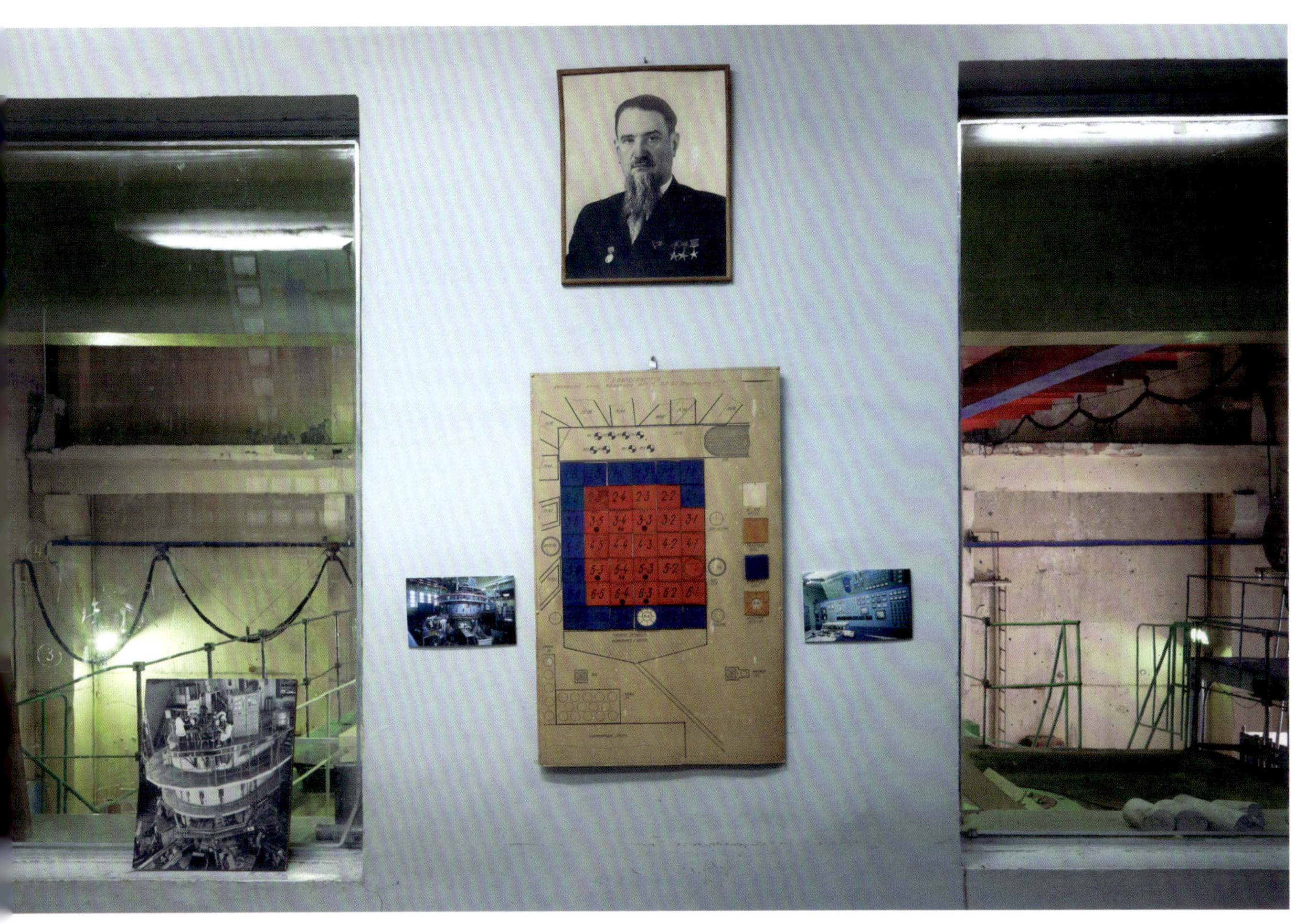

A view of the control room looking towards the pool. A diagram of the reactor core layout hangs on the wall with a portrait of Igor Kurchatov (1903–1960), lead scientist of the Soviet nuclear programme, above it.

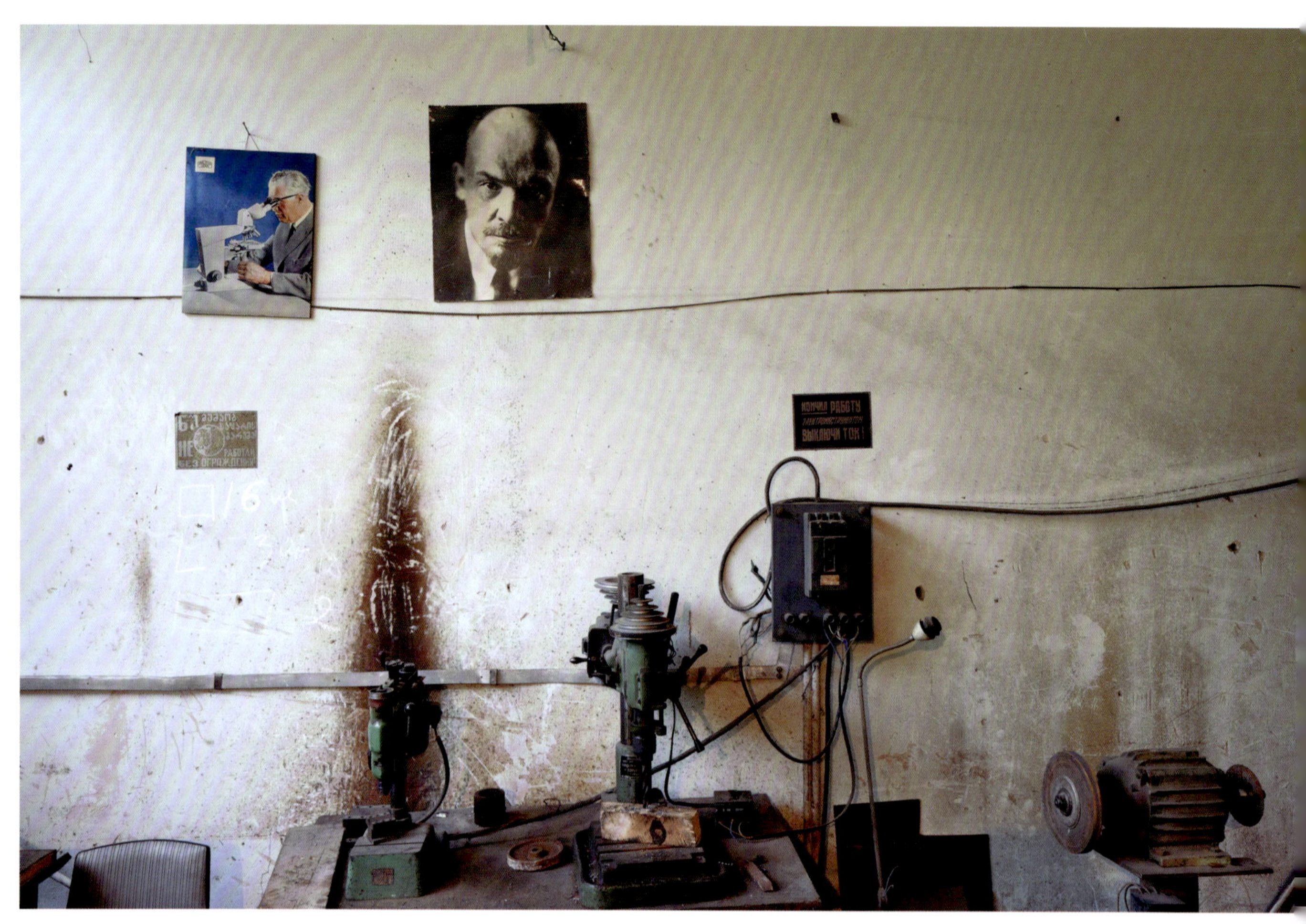

In the workshop next to the reactor hangs a portrait of Lenin (1870–1924), founder of the Soviet state. On the left is a photograph of a scientist using a Carl Zeiss microscope manufactured at their factory located in Jena, in the former German Democratic Republic (GDR).

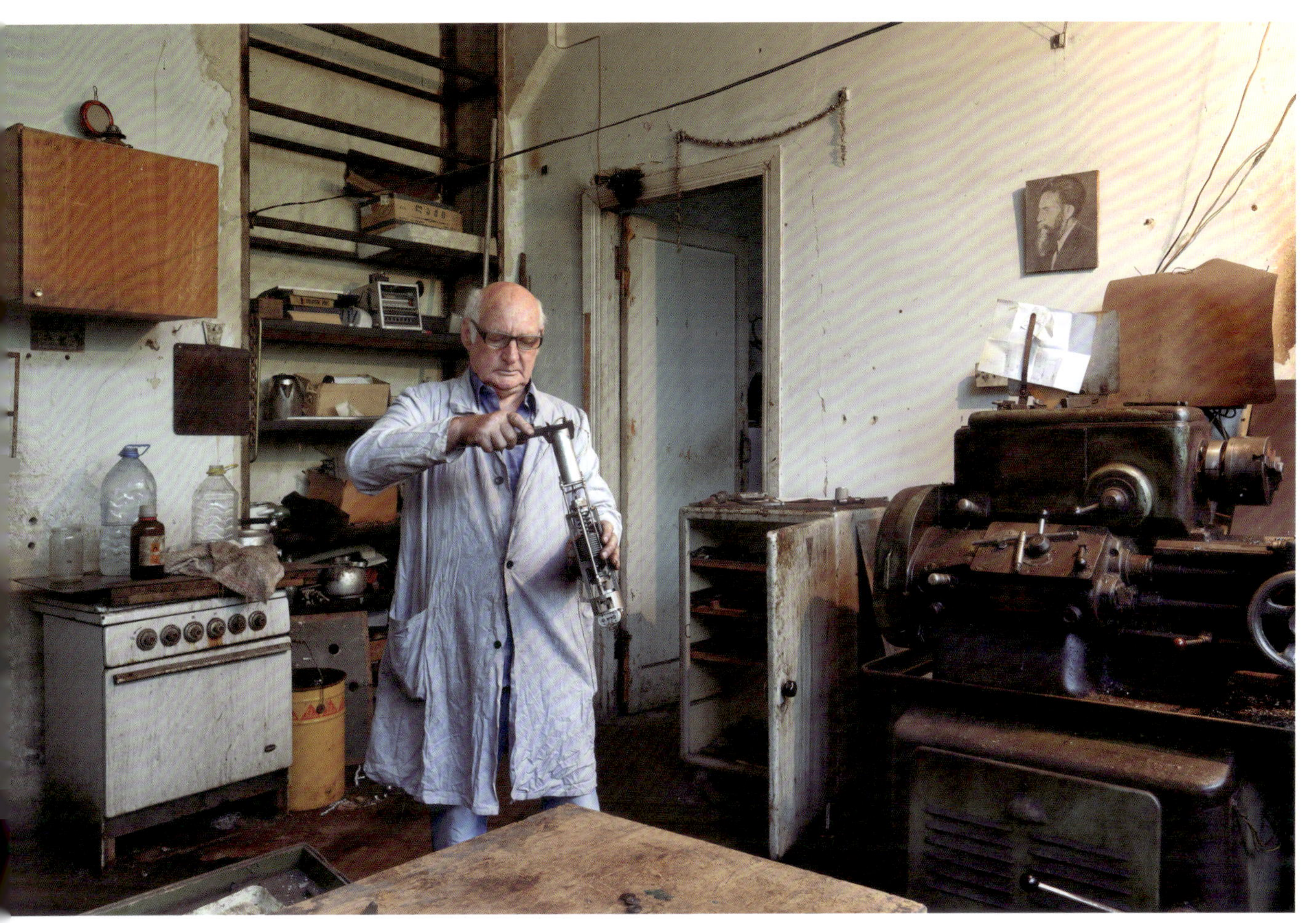

Engineer Giorgi Gabashvili demonstrates an instrument he built to determine the conditions of metals after irradiation.

CENTRE FOR ENERGY RESEARCH

Hungarian Academy of Sciences

Budapest, HUNGARY

In the early stages of the Cold War, leaders of the Hungarian Communist Party believed that World War III was inevitable. The authorities wanted to understand the consequences of atomic attacks, and to accurately measure radioactivity and treat its effects. The Central Research Institute for Physics (KFKI) was set up in 1950 on the outskirts of Budapest with the aim of advancing the country's scant capabilities in various fields of the discipline.

In response to the US 'Atoms for Peace' initiative of 1955 (a government campaign to enlighten the American public as to the risks and hopes of a nuclear future), the Soviet Union offered scientific and technical assistance to socialist countries for the construction of nuclear research facilities. In Hungary this programme included plans for a nuclear reactor, with Hungarian authorities responsible for the organisation and funding of the project.

The resulting Budapest Research Reactor, a Water-cooled, Water-moderated Reactor (VVR-S), was Hungary's first nuclear facility and remains one of the country's top research infrastructures. It reached operational criticality in 1959 and was hailed as a symbol of a successful, modern Hungary. This type of installation was designed for studying the characteristics of radiation shielding materials, among other physical research activities, and for the production of radioactive isotopes. It is a tank-type reactor with light-water (H_2O) moderation and cooling with an initial thermal power output of 2 megawatts (MW). It was first upgraded in 1967, increasing the power to 5 MW using a new type of fuel and a beryllium reflector surrounding the core. In 1972, Ferenc Mezei (1942–), previously a researcher at the institute, invented the neutron spin echo principle which became a globally adopted spectroscopic method.

With a projected lifespan of 30 years, discussions began in the 1980s as to whether to extend the reactor's life or prepare for decommissioning. As it was still in high demand, the government approved its further development. Design work began in 1984 and on 9 May 1986 – just two weeks after the Chornobyl accident – it was shut down in order to receive major upgrades. The reconstruction was completed in 1990, increasing its power to 10 MW. However, the uncertain political climate meant that it wasn't restarted until 1993.

A great part of Hungarian nuclear culture was developed here and, with the demise of communism, more attention is being paid to transparency and communication with the general population. Today the reactor, with its many and various scientific instruments distributed around it, serves as a high-power neutron source for research, as well as producing medical isotopes used in pharmaceutical products for the treatment of metastatic tumours. Authorisation to operate the Budapest reactor has been granted until 2033.

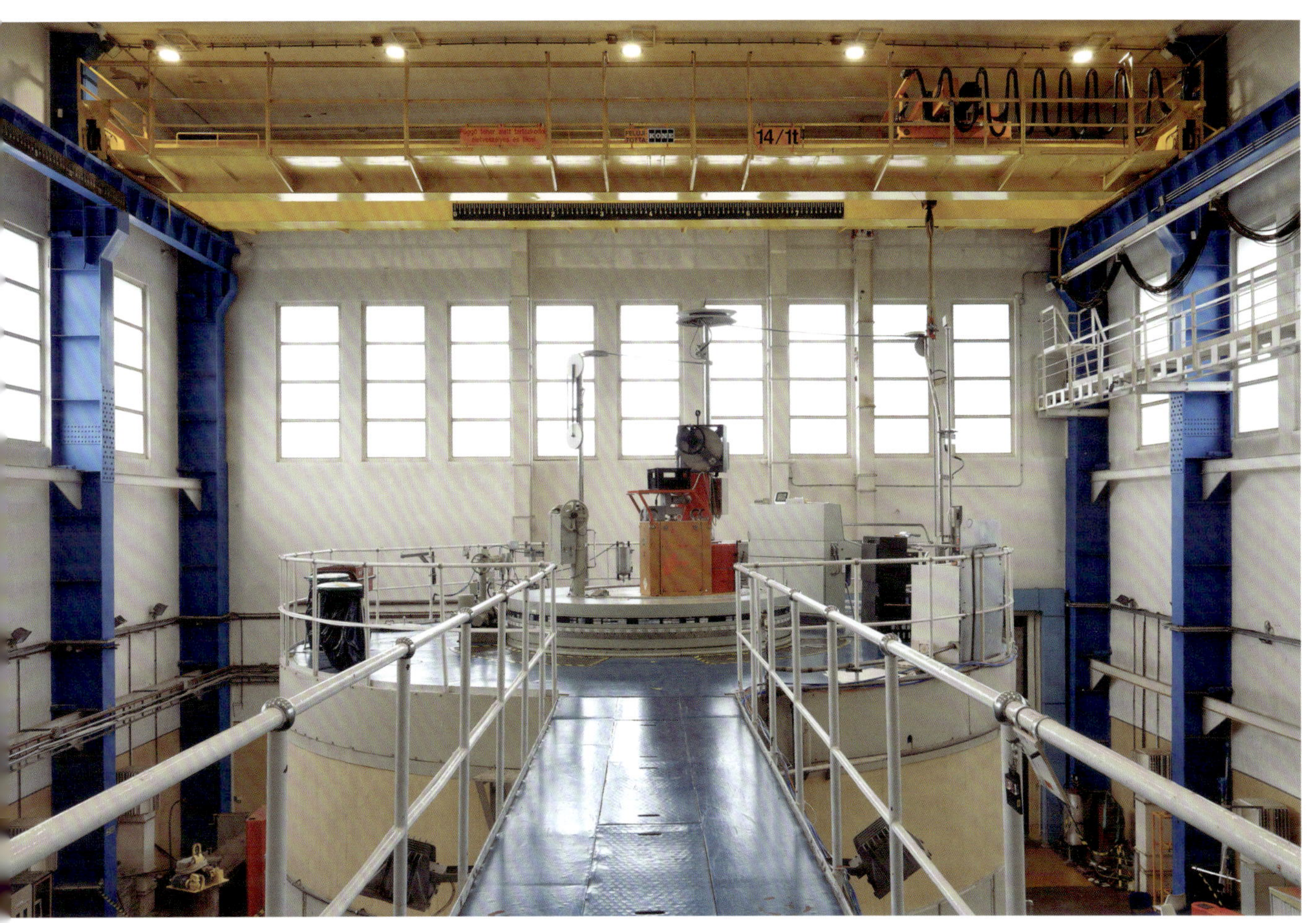

The walkway leading to the top of the reactor.

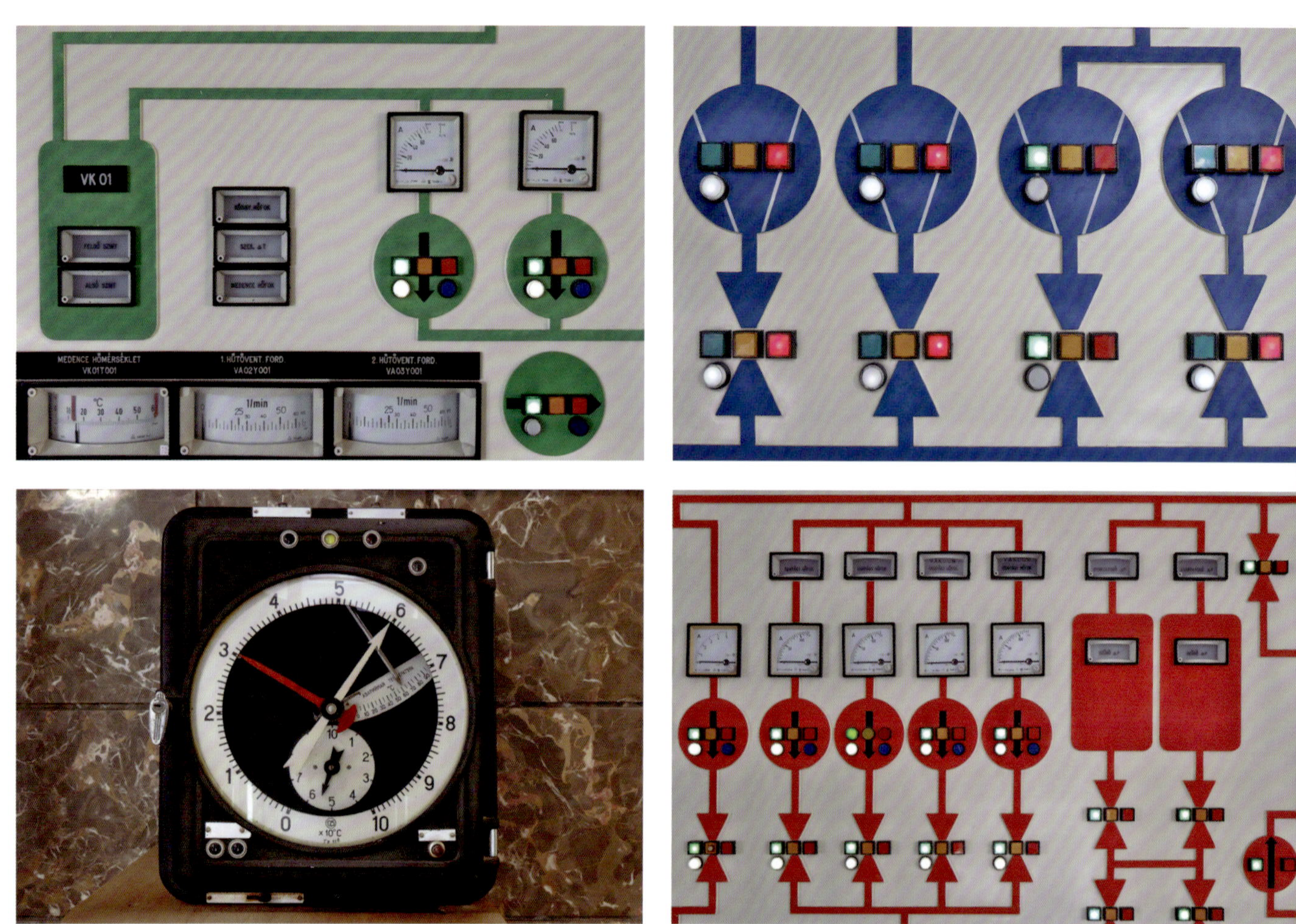

Details of various control panels in the modernised control room. An original gauge used to measure the temperature of bearings is exhibited at the entrance to the reactor hall (bottom left).

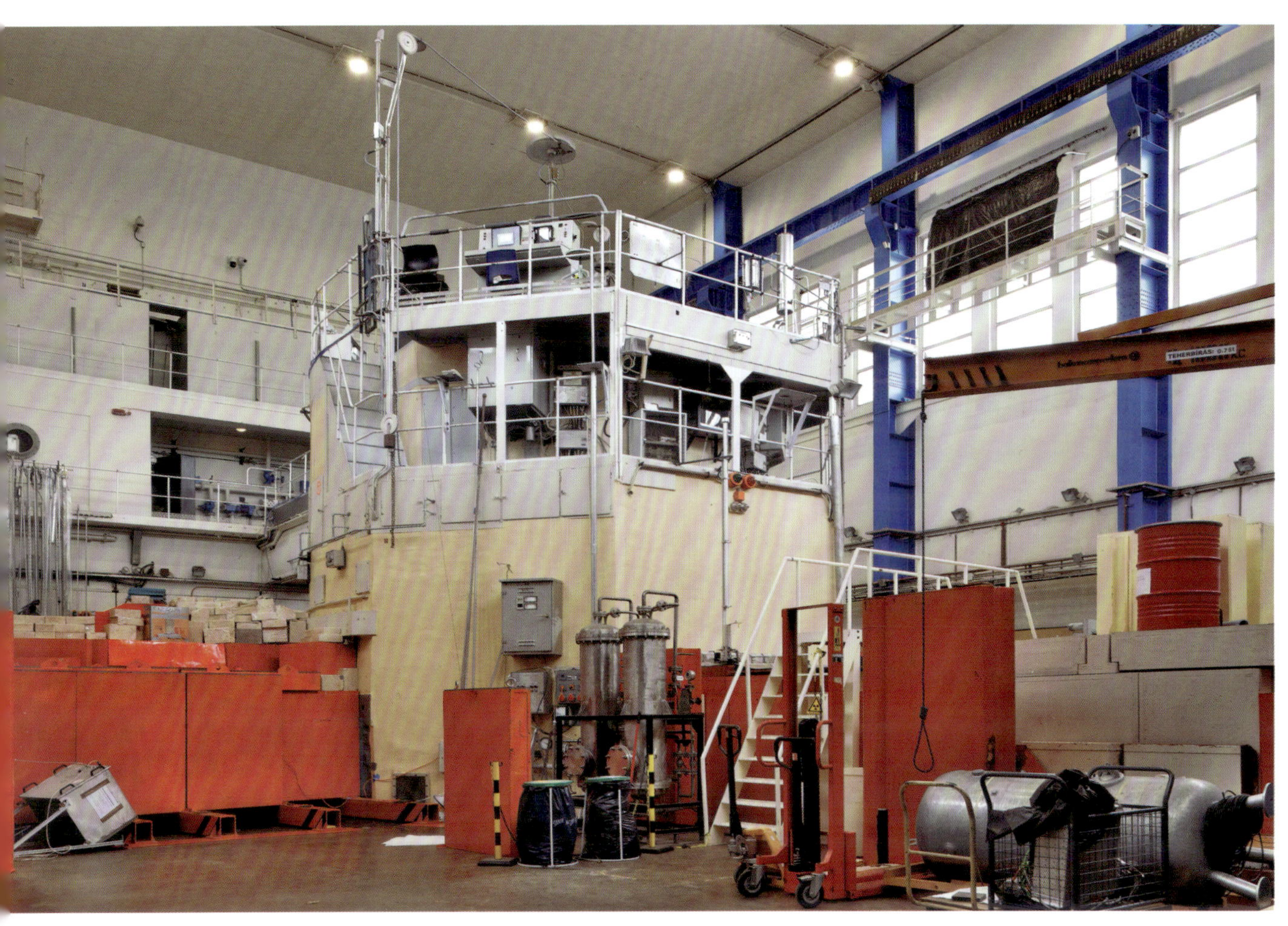

The reactor is housed in a tank 2.3 metres in diameter and 5.685 metres high, constructed from a special aluminium alloy. This is enclosed in a heavy concrete block, located within the rectangular, semi-hermetically sealed reactor hall.

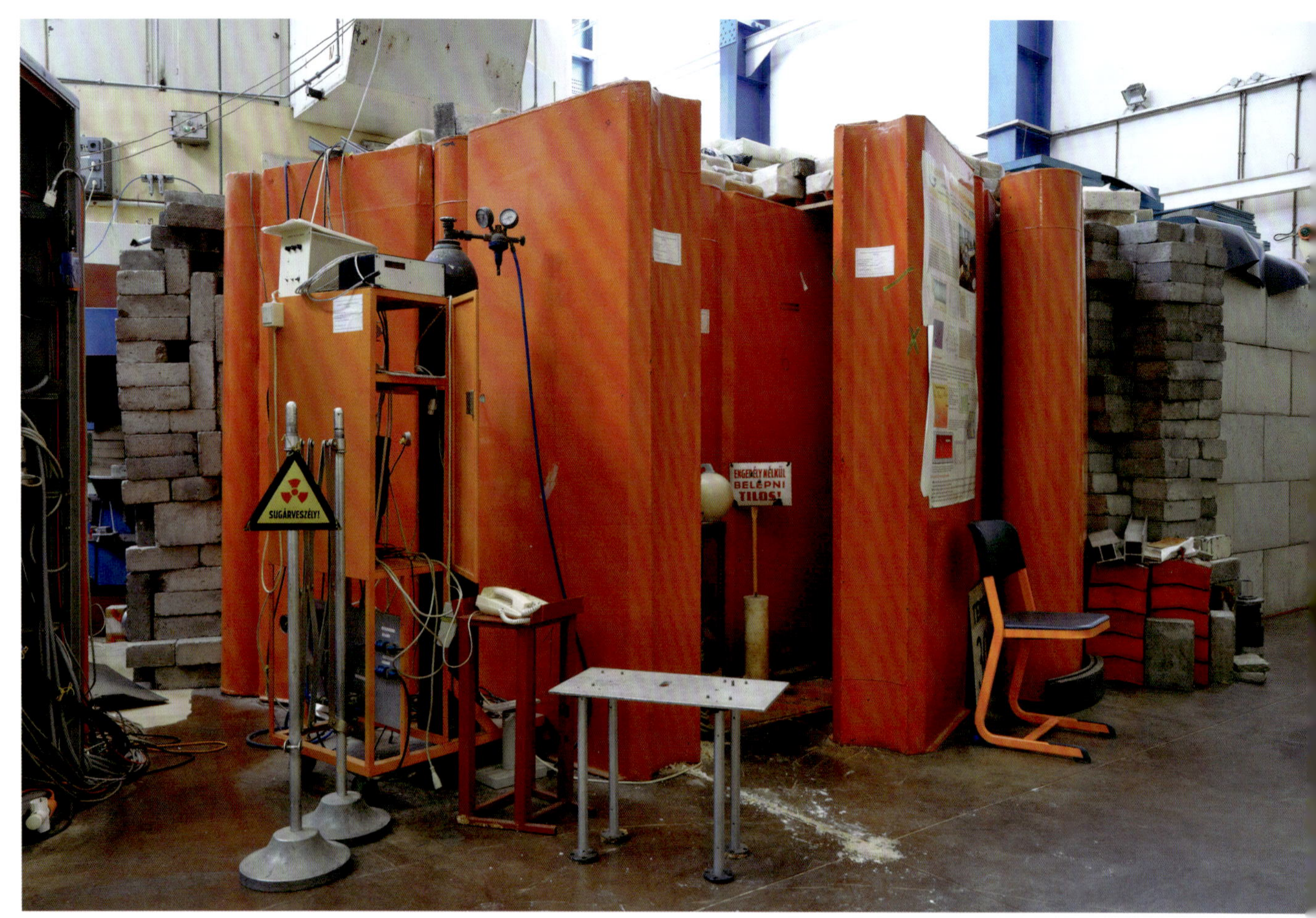

The access to this bunker, which contains an experimental device connected to the reactor, is designed like a labyrinth to protect personnel from radiation. Multiple bends absorb radiation along the length of the passageway, reducing the dose rate to an acceptable level at the entrance, eliminating the need for a single, complex and expensive shielded door.

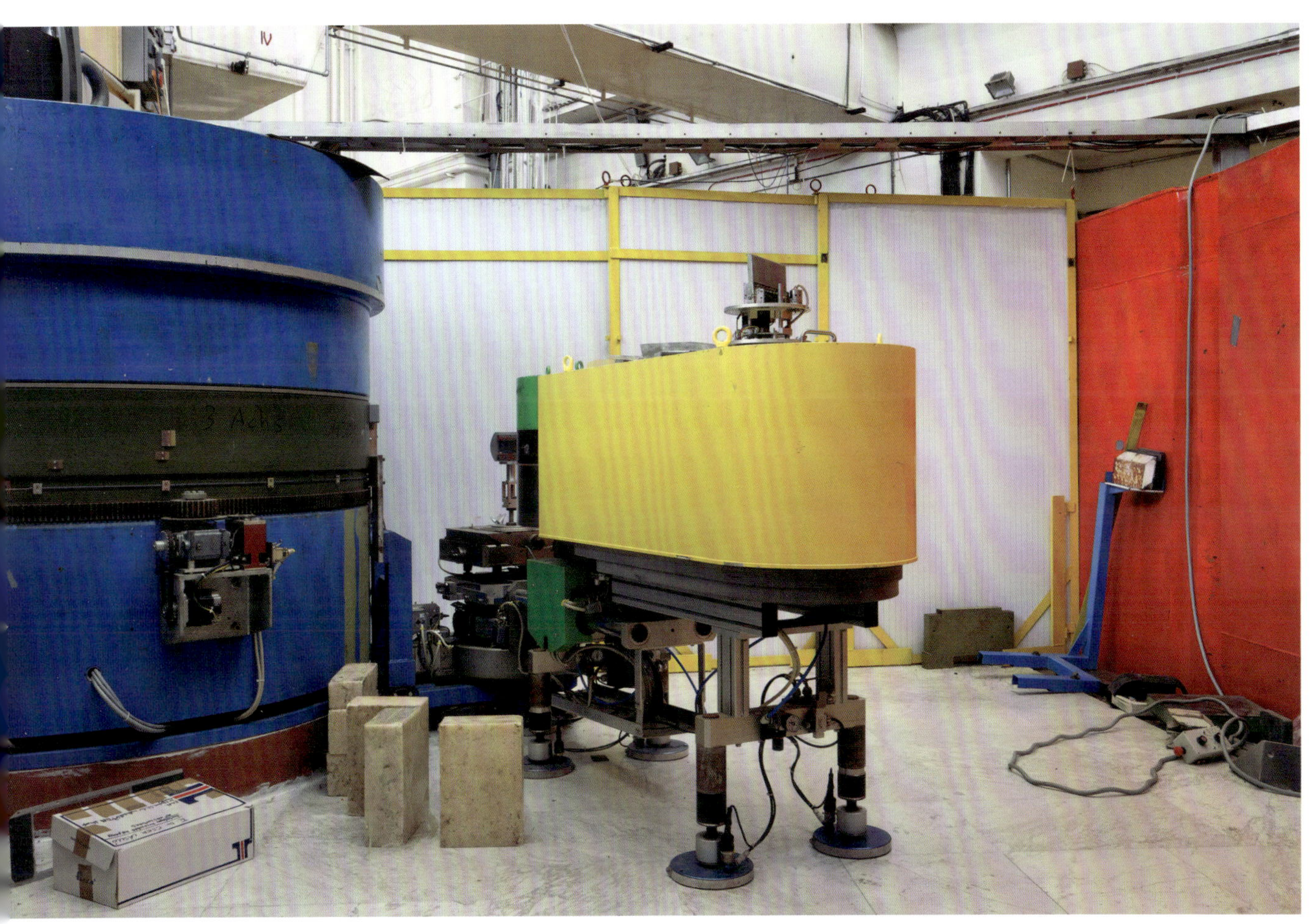

The Thermal Neutron Three-Axis Spectrometer and Neutron Holographic Instrument (TAST/HOLO) is used to investigate structural and magnetic properties in the field of condensed matter physics. The scientific utilisation of the reactor is directed by the Budapest Neutron Centre, a consortium established by various academic institutions in 1993.

INSTITUTE OF NUCLEAR TECHNIQUES

Budapest University of Technology and Economics

Budapest, HUNGARY

'Small but powerful! (At least enough.) And what's most important: very safe.' This sentiment was recorded by physicist Edward Teller (1908–2003) in 1990, in the visitors' book of the Budapest Training Reactor. Teller, who played a key role in the Manhattan Project developing the atomic bomb, and was known as the father of the hydrogen bomb, was visiting his native city for the first time in 54 years, just months after the fall of the communist regime.

In the 1960s the Hungarian government decided to use nuclear energy to supplement the country's needs. This required the construction of a new training facility to provide practical instruction for future specialists at the planned atomic installation, known today as the Paks Nuclear Power Plant.

The Budapest Research Reactor (BRR), which began operating in 1959, was Hungary's first nuclear facility (page 68). The reactor provided valuable operational experience, giving technicians and researchers the expertise to design and build the new training reactor. The first plans were completed in 1962 and approved by the Soviet Union in 1963. Construction began in 1967, and the Budapest training reactor was commissioned in 1971, becoming the country's second nuclear facility.

Initially, the training reactor was licensed for a thermal power rating of 10 kilowatts (kW). However, in 1980, as demand rose, its core and control systems were modified, increasing maximum power to 100 kW. The nuclear fuel EK-10, which contains 10% enriched uranium and was manufactured in the 1960s, has not needed replacing since the reactor was commissioned. This longevity is attributed to it operating at low power with optimised management, and it is expected to last for several more decades.

The fission of the training reactor core utilises the same physics as the Paks Nuclear Power Plant, and a high level of safety has been engineered into it to ensure that it can be operated on the university campus in the centre of the capital. Its pedagogical design allows students to directly understand how a nuclear reactor works, and to carry out exercises without fear of unintended consequences. As early as the 1970s, groups of students from countries such as Algeria, Cuba, Czechoslovakia and Russia would regularly study at the facility.

Today such cooperation continues, with the International Atomic Energy Agency (IAEA) running an annual training course for nuclear safety inspectors. The reactor is also used extensively as a source of neutron and gamma radiation for research purposes. The institute is conducting research into plausible Generation IV reactors, the Monte Carlo method of risk calculation, and magnetic confinement fusion devices in the context of ITER (International Thermonuclear Experimental Reactor) and EUROfusion (an international fusion research consortium). The institute has plans to continue using the training reactor for the next 20 years.

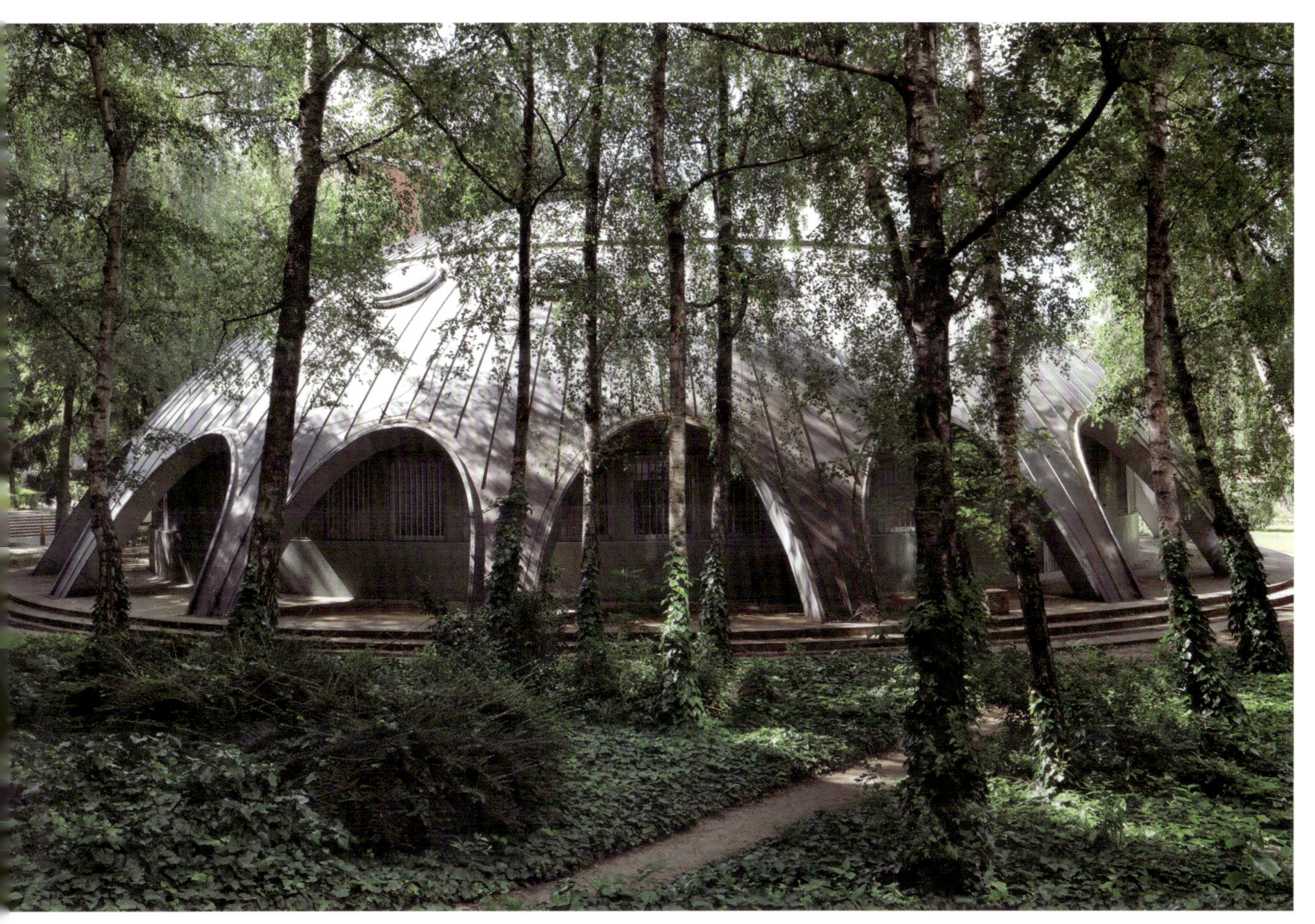

The facility, designed by Hungarian engineers and physicists in the 1960s, is located on the university campus in the centre of Budapest. Unfortunately, the inspiration behind its unique architecture has not been documented.

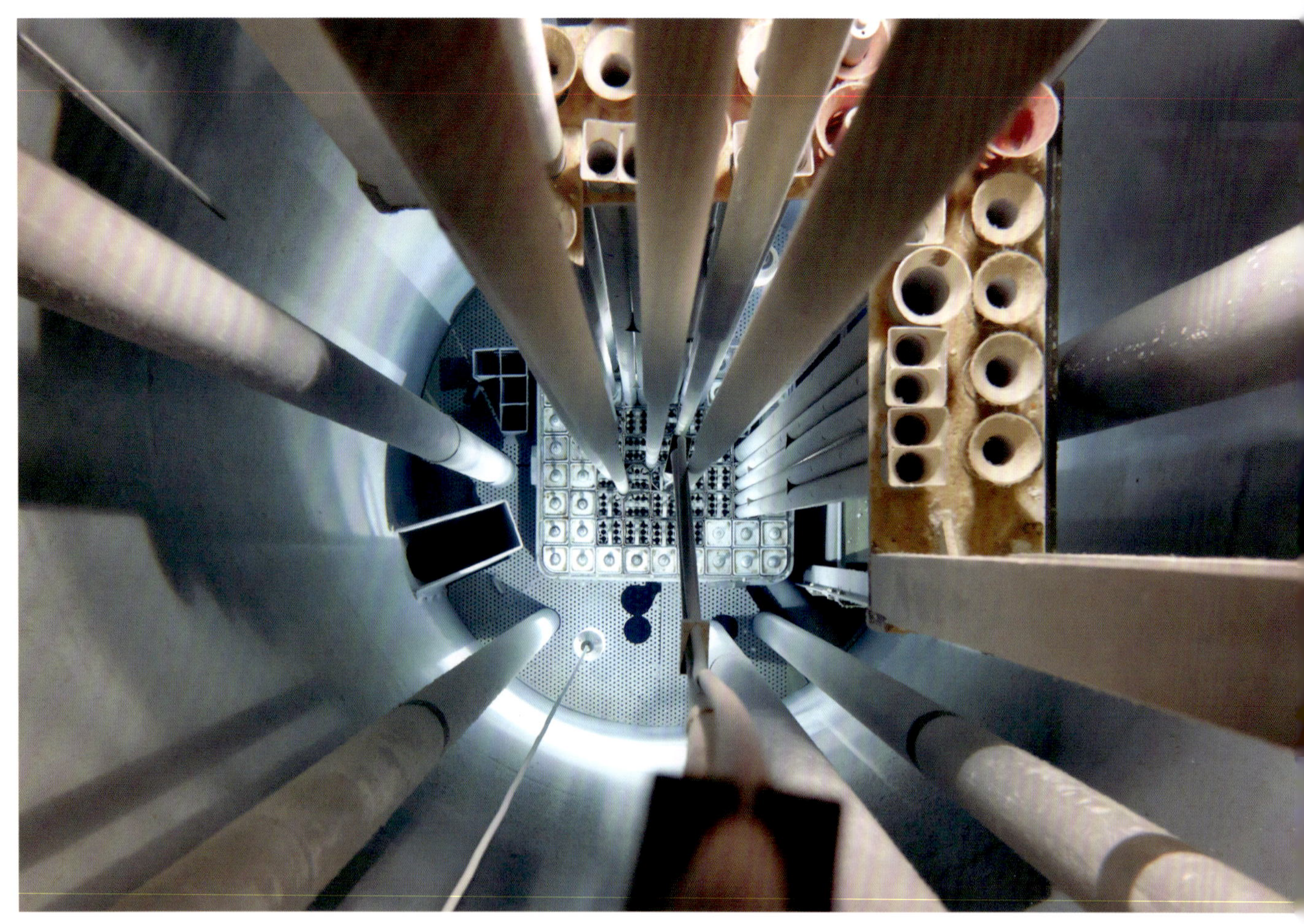

A view of the reactor core, looking down into the pool. Containing 24 fuel assemblies, comprising 369 fuel pins in total, it is surrounded by 41 solid graphite blocks with aluminium cladding, which serve as a neutron reflector around the core, increasing efficency. Control rods inserted into aluminium guiding tubes modify the rate of the nuclear reaction by absorbing neutrons.

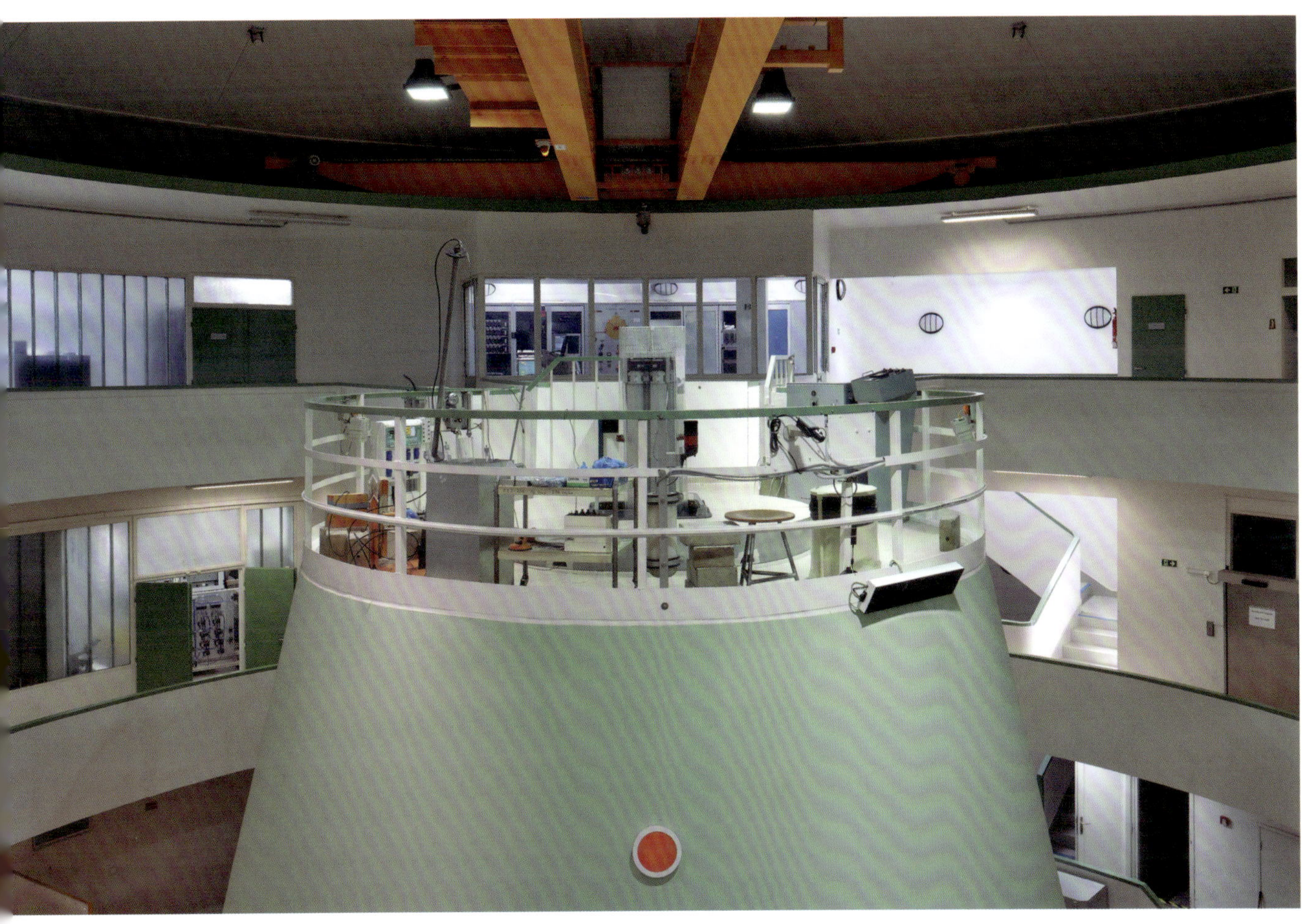

The reactor core is located at the bottom of a sealed aluminium tank containing demineralised water, which acts as a moderator, coolant and biological shield. The tank measures 1.40 metres in diameter by 6 metres in height, with 2-centimetre-thick walls and is encased in 2-metre-thick concrete .

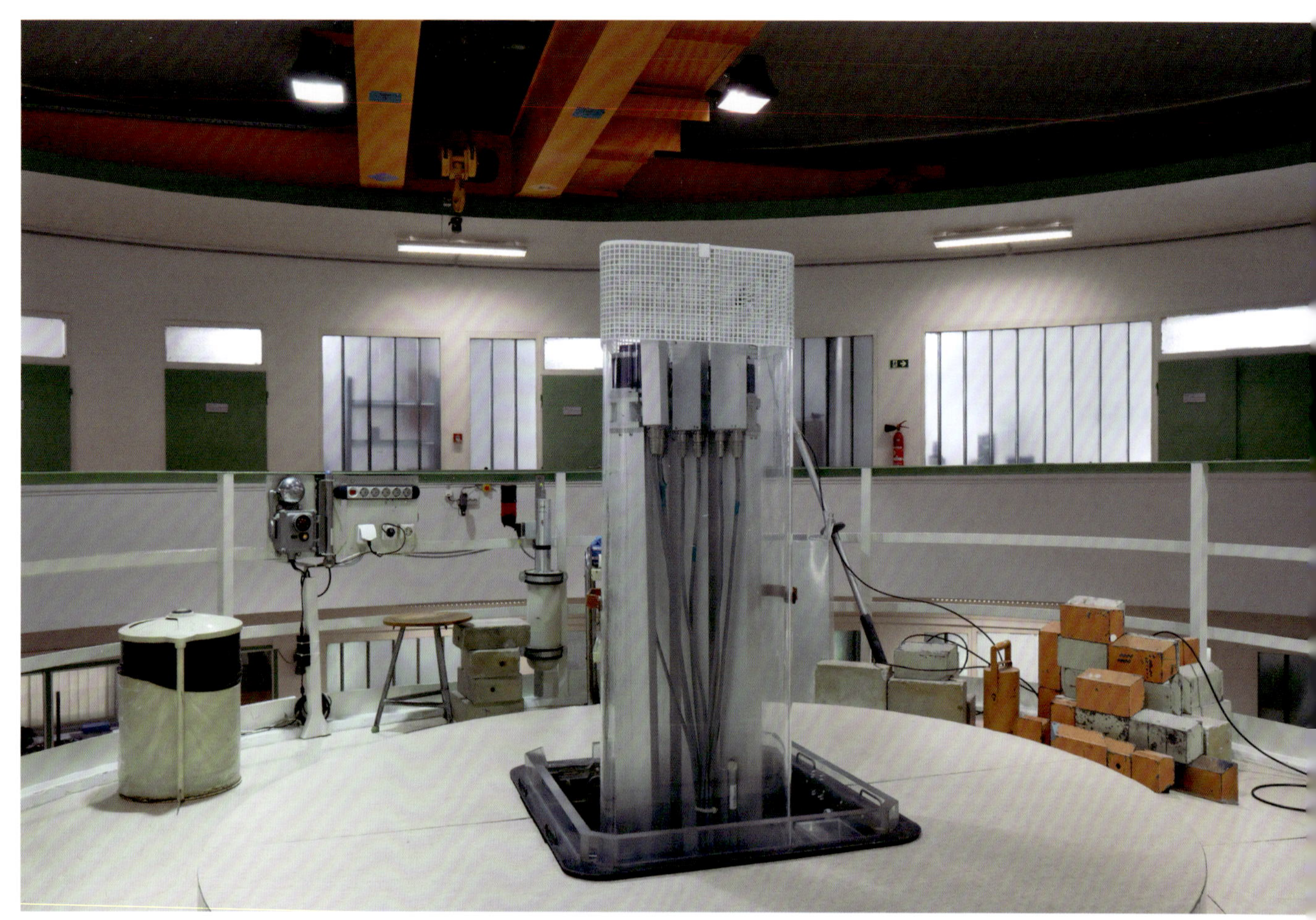

An opening at the top of the structure allows for manipulation of the reactor core components.

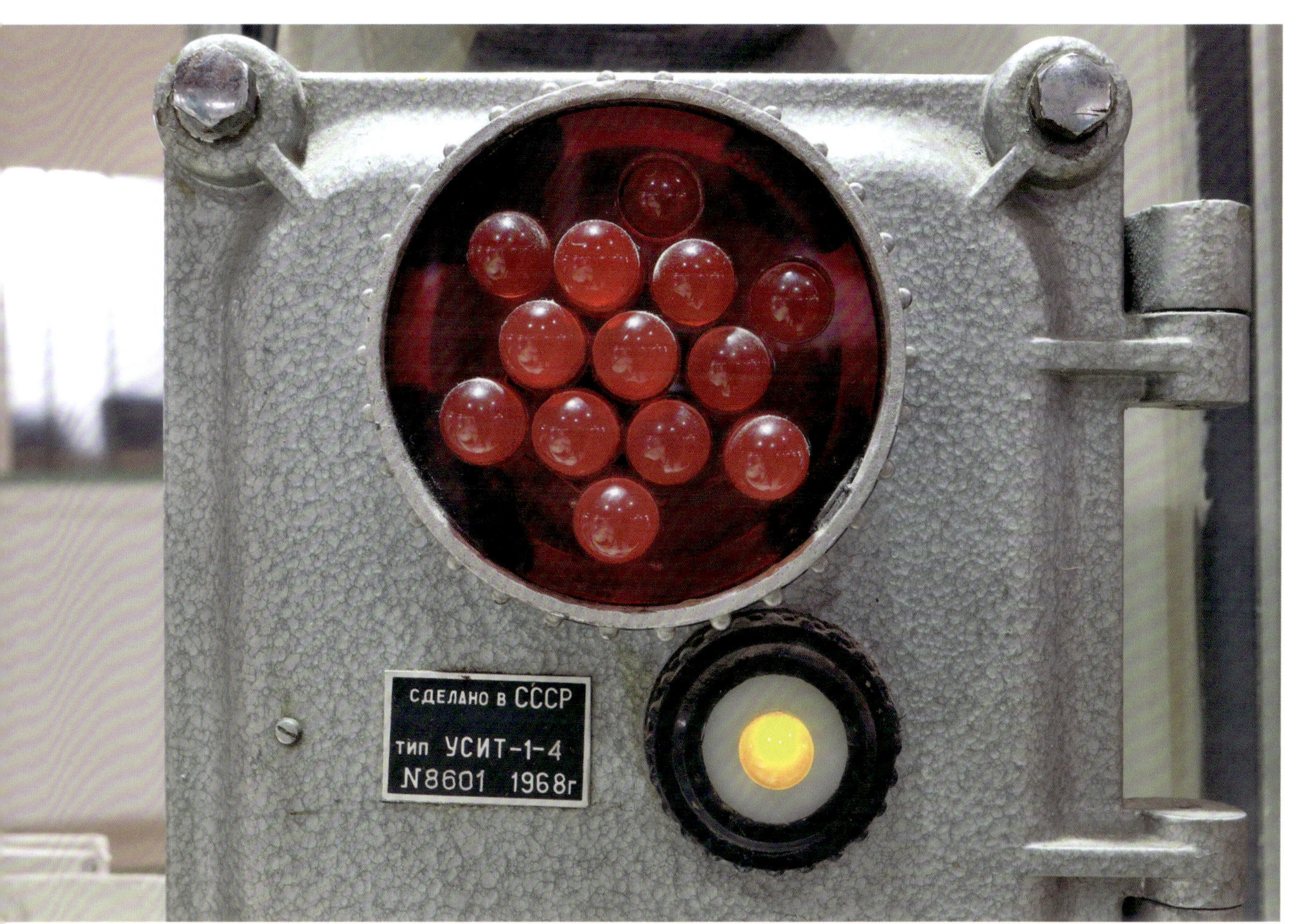

An operational Soviet era alarm, manufactured in 1968, located at the top of the reactor.

FESENKOV ASTROPHYSICAL INSTITUTE

Assy-Turgen Observatory, KAZAKHSTAN

In 1940, several teams of Soviet astronomers organised expeditions to Kazakhstan to document the imminent total solar eclipse on 21 September 1941. However, Germany's invasion of the USSR in June 1941 turned what had been planned as a short-term study of an astronomical phenomenon into the start of a prolonged evacuation.

The scientists arriving at Almaty found exceptional conditions in which to work and, with the impossibility of their return, Vasily Fesenkov (1889–1972), a key figure in Soviet astrophysics, convinced the authorities to create a new institute that would provide a sanctuary for the astronomers and allow their research to continue uninterrupted.

The difficult situation during and after the war delayed construction of the observatory, and it wasn't until 1947 – using a workforce of Japanese prisoners – that it was finally built. In addition, several telescopes arrived from Germany as part of its war reparations duties.

The facility developed high-precision hardware and software necessary for tracking Sputnik and subsequent artificial satellites. For the Soviet military-industrial complex its scientists were tasked with drawing up astronomical catalogues for spacecraft navigation systems. Stars with known absolute energy distribution serve as 'beacons' for rockets and space vehicles. In 1978, the institute published the 'Consolidated spectrophotometric catalogue of stars', which documented the data of 602 stars. In 1988, a second edition presented data on 1,159 stars. At the time of release, these catalogues were the most comprehensive of their kind in the world.

The institute was set in the foothills of Almaty, on the Kamensky plateau at an altitude of 1,450 metres. Despite this remote situation, the rapid growth of the city and resulting increase in glare and smog impacted negatively on the work, and in 1975 the decision was made to build the Assy-Turgen Observatory at a location about 85 kilometres east of Almaty. At an altitude of 2,750 metres, it offers a high degree of atmospheric transparency, minimal light pollution and low air turbulence – all essential prerequisites for astronomical study.

In 1981, continuous observations began using a 1-metre Carl Zeiss telescope. In the late 1980s, construction started on a 45-metre-high pavilion for the observatory's new 1.5-metre AZT-20 telescope. The dome and the building structure were completed, but funding was suspended following the collapse of the Soviet Union, and the telescope lay in a disassembled state for decades. In 2014, the institute was able to resume construction using its own resources, and on 27 July 2017, after a quarter-century hiatus, it finally began operating, in effect becoming the largest telescope in Kazakhstan and bridging the gap in this field between Europe and Asia. Ongoing work includes the installation of automating systems and yet higher-resolution equipment to further improve the quality of the observations.

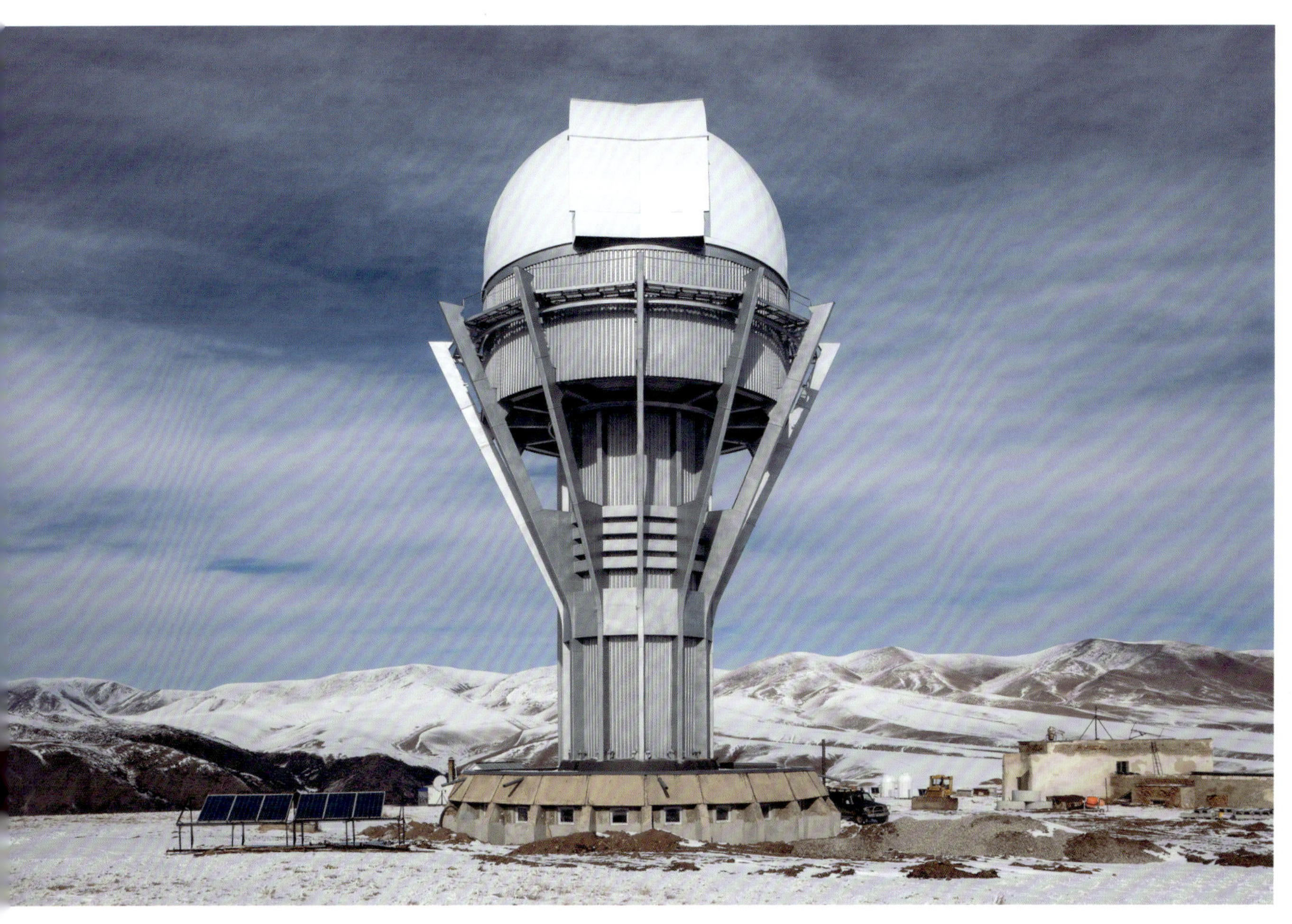

The 45-metre-high tower housing the AZT-20 telescope.

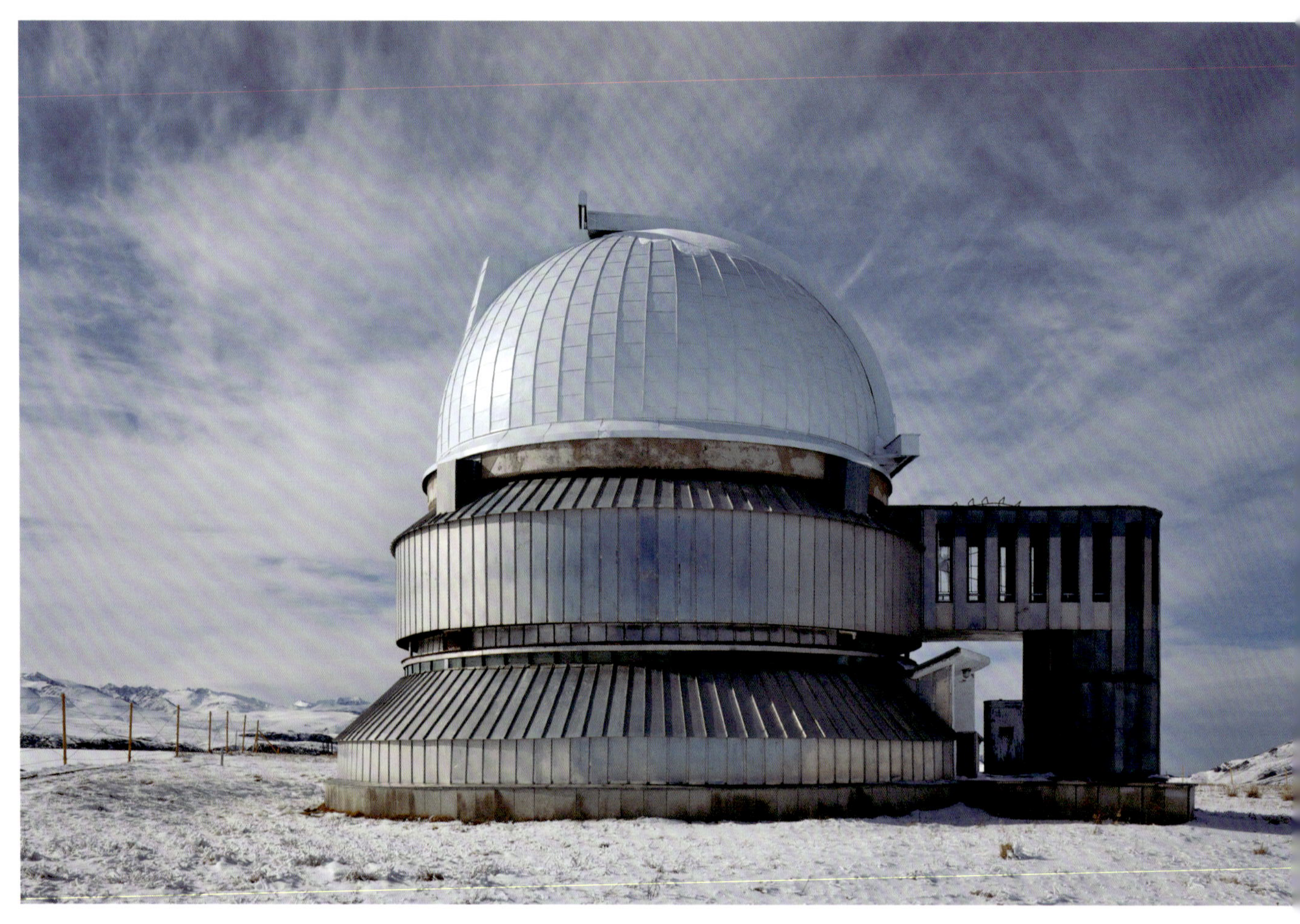

The Carl Zeiss telescope pavilion. Seeing first light in 1981, this was the first operational telescope at the institute's high-altitude Assy-Turgen Observatory site. Used for research into non-stationary active stars and galaxies, it is currently under reconstruction.

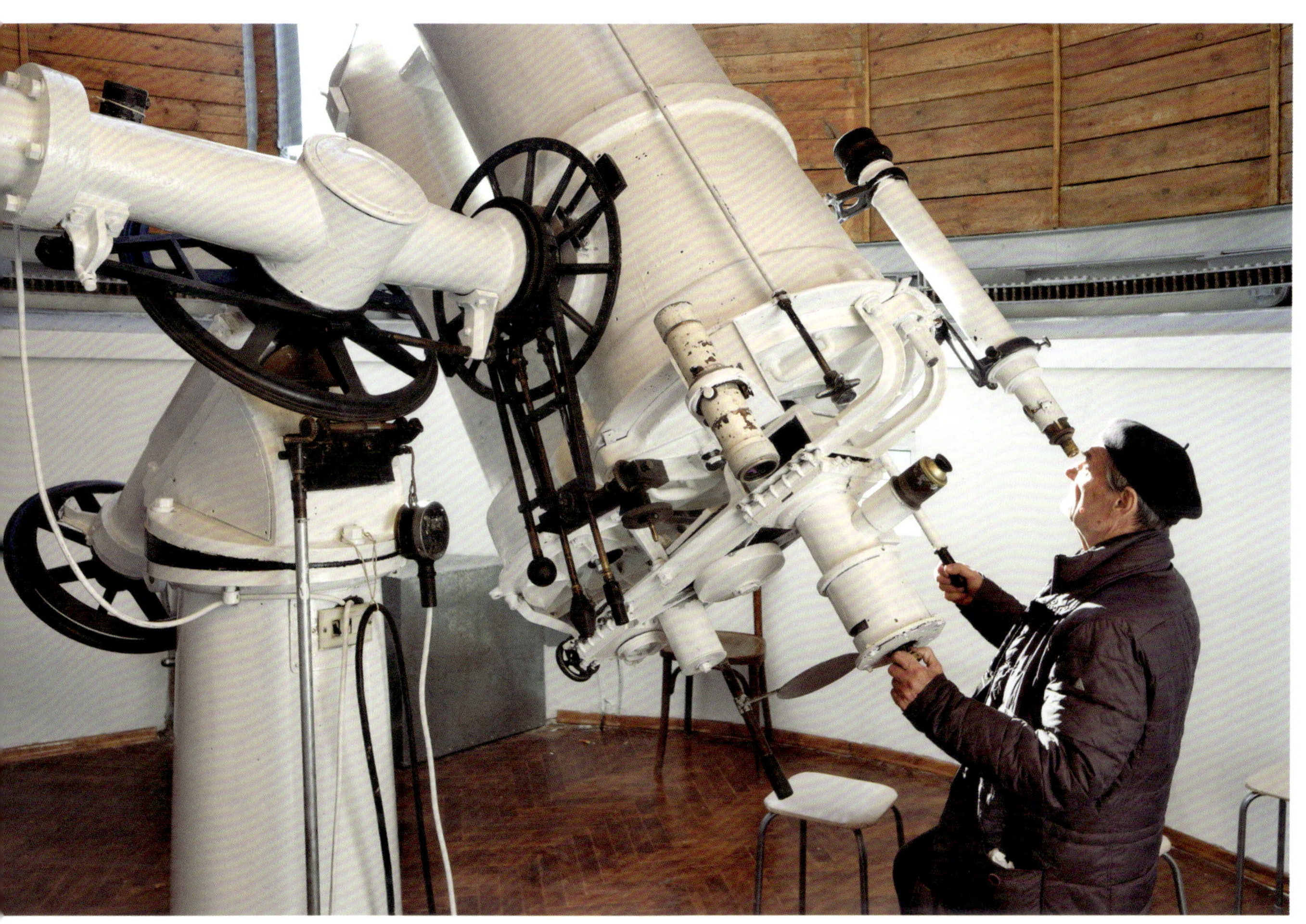

Located at the observatory's Kamensky plateau site, this Hertz telescope has been used by astronomer Vladimir Tereshchenko for almost 50 years. Built at the beginning of the 20th century, it was acquired by the institute in 1947 from the Potsdam Observatory in Germany, as part of war reparations. It is now mostly used for educational purposes.

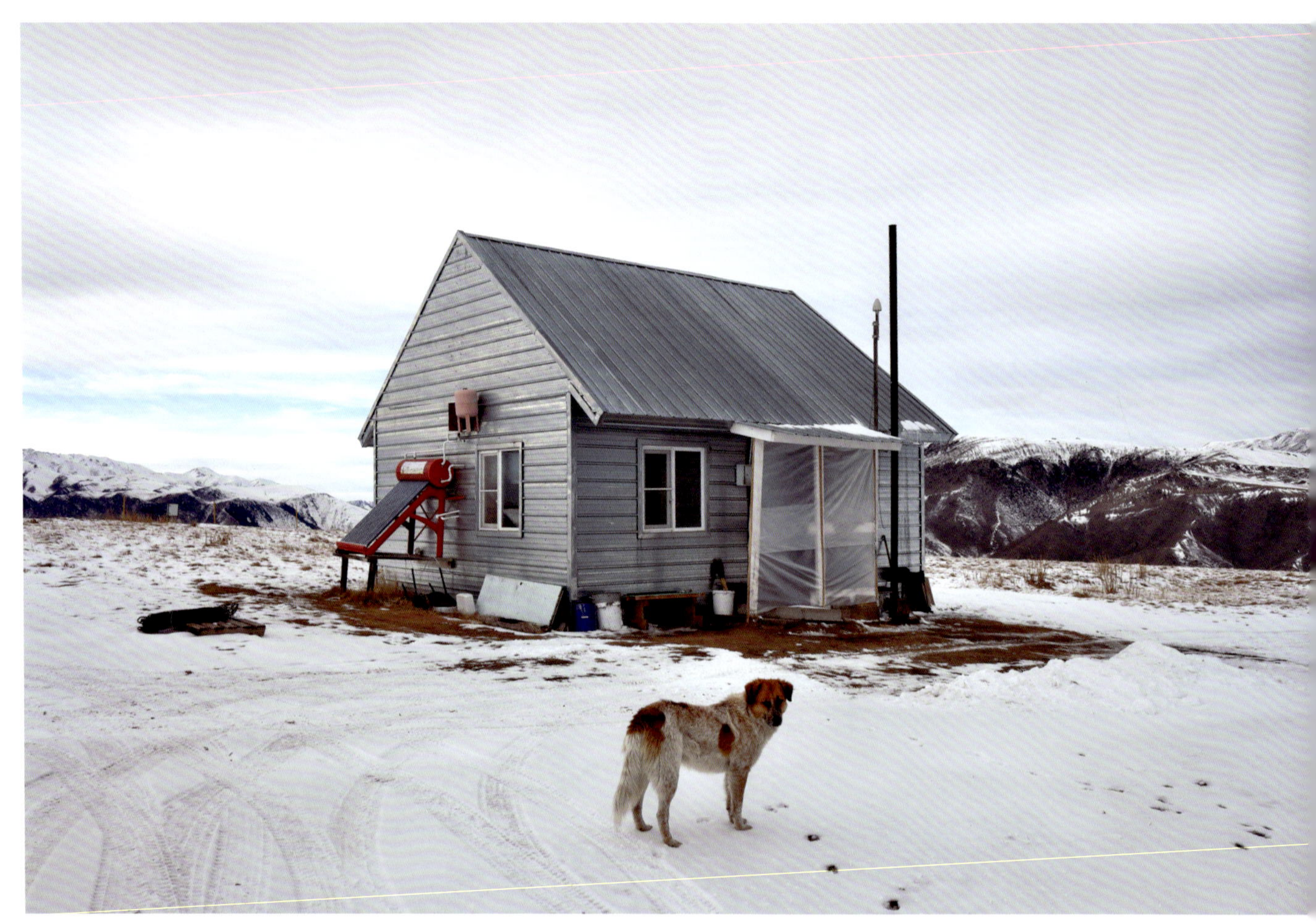

The staff house, with a view of the Zailiyskiy Alatau mountain range beyond.

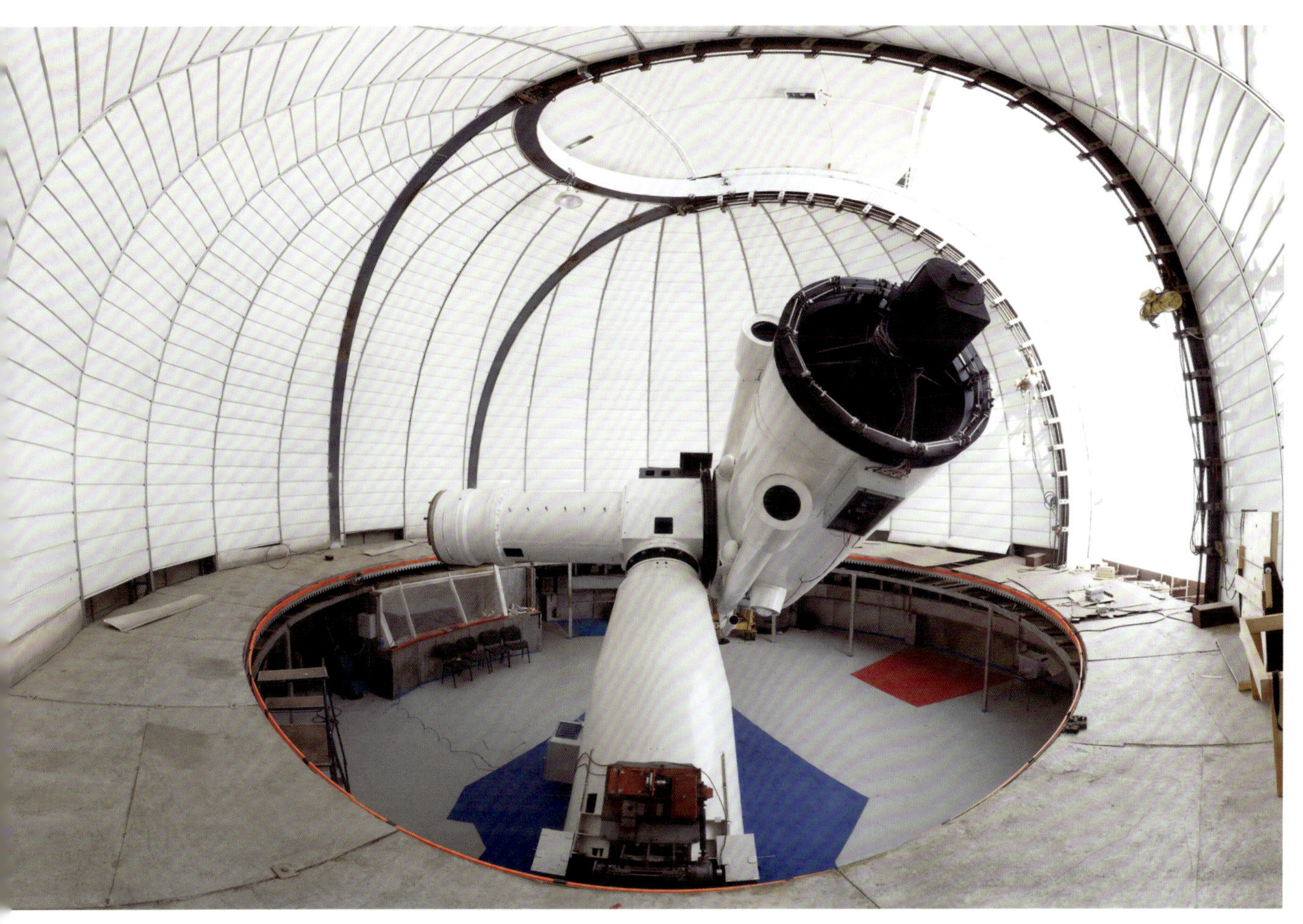

The AZT-20 telescope and its protective dome.
Overleaf: Looking north from the AZT-20 tower, with newly installed equipment in the foreground.

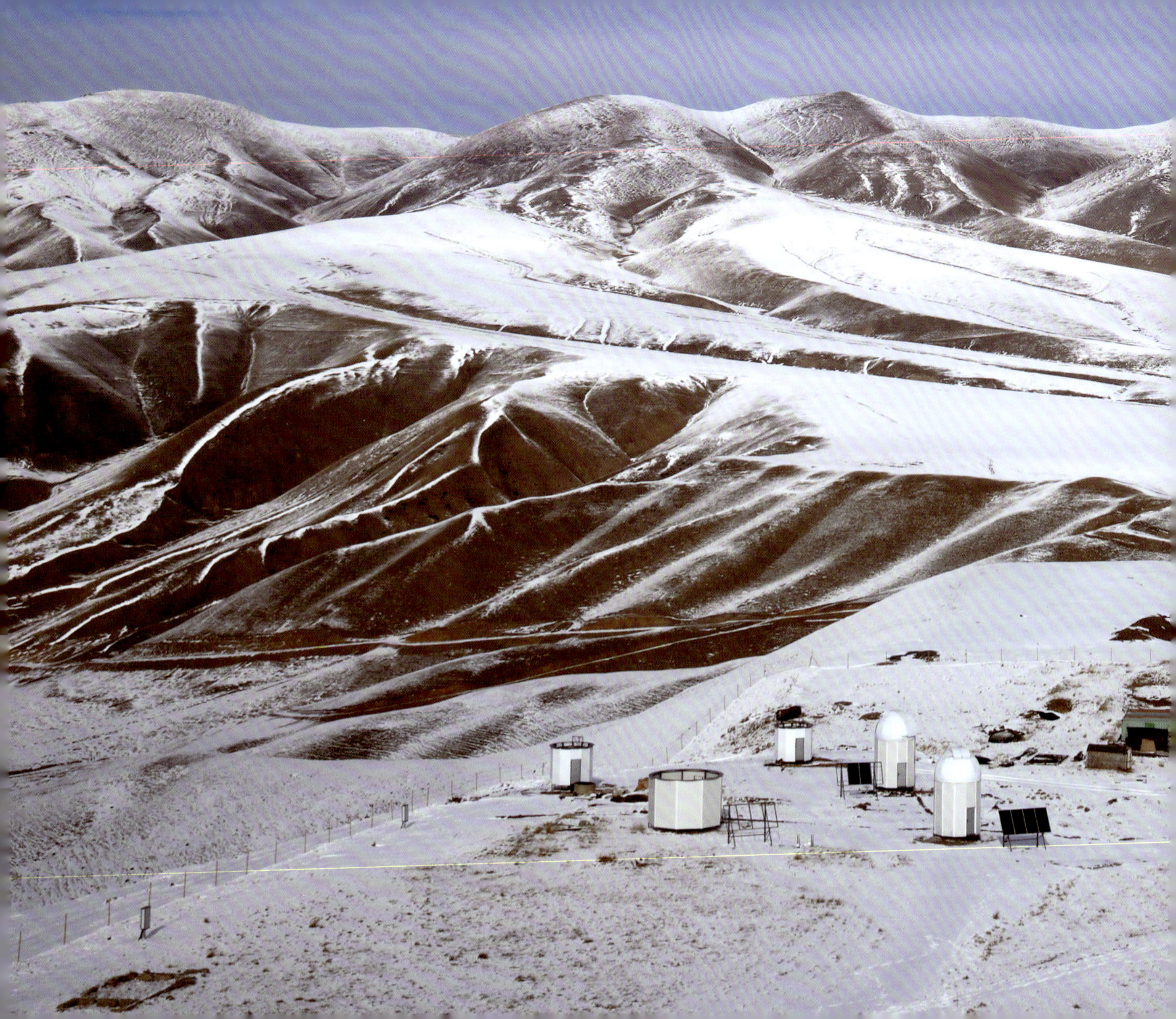

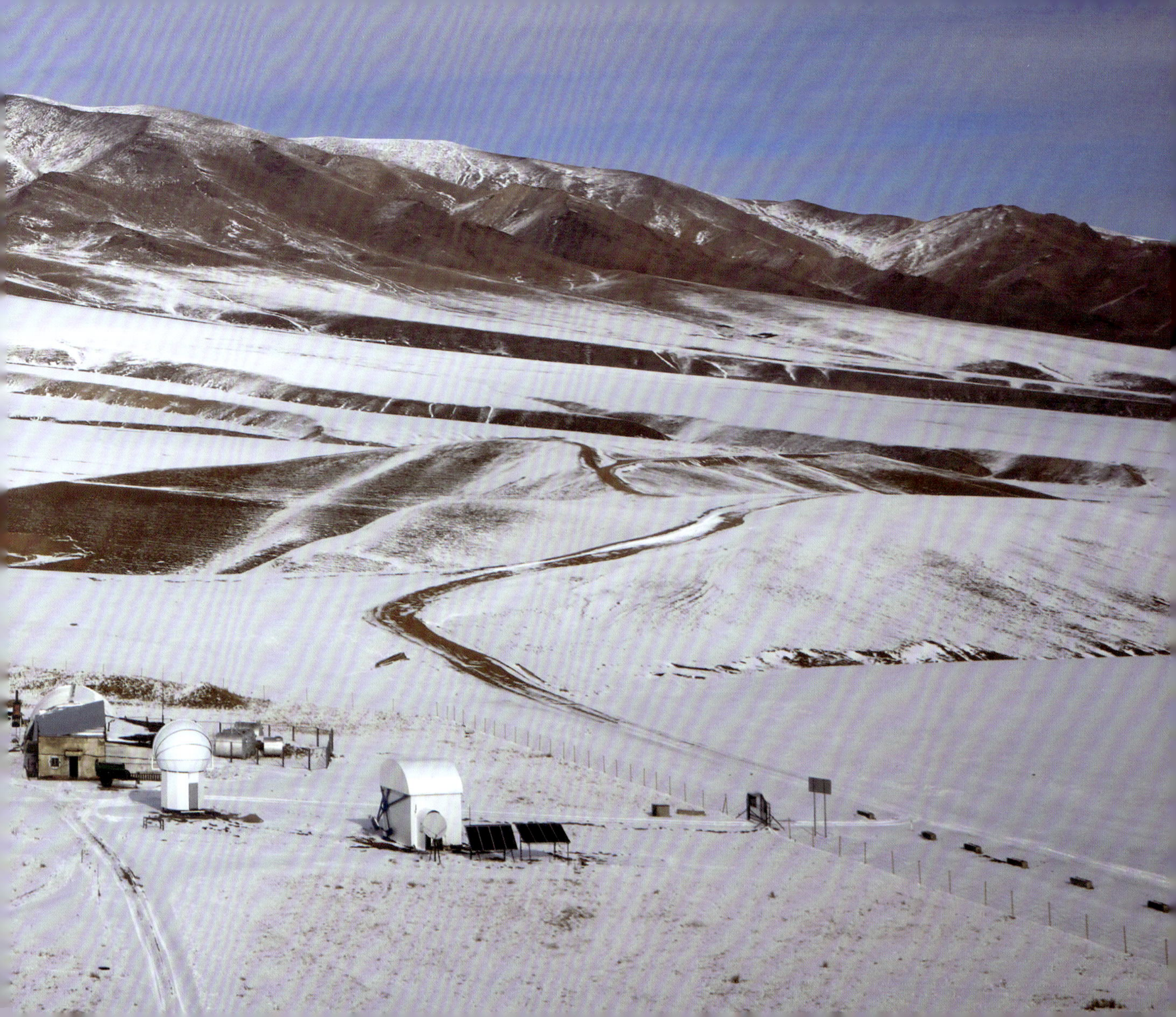

VENTSPILS INTERNATIONAL RADIO ASTRONOMY CENTRE

Engineering Research Institute, Ventspils University of Applied Sciences
Ventspils, LATVIA

In 1967 the Soviet authorities started building a secret military complex on the Baltic coast, 30 kilometres from the port city of Ventspils, in a forested location within the restricted border zone, ideal for concealing its purpose. Nicknamed 'Zvezdochka' ('Little Star'), it was home to the 649th Independent Radio and Space Intelligence Station. At its peak during the Cold War, an entirely self-sufficient town (with the coded address 'Ventspils-8') complete with a school, a shop, a house of culture and a sports hall was built for the 2,000 soldiers, scientists and staff employed there.

Its operations were controlled by the Main Intelligence Directorate (GRU), while the Committee for State Security (KGB) conducted parallel procedures to correlate acquired intelligence. In addition to other equipment and receivers, the complex features two large, fully rotatable parabolic antennas: the RT-16, nicknamed 'Pluto', with a diameter of 16 metres, and the RT-32, 'Saturn', commissioned in 1971, with the largest dish in Northern Europe at 32 metres. The station was used to monitor NATO communications from satellites, aircraft and submarines. While some of its activities are still unknown, US technical intelligence suggests that, for an extended period, the station successfully intercepted communications from every Western submarine active in Norwegian waters. The operators who managed to record communications from *Air Force One*, the aircraft on which the US president was travelling, were rewarded with 10 days' leave.

In 1991, Latvia gained independence from the crumbling Soviet Union. However, the existence of the installation was only publicly revealed in 1993, and troops remained there up until 1994 when withdrawal was finally negotiated. On leaving, the Russians caused a great deal of damage, smashing equipment, cutting cables, hammering nails into wires and pouring acid into motors – though the two largest antennas, the RT-16 and RT-32, survived. When Latvian scientists began the lengthy restoration process, their task was made all the more difficult by the lack of technical documents.

Today a dedicated team works constantly to improve the radio telescopes. In 2015 the facility benefitted from a 16 million-euro injection of funds, and, in a collaboration between the European Union, the Latvian government and local Ventspils authorities, it is undergoing a major programme of modernisation. Approximately 20,000 structural parts of the RT-32 have been replaced, along with the drive motors and electrical control system. In addition, an advanced, cryogenically cooled radio receiver has been installed, that significantly reduces signal noise during astronomical observations. This large-scale refurbishment marks the successful conversion of a former Soviet military facility to civilian scientific use, and, thanks to these efforts, the RT-32 now participates in international research programmes on a wide range of topics, from the near-Earth ionosphere to Jupiter, the Sun and the farthest reaches of space where stars are formed.

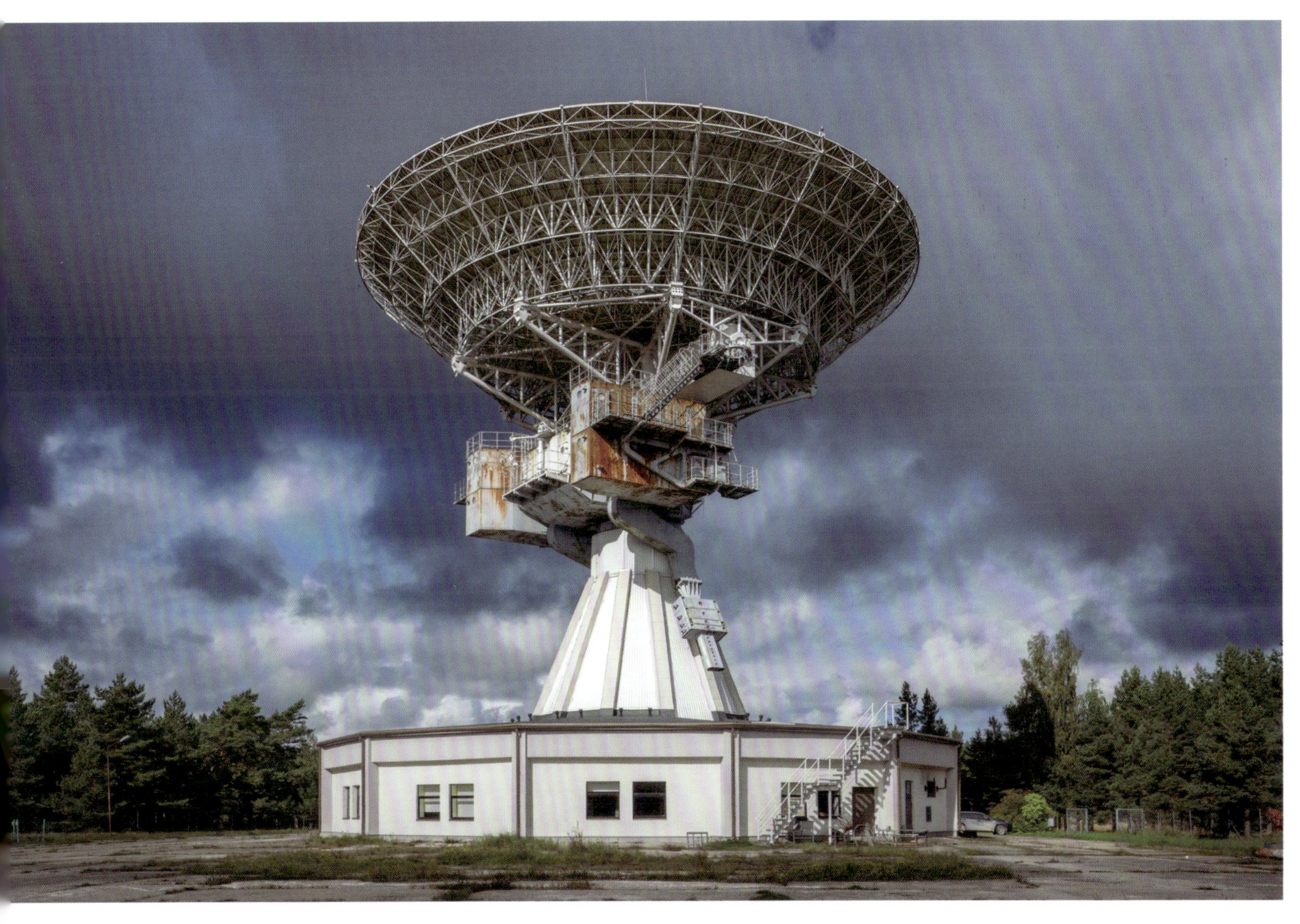

The RT-32 radio telescope is a fully steerable 32-metre parabolic antenna. The moving part of the structure weighs 600 tonnes. The antenna itself weighs 58 tonnes and is mounted on top of a 25-metre tower. Today it is used solely for scientific purposes including very-long-baseline interferometry, solar observations and the tracking of space debris.

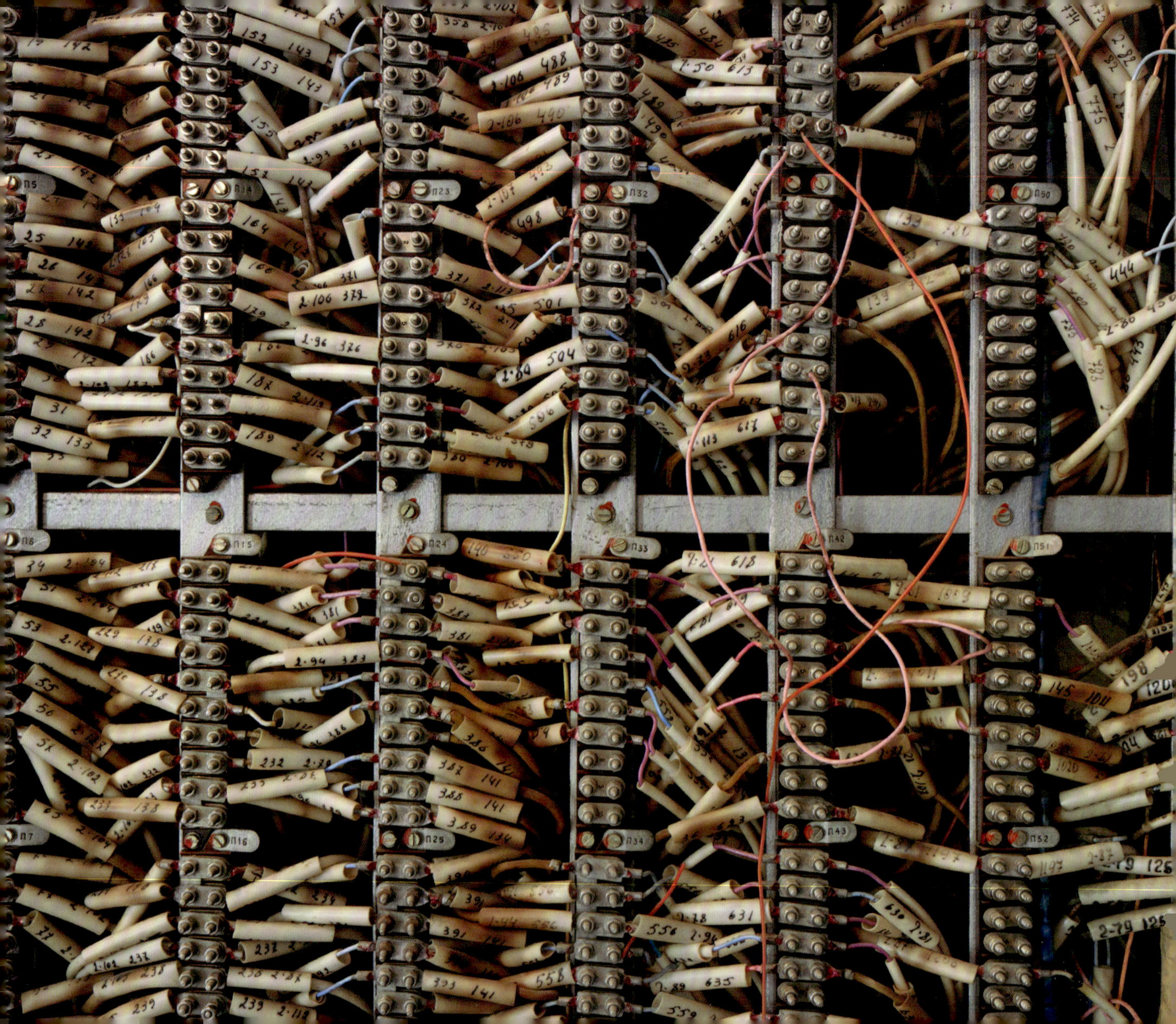

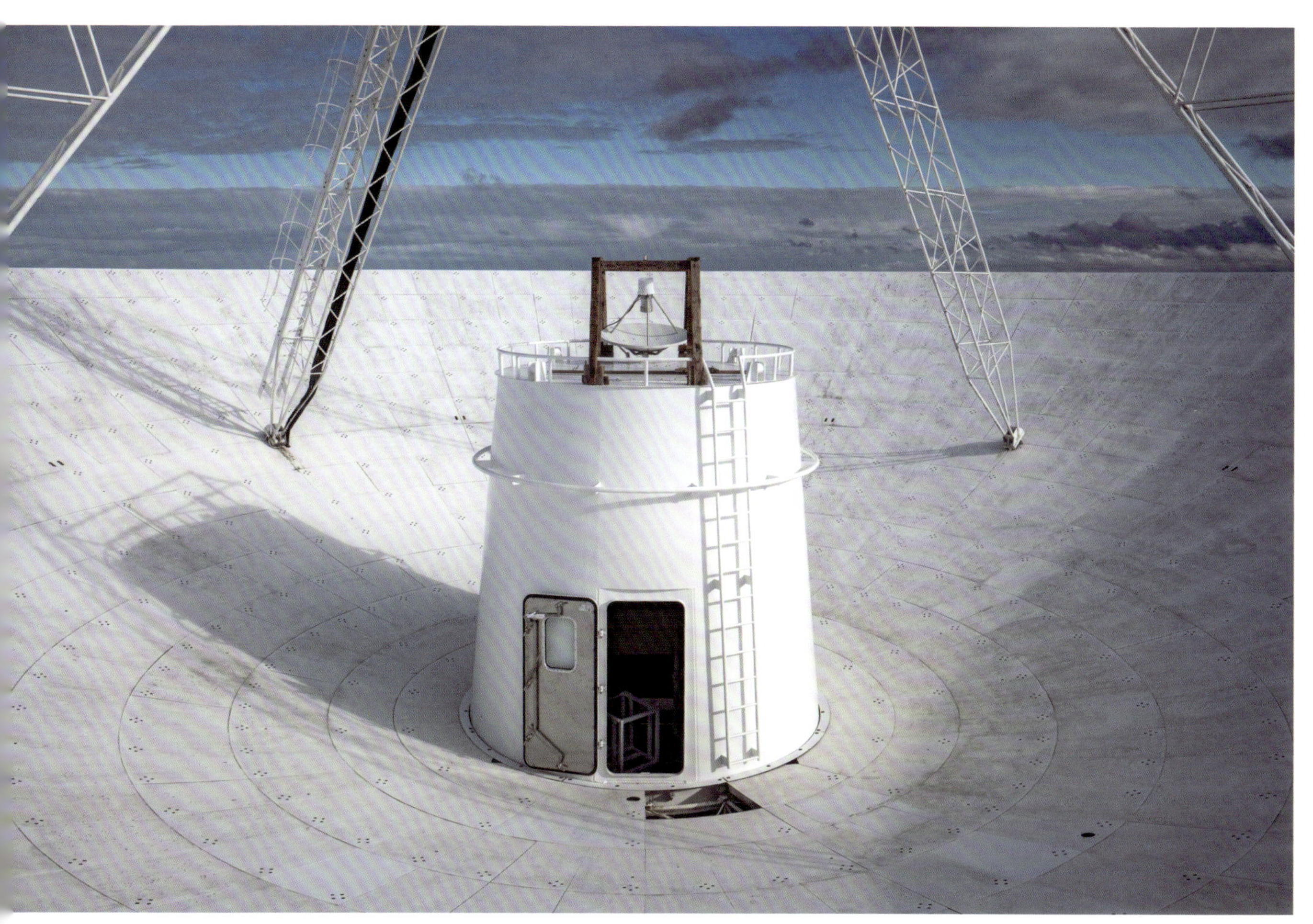

A 4.4-metre cone in the centre of the main mirror houses modern receiving equipment. The renovated dish was painted with a special white paint from the USA that reflects sunlight and heat to minimise thermal expansion, helping to maintain its shape.
Left: An electrical panel from the RT-8 radio telescope control room.

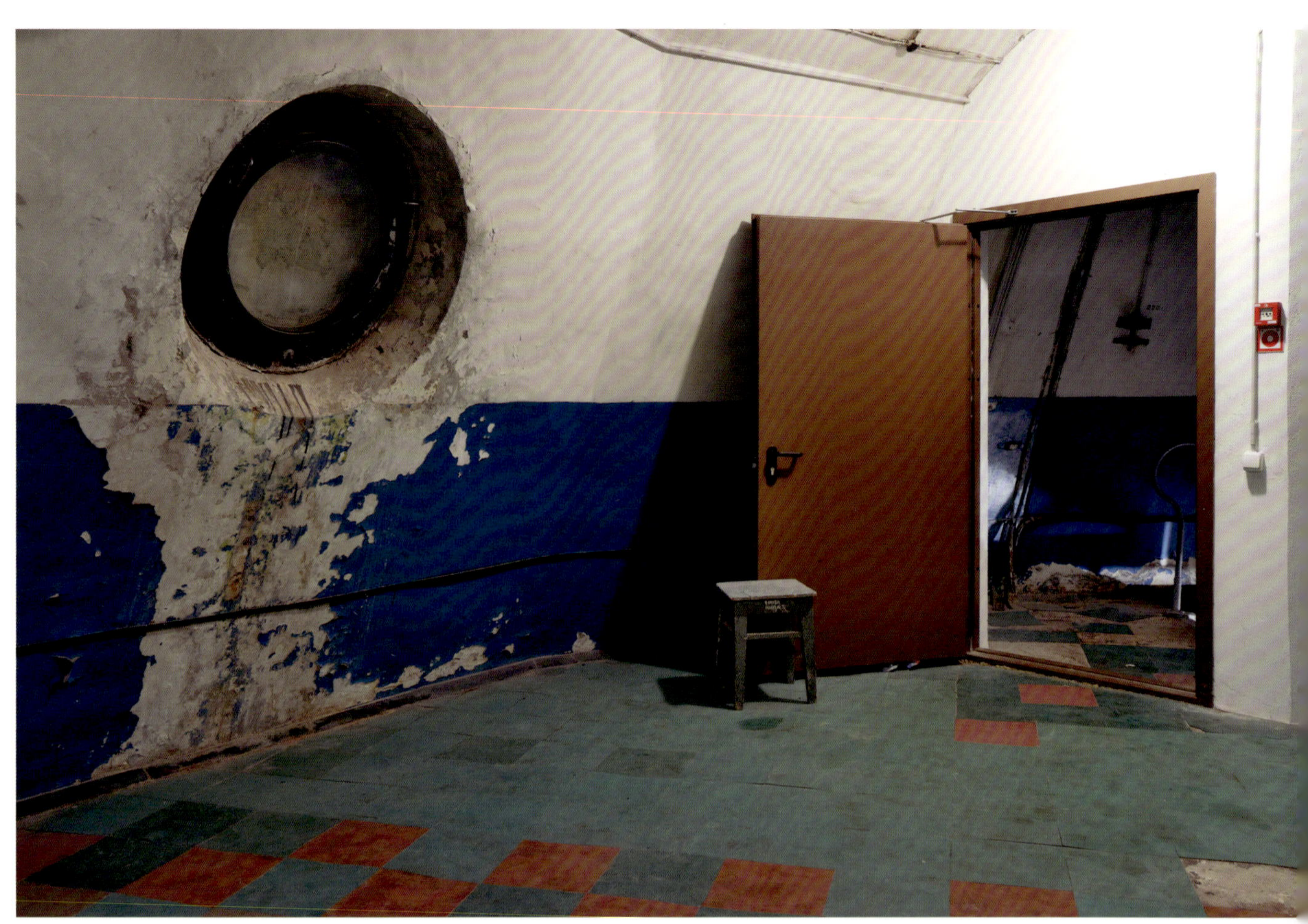

The structure was built at a naval yard in Ukraine and elements of it resemble a ship.

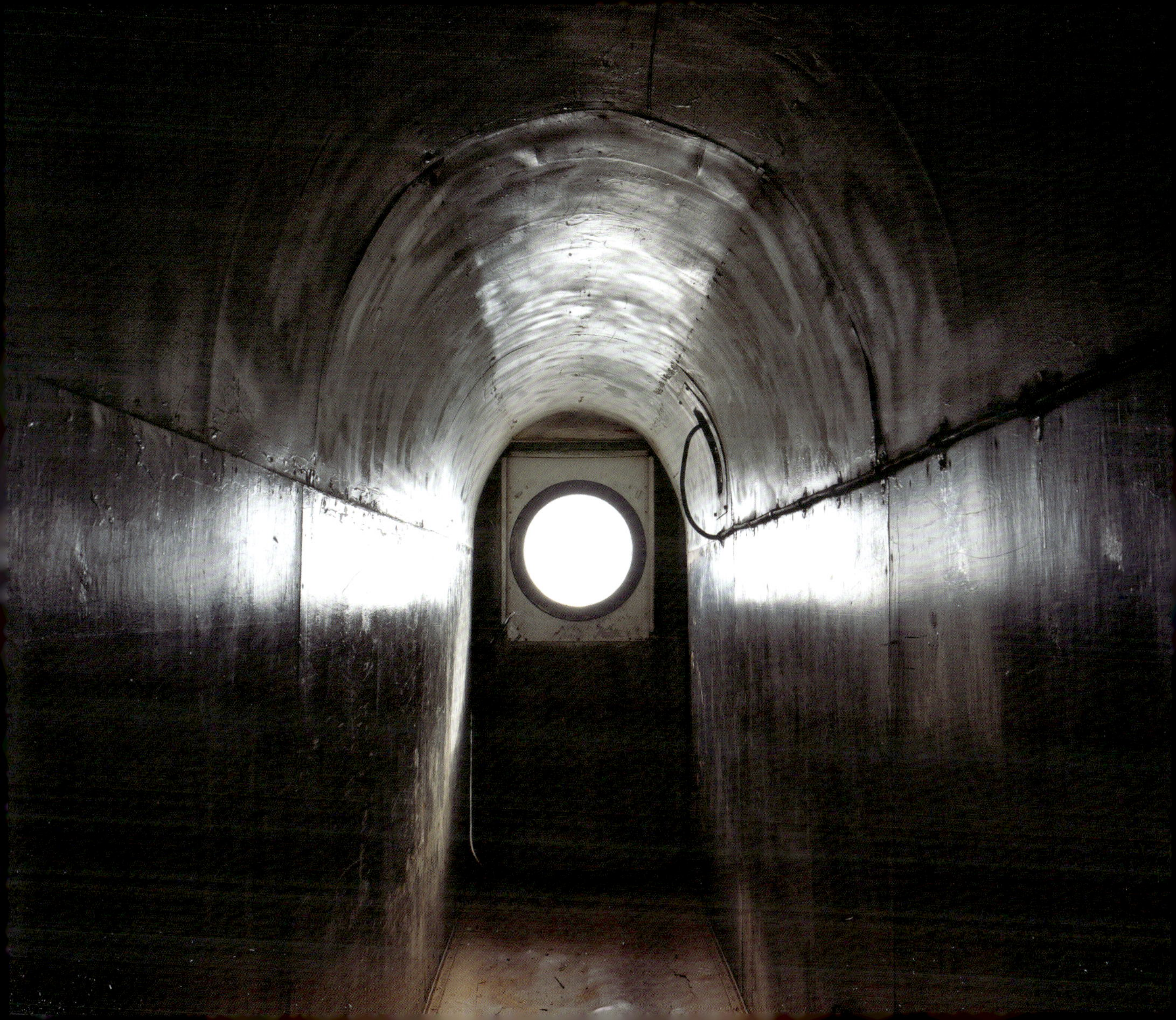

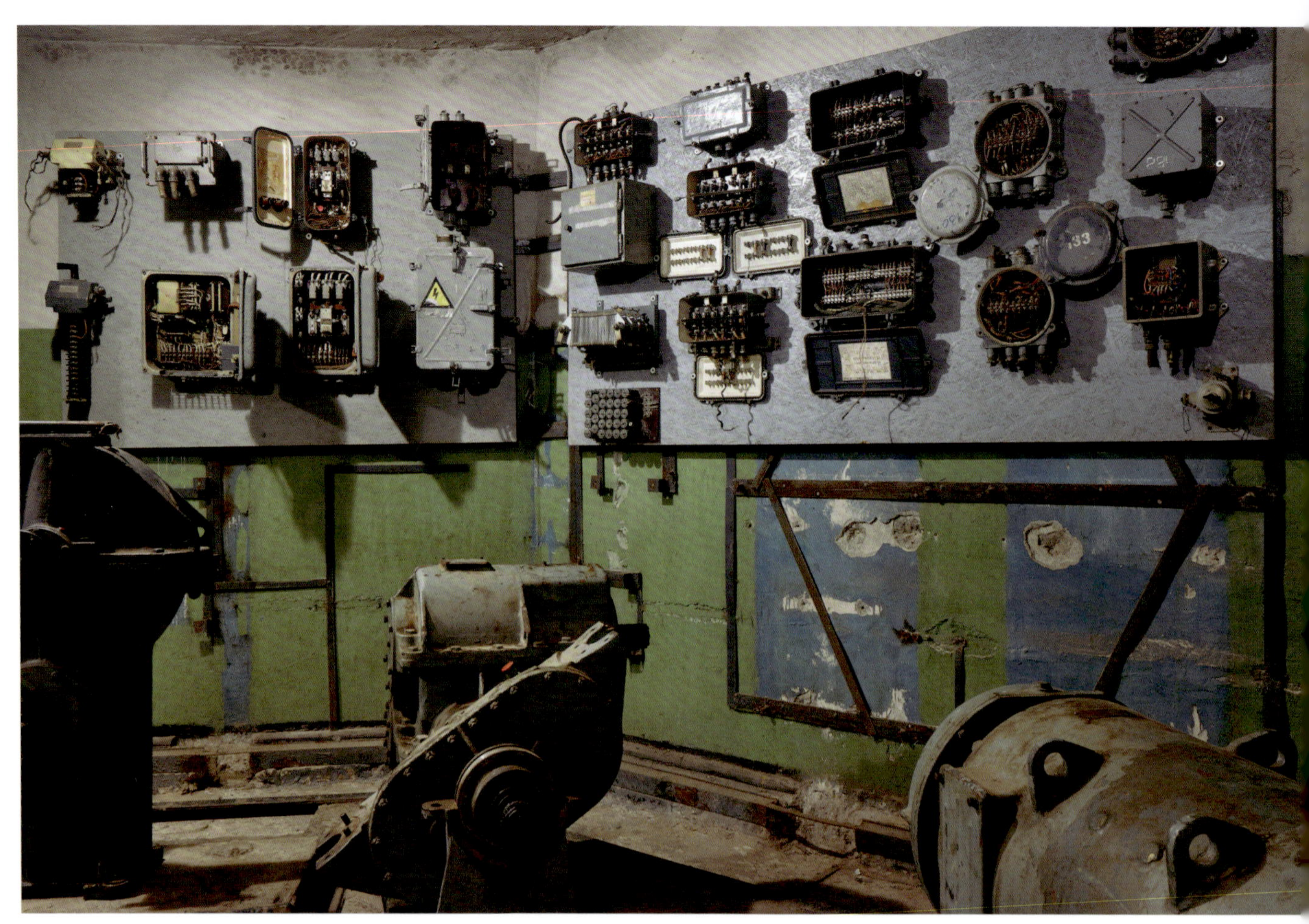

The former engineering room of the RT-8 radio telescope. Unlike the RT-32 and RT-16, the antenna of the smaller RT-8 telescope was taken by the Russian military when they withdrew in 1994.

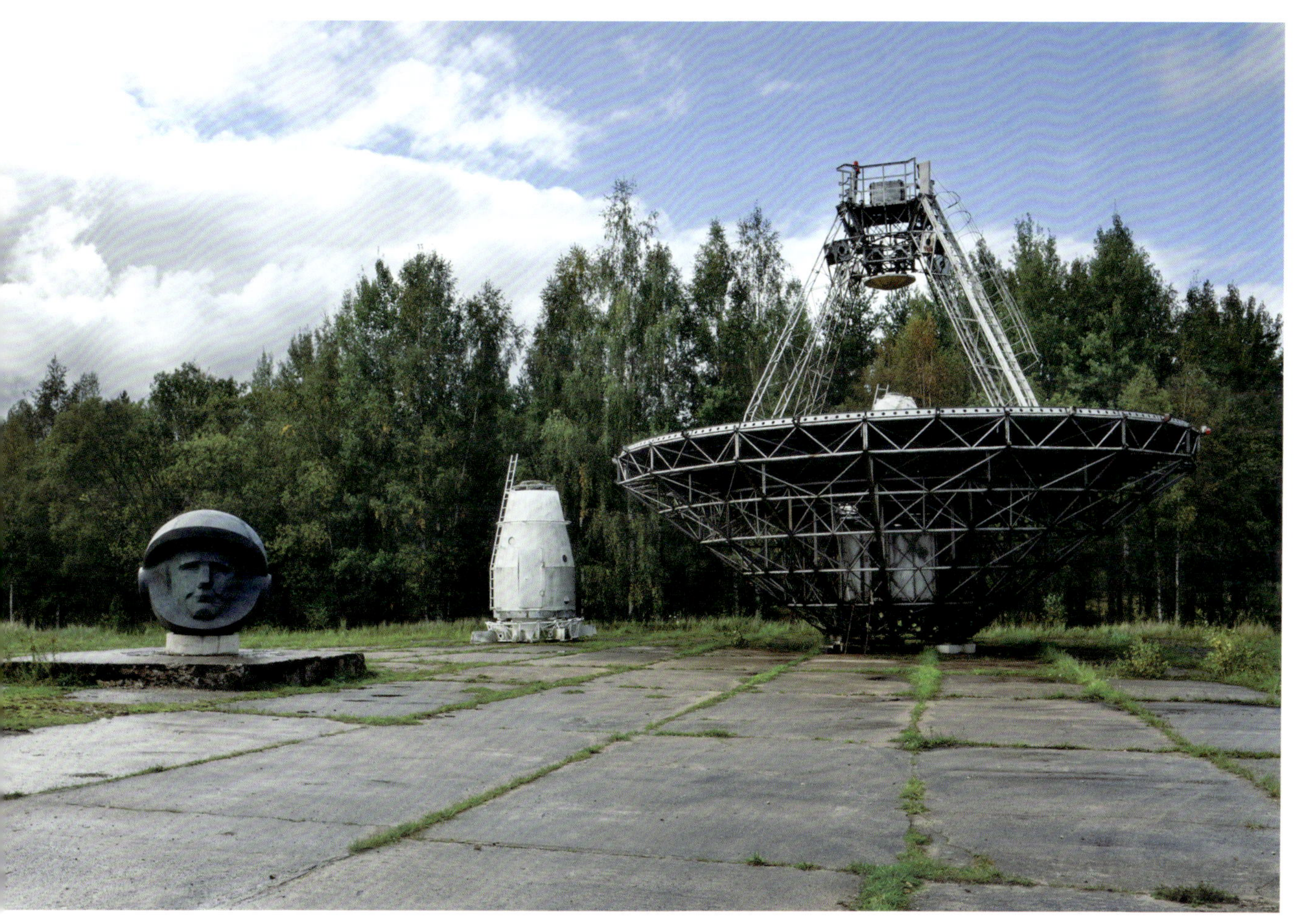

The old RT-16 dish lies next to the original RT-32 cone and a Soviet-era bust of Yuri Gagarin, the first man in space.

NATIONAL INSTITUTE FOR RESEARCH, DEVELOPMENT AND TESTING IN ELECTRICAL ENGINEERING
Craiova, ROMANIA

During the Cold War, Romania under communist rule gradually adopted an independent political line that distanced the country from the Soviet Union. This shift, accompanied by increased domestic authoritarianism and repression, began in the 1960s under Gheorghe Gheorghiu-Dej (1901–1965) and was consolidated by his successor, Nicolae Ceaușescu (1918–1989).

In 1968, Romania was the only Soviet-aligned country within the Warsaw Pact not to participate in the invasion of Czechoslovakia. Its open condemnation of the action, which had been orchestrated by the USSR to surpress the liberal reforms of the Prague Spring, exacerbated the schism between the two countries, prompting a temporary improvement in relations between Romania and the West. These political constraints shaped the development of science in the country. Equipment for institutes was initially supplied from the USSR and other socialist countries, with Western technologies being introduced gradually from the 1970s onwards.

Following the examples of China and North Korea, Ceaușescu intensified the programme of economic and social transformation. To convert Romania from a predominantly agricultural country into an industrial one, a series of highly centralised five-year plans was implemented, involving massive investments in large quantities of equipment for infrastructure and electrification.

Founded in 1949 in Craiova, Electroputere was one of Romania's largest companies, specialising in the production of heavy electrotechnical equipment including electric engines, high-voltage transformers and locomotives. In 1962, while on a visit to the Electroputere factory, the Soviet leader Nikita Khrushchev was irritated to discover that Romanian locomotives were being manufactured under a Swiss licence, thus challenging the idea that the USSR was technologically supreme and that other Eastern bloc nations should rely exclusively on it for any assistance. Over the course of its history, Electroputere became a major manufacturer of trains for Romanian, Bulgarian, Chinese and Polish railways, producing more than 2,400 diesel and 1,050 electric locomotives.

In 1974, the research and development department of the Electroputere plant was transformed into the Scientific Research and Technological Engineering Centre – CCSIT Electroputere Craiova. Its purpose was to test equipment intended for both domestic use and export. In 1989, the Ceaușescu dictatorship was overthrown at the start of the Romanian revolution and in 1990 the Centre became an independent entity.

Today, the institute is an internationally recognised centre of excellence with extensive experience in the evaluation of high-voltage research, development and testing technology, the monitoring and diagnosis of electrical power equipment, and electromagnetic compatibility. Its two flagship laboratories, the High Voltage Laboratory (HVL) and the High Power Laboratory (HPL), are critical in developing equipment for the functioning and safety of the national electrical energy system. Since its inception it has tested almost all the equipment produced in Romania for the transmission and distribution of electricity, and has developed an extensive catalogue of international clients.

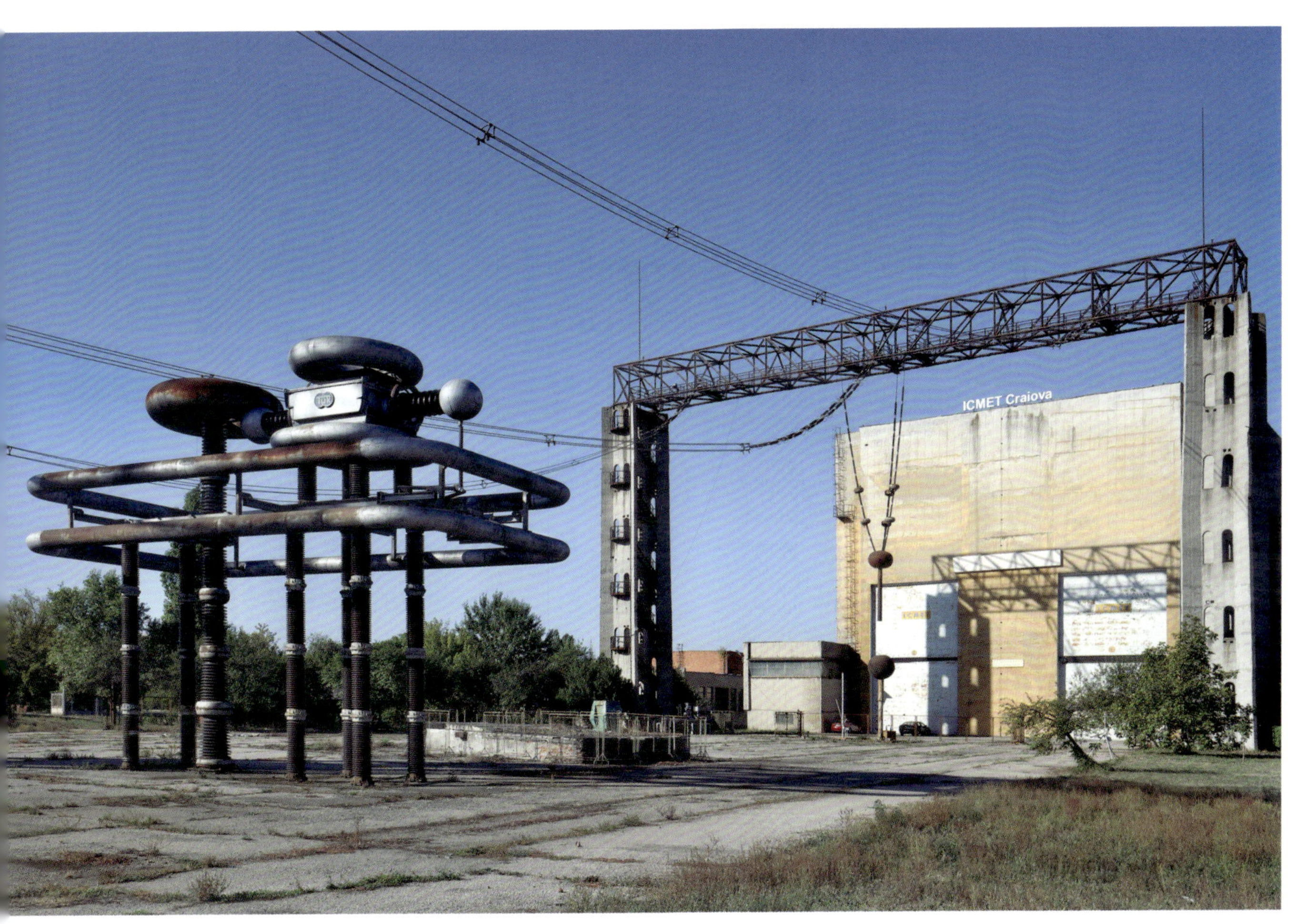

The outdoor test platform. The mobile design of the pulse generator and transformer cascade means they can be taken outdoors to test equipment mounted directly on the platform or on a rail car or trailer.

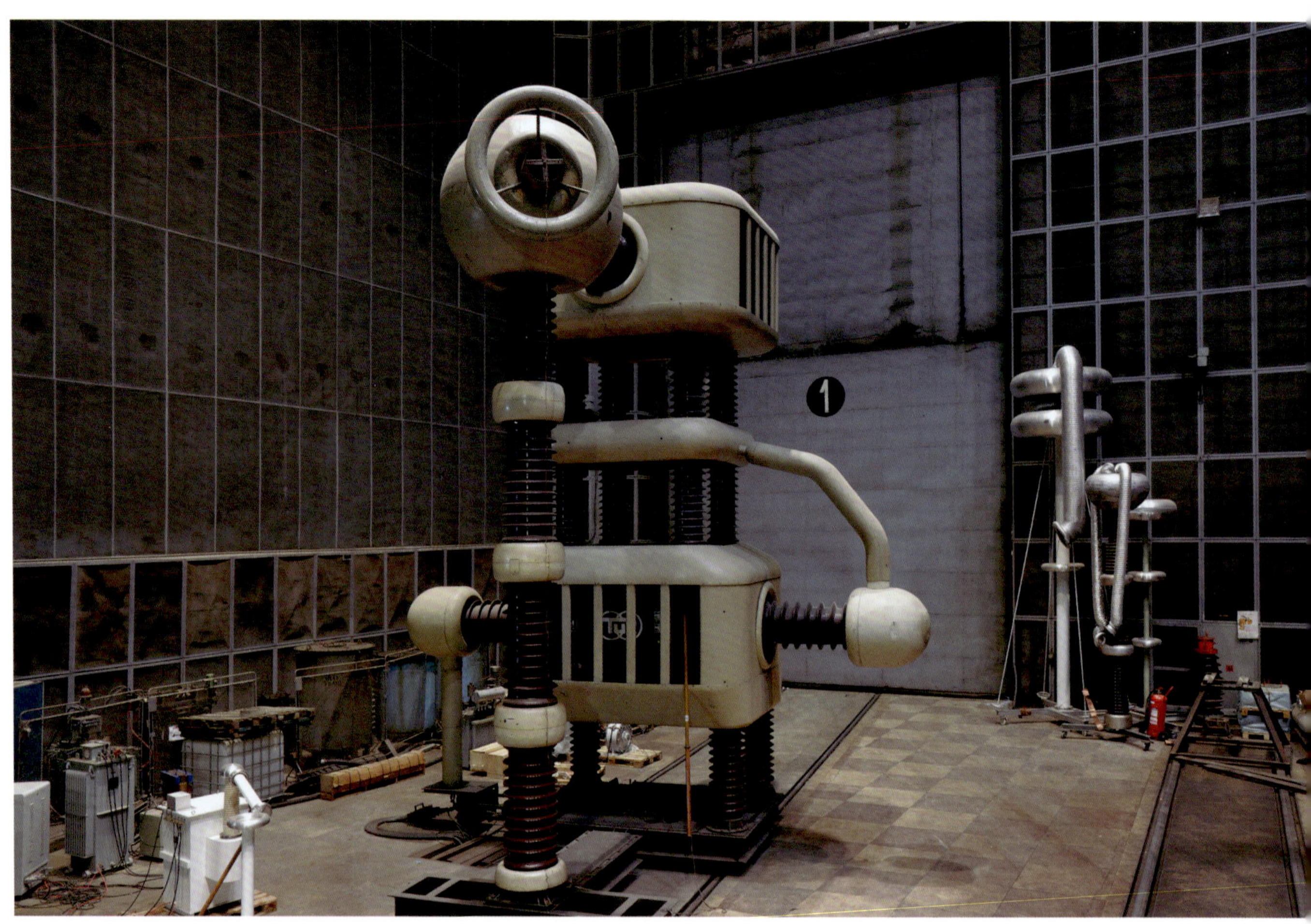

The High Voltage Laboratory comprises the main test hall, a shielded chamber measuring 48 x 32 x 27 metres. This area is used for type tests (to validate the standards of a product design type) and special tests (to provide specific information about equipment or products that falls outside that covered by type tests).

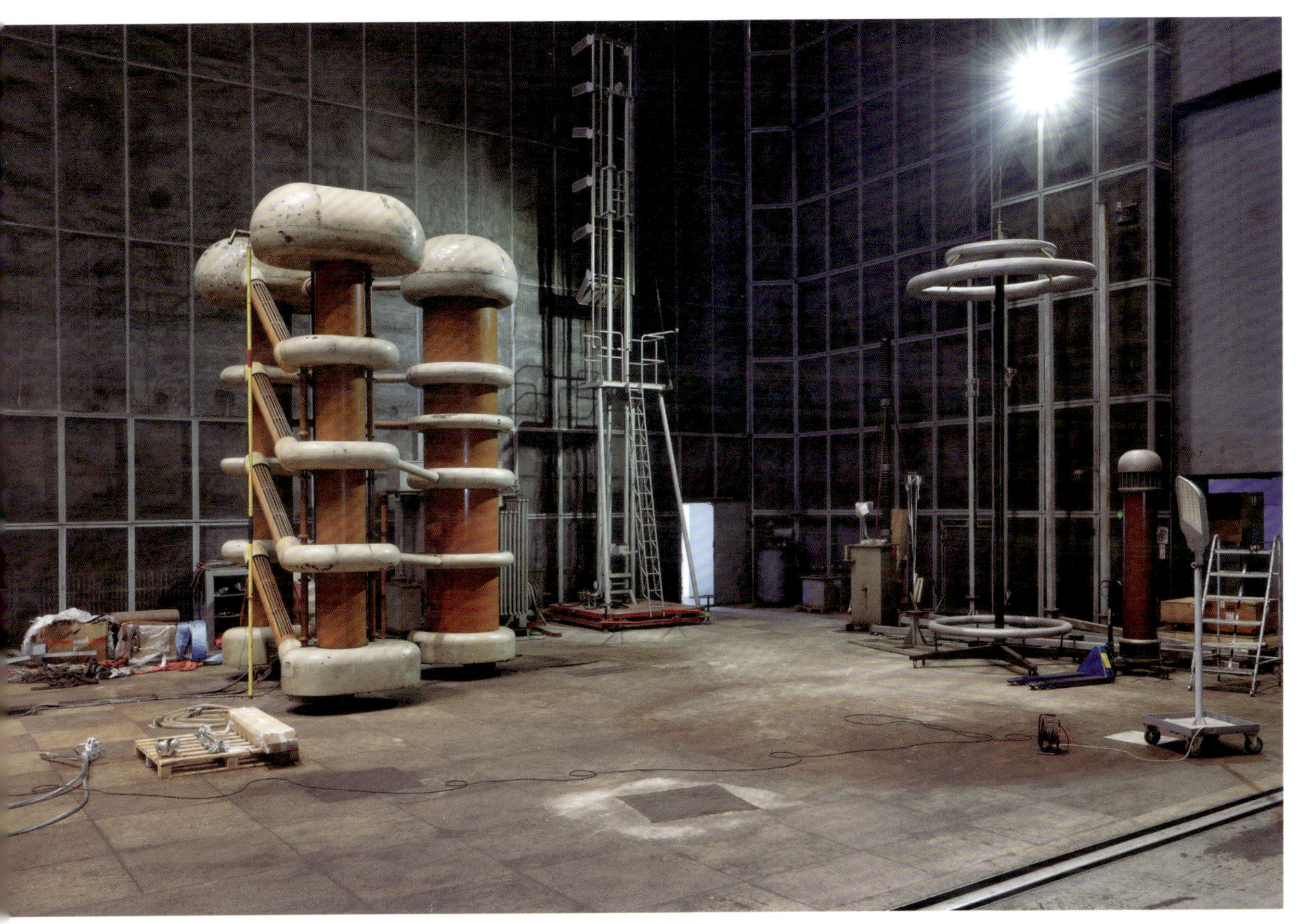

The equipment includes a 4.2 MV impulse generator, a 1.2 MV AC transformer cascade and a 1.1 MV DC rectifier cascade, as well as an artificial rain device.

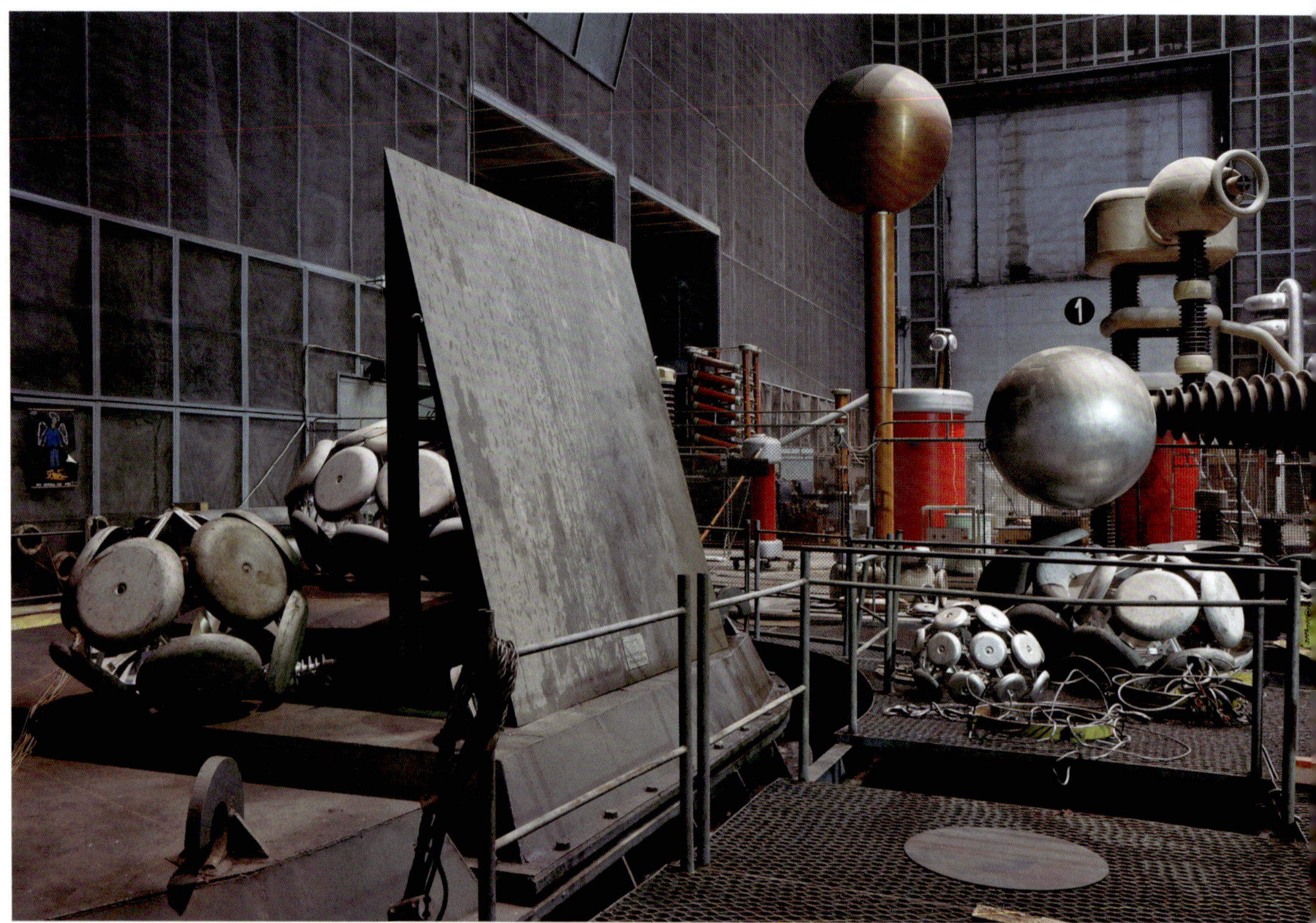

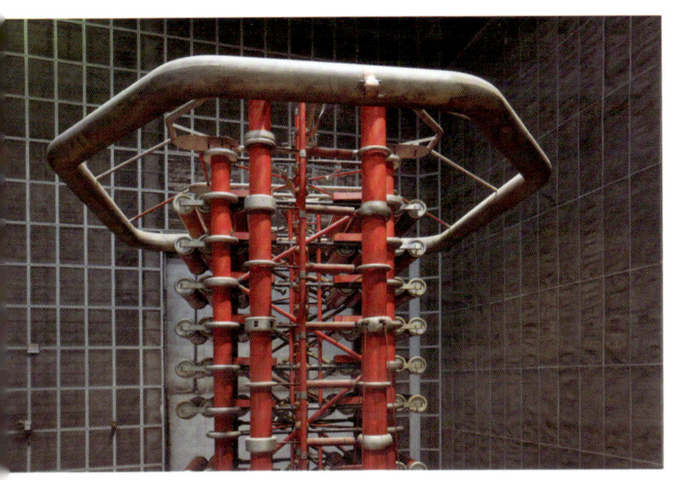 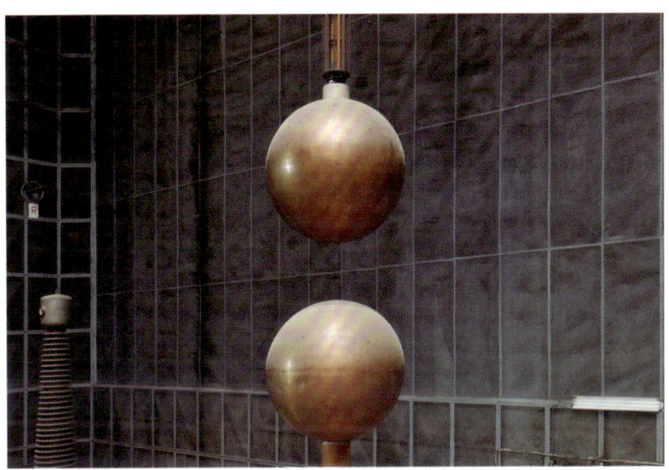

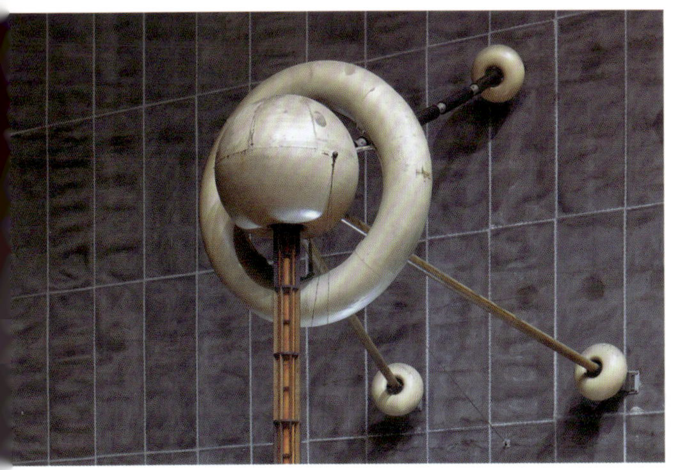 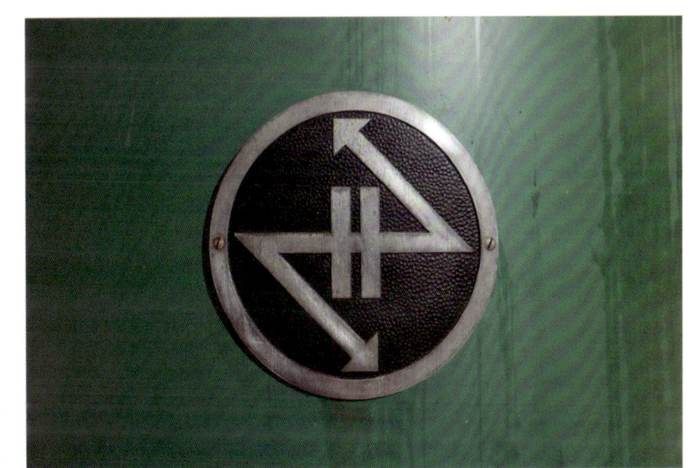

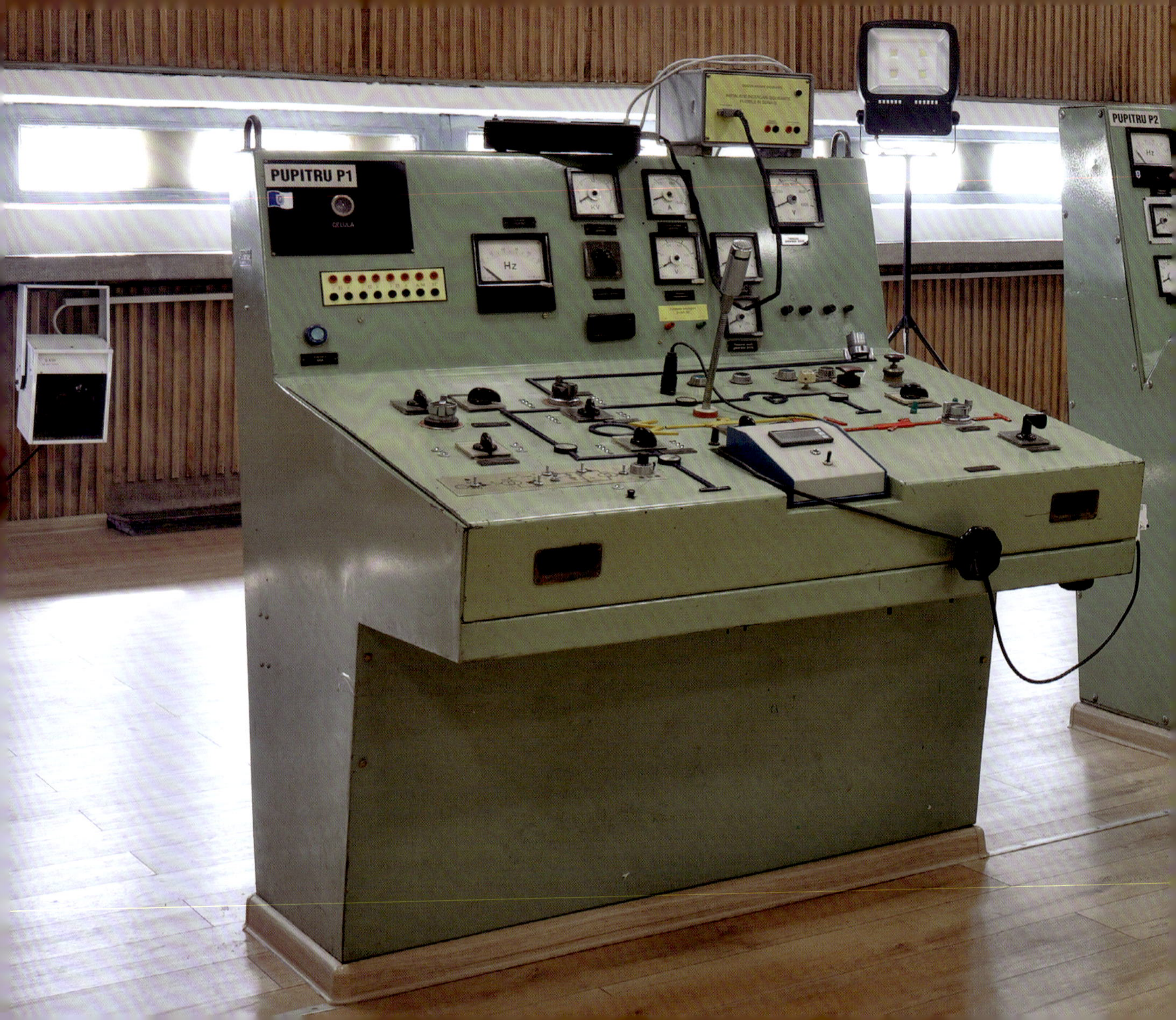
PUPITRU P1
CELULA
KV
A
V
Hz
V
PUPITRU P2
Hz

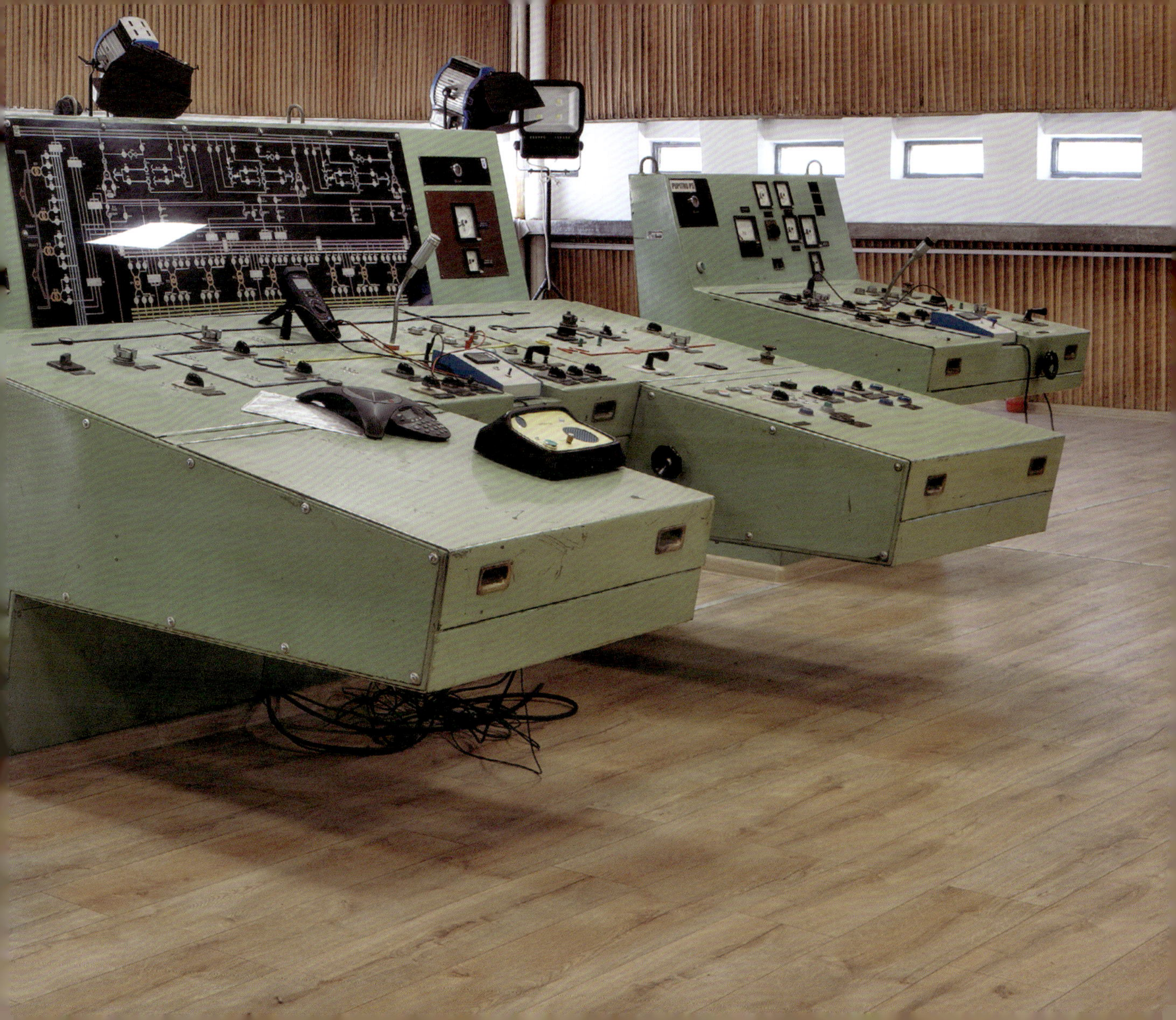

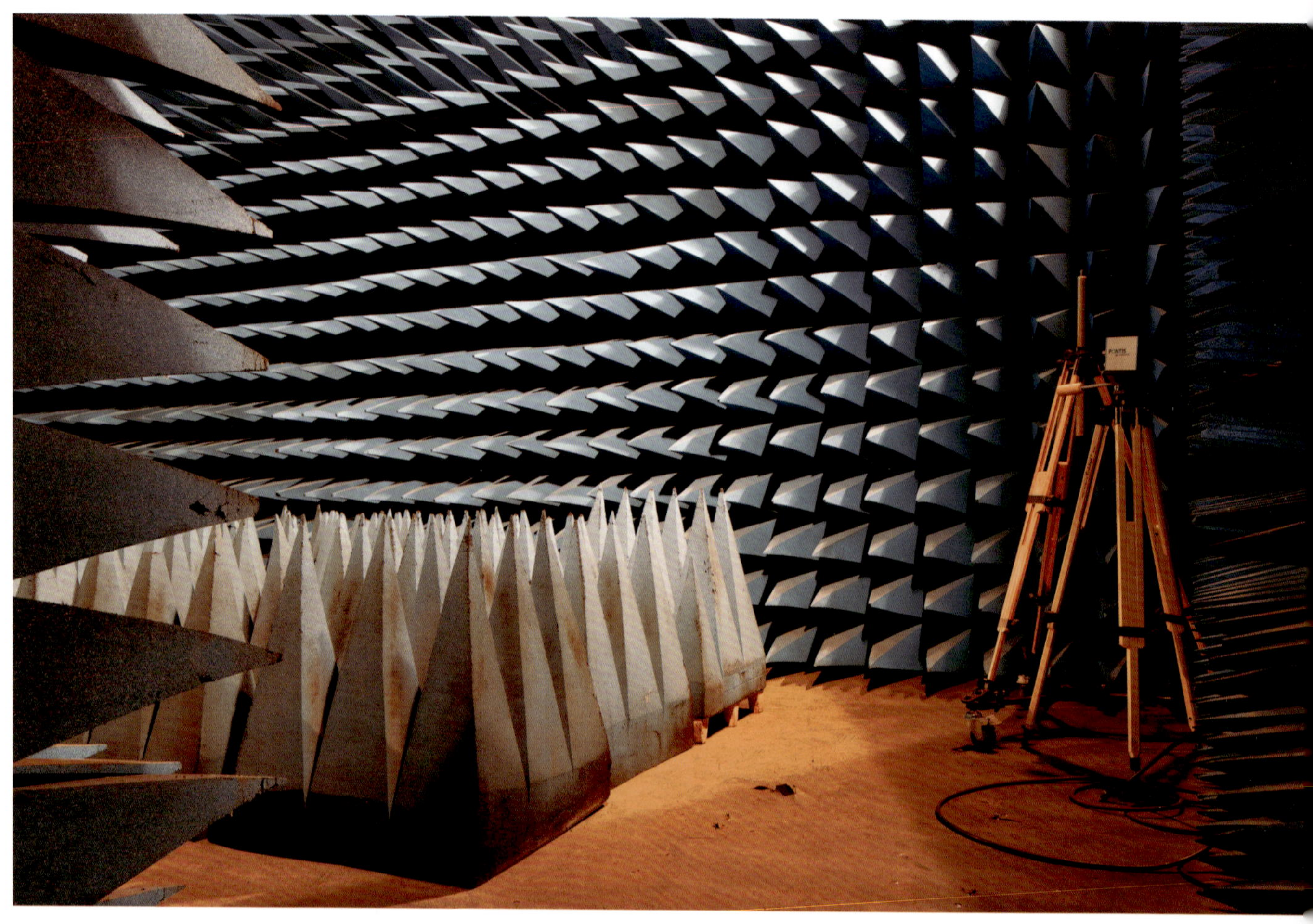

Previous pages: The High Power Laboratory control room. The equipment and technical assistance for its installation was provided by the All-Russia Electrotechnical Institute named after V. I. Lenin (VEI).

In 2000, the institute set up Romania's first modern semi-anechoic chamber to test equipment for electromagnetic compatibility.

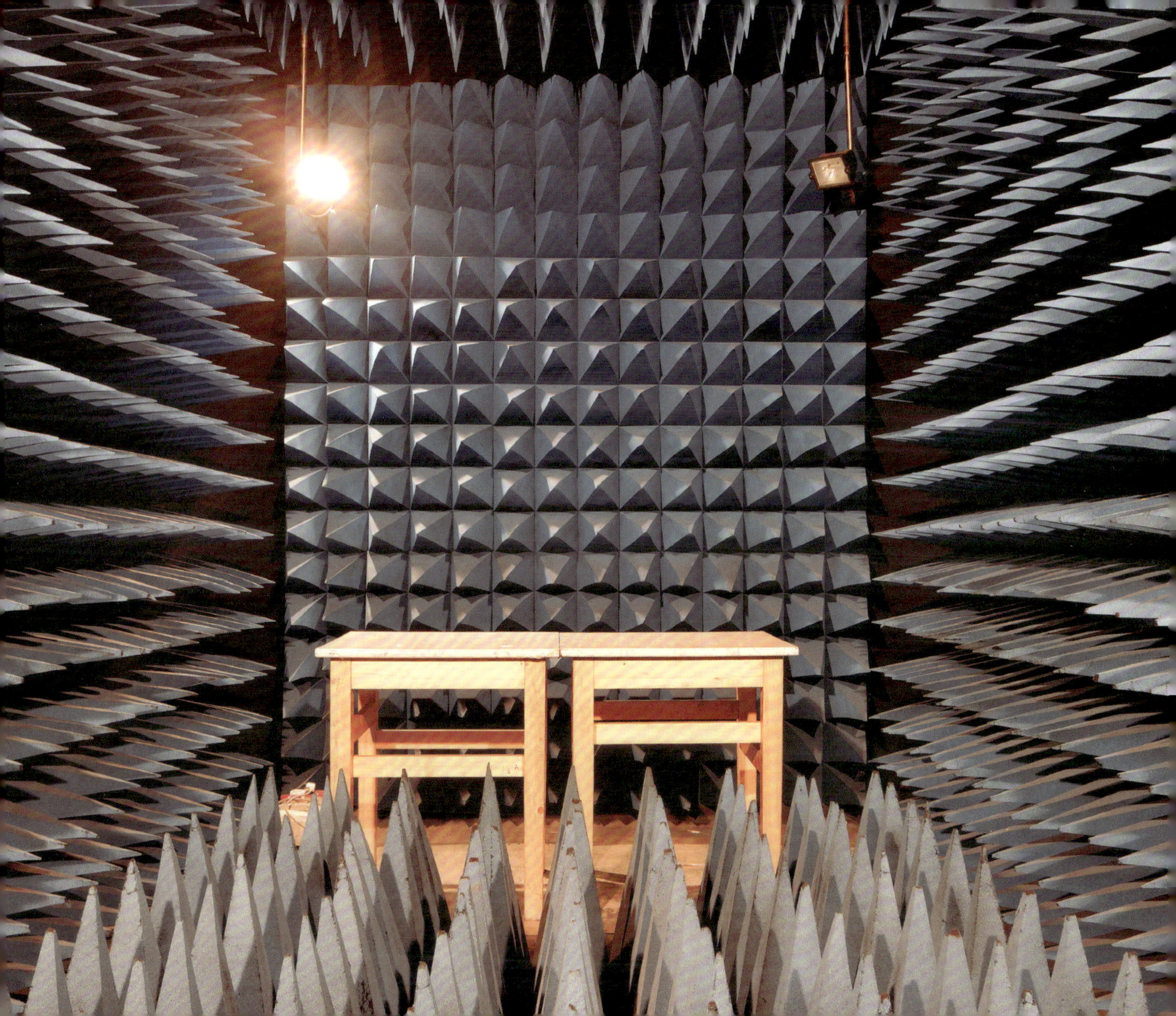

HORIA HULUBEI NATIONAL INSTITUTE FOR RESEARCH AND DEVELOPMENT IN PHYSICS AND NUCLEAR ENGINEERING

Măgurele, ROMANIA

Led by eminent physicist Horia Hulubei (1896–1972), the Institute of Physics was established in Bucharest in 1949. Like many other Romanian intellectuals, Hulubei had strong links with the French scientific community. In 1933, he earned his PhD in Paris under the supervision of the atomic physicist and Nobel Prize winner Jean Perrin (1870–1942), while his doctoral committee was headed by physicist and chemist and twice Nobel Prize winner, Marie Curie (1867–1934). Hulubei became renowned for his exceptional contributions to atomic and nuclear physics, particularly in the field of X-ray spectroscopy (a technique determining material composition through X-ray interactions).

The Romanian nuclear programme began in 1955, following a bilateral agreement with the USSR regarding cooperation in the peaceful use of nuclear energy. In 1956, construction began on the country's first two major research facilities, the VVR-S nuclear reactor (a Water-cooled, Water-moderated Reactor) and the U-120 cyclotron (a 120-cm-diameter particle accelerator). The VVR-S was the first reactor to be approved by the USSR outside of its own borders. Designed with a power output of 2 MW, it was operational from 1957 until its shutdown in 1997, remaining largely unmodified throughout this 40-year period.

At these installations Romanian physicists conducted scientific research into nuclear reactions and structures, the better to understand atomic nuclei and their behaviour. The reactor was also employed in the production of radioactive isotopes for various industrial and medical applications. Contrary to speculation, the institute did not conduct military research. After the fall of the Ceaușescu regime, inspections by the International Atomic Energy Agency and Euratom found no evidence of military applications at this site.

Between 1997 and 2002, following a period of maintenance, a series of studies was conducted to determine whether to upgrade or decommission the reactor, and in 2002 the government decided on decommissioning. Such a process is of necessity a lengthy one, involving regulatory, legislative, technical and environmental concerns. In 2009 and 2012, the enriched uranium spent fuel was repatriated in two batches to Russia. Decommissioning was initiated in 2010, and the reactor block demolished in 2017. Finally, a certificate of release, showing that the site was no longer classified as a nuclear territory, was issued in 2020.

During this process, the Institute was simultaneously developing Romania's new flagship research facility, the Extreme Light Infrastructure – Nuclear Physics (ELI-NP), which uses the world's largest and most advanced high-power laser system. And currently, the old reactor building stands ready to be converted into an extension of the ELI-NP.

Today, through multidisciplinary research activities carried out in collaboration with international partners, the institute continues to pursue its goals of understanding nature, developing beneficial applications and training a new generation of nuclear physicists.

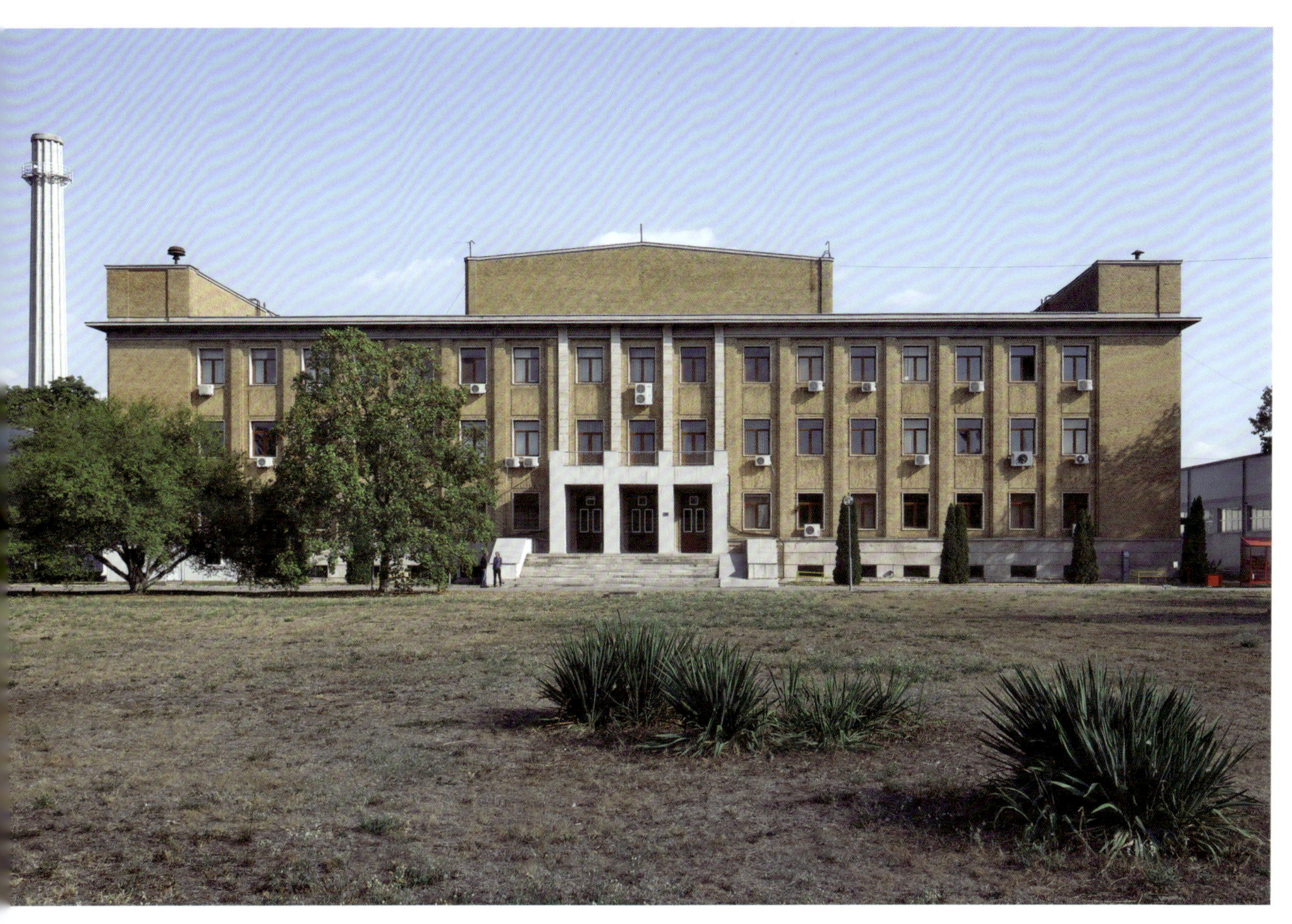

The original reactor building. It is intended that this will be used as part of the nearby Extreme Light Infrastructure – Nuclear Physics facility.

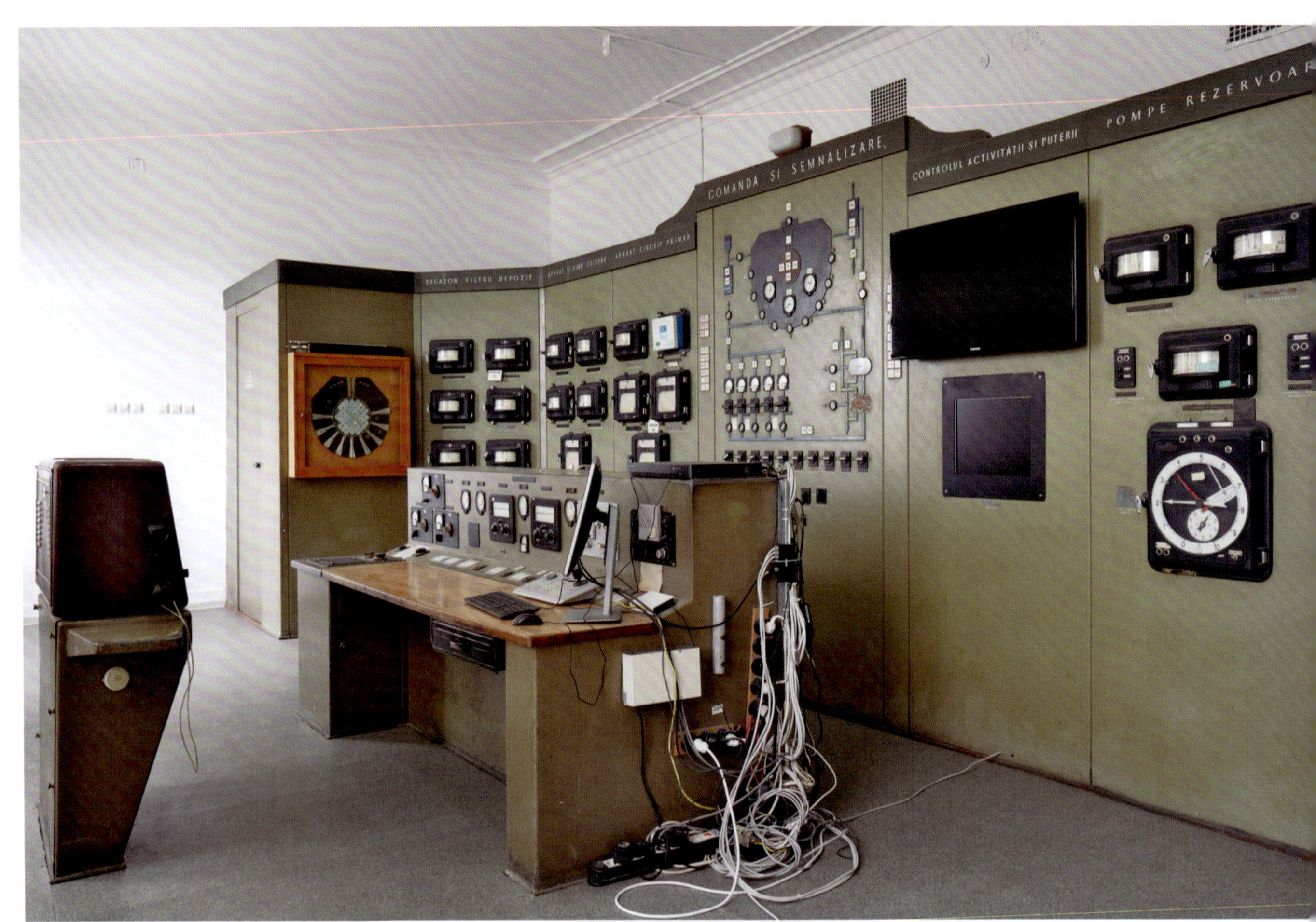

The reactor control room has remained largely unchanged since its construction in the 1950s. (The gauge on the bottom right is the same as that on display in the entrance hall of the Centre for Energy Reseach, Budapest, see page 70.)

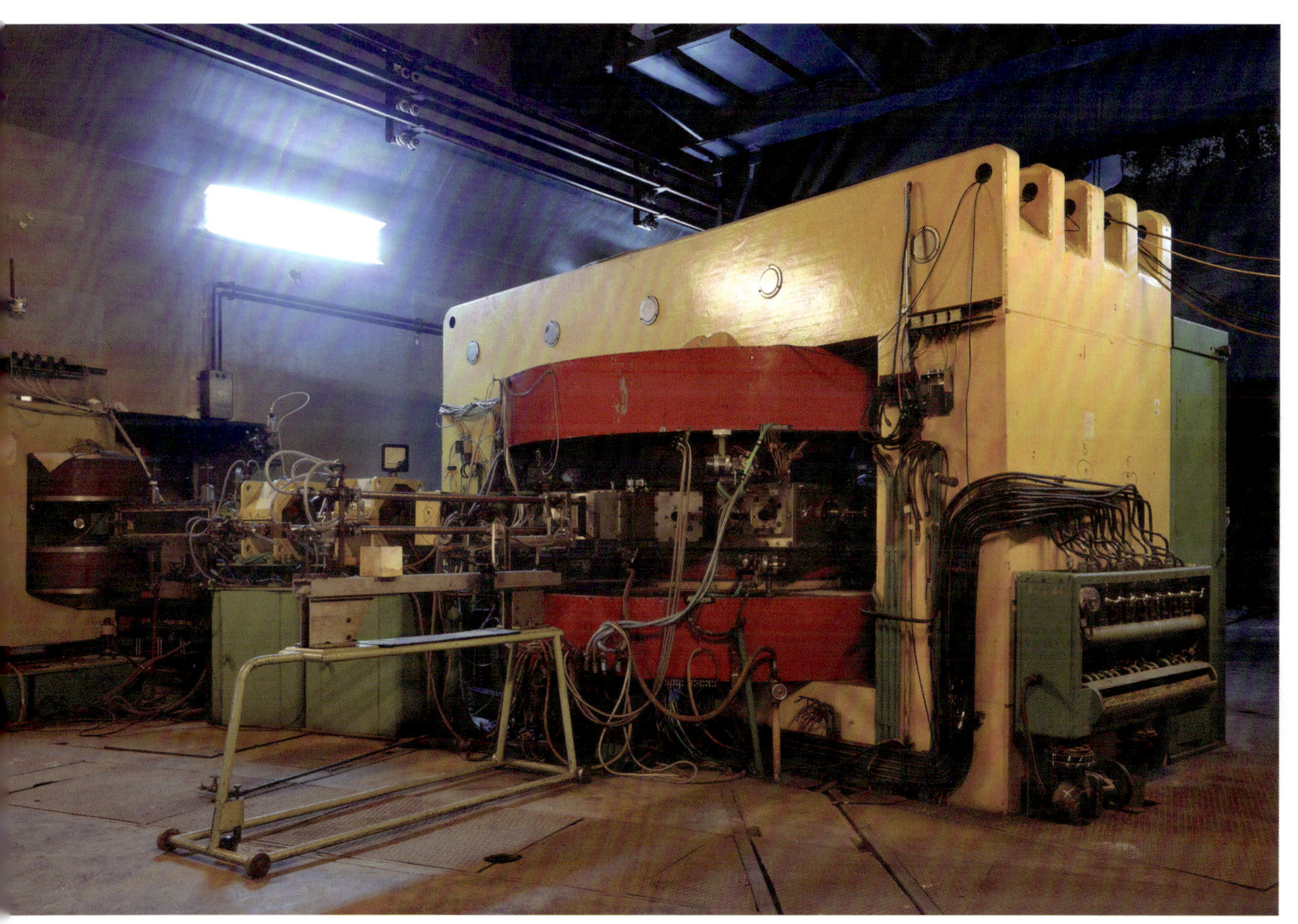

The cyclotron U-120 (a 120-centimetre particle accelerator) is in the process of being decommissioned.

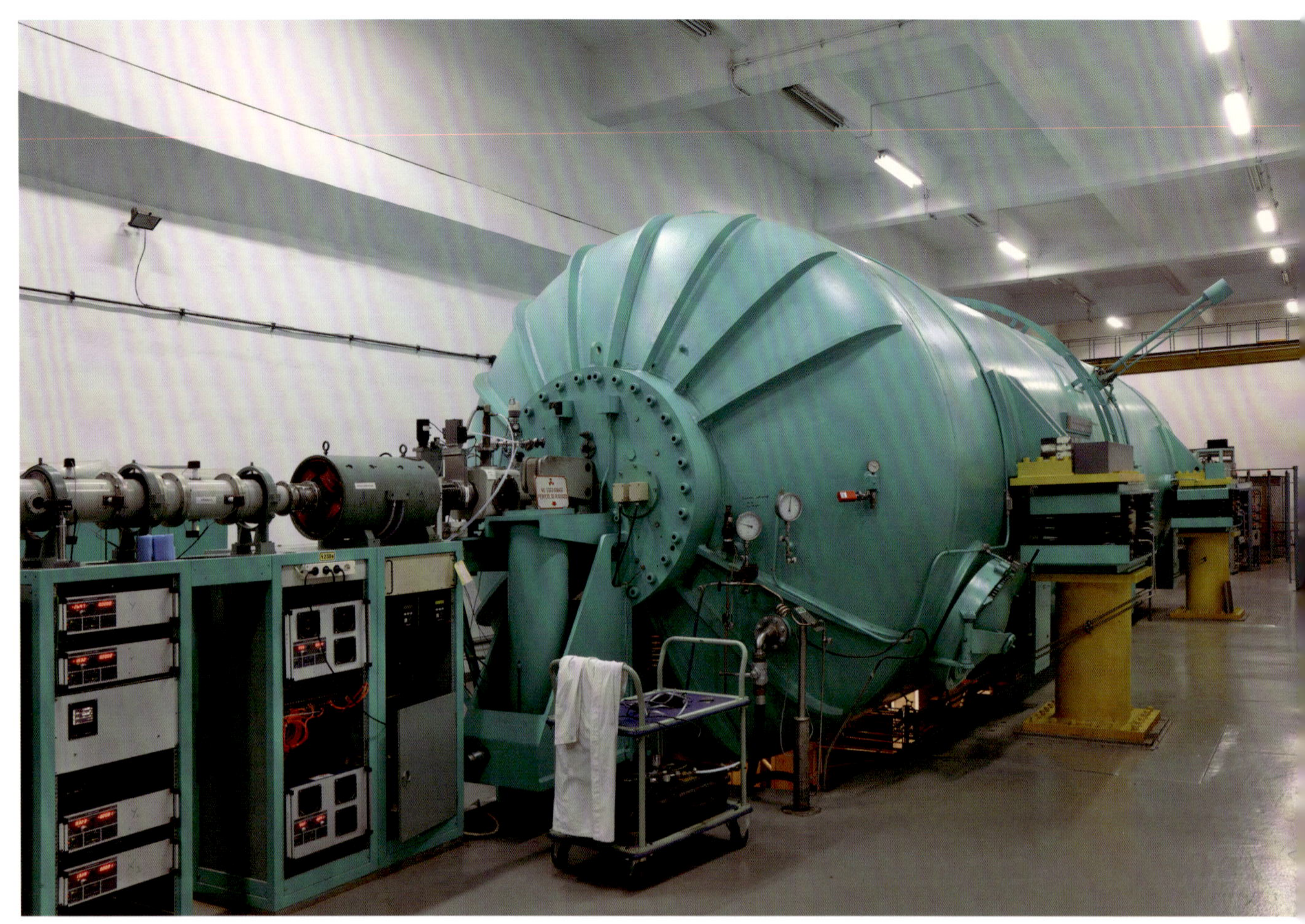

This American 9 MV FN Pelletron Tandem Accelerator was installed in 1973, as Romania opened up to the West. Today it is used for basic and advanced research (mainly in nuclear structure physics and nuclear reaction physics). Having undergone extensive modernisation to enhance its reliability, stability and capabilities it currently operates at an average rate of 5,500 hours a year.

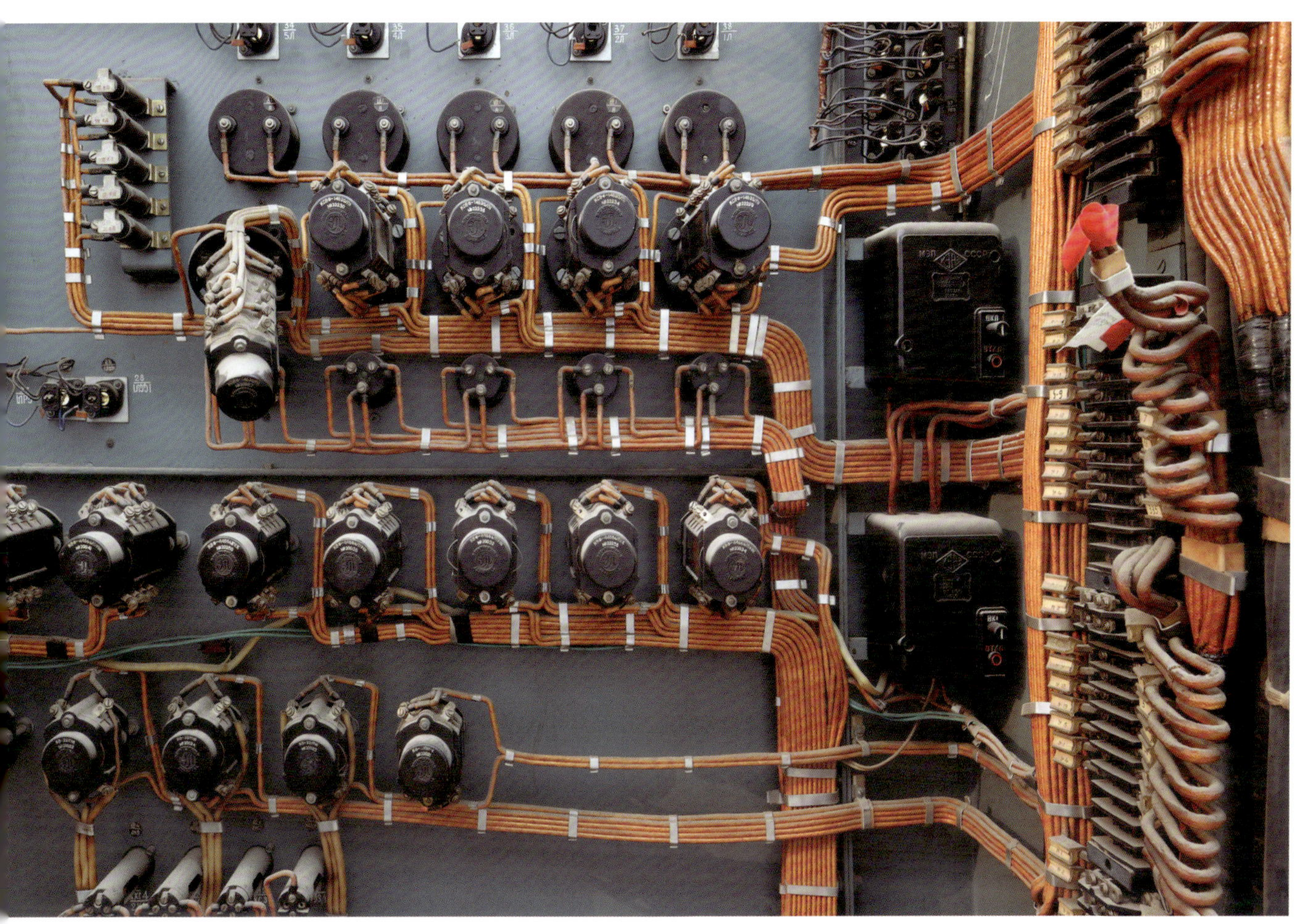

An electrical panel in the reactor control room.

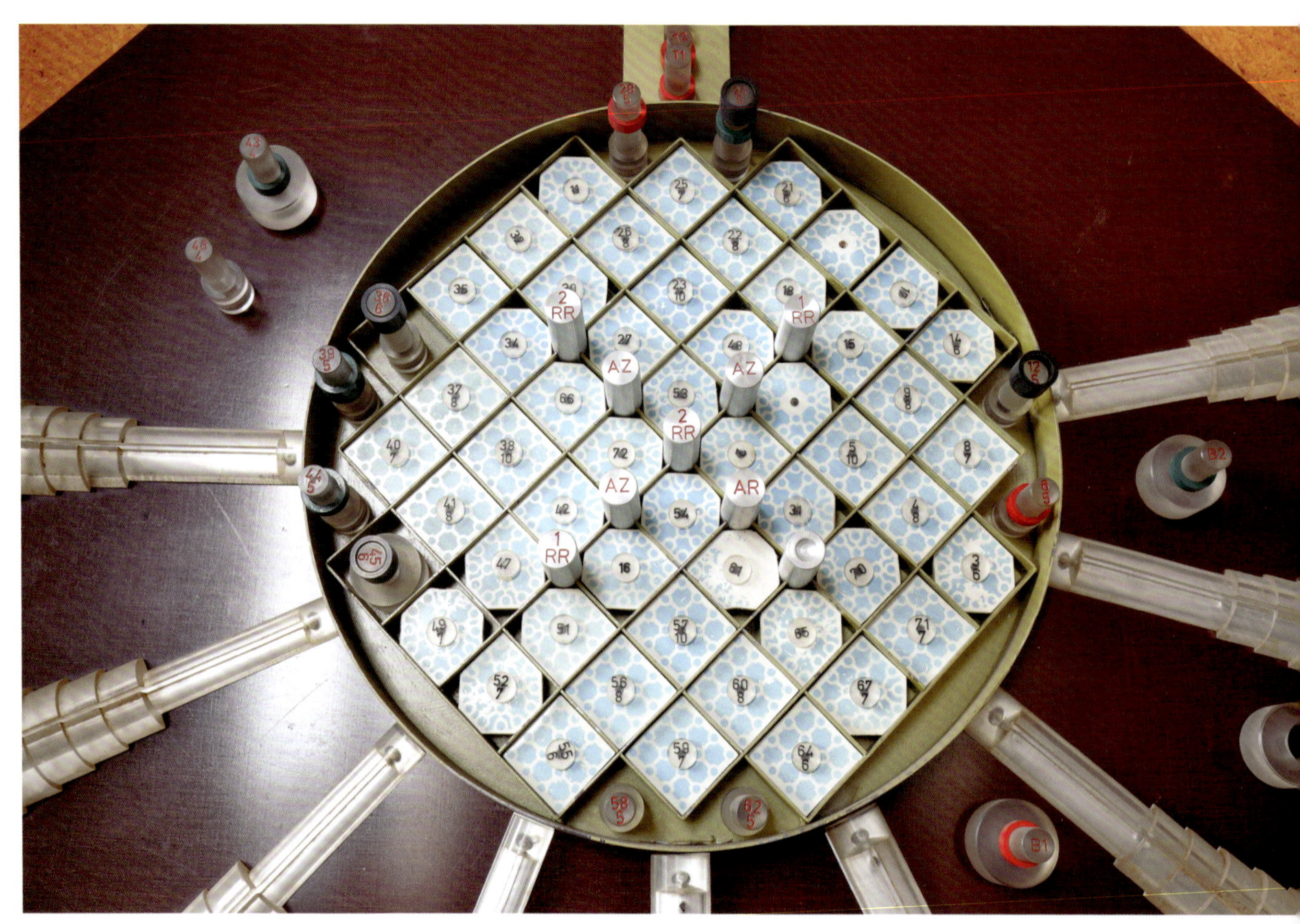

A model diagram of the reactor core forms part of the control room instrument panel.
Right: The reactor hall after dismantling had been completed.

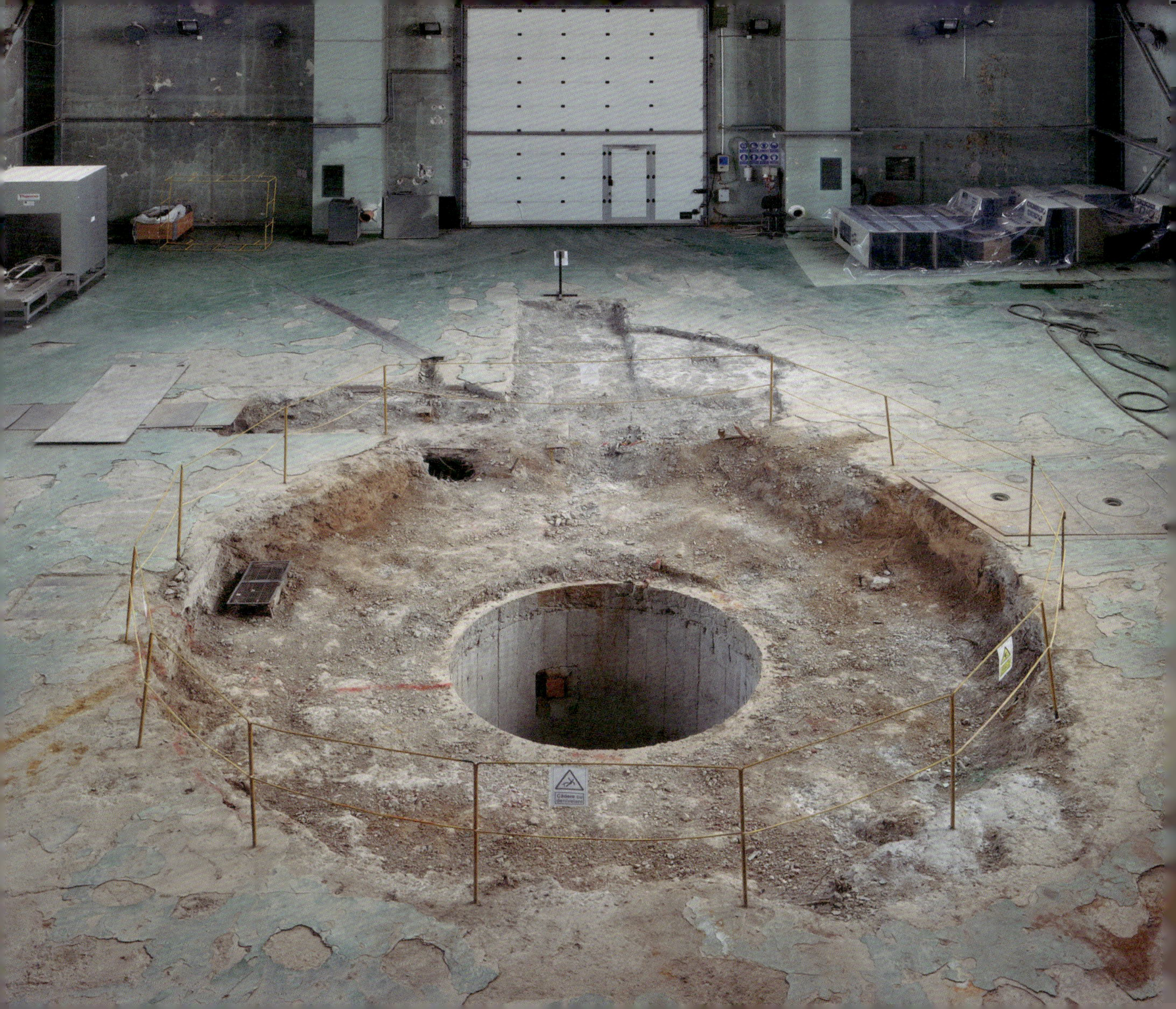
Căderea cu
denivelare

INTERDEPARTMENTAL TRAINING AND TECHNOLOGY CENTRE FOR HIGH-VOLTAGE PULSE ENGINEERING

Kharkiv Polytechnic Institute

Kharkiv, UKRAINE

Between 1919 and 1934, Kharkiv served as the capital of Soviet Ukraine. With this status came ambitious and radical urban transformation. The city's population almost quadrupled over a period of 20 years, and it became one of the largest industrial, cultural, scientific and educational centres of the USSR.

In 1920, Vladimir Lenin (1870–1924), first head of the Soviet state, famously declared that 'Communism is Soviet power plus the electrification of the whole country,' thus asserting the link between the new political authority of the Soviets and the modern industrial progress of electricity. In 1928, the Soviet government under Joseph Stalin (1878–1953) launched its first five-year plan, a massive, ruthlessly accelerated industrialisation project, initiating the construction of expansive networks for the transmission of electric power. However, this futuristic policy was threatened by lightning – a serious problem, with power grids vulnerable to strikes that damaged equipment, causing malfunctions and triggering outages.

In 1930, Professor Pavel Kopnyaev (1867–1932) founded the Electrotechnical Institute, designed in the Constructivist style by renowned Kharkiv architect, Oleksiy Beketov (1862–1941). The new scientific departments were tasked with studying the causes of lightning accidents and developing means of protecting the country's first unified energy system, named 'Donbasenergo', from this natural phenomenon. The research required the creation of specialised scientific equipment and was led by prominent young scientist Saul Fertik (1903–1972). He developed a unique 'lightning machine', a generator combining high impulse voltages with large impulse currents. When completed in 1933, it was the world's largest mobile pulse generator, enabling the study of overvoltages in electrical networks, and testing Donbasenergo's power equipment for its capacity to resist lightning strikes. Author of several hundred scientific publications and creator of over a hundred inventions, Fertik is known today as the 'conqueror of lightning'.

The high-voltage laboratory is equipped with cascade transformers that can produce up to 1 million volts (MV), and a pulse generator of 2.4 MV. It was designed by Kopnyaev to be used as both a scientific and an educational facility. Its primary research focuses on the physics and engineering of high-voltage systems, electrical insulation and lightning protection, with the aim of enhancing the reliability, safety and efficiency of power systems and installations. Students learn how electric fields behave under extreme conditions and how to ensure insulation integrity and equipment reliability under harsh conditions.

The Department of Electric Power Transmission and the Department of Engineering Electrophysics continually train personnel to a high level of expertise to work in Ukraine's electric power industry, the networks and critical infrastructures of which have been specifically targeted and heavily damaged by Russian forces since the large-scale invasion of 2022.

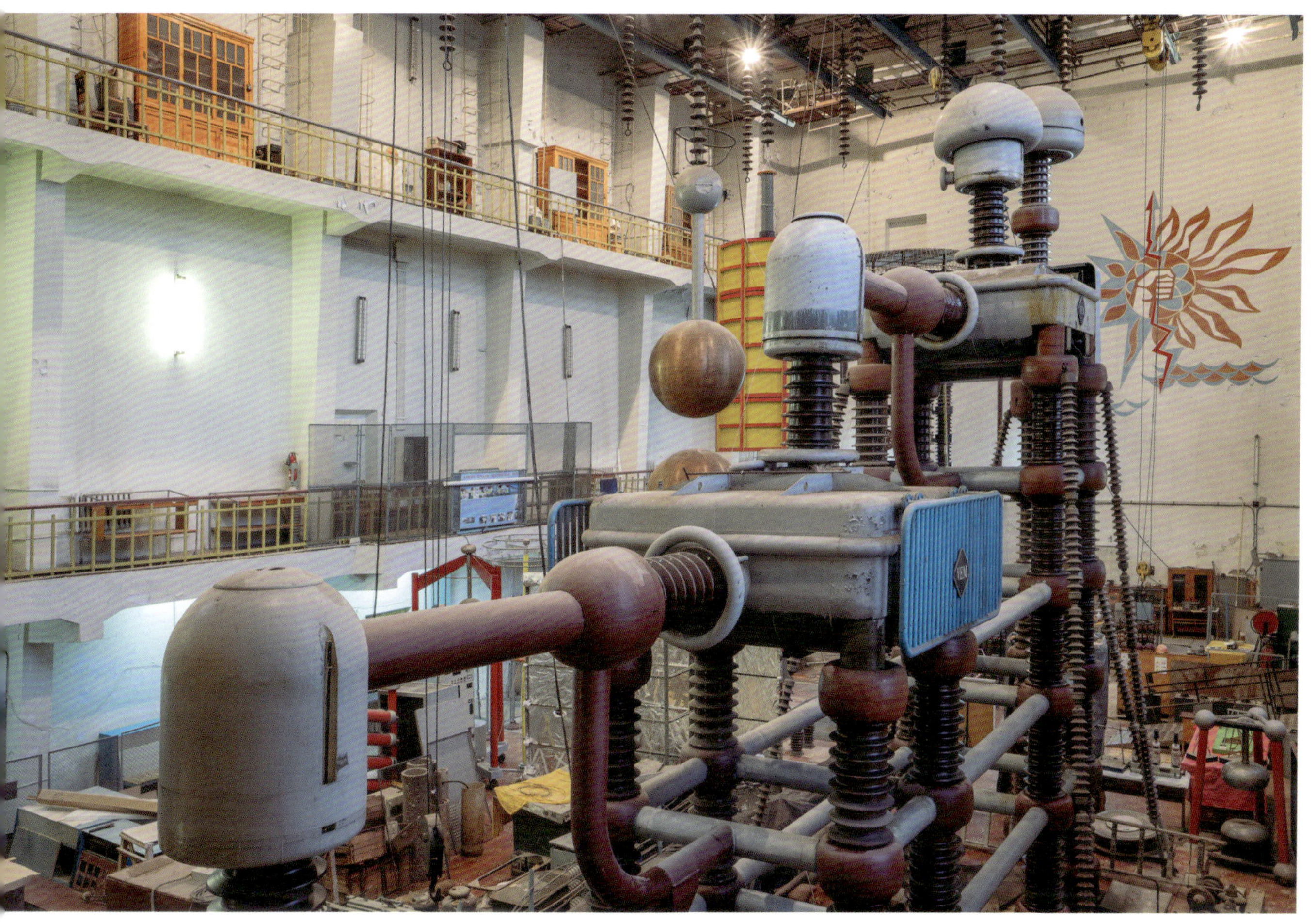

The high-voltage hall has remained almost unchanged for a century. A Soviet-era mural depicts a hand grasping a lightning bolt.

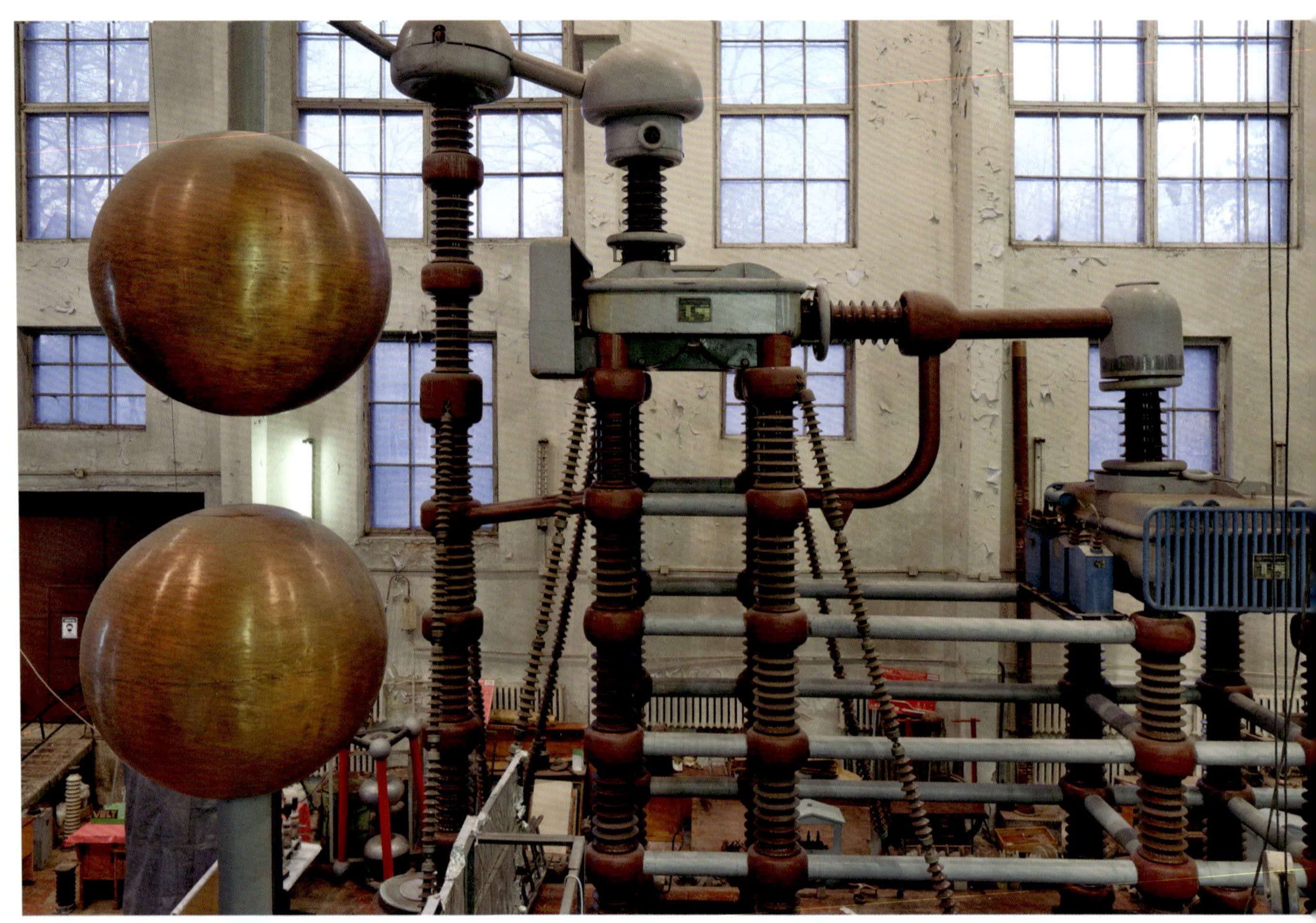

Sphere gaps are used to measure high voltages and the output of transformer cascades up to 1 million volts. They determine the peak voltage at which an electrical sparkover (a spark jumping across the known gap between the spheres) occurs. This is a reliable method for calibrating other measuring devices.

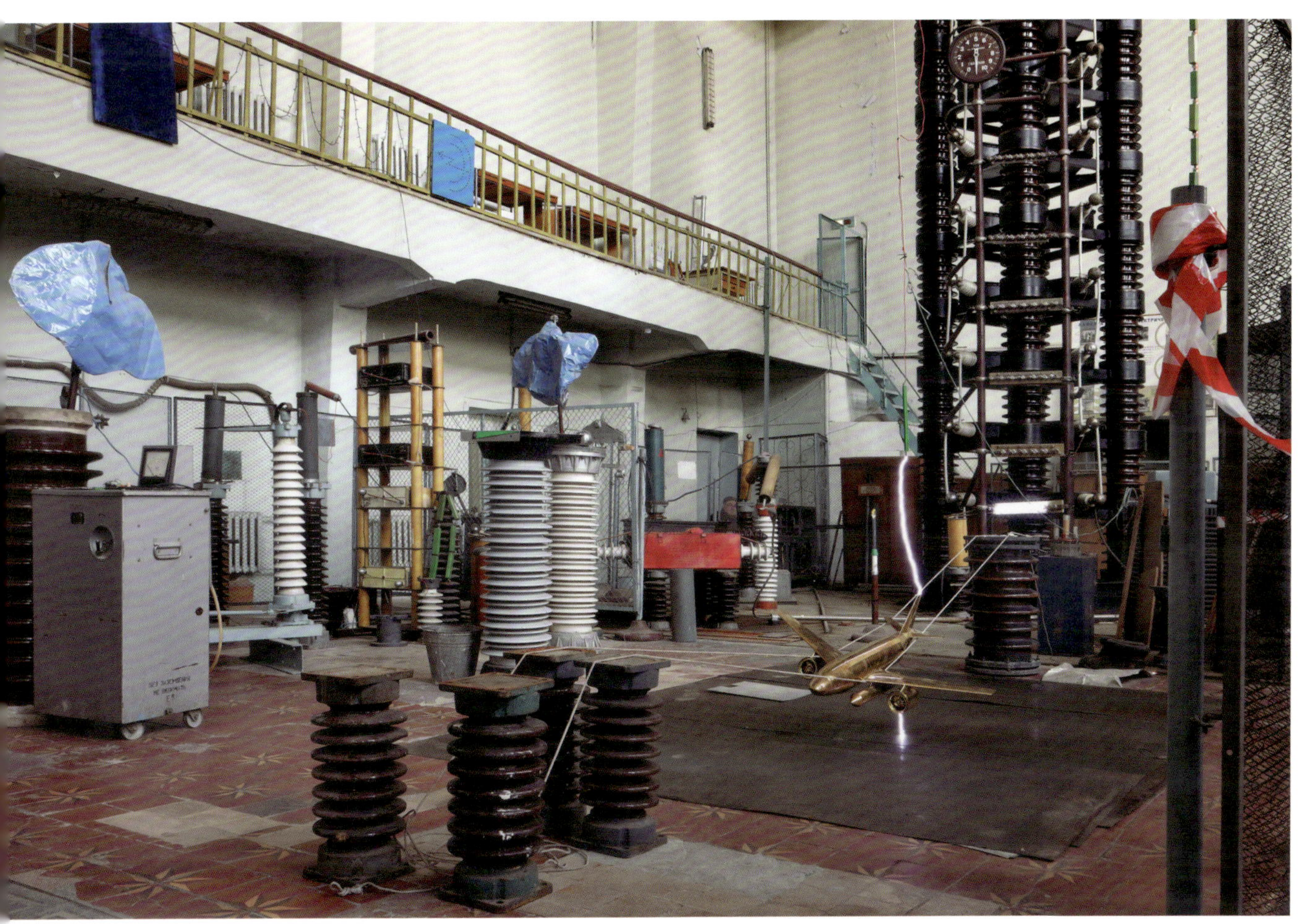

An experiment in the high-voltage hall uses a model aircraft to determine the effects of lightning strike.

'LIGHTNING' RESEARCH AND DESIGN INSTITUTE

Kharkiv Polytechnic Institute

Kharkiv, UKRAINE

In 1966, Yakov Zeldovich (1914–1987) and Yulii Khariton (1904–1996), both leading scientists in the Soviet nuclear weapons programme, approached fellow scientist Saul Fertik (1903–1972) who specialised in the electrophysics and engineering of high voltages. They proposed a significant technical challenge, asking Fertik to design and construct a large-scale simulator capable of replicating the electromagnetic pulse of a nuclear explosion – a burst of energy with the power to disable electronic circuits hundreds of kilometres away. This would allow for realistic testing without violating the 1963 Limited Test Ban Treaty, which prohibited above-ground nuclear explosions. Ultimately, Fertik developed a unique set of high-voltage pulse facilities across a 27-hectare site in a pine forest. This location became the state centre for the testing of radio and electrical apparatus, assessing the equipment's resistance to the shock effects of extreme electromagnetic factors and lightning-like conditions.

Throughout the 1970s and 1980s, the centre became embedded within the military-industrial complex, with over 3,500 individual items being tested. These ranged from electronic equipment for ground forces and the navy, to the warhead of the SS-18 Satan intercontinental missile and parts used in rocket and space technology equipment – such as sections of the Soyuz and Progress launch vehicles, the Energia and Proton launchers and the Buran reusable spaceplane (the Soviet version of the US Space Shuttle). Elements from practically all the Soviet Union's rocketry, space systems and modules were tested at the site, although details remain classified.

This period also saw the development of mobile testing units that could be deployed to assess large structures on site, such as silo launchers, missiles, aeroplanes, ships, submarines, radar stations and underground command posts. From 1970 to 1990, more than 75 testing centres in the USSR were equipped with similar high-voltage evaluation installations, including those in the closed cities of Arzamas-16, Semipalatinsk, Chelyabinsk-70, Tomsk-4 and others. Until the 1990s, the institute was known only to a narrow circle of specialists due to the specific nature of its activities.

After the collapse of the Soviet Union in 1991, orders for the testing of military systems dried up completely. Staff numbers decreased and, as the facility struggled to pay its utility bills, its equipment was mothballed. The experimental base was kept in a state of preservation for around 10 years, while the institute reoriented its activities towards civilian research. Eventually, it became one of the few centres in Ukraine capable of conducting electromagnetic compatibility certification. It continues to specialise in lightning protection and the testing of aircraft electronics, as well as evaluating nuclear power plant systems. The institute has even partnered with Boeing to help develop lightning-resistant composite materials for modern aircraft. Today, Russia's war against Ukraine is once again forcing the facility into preservation mode.

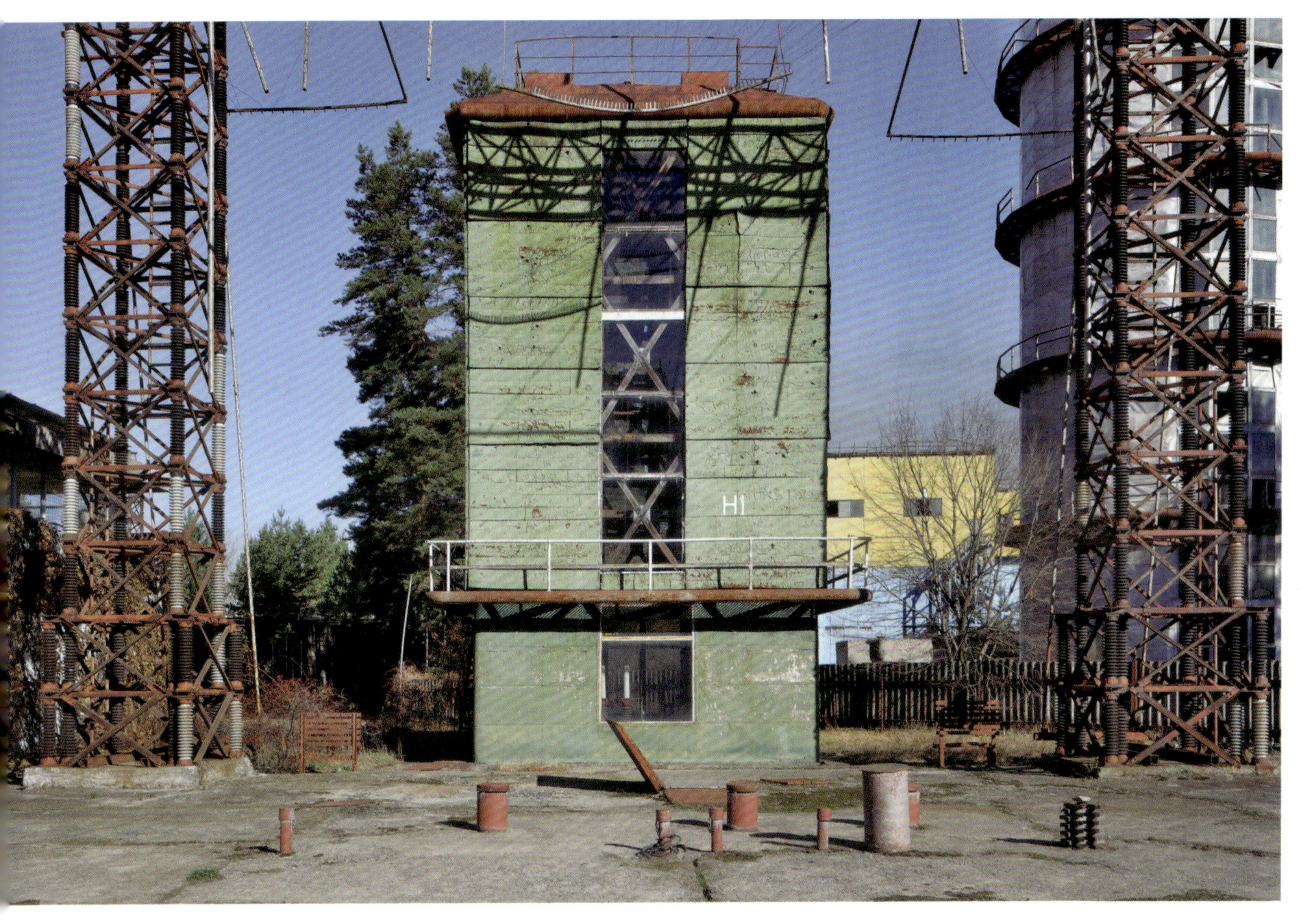

The IEMI-10 high-voltage test facility is designed for testing medium-sized objects.

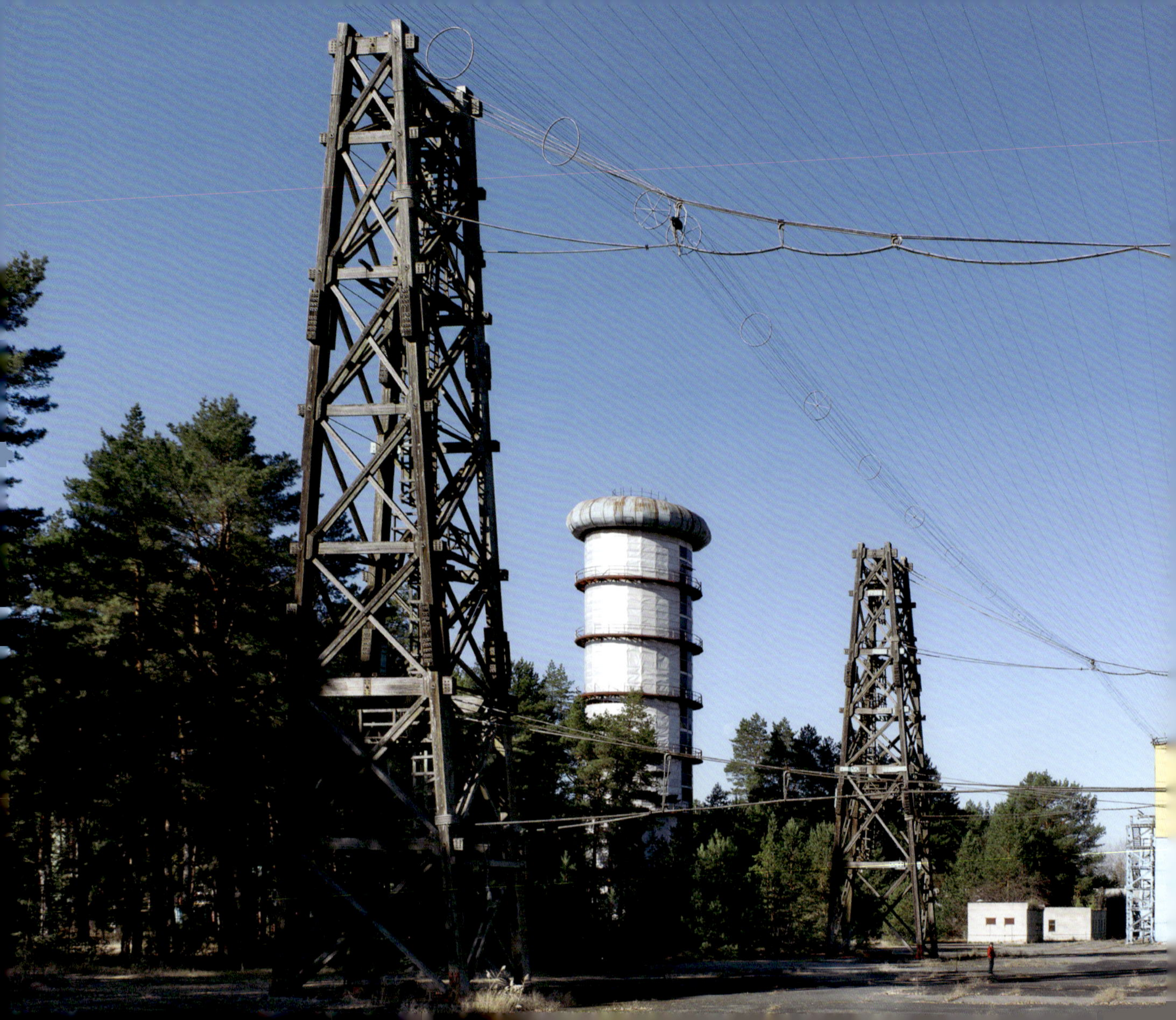

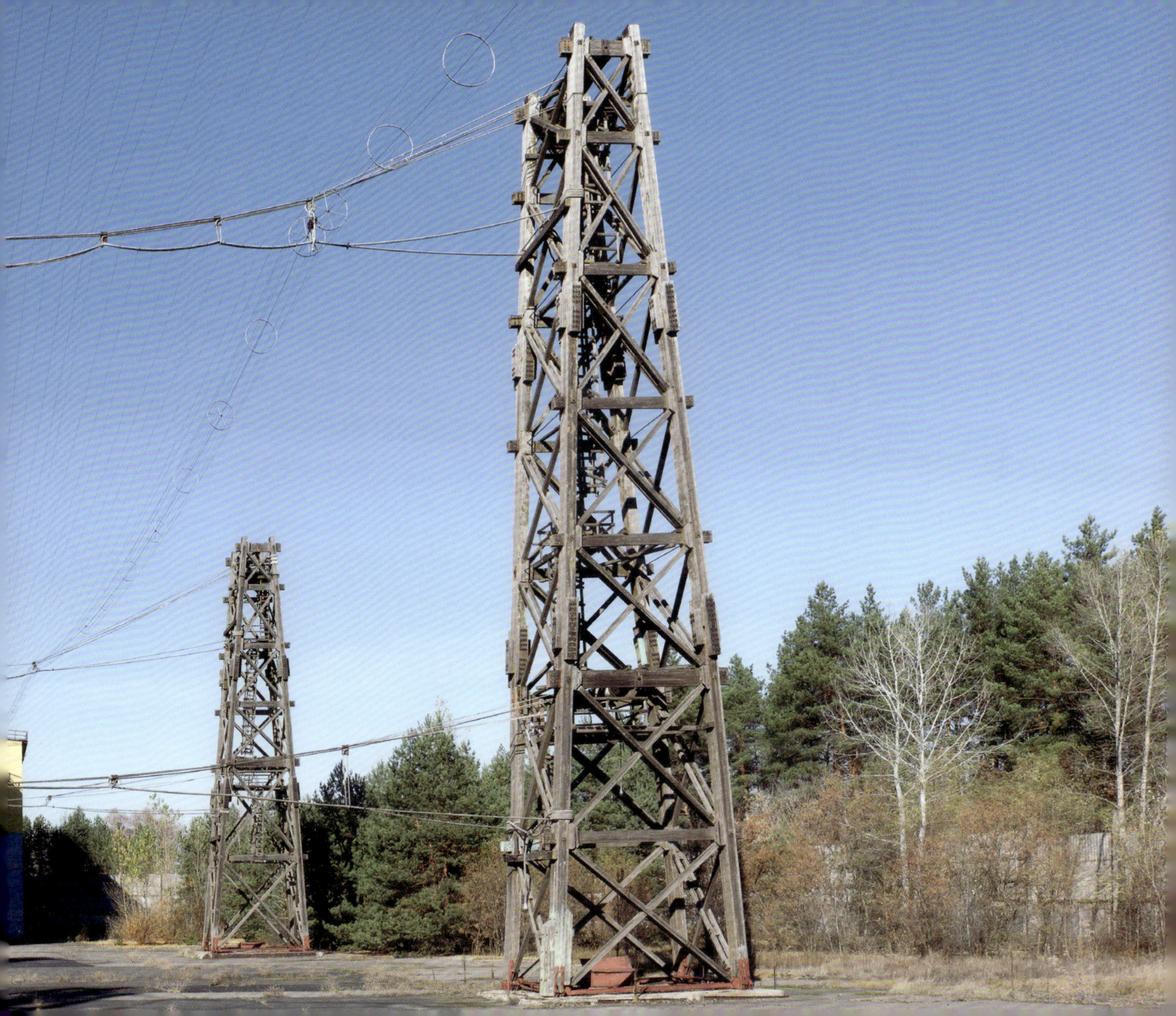

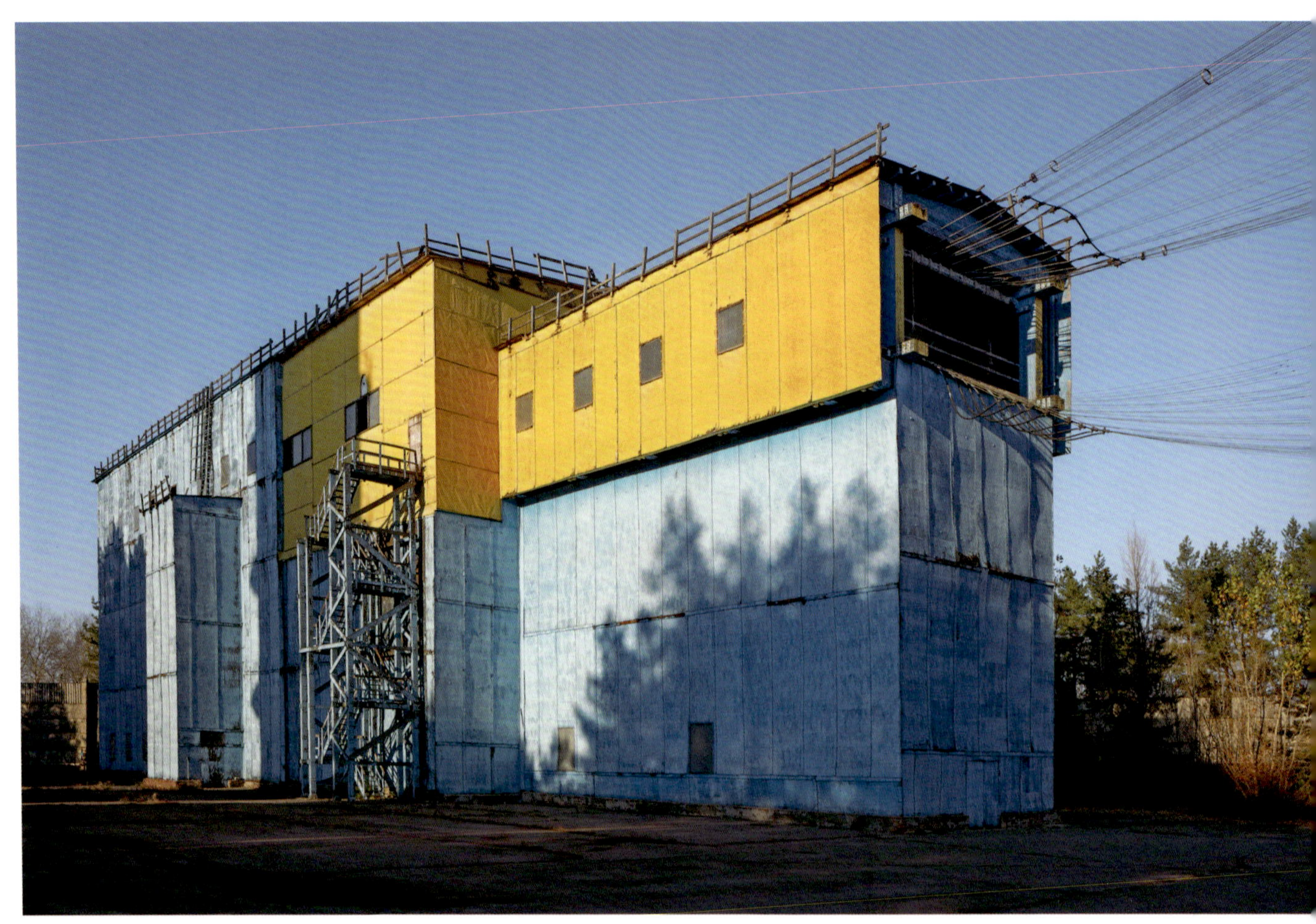

Previous pages and above: the GINT-12-30 ultra-high voltage test installation for experiments on large-scale objects. It comprises a GIN-14 (14 million volt) impulse generator, a pulse generator building, and a 254-metre transmission line that propagates electromagnetic waves to the terminator. The conductors consist of parallel wires supported by six laminated wood towers.

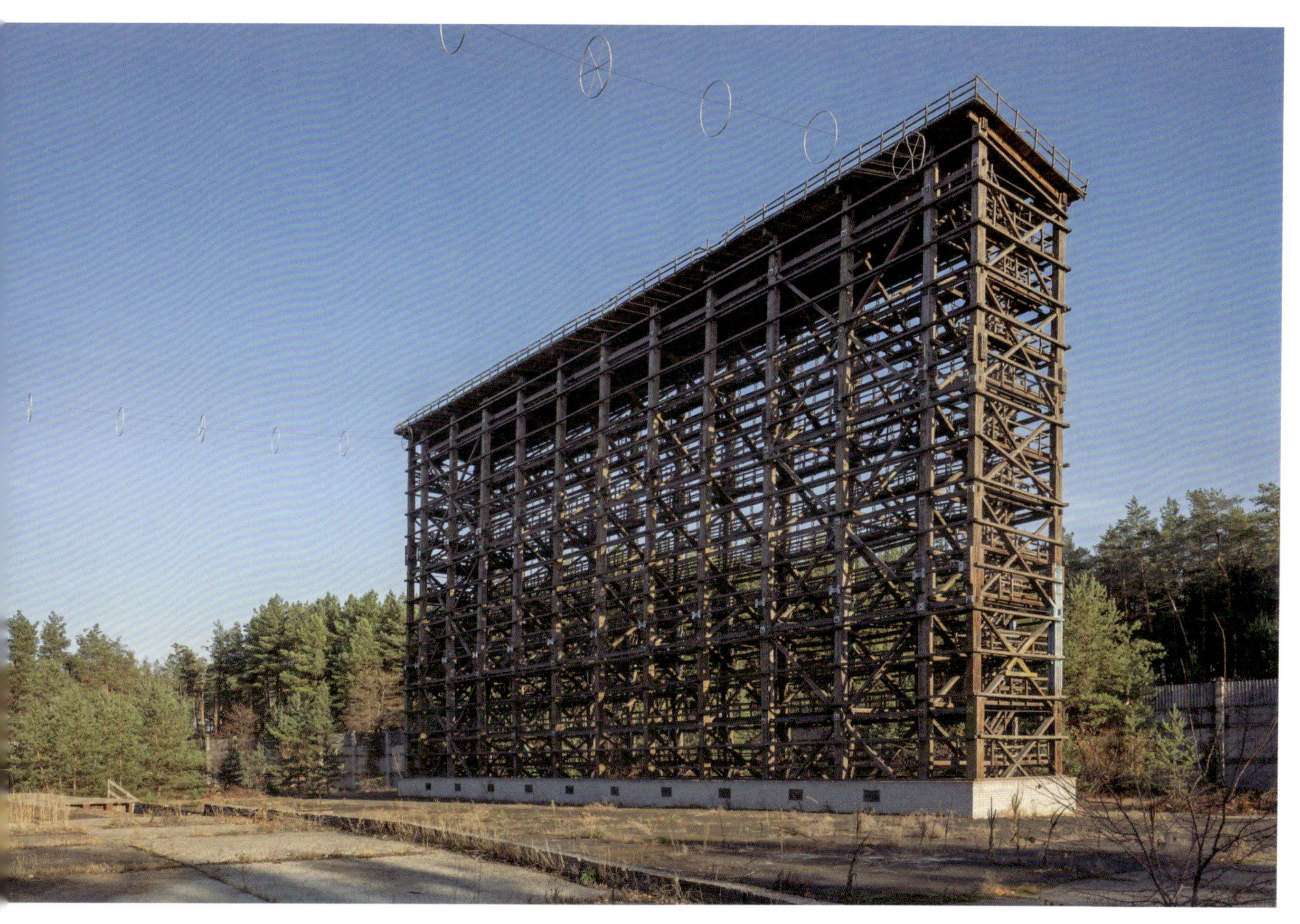

The large terminator is constructed from laminated wood and is used to safely absorb the massive amount of energy discharged during high-power impulses. The test object is placed on the wooden platform at the bottom-left.

INSTITUTE OF IONOSPHERE

Kharkiv Polytechnic Institute

Kharkiv, UKRAINE

In 1957, the Soviet Union launched Sputnik, the world's first artificial satellite. This marked the beginning of both the Space Age and the Space Race between the USSR and the United States. Sputnik was used to study the ionosphere, a dynamic layer of Earth's upper atmosphere which constantly changes, reacting to solar activity. This action reflects and modifies the radio waves used for communication, navigation and missile detection – making the accurate interpretation of its properties crucial for military applications.

The most accurate ground-based method for studying the ionosphere is the incoherent scatter technique, developed in the 1960s by American physicist William E. Gordon (1918–2010). Incoherent scatter radars (ISR) measure full altitude profiles of ionospheric parameters such as electron density and temperature. Requiring complex construction, high power consumption and specialist operation and maintenance, there are very few currently in use.

Inspired by these pioneering studies, Vitaly Taran (1929–2015) began developing the first Soviet ISR in Kharkiv in 1966. Initial experimental results were obtained in 1972 with a fixed 30-metre parabolic antenna that utilised repurposed equipment from the 'Dnepr' early-warning missile radar system. Subsequently, the radar was improved with a 100-metre dual-reflector Cassegrain antenna (named after Laurent Cassegrain (1629–1693)), the world's largest at that time.

Regular ionospheric observations commenced in 1975. Since the 1980s, the radar has been used to study disturbances in the ionosphere caused by powerful explosions and spacecraft launches, the effects of which can be observed from distances of a few thousand kilometres. Inhabitants of neighbouring villages, struggling to understand the station and its huge antenna pointing skywards, invented explanations such as it being a geophysical climate weapon, with the power to control the weather.

In 1991, following the dissolution of the Soviet Union and Ukrainian independence, the institute experienced difficulties, but ionospheric studies continued. At this time, cooperations began with the Massachusetts Institute of Technology, and gradually, the institute's capabilities have extended significantly. Today it participates in numerous international research programmes and is known worldwide as one of the most prominent scientific centres researching near-Earth space.

The radar was last used on 24 December 2021, prior to Russia's full-scale invasion of Ukraine. Its operation will be resumed when security requirements can be met. On 3 February 2022, SpaceX launched 49 Starlink satellites, 38 of these were caught in a geomagnetic storm and consequently burnt up in Earth's atmosphere, resulting in an estimated loss of 100 million dollars. Despite working under war conditions, scientists from the institute collaborated with an international team to analyse the latest data, discovering that the density of atomic oxygen in the upper atmosphere was up to 30 per cent higher than predicted, which ultimately led to the loss of the satellites, demonstrating the importance of accurate space weather models.

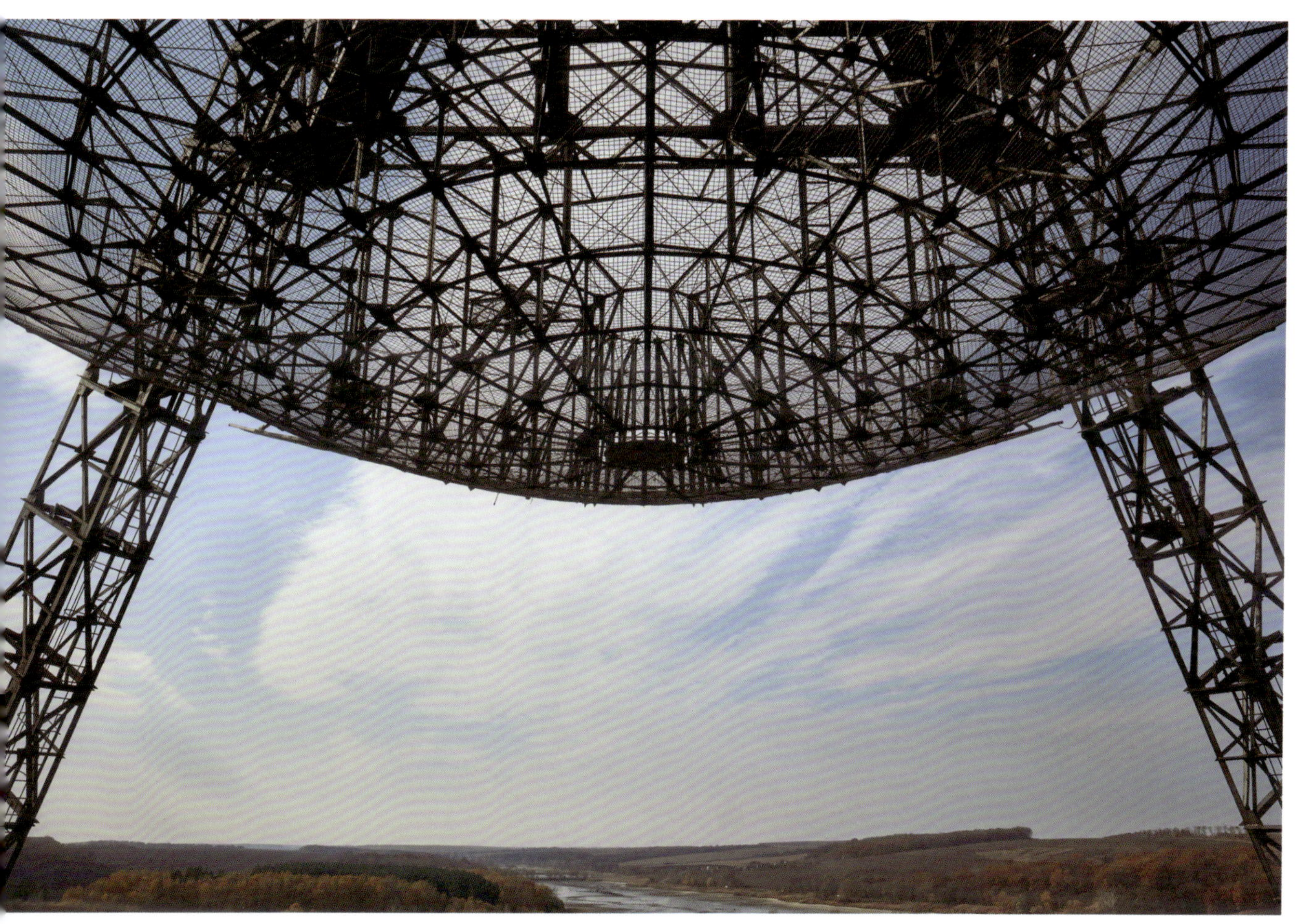

The counter-reflector, supported by a 43-metre tripod, is positioned at the focus of the large primary reflector. It redirects incoming waves collected by the primary reflector towards the radio receiver.

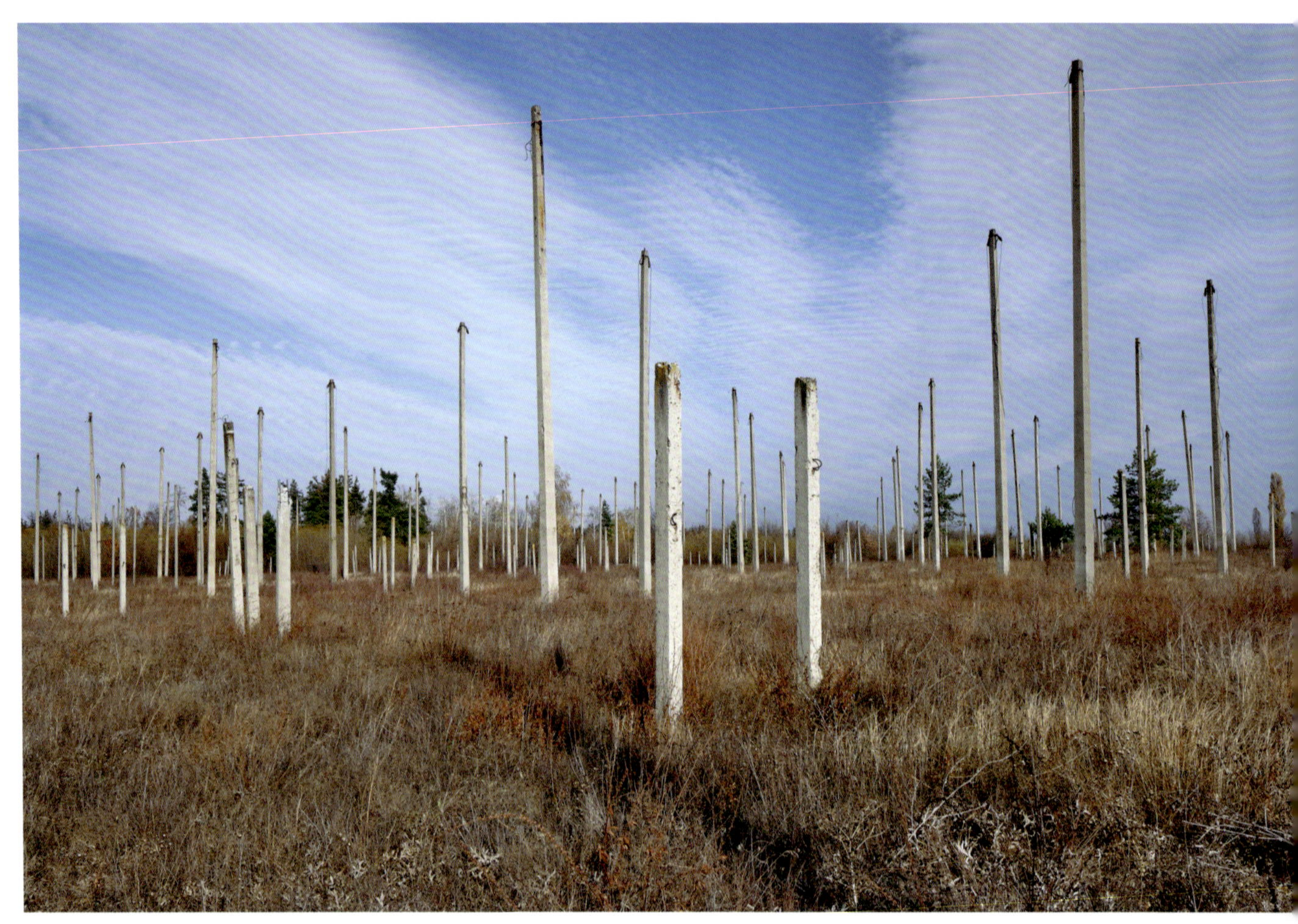

The remains of the Decameter Zenith Radiation Antenna Array. Built in the 1980s and covering an area of 300 x 300 metres, this heating stand with a vertical radiation antenna was stripped of its copper in the 1990s as Ukraine suffered from a severe economic crisis. In the 2010s, the institute considered its reconstruction, but the costs proved too prohibitive.

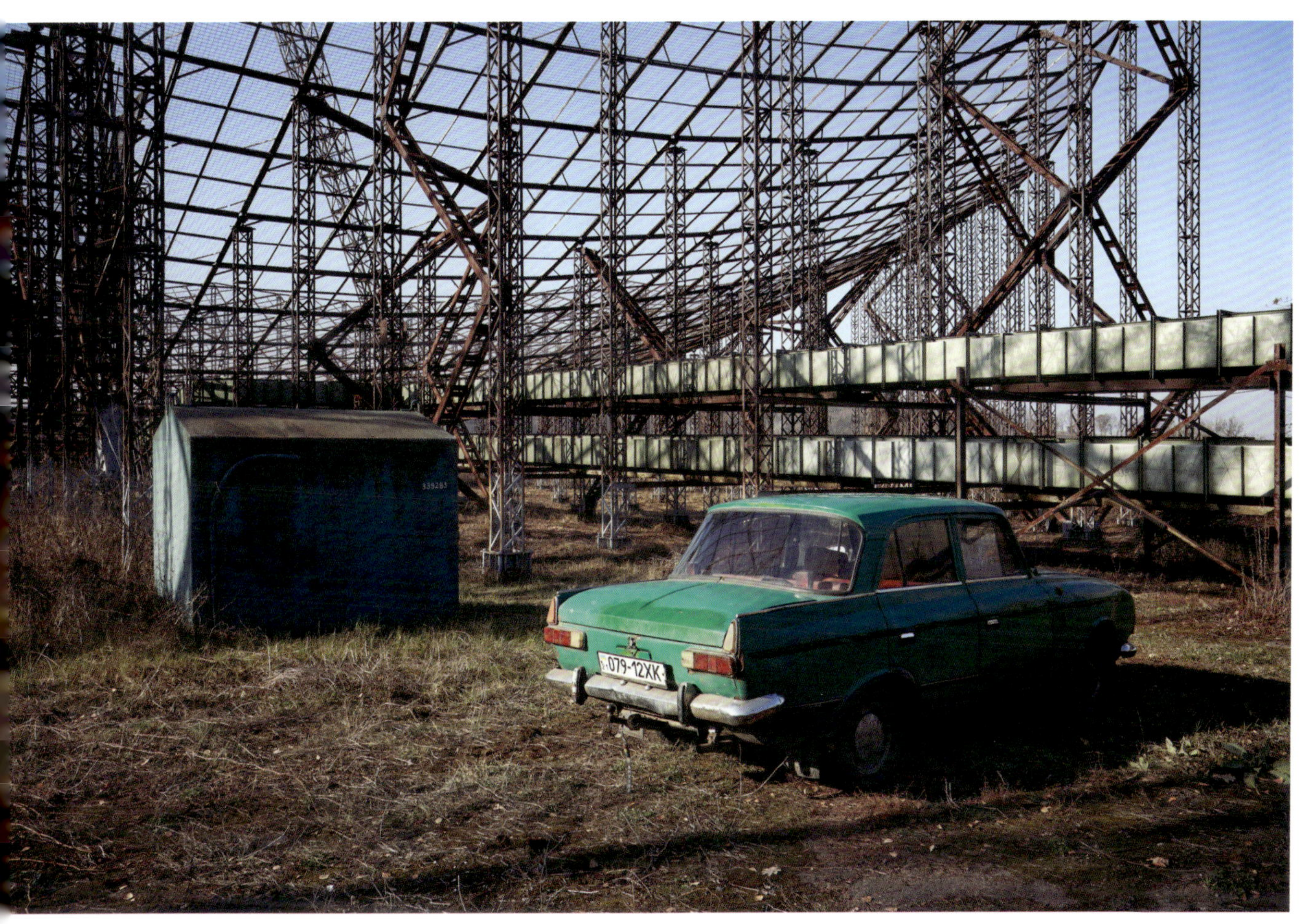

An employee's Moskvich-412 is parked in front of the power and transmission lines, at the foot of the antenna.

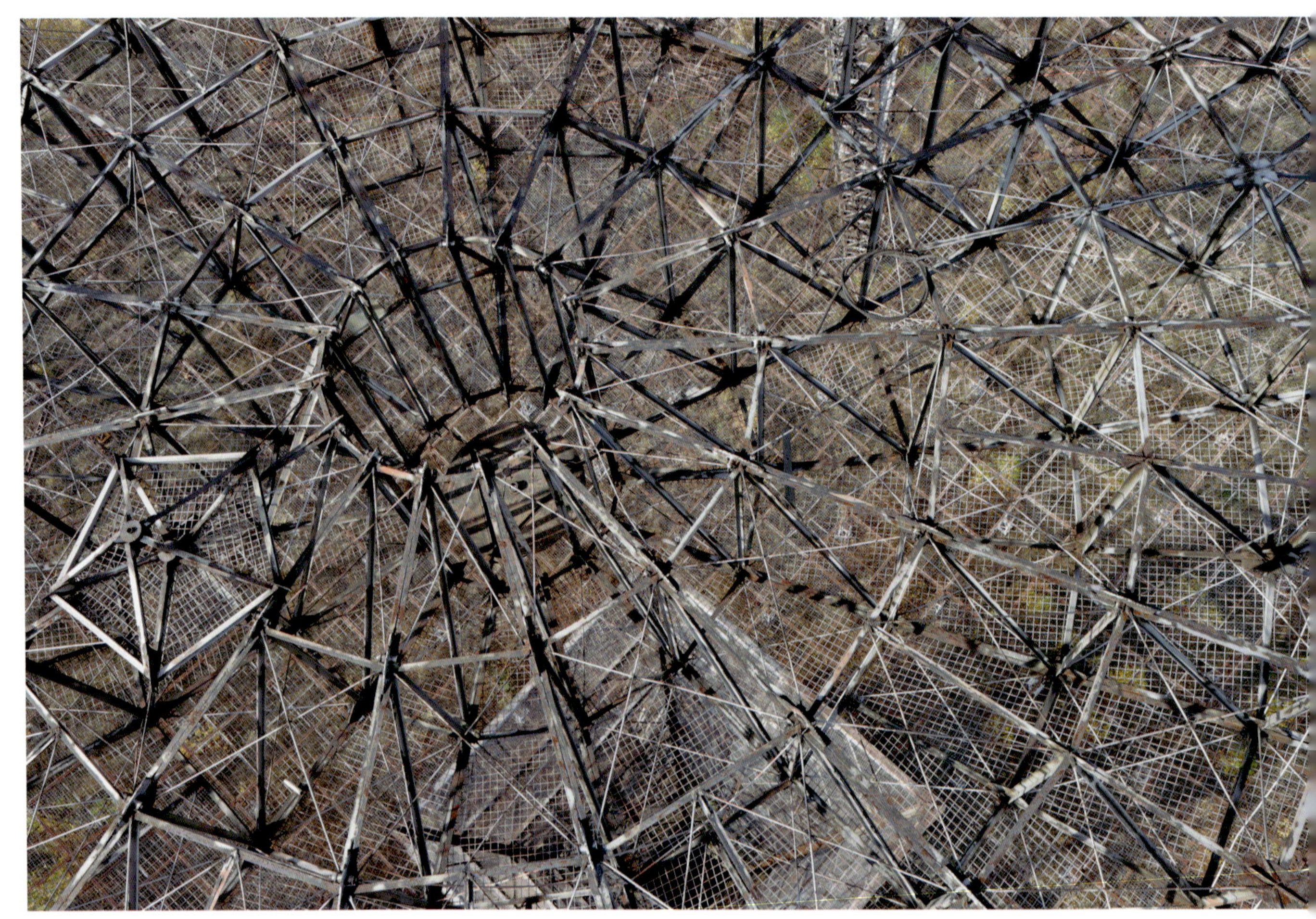

Looking down onto the counter-reflector.

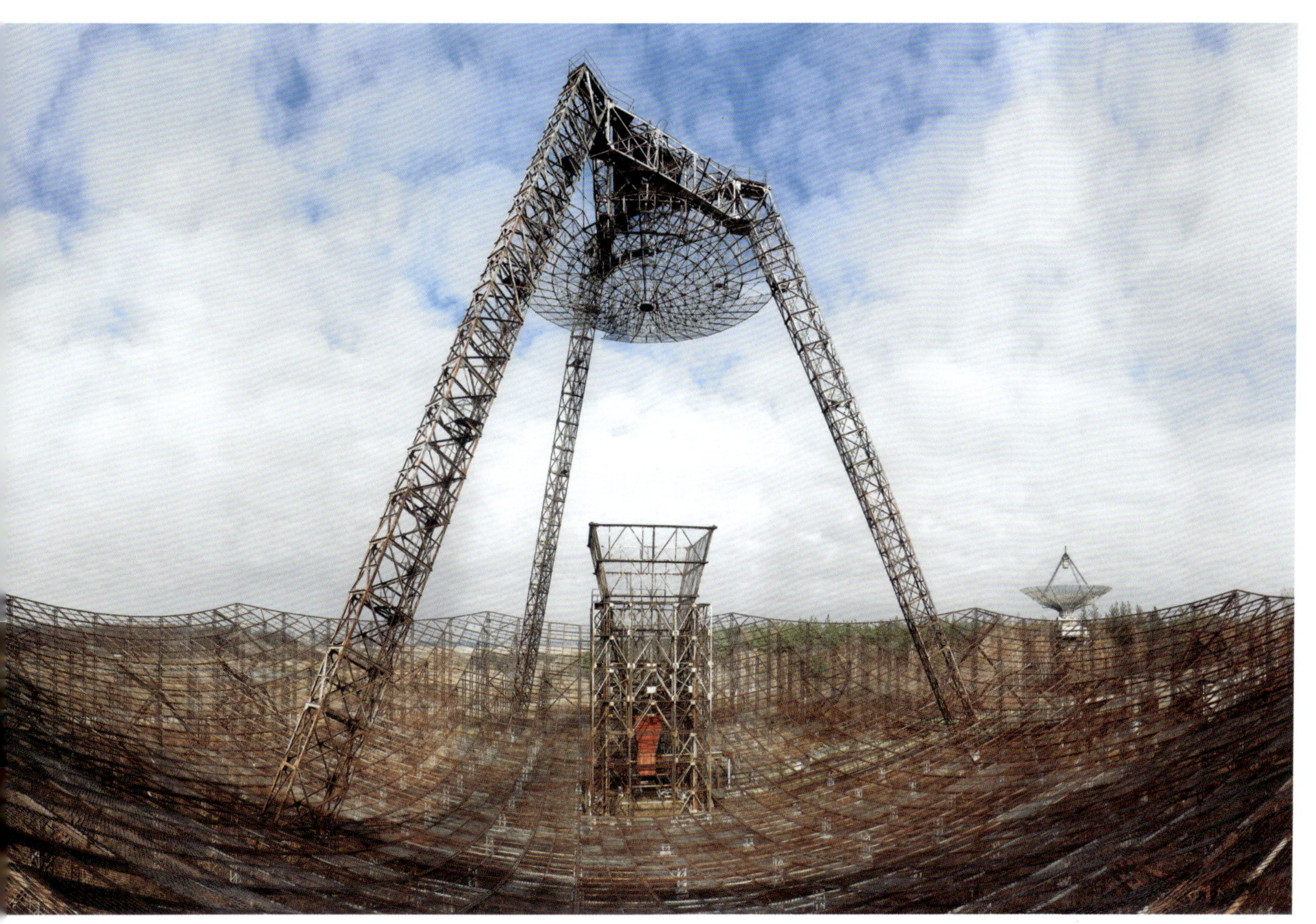

The 100-metre, dual-reflector, parabolic antenna, with its transmitter feed located at the centre of the bottom dish.

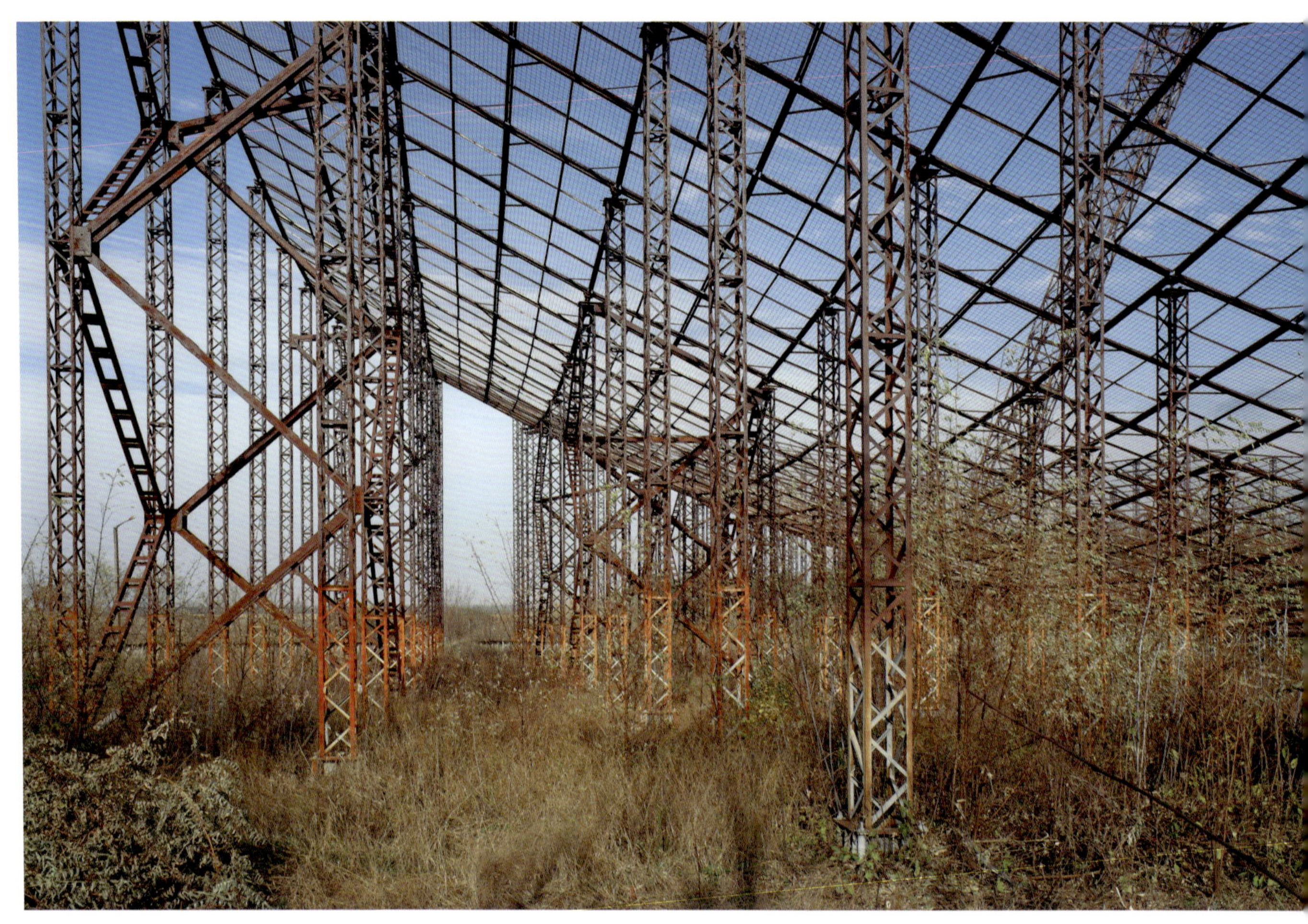

Underneath the antenna structure. The main reflector is a vertically directed, parabolic antenna, 100 metres in diameter, curved in a hyperbolic shape.

Right: Installed in 1989, the PPA-25 antenna, with a diameter of 25 metres, is used to measure parameters of geospace plasma.

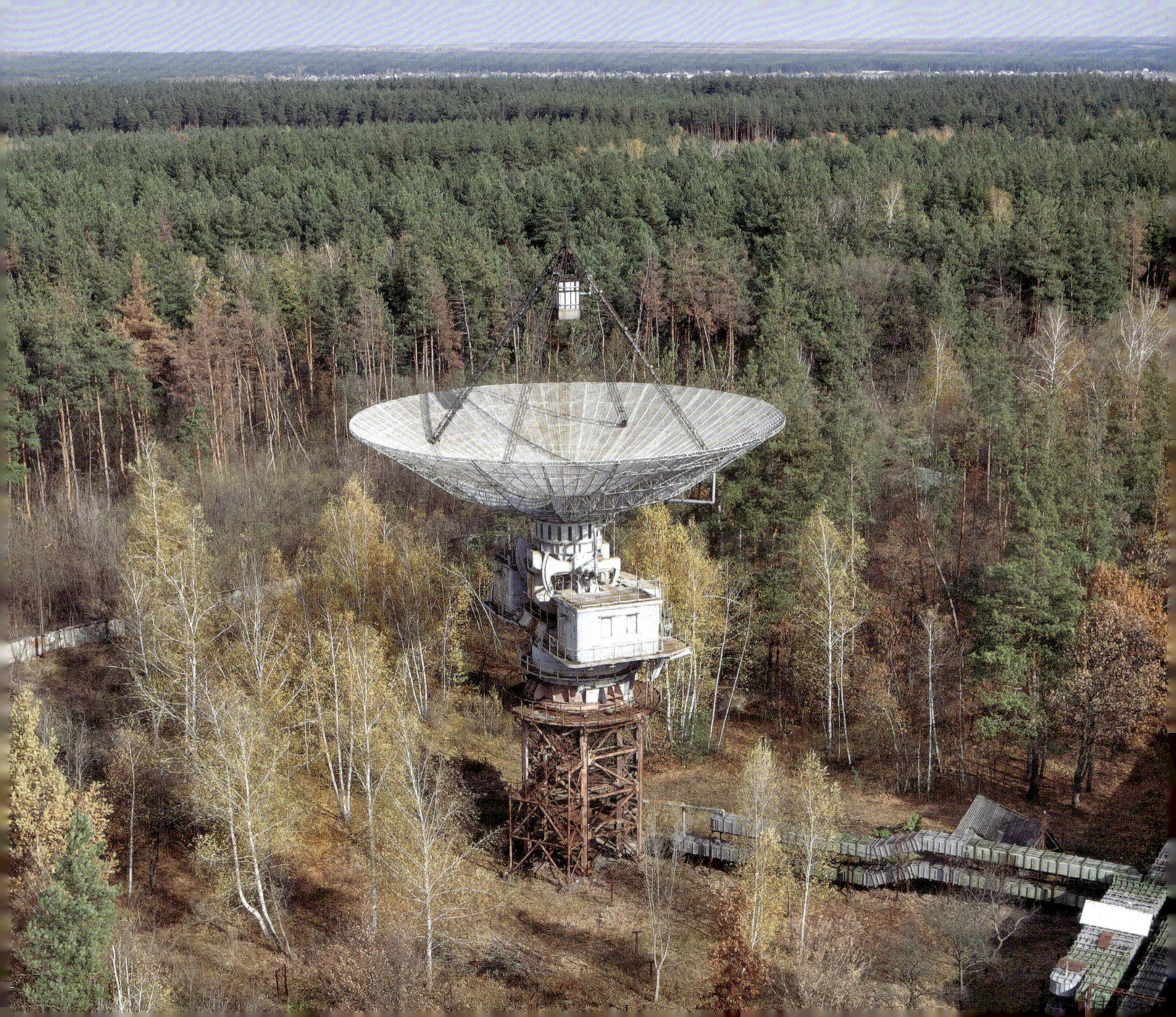

B. VERKIN INSTITUTE FOR LOW TEMPERATURE PHYSICS AND ENGINEERING

National Academy of Sciences of Ukraine

Kharkiv, UKRAINE

The institute was founded in 1960 to continue the work of the cryogenic laboratory established by Lev Shubnikov (1901–1937) at the Ukrainian Physics and Technology Institute (UFTI) in the 1930s.

The scientific direction of the laboratory – that of pioneering investigations into liquid helium – was decided in close cooperation with the physicist Lev Landau (1908–1968), who came to Kharkiv in 1932. The two Levs – 'Lev the Stout' and 'Lev the Slim' as they were known – were not only co-workers but also close friends. However, in 1937, after being falsely accused of anti-state activities, Shubnikov was arrested and executed by firing squad. Over the next two decades, all mention of him and his work was forbidden, and it was not until 1957 that he was posthumously rehabilitated. Boris Verkin (1919–1990), head of the newly formed Institute for Low Temperature Physics and Engineering, brought in scientists who had previously been at UFTI to continue their research, creating a supportive and enthusiastic working environment.

An understanding of low temperature physics is critical to maintaining the stability and functionality of spacecraft and instruments in the extreme operational environment of outer space. This is why Sergei Korolev (1907–1966), the Soviet Union's lead rocket engineer and spacecraft designer, requested that the institute conduct intensive research and testing to assist in the development of the Soviet space programme.

The sensitive nature of these works meant that they were generally carried out in strict secrecy, although in 1971 it was disclosed that the institute had spent five years researching the design and materials used on the chassis of Lunokhod-1, the first lunar rover to land on the Moon in 1970. In addition, it developed the mass spectrometers used on the unmanned probes Venera-9 and Venera-10, both launched in 1975 to analyse the atmosphere of the planet Venus. Also in 1975, Verkin established the journal *Low Temperature Physics*, which is still being published today, with an English language version produced by the American Institute of Physics.

After 1985, Verkin took advantage of the freedom of speech reforms of the Perestroika period to collect documents and testimonies about Shubnikov's life and work, which were published in 1990. Verkin considered his three main achievements to be the founding of the institute, the launching of the journal, and the restoration of Shubnikov's reputation.

Since the 1980s, the institute's Department of Physics of Quantum Fluids and Crystals has produced special, ultra-low temperature refrigerators that allow the observation of quantum effects. From its inception, the institute has made significant contributions to low-temperature applications in the fields of instrumentation, electrical engineering, space technology, medicine, biology and the food industry. The reach of the institute's activities, extending from the depths of the oceans to near outer space, encompasses in this respect Verkin's original ideas and ideals.

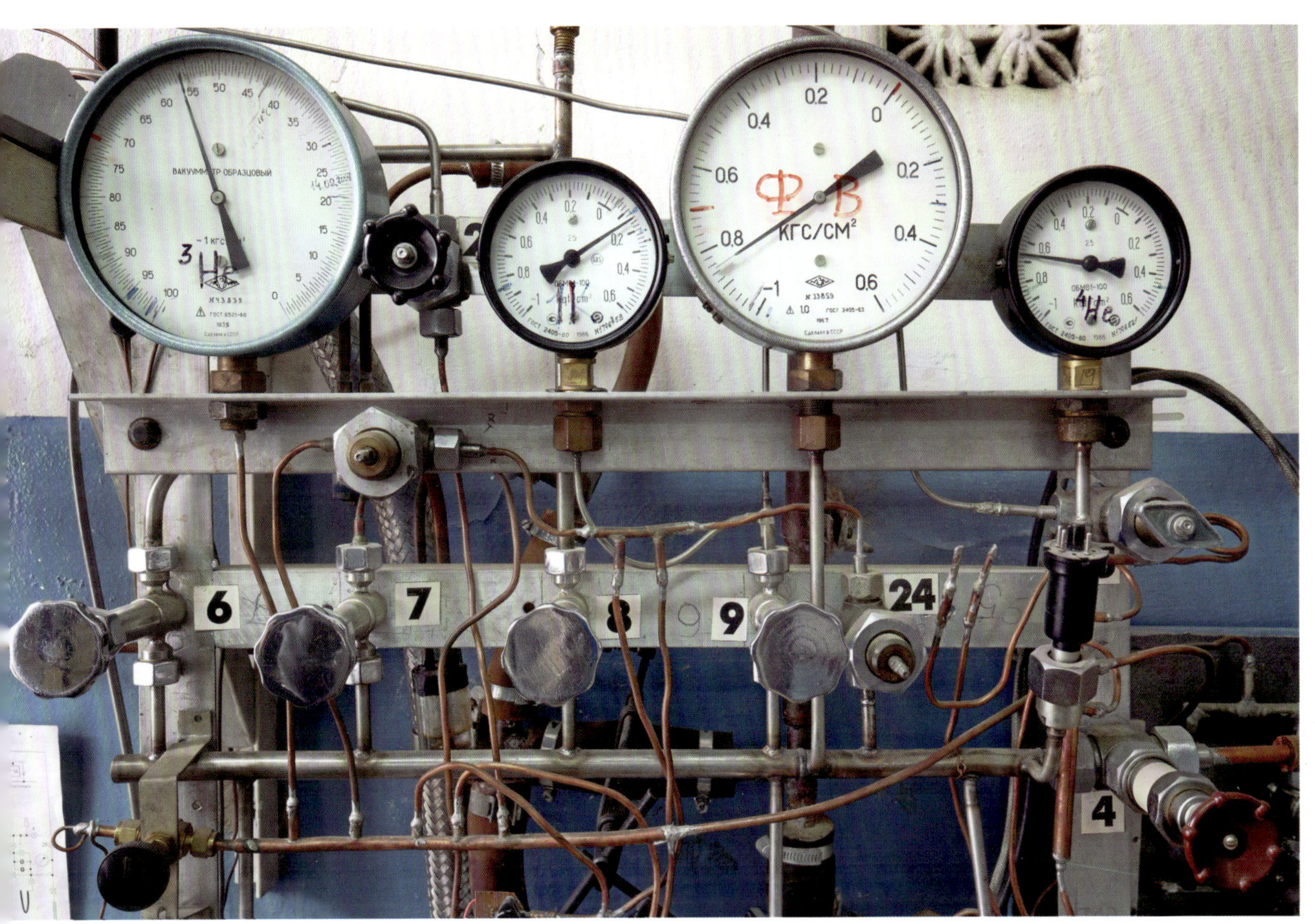

Manometers are used to measure the pressure of helium-3 and helium-4 within a dilution refrigerator. By using these liquefied gases, this specialised cryogenic device is capable of reaching extremely low temperatures, often just thousandths of a degree above absolute zero (−273.15 °C or −459.67 °F), in order to study quantum phenomena.

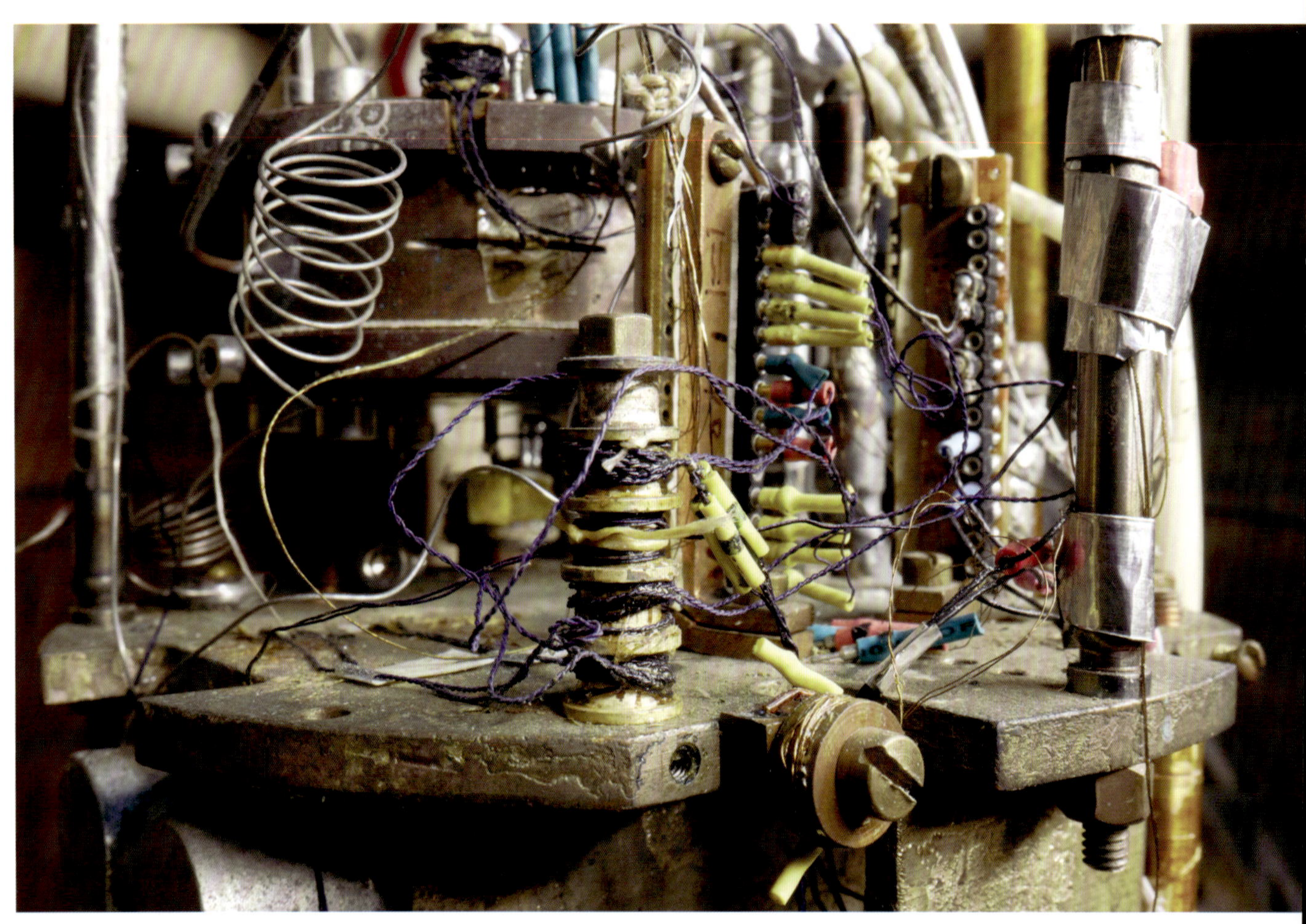

A dilution refrigerator chamber, without its outer vacuum shield. Cooling is achieved through the enthalpy of mixing helium-3 and helium-4 isotopes, rather than relying on traditional refrigerants or compression cycles. The helium mixture passes through various chambers in a closed-loop circulation, enabling continuous operation for days at ultra-low temperatures.

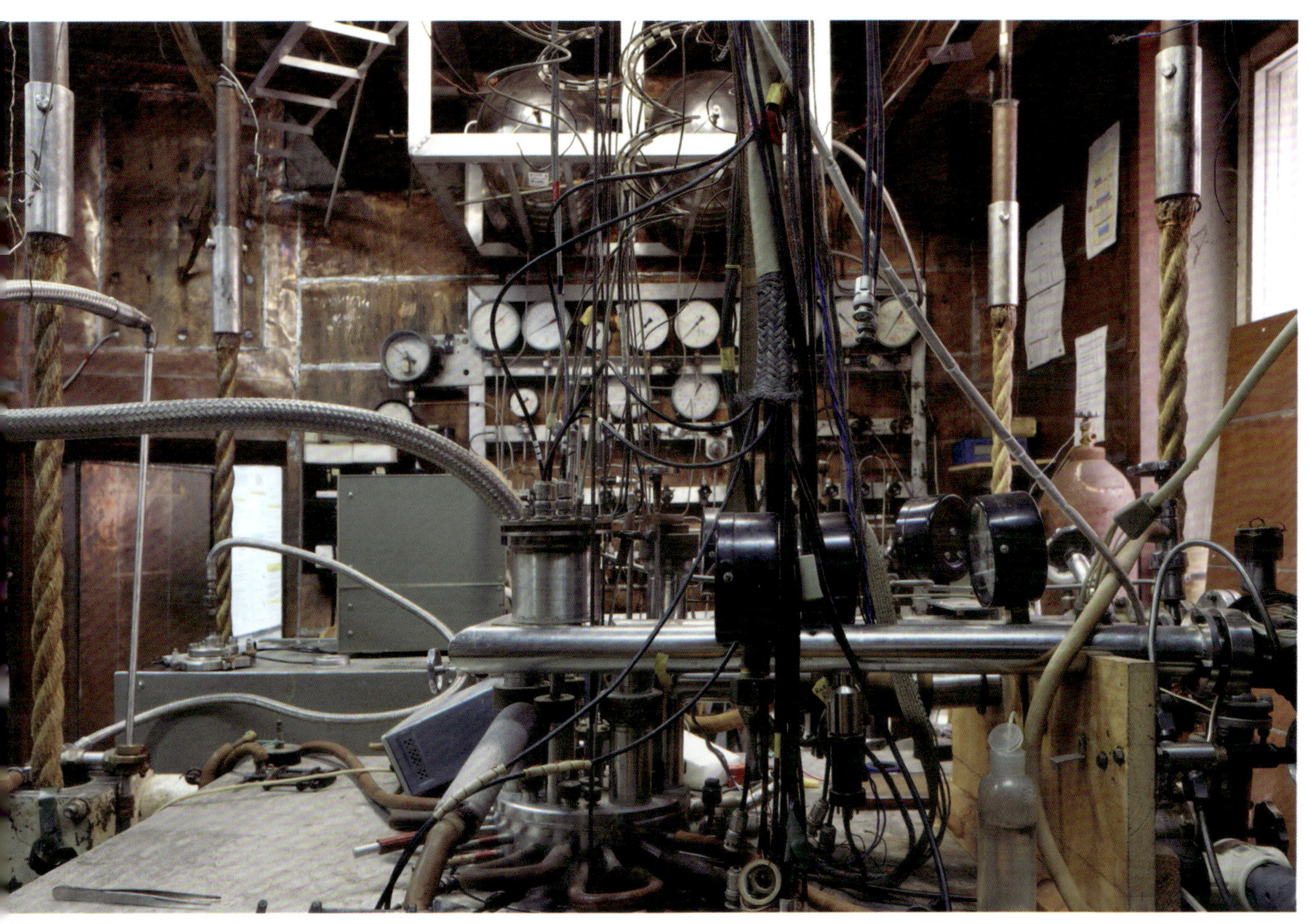

The upper section of the dilution refrigerator with a hybrid helium-3 circulation system. To eliminate vibration this apparatus is housed in a separate small building. The refrigerator is used to study kinetic processes in quantum crystals.

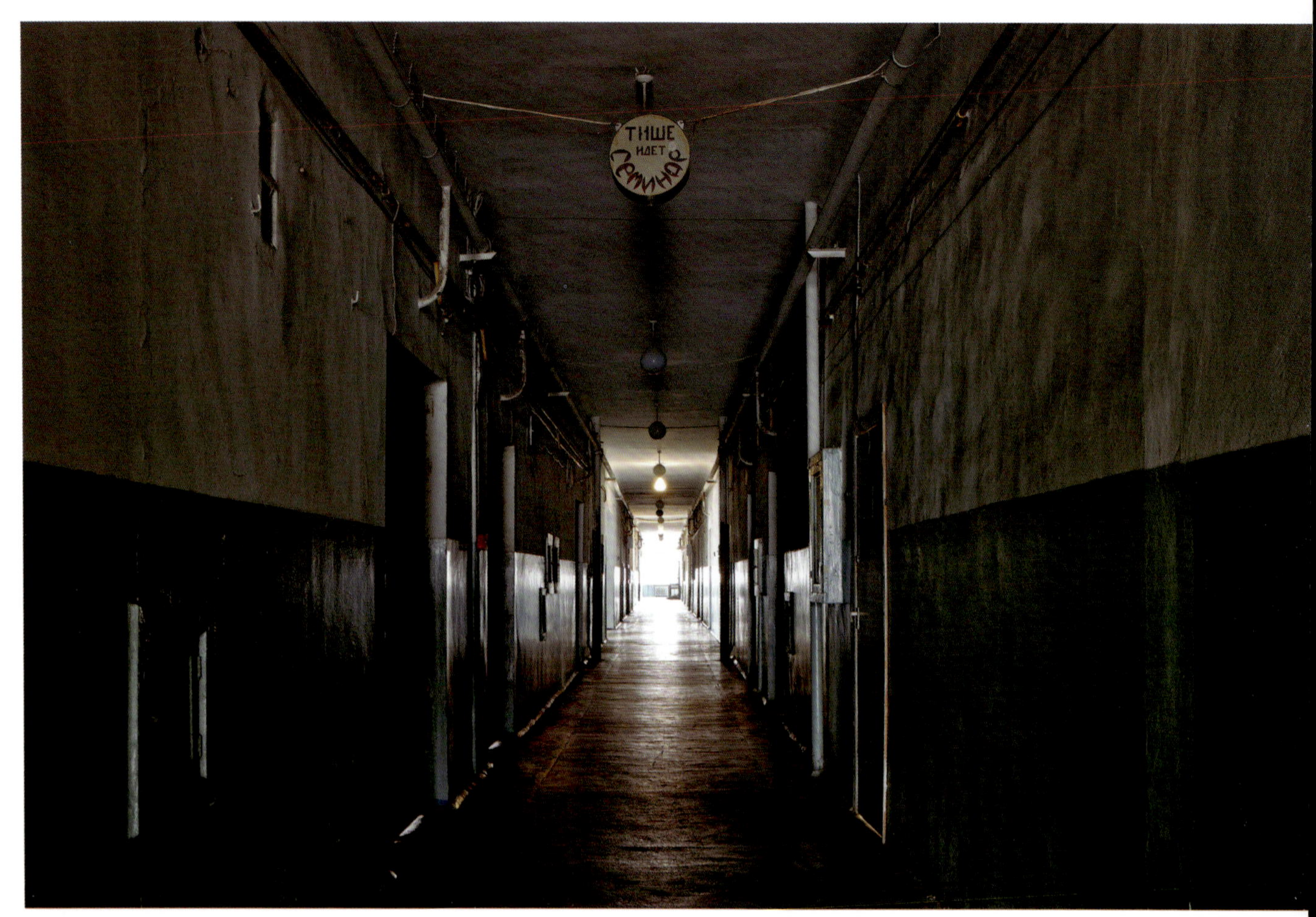

A corridor inside the institute with rooms used for workshops and lectures. The Soviet-era sign reads: 'Quiet, seminar in progress'.

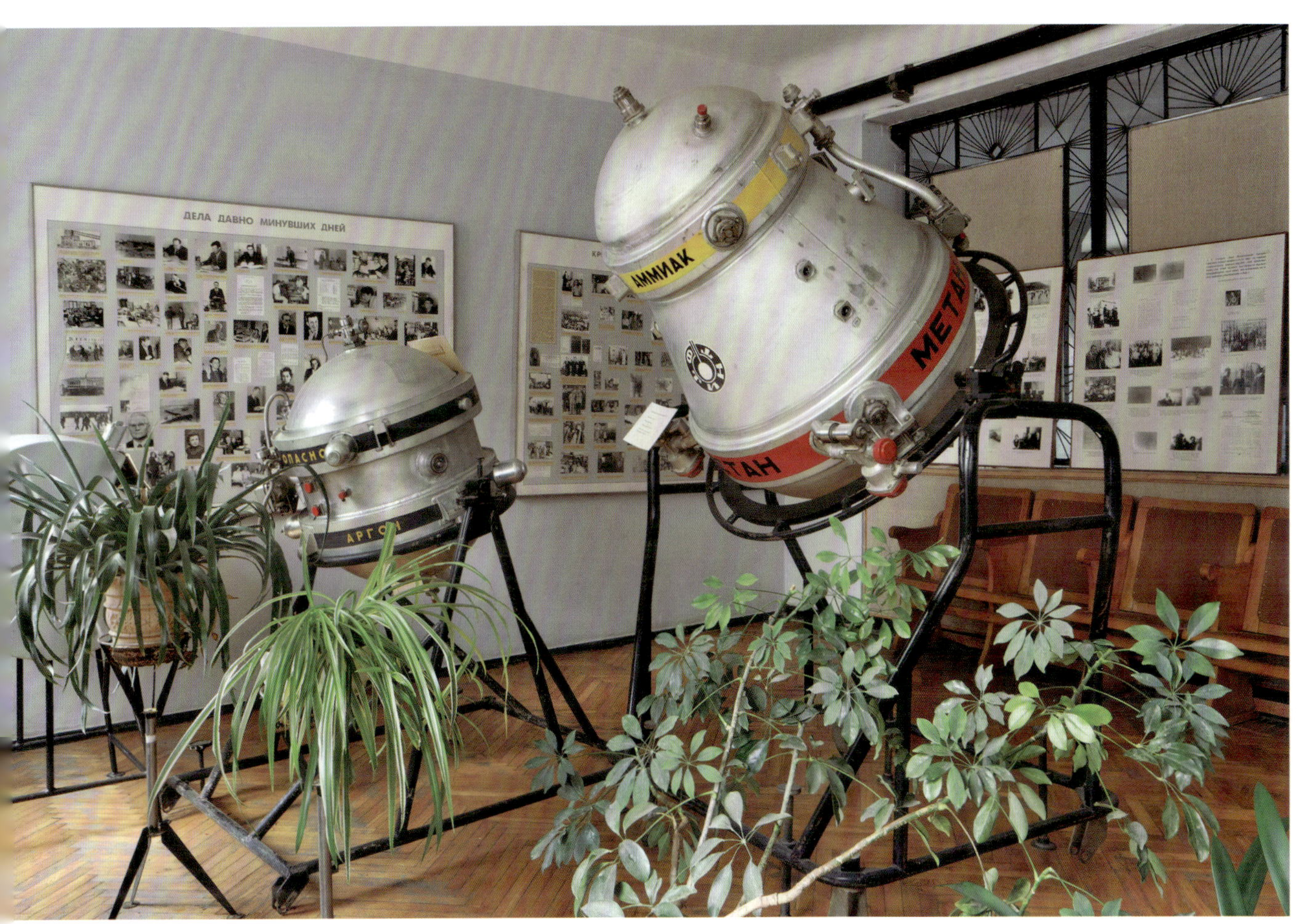

The exhibition hall displays the history of the institute alongside past cryogenic equipment.

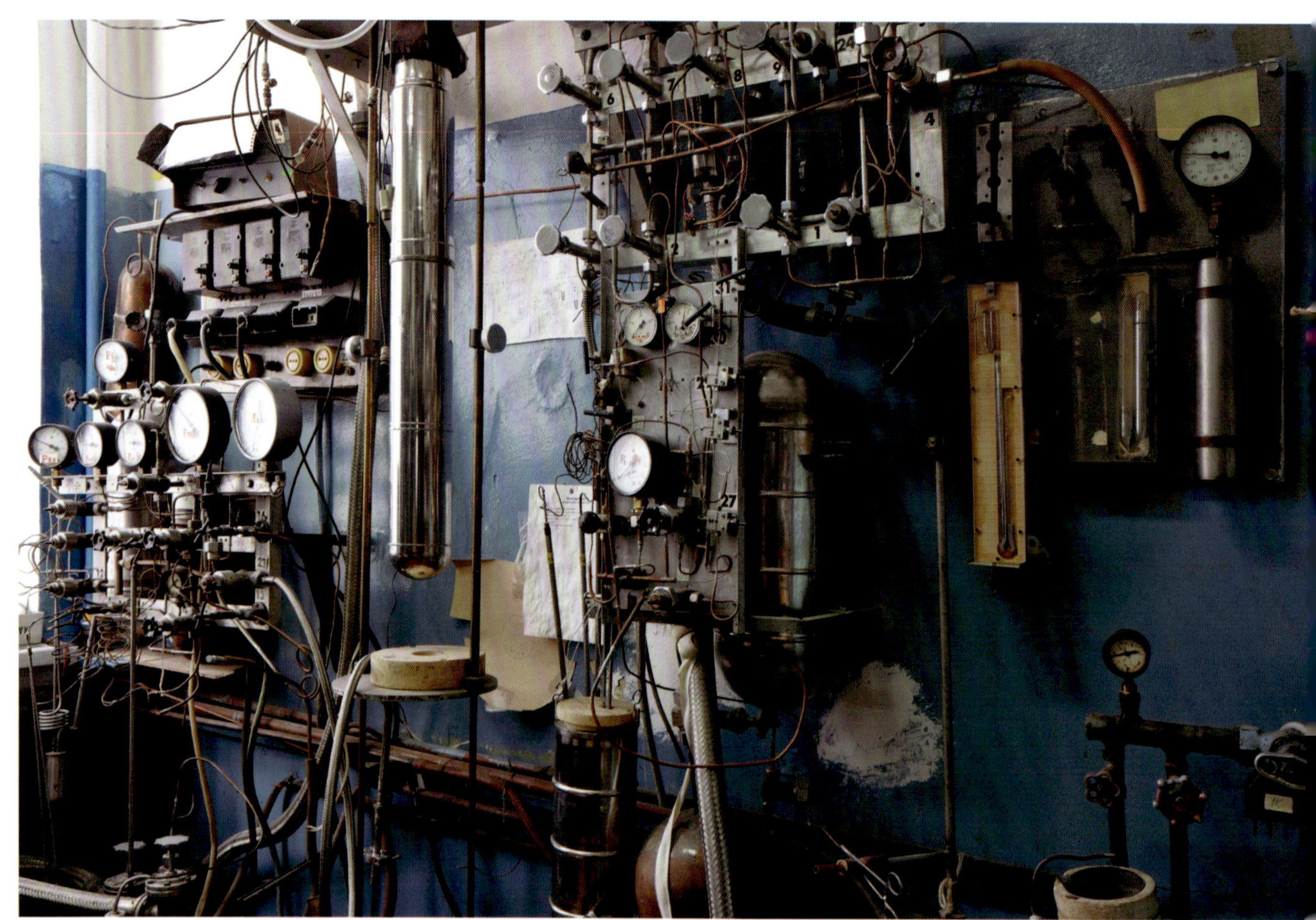

The control and monitoring system of a dilution refrigerator.

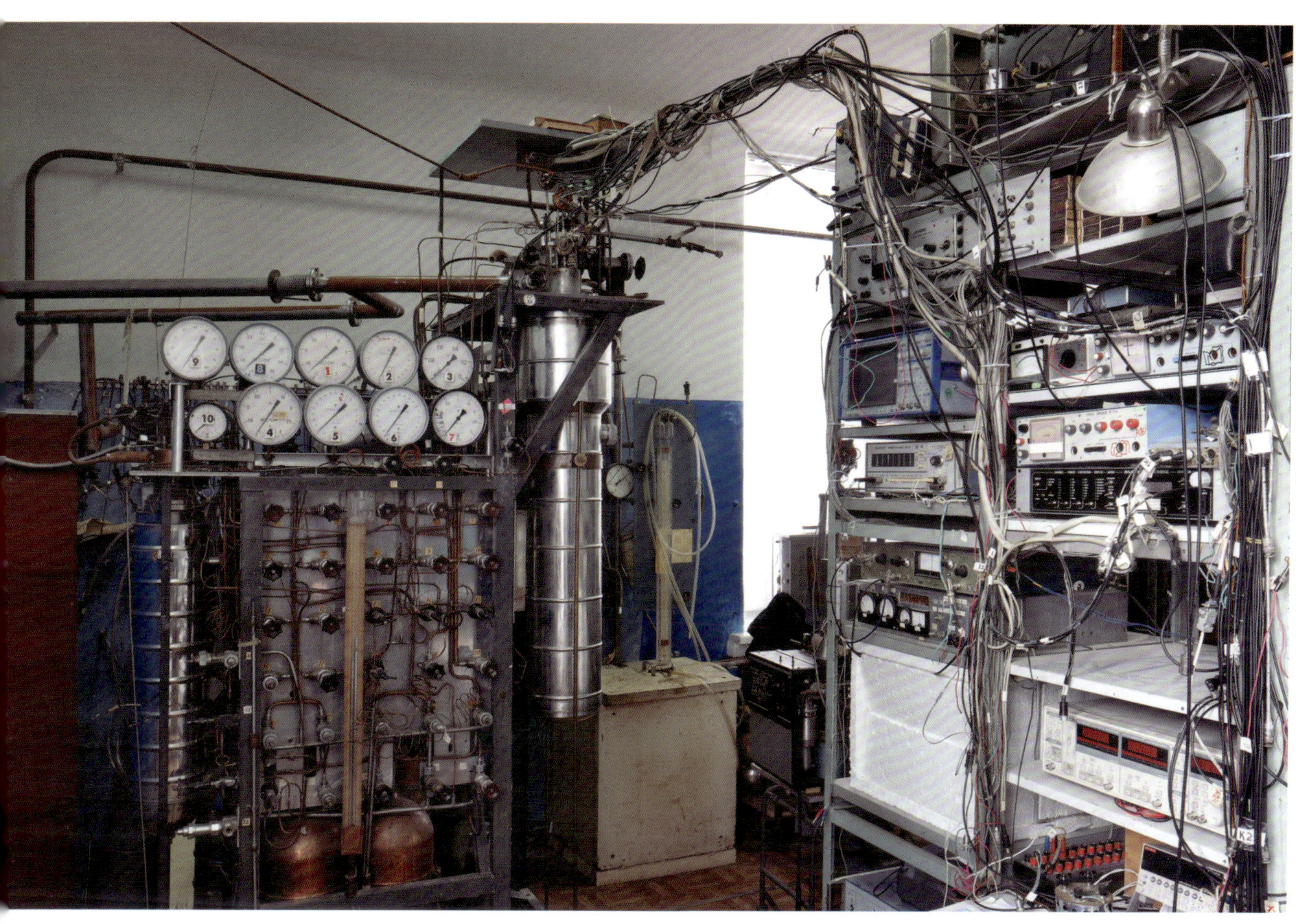

The outer circulation dilution refrigerator began operating in 1980. It is used for the study of superfluid helium isotope solutions, incorporating an ultrasound spectrometer to analyse their acoustic properties.

INSTITUTE FOR SCINTILLATION MATERIALS

National Academy of Sciences of Ukraine

Kharkiv, UKRAINE

The Institute for Single Crystals was founded in 1955 as a scientific and technological complex for the production of radiation detectors in the developing field of nuclear research as well as in the aeronautic and space industries. During the Soviet period, 80 per cent of the institute's output was for military purposes. In 1992 leading Ukrainian scientist Lyudmyla Nagorna (1932–2013) proposed the use of lead tungstate crystals ($PbWO_4$) in particle physics experiments, recognising their superior characteristics in these applications.

A collaboration began with the European Organization for Nuclear Research (CERN) in Switzerland, which implemented thousands of these crystals in the A Large Ion Collider Experiment (ALICE) and Compact Muon Solenoid (CMS) particle detectors of the Large Hadron Collider. In 2002, the offshoot Institute for Scintillation Materials was established. A world leader in the creation, study and deployment of new materials in this field, it successfully combines exceptional research and production skills with the manufacture of high-tech apparatus for various scientific and industrial sectors.

Scintillating materials, such as zinc selenide, strontium iodide, bismuth germanate, etc., emit flashes of light when exposed to ionising radiation (X-rays, gamma rays and so on). These materials are crucial for developing particle detectors in nuclear medicine and high-energy physics, and are manufactured in a range of similar ways. The precisely shaped and polished lead tungstate crystal components are initially cut from large, artificial, single crystal ingots measuring over 500 mm in diameter and 500 kg in weight, grown in special furnaces, and are extremely sensitive to temperature variations, impurity levels and growth rate – the slightest inaccuracy potentially compromising the result. Hence the specific automated cultivation technologies formulated for this purpose.

In 2022, during the first months of the war against Ukraine, the Russian bombardments were so intense that around 50 members of staff and their families were forced to live in the institute's basement, their beds laid out amongst the equipment in the laboratories. A further 300 people from the local neighbourhood sought refuge from the bombs in the institute. During these attacks, some of the facilities were destroyed, including the main crystal production workshop. However, far from being defeated by these adverse circumstances, between alarms and shelling the teams managed to move the crystal furnaces to better protected areas to maintain production.

The institute's current research involves innovative production methods such as a 3D-printed detector, which is being developed to greatly simplify the construction of new scintillators. The institute continues to export its products worldwide and participate in various CERN research programmes alongside other cooperative international projects.

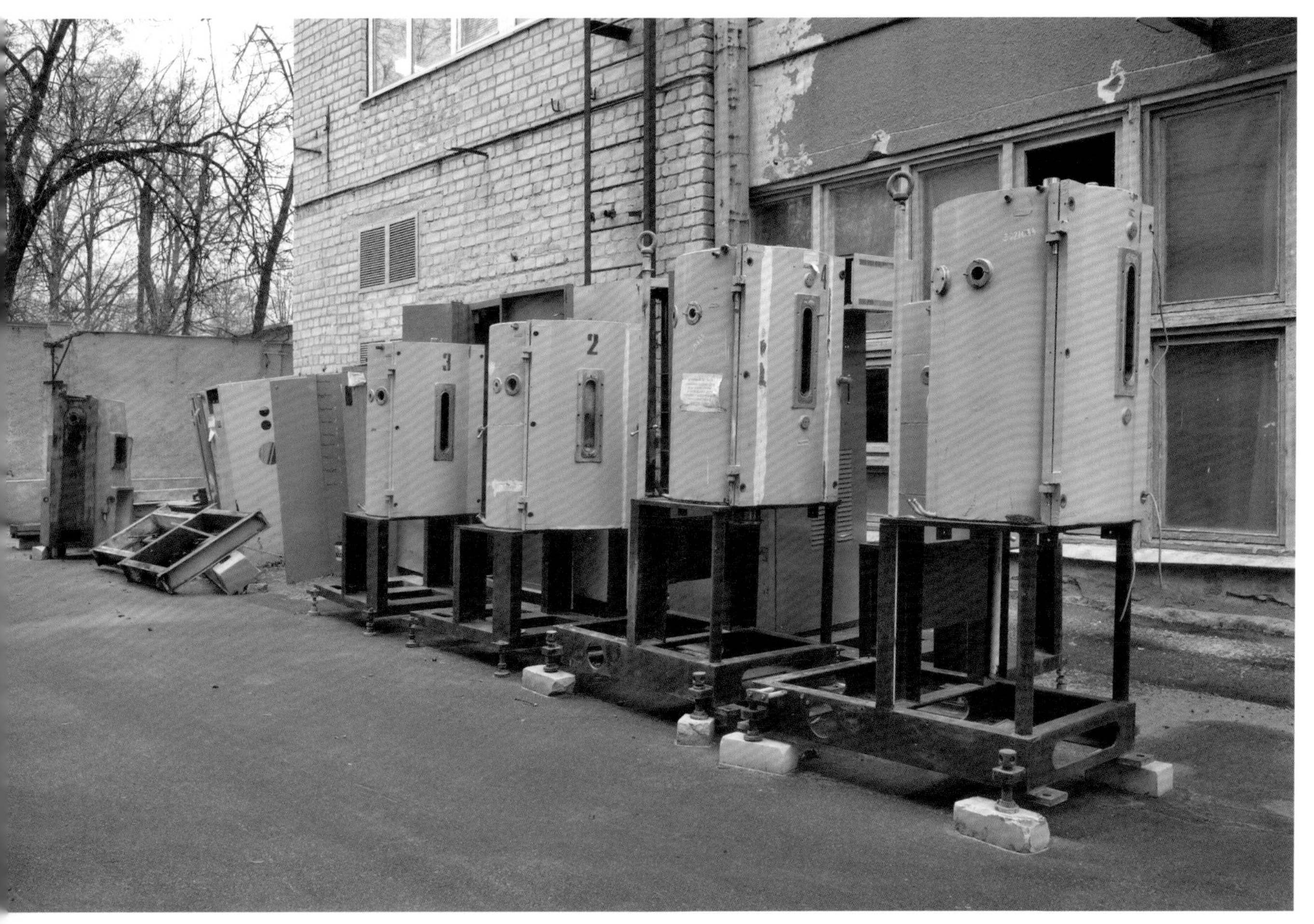

These Soviet-era crystal furnaces have been taken out of service.

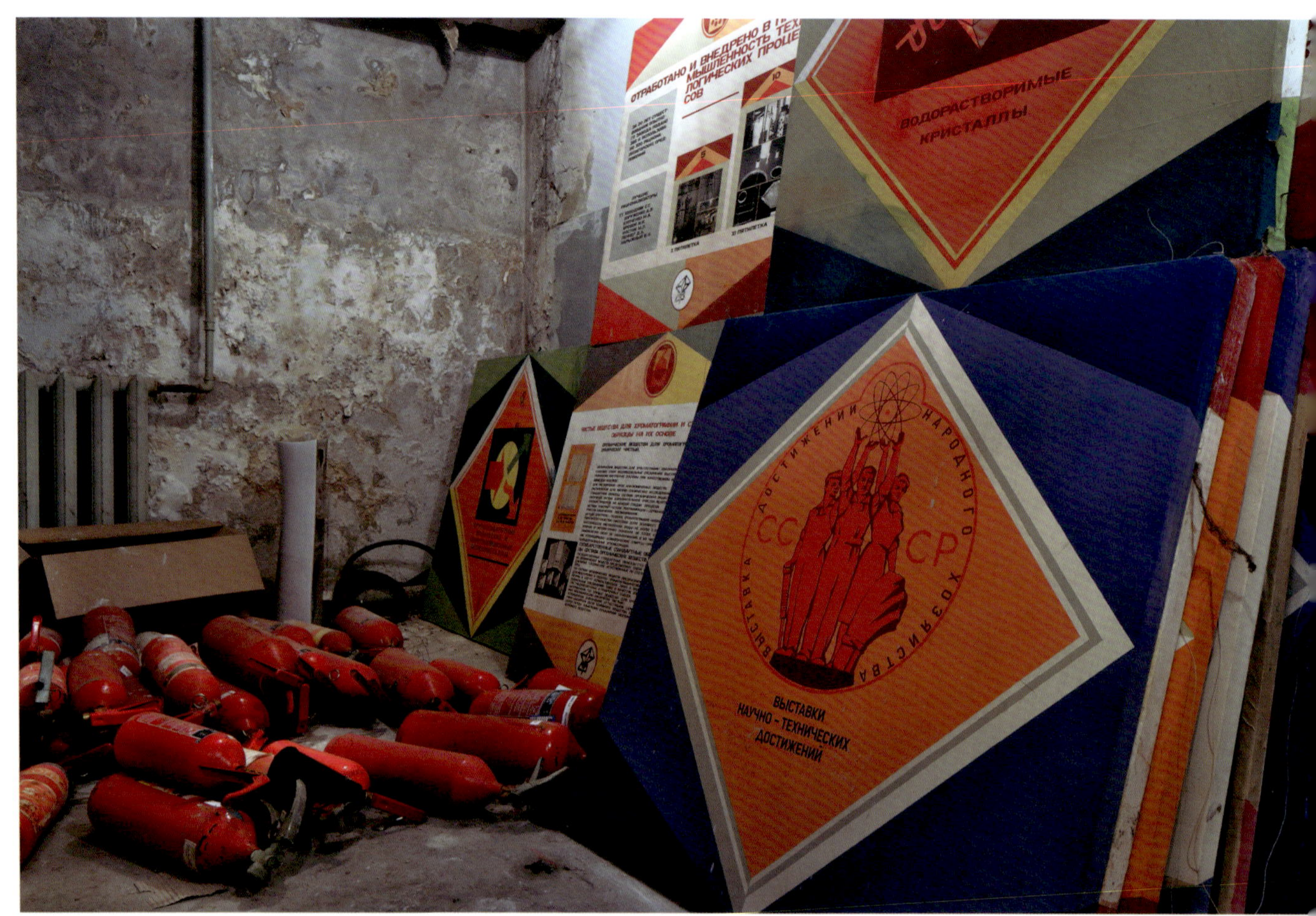

Display boards from a Soviet-era scientific exhibition are stored in a cellar.

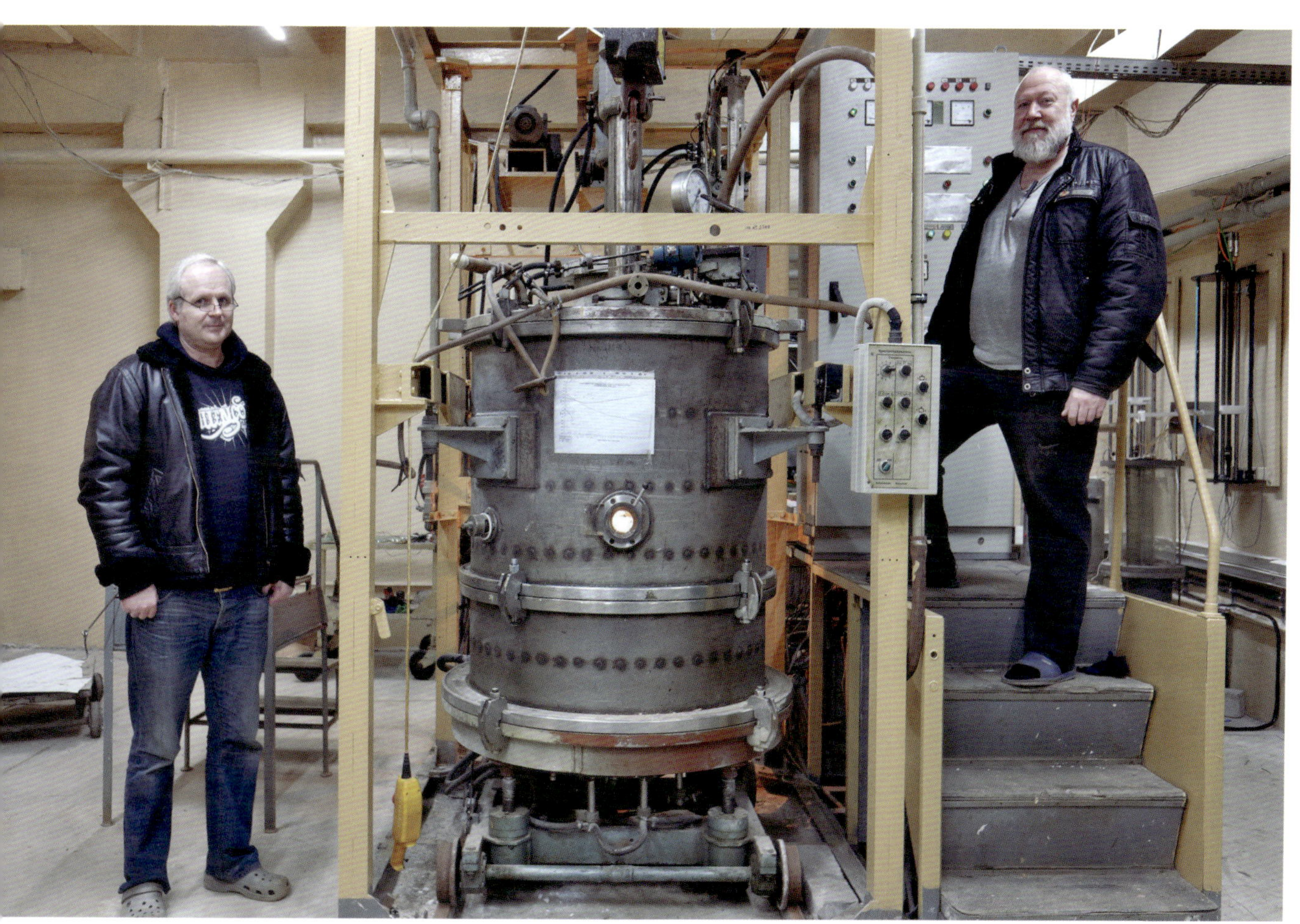

Technicians Oleg Syzov and Stanyslav Zyusko with their large-scale alkali-halide crystal growth furnace, an apparatus which they set up and made operational during the Russian invasion. Their effort has gained recognition as an example of the resilience of Ukrainian scientists and technicians at a time of conflict.

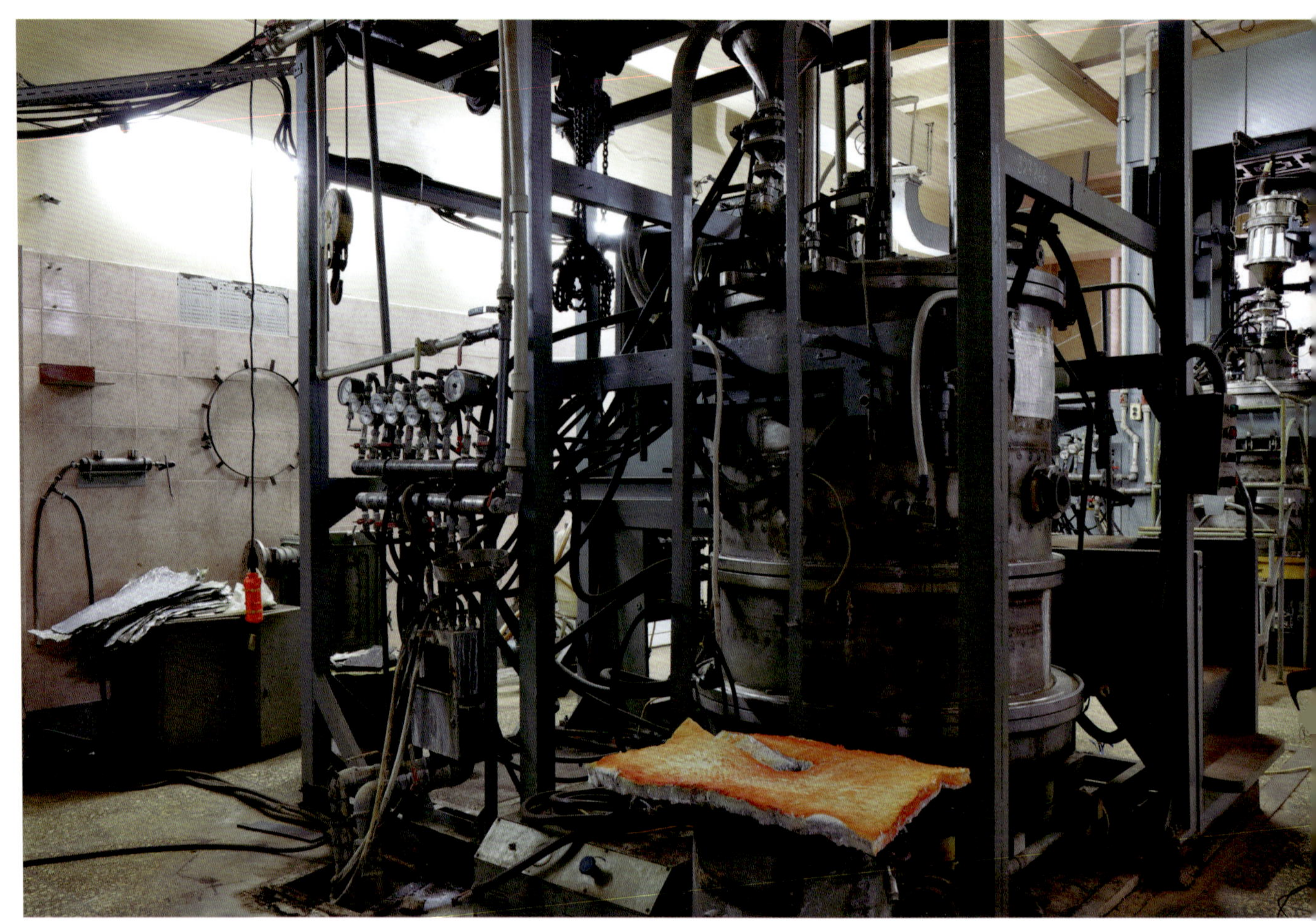

The crystal production workshop.

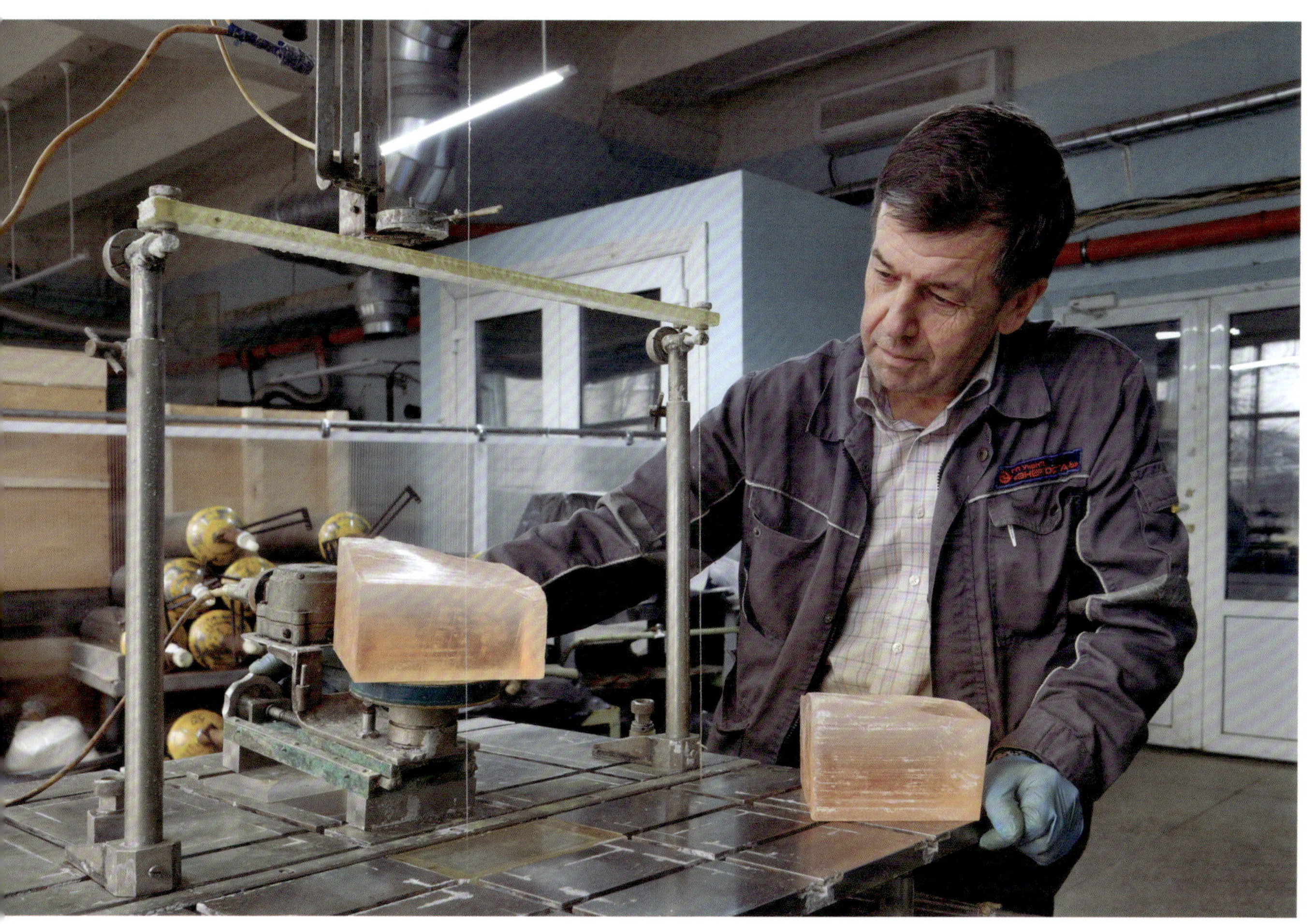

Technician Ahdriy Shille processes alkali-halide crystals. These crystals are used as scintillation detectors for ionising radiation, with applications in nuclear physics, medical imaging and geological prospecting.

RADIOPHYSICAL OBSERVATORY OF THE DEPARTMENT OF SPACE RADIO PHYSICS

V.N. Karazin National University

Kharkiv, UKRAINE

The Department of Space Radio Physics was founded in 1964 to train radio physicists who were to be assigned to various sectors such as research institutions, higher education institutions and programmes undertaken by ministries of the USSR, as well as to establish a new scientific school.

The Radiophysical Observatory is a unique resource in Ukraine for the study of fundamental environmental physics processes, using apparatus for the remote examination of near-Earth space. Situated in a secluded countryside location in order to avoid signal interference, the entire observatory complex covers an area of 27 hectares. Created in 1980, it serves as a scientific and technical base for comprehensive research into radio wave propagation and ionospheric and space weather.

Space weather research focuses on changing environmental conditions in space, driven by the Sun's activity, and the effects of these conditions on Earth. Phenomena such as solar flares and coronal mass ejections release high-energy particle radiation that can disrupt satellites, power grids, communications systems and navigation. A powerful solar storm might have devastating consequences for humankind, and the more developed the civilisation, the more vulnerable its critical infrastructure is to variations in such weather.

As well as monitoring space weather to predict the effects of solar processes on Earth within a few days or hours, the observatory also works to improve the reliability of seismic forecasts, providing early warnings of earthquakes. The ionosphere acts as a kind of mirror for radio waves, allowing physicists to detect disturbances caused by natural events such as earthquakes and volcanic eruptions, as well as man-made events such as rocket launches and powerful industrial explosions. Even the flights of large aircraft can be tracked through secondary manifestations. However, this mirror is constantly and randomly distorted, so that particular skill is required to decipher relevant information amid ever-changing parameters.

A wide range of equipment, such as medium-frequency radars, high-frequency Doppler radars, satellite beacon receivers, a magnetometer and an ionosonde, are used for remote radio sensing tasks. The observatory's capabilities for conducting ground-based research had no equal in the rest of the former USSR. The monitoring of satellite signals for ionosphere diagnostics is a powerful means of studying the impact of space weather. To conduct such studies, the complex operates receivers that can record signals from navigation satellites such as GPS (the US-based Global Positioning System), GLONASS (Global Navigation Satellite System, the Soviet version of GPS) and its predecessor Tsikada (after the insect known for its pulsing sound; used for the Soviet navy and commercial shipping, it was concluded in 2008).

The Radiophysical Observatory cooperates internationally with universities in the United States, Canada and Japan. To date, it has not been damaged by the war in Ukraine.

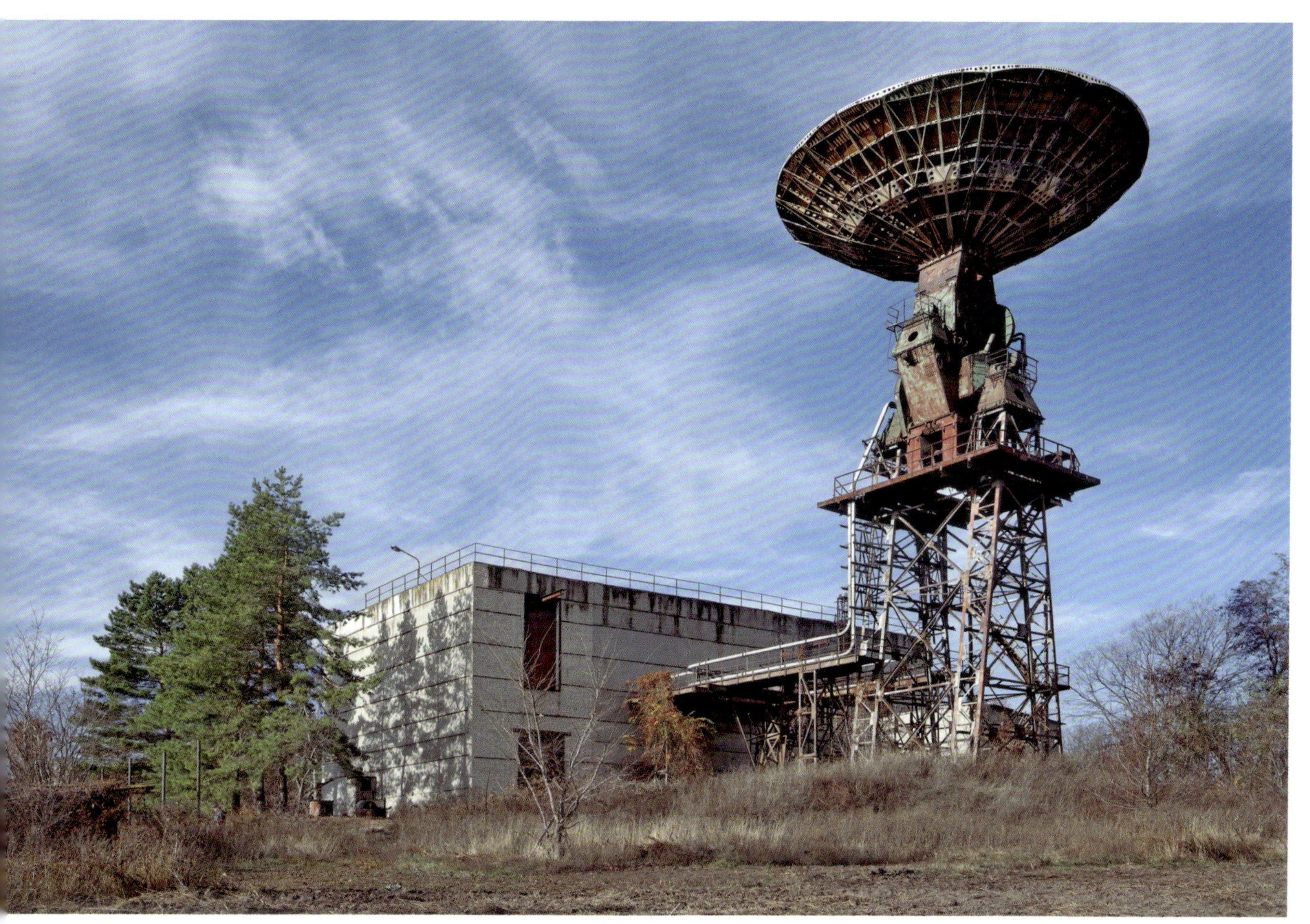

The fully steerable 15-metre ultra high-frequency antenna. It is used to study the ionosphere, in particular various interacting processes within the altitude range of 60 to 1,000 kilometres.

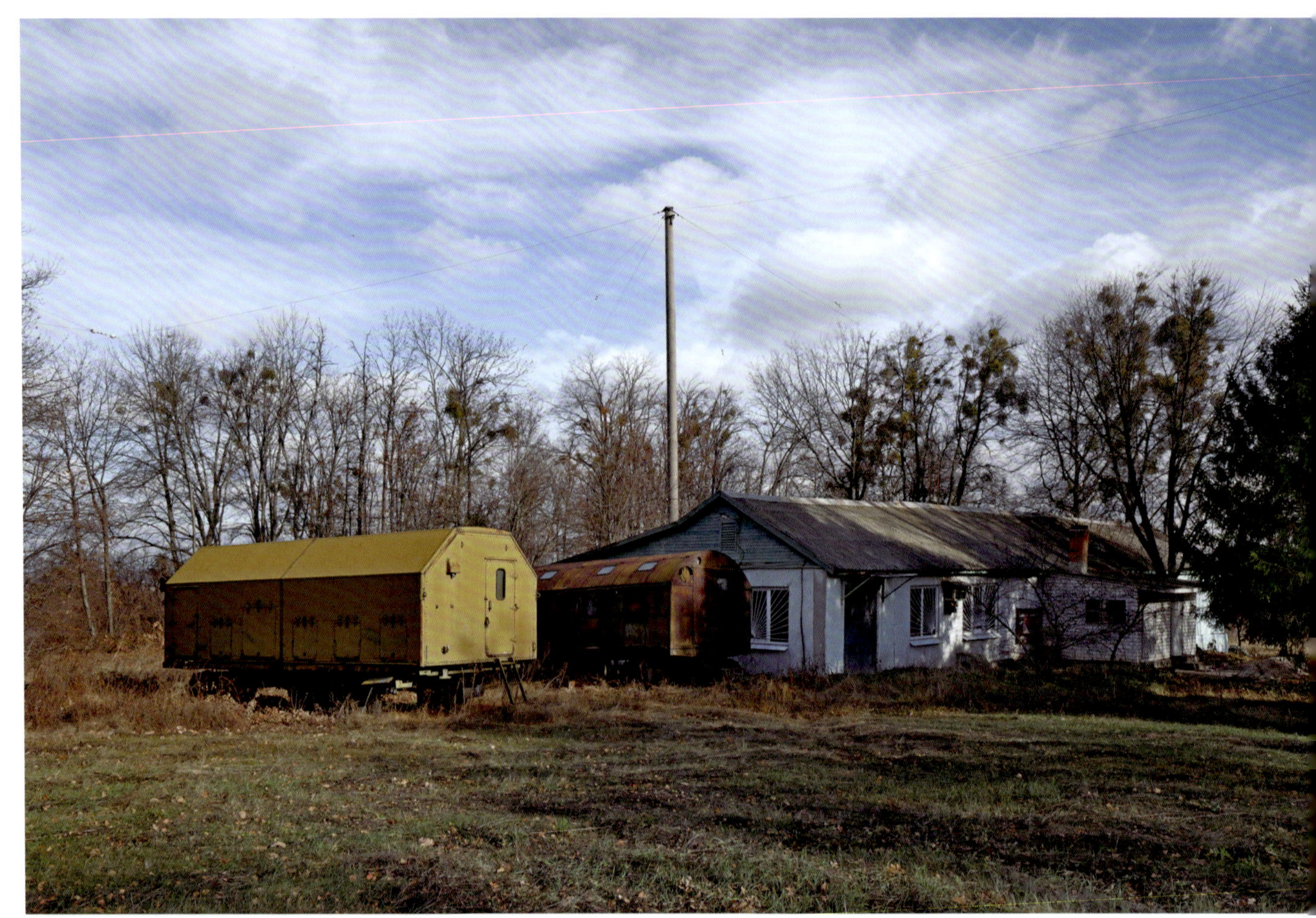

One of the observatory's laboratories housing radio engineering systems.

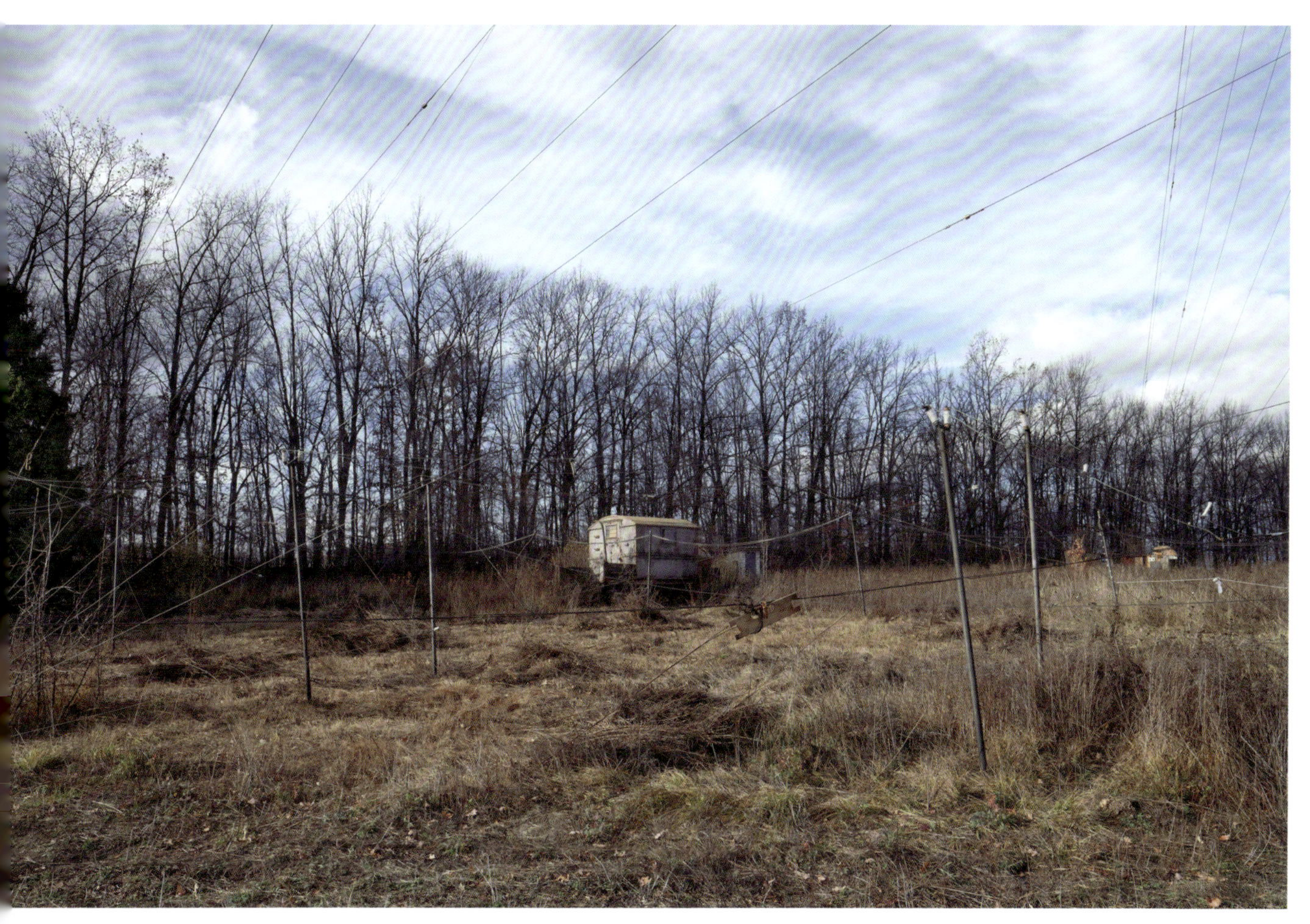

High-frequency antennas positioned in a field within the grounds of the observatory.

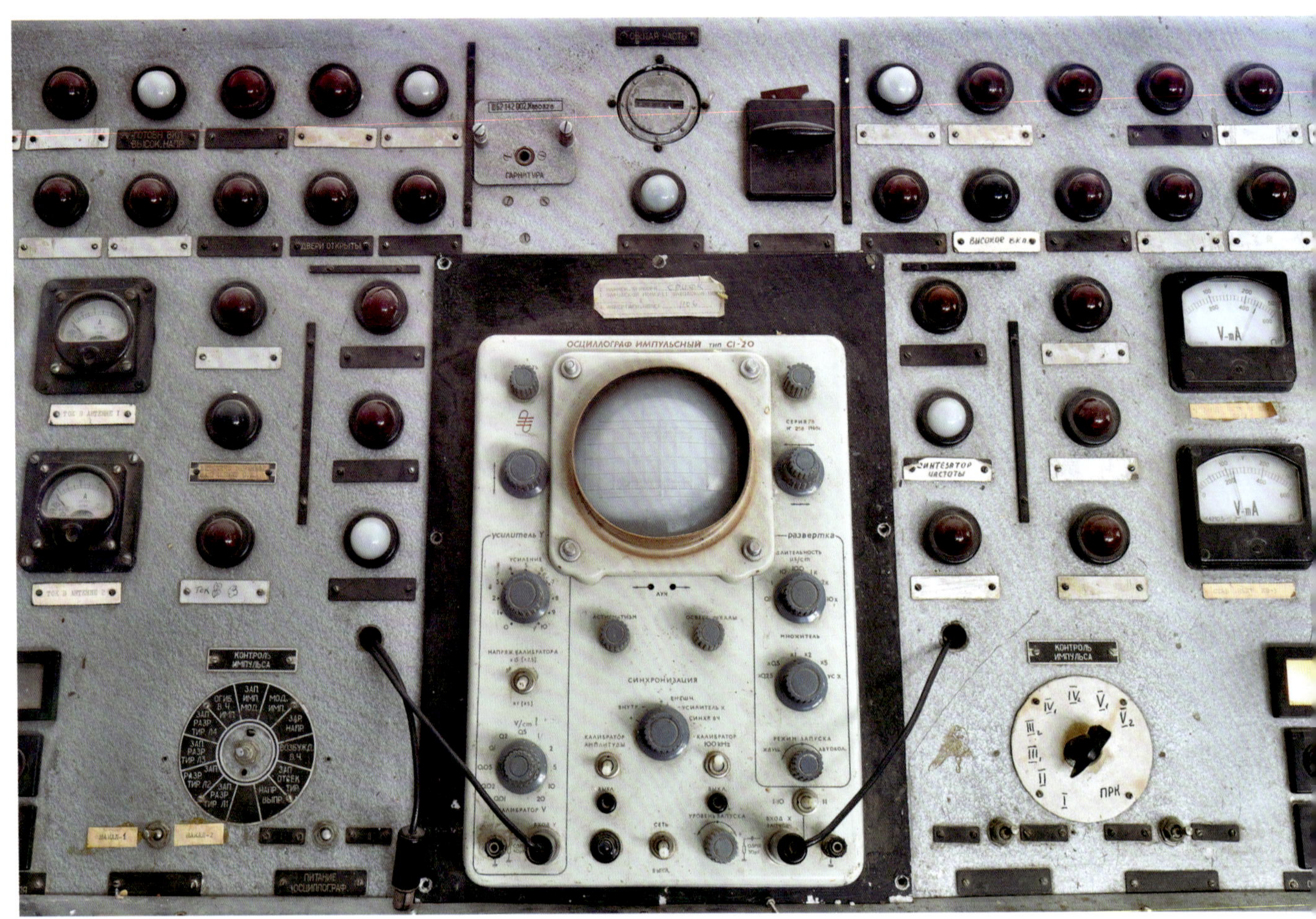

The partial reflection radar control panel. This medium-frequency radar allows researchers to monitor and take various measurements in the Earth's upper neutral atmosphere. It is used to study the mesosphere and the lower thermosphere (MLT) region, which is between 50 and 110 kilometres in height.

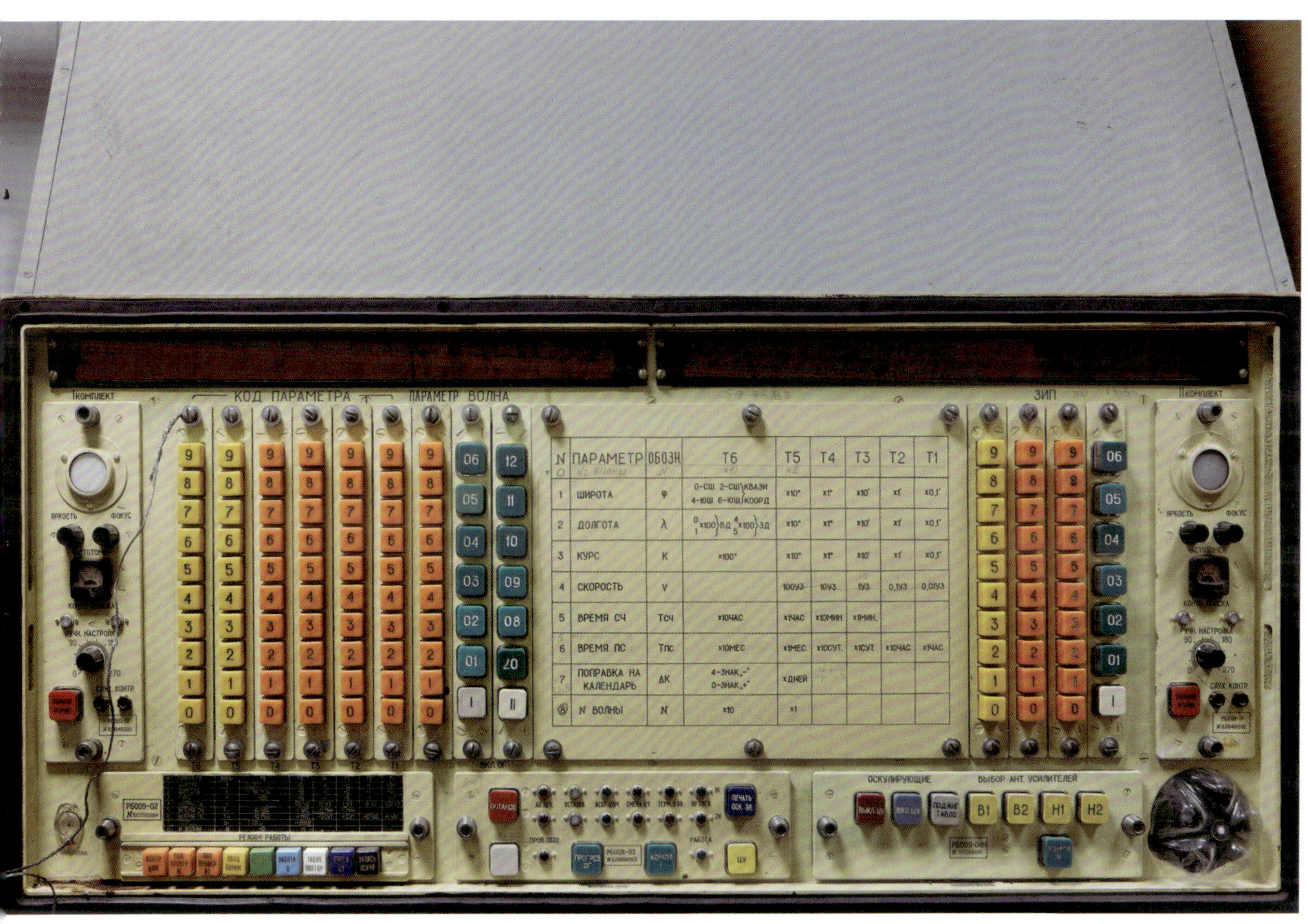

A control console used to receive and process Doppler signals from the Tsikada satellite navigation system. An operator would set geodetic parameters and calibration values, entering them in a specific sequence. These would include: latitude, longitude, course, speed, time and calendar corrections.

USIKOV INSTITUTE FOR RADIOPHYSICS AND ELECTRONICS

National Academy of Sciences of Ukraine

Kharkiv, UKRAINE

Kharkiv is known for its School of Radiophysics, founded in 1921 by Dmytro Rozhansky (1882–1936). He was imprisoned in 1930 after publicly opposing the death penalty for engineers who had been wrongly accused of sabotage. Thanks to the efforts of influential physicist Abram Ioffe (1880–1960), Rozhansky was released after nine months. He stated his interrogators attempted to make him confess that he was 'inventing a device capable of reading the thoughts of Comrade Stalin from a distance.'

A new department of the Ukrainian Institute of Physics and Technology (UFTI) – the Laboratory of Electromagnetic Oscillations (LEMO) – was established in 1930. Led by Rozhansky's finest student, Abram Slutskin (1891–1950), it pioneered research into electrical engineering and electromagnetic waves. Effective microwave oscillators, magnetrons in particular, became key components of radar systems, a priority of the Red Army.

The Zenit experimental radar was created in 1937 by Slutskin and two of his students: Olexander Usikov (1904–1995) and Semyon Braude (1911–2003). This innovative apparatus used a pulsed radio-location method instead of a continuous wave, enabling it to accurately determine the three necessary coordinates of an airborne target. During World War II, the team was evacuated to Bukhara in Uzbekistan where, in 1942, they developed an improved battlefield version named Rubin. However, this adaptation never entered production, as the Soviet military adopted the British GL Mk II radar instead, which was supplied under the Lend-Lease Programme.

In 1955, Usikov founded the Institute for Radiophysics and Electronics, with Braude as deputy director. The institute focused on millimetre and sub-millimetre wave technology, with most of the research concentrated on defence applications. Although difficult to master, these frequencies promised improved radar capabilities, allowing them to detect smaller objects with greater accuracy. In the 1970s, Usikov developed new methods of processing digital radar images. This resulted in the first three-dimensional images of large areas of Venus, Mars and the Moon. Over the years, the scope of the institute expanded to include biophysics, quantum electronics, cold plasma physics and acoustics.

Due to the sensitive nature of the institute's activities, permission was granted to photograph a single site which houses the unique Large Ukrainian Radio Spectrometer of the Academy of Sciences (BURAN). This facility acts like a super-powered microscope — not for seeing shapes, but for revealing the hidden magnetic and electronic behaviour of advanced materials. It helps scientists explore the building blocks of future technologies. BURAN is especially valuable for research on semiconductors, magnetic materials, nanostructures, and quantum-related phenomena.

In 2022, the institute was targeted by the Russian army and although BURAN was spared, the larger buildings were destroyed and much of the scientific equipment lost. The critical situation forced the staff to continue their work remotely until conditions are such that the institute can be revived and rebuilt.

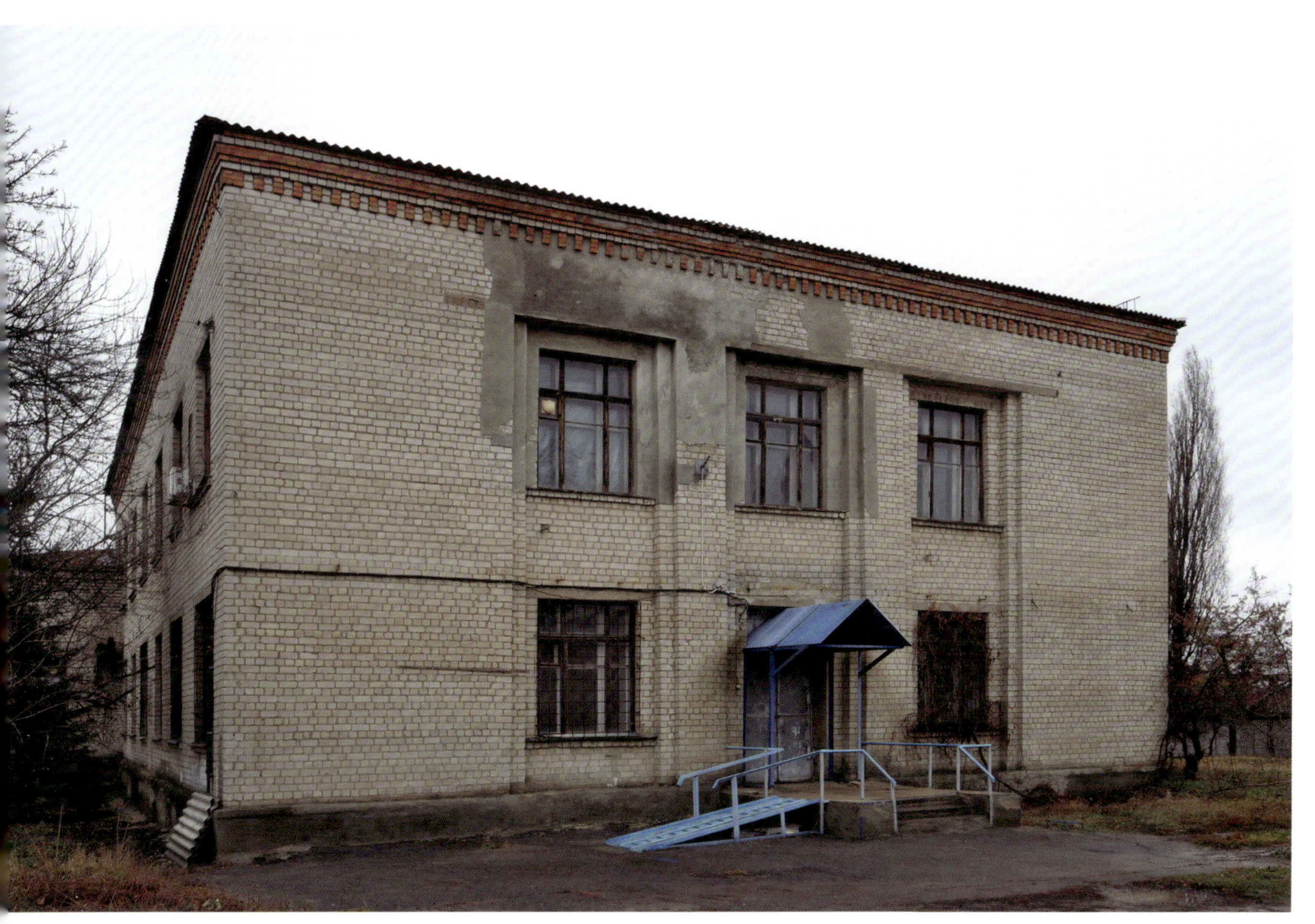

This building houses the Large Ukrainian Radio Spectrometer of the Academy of Sciences (BURAN).

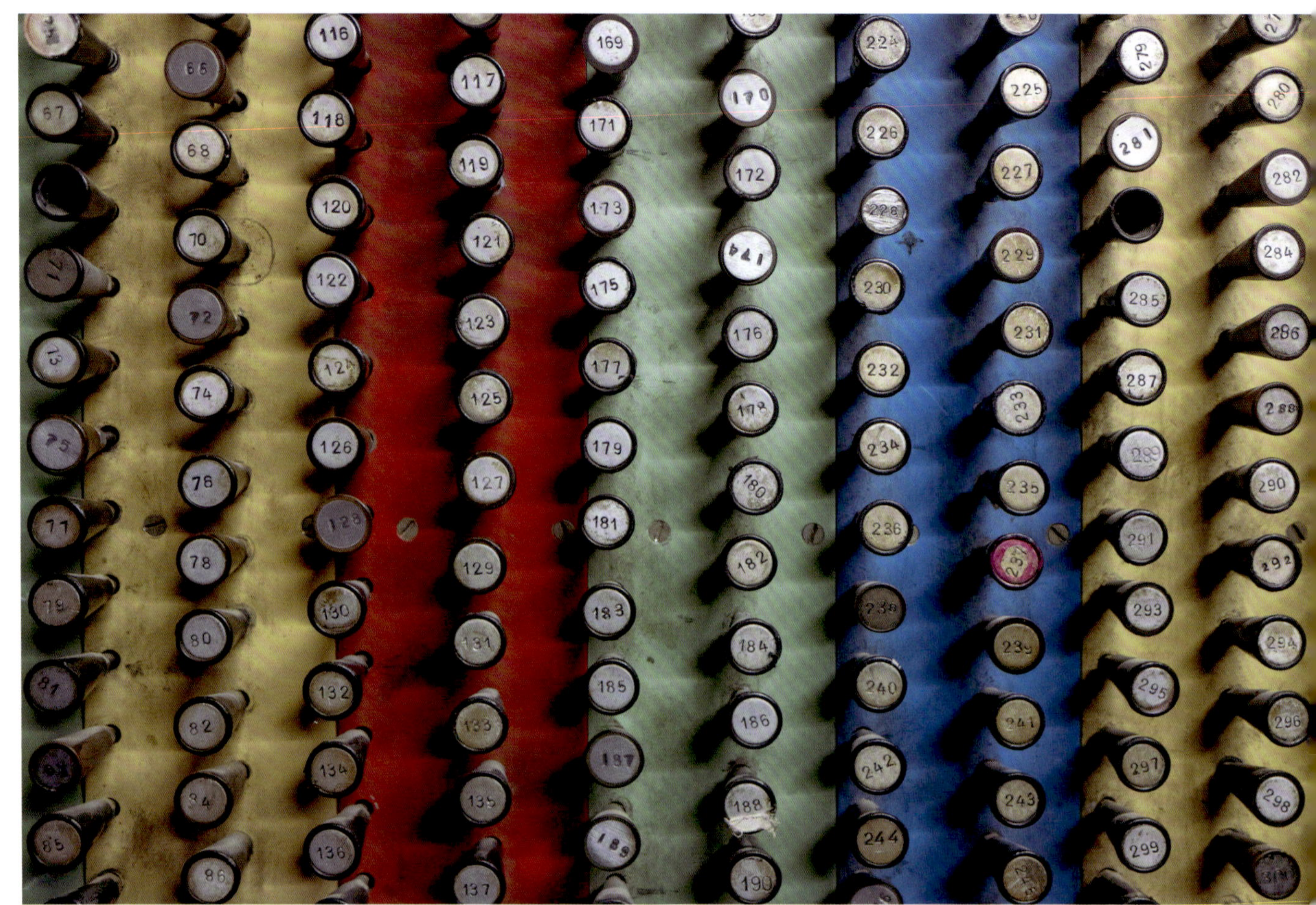

The original Soviet-era staff attendance board is still a fixture at the entrance to the institute.

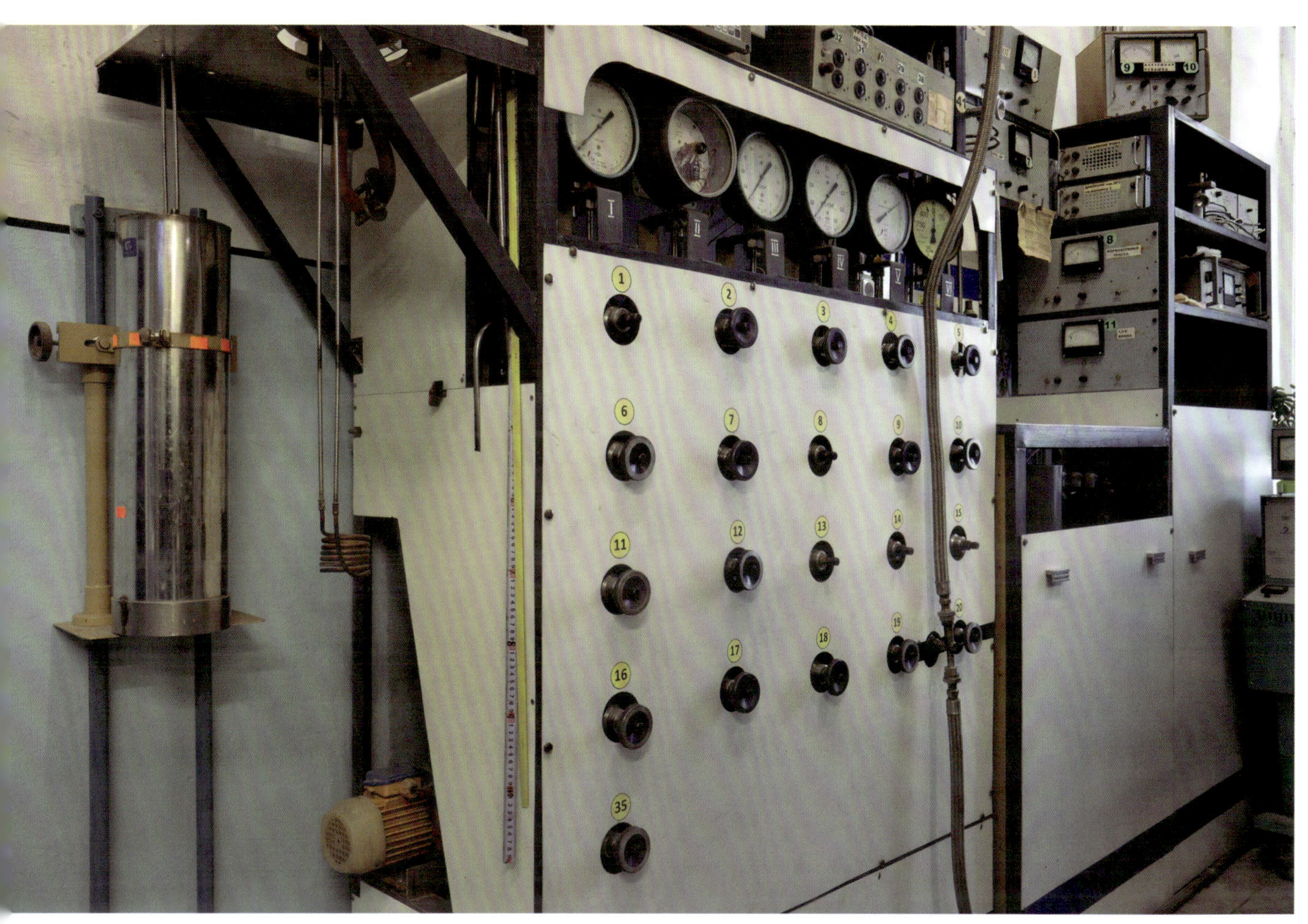

Control and monitoring panels at the BURAN complex, showing the array of tuning apparatus, pressure gauges and supporting electronics used to regulate the vacuum system.

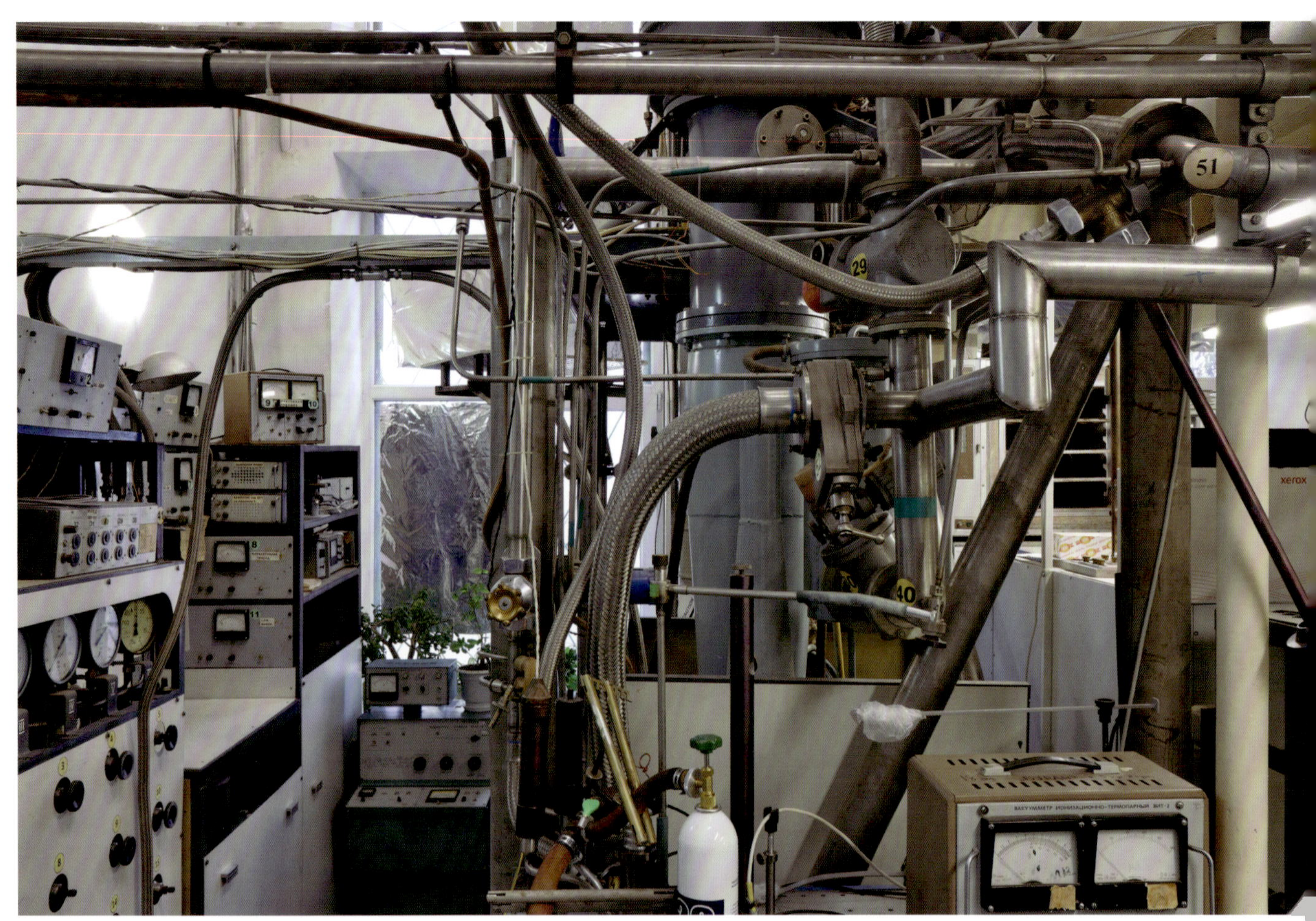

Investigations can be carried out at very high frequencies, at temperatures near absolute zero and under very strong magnetic fields. This process reveals physical effects that cannot be observed under normal conditions.

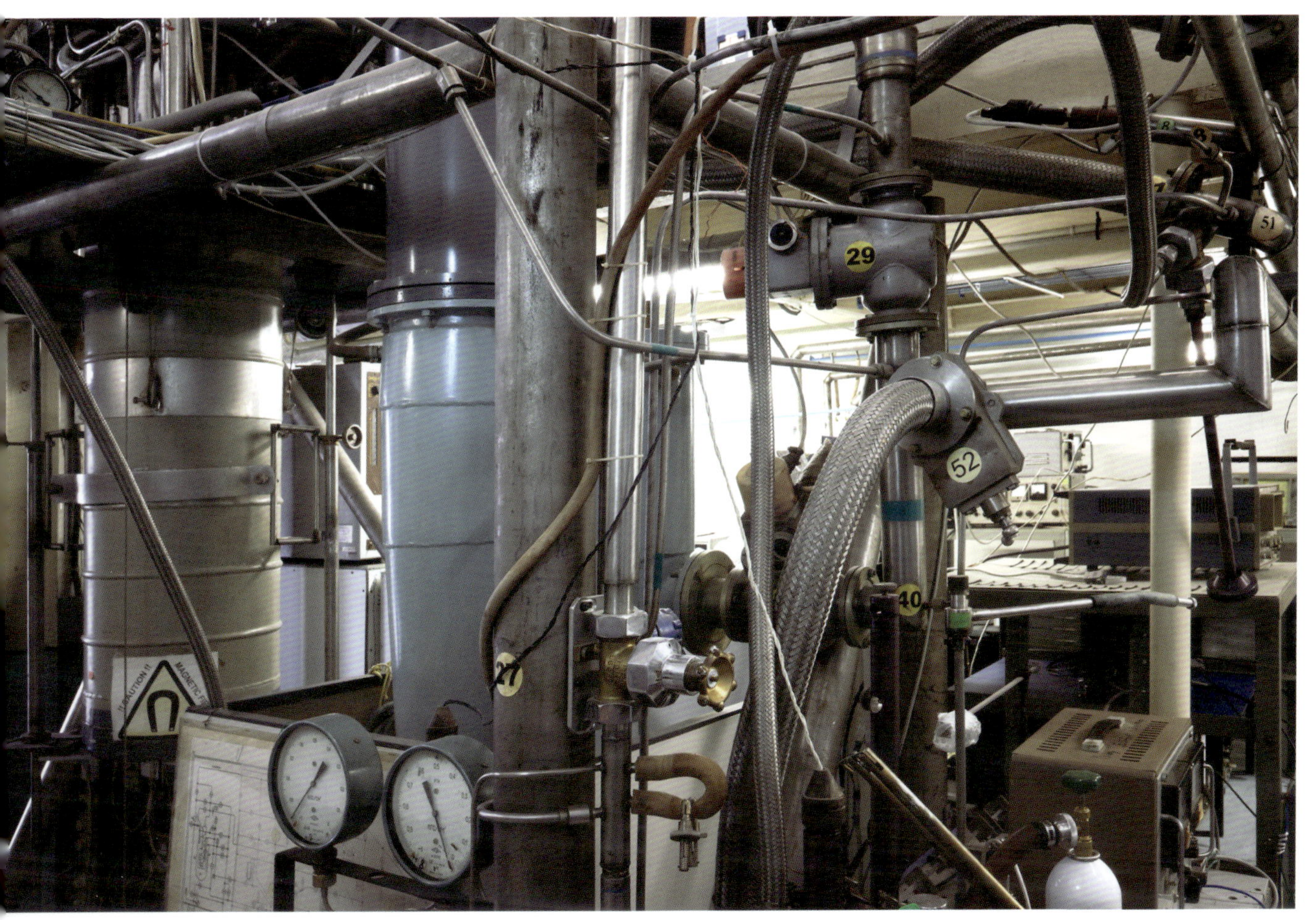

The BURAN complex is dedicated to advanced studies of nonlinear processes in nuclear systems.

INSTITUTE OF RADIO ASTRONOMY

National Academy of Sciences of Ukraine

Kharkiv, UKRAINE

The rapid development of radar during World War II greatly advanced the techniques required for radio astronomy, at that time a promising new branch of the discipline. Radio astronomy detects celestial objects invisible to optical telescopes by analysing the radio waves they emit. Astrophysicists were interested in measuring cosmic radio emissions in the decametre (10-metre) range – a portion of the electromagnetic spectrum that offers valuable scientific insights difficult to obtain at higher frequencies. However, due to significant experimental obstacles, by the end of the 1950s the decametre range had still not been completely mastered.

The Institute of Radio Physics and Electronics (IRE) created a radio astronomy division headed by Semyon Braude (1911–2003). In 1957, Braude began developing radio telescopes capable of providing noise-resistant measurements for various scientific programmes, and by the end of the 1960s, a number of original instruments had been designed and constructed. Introduced in 1971, the Ukrainian T-Shaped Radio Telescope, Second Modification (UTR-2) is the world's largest low-frequency radio telescope, operating at decametre wavelengths corresponding to a frequency range of 8 to 33 megahertz. Made up of a network of 2,040 antennas known as dipoles, the entire structure covers 15 hectares and takes the form of a giant letter 'T'. The UTR-2 is the main component of the URAN (Ukrainian Radio Interferometer of the National Academy of Sciences) system, which comprises four smaller low-frequency radio telescopes located across Ukraine. The telescope is used to analyse radio signals from a range of cosmic sources, particularly those from the Sun, lightning on Saturn and pulsars, as well as emissions from interstellar and interplanetary space.

In 1985, Braude and Leonid Litvinenko (1938–2023) founded the Institute of Radio Astronomy, with Litvinenko serving as director for the next 32 years. Unlike the IRE, the new institute was not involved in military research and was therefore free from restrictive security concerns. This allowed it to focus on academic, civilian radio astronomy research and the development of international scientific cooperation. These connections proved crucial to the institute's survival after 1991, when foreign grants and participation in international programmes helped overcome the challenges of the post-Soviet period.

On 24 February 2022, the first day of Russia's large-scale invasion of Ukraine, institute researchers were intending to work with NASA on the Juno mission to study Jupiter. However, the next day, a Russian army battalion occupied the Braude Observatory, which houses the UTR-2 and GURT radio telescopes. They used it as a military base for six months, until Ukrainian armed forces carried out a counter-offensive in autumn 2022. The observatory has been rendered inoperable by looting and destruction, but undeterred, resolute Ukrainian astronomers are actively repairing and modernising their flagship facility.

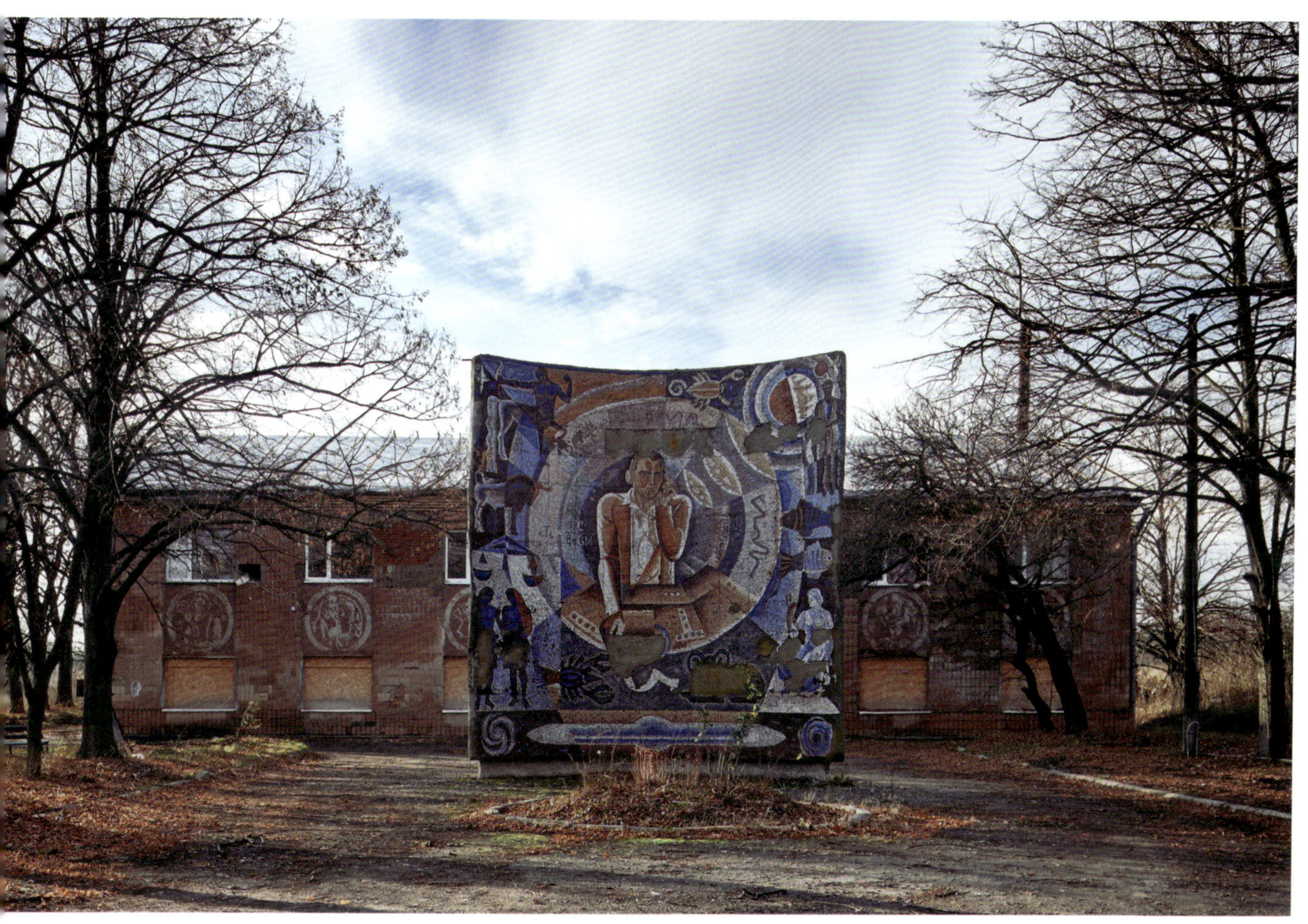

This mosaic at the entrance to the Braude Observatory, which houses the UTR-2 and GURT radio telescopes, depicts a man listening to signals from space. He is surrounded by the 12 signs of the zodiac and various mathematical formulae, including that for calculating the temperature of radiation emitted by a black hole, developed by Stephen Hawking (1942–2018) in 1974.

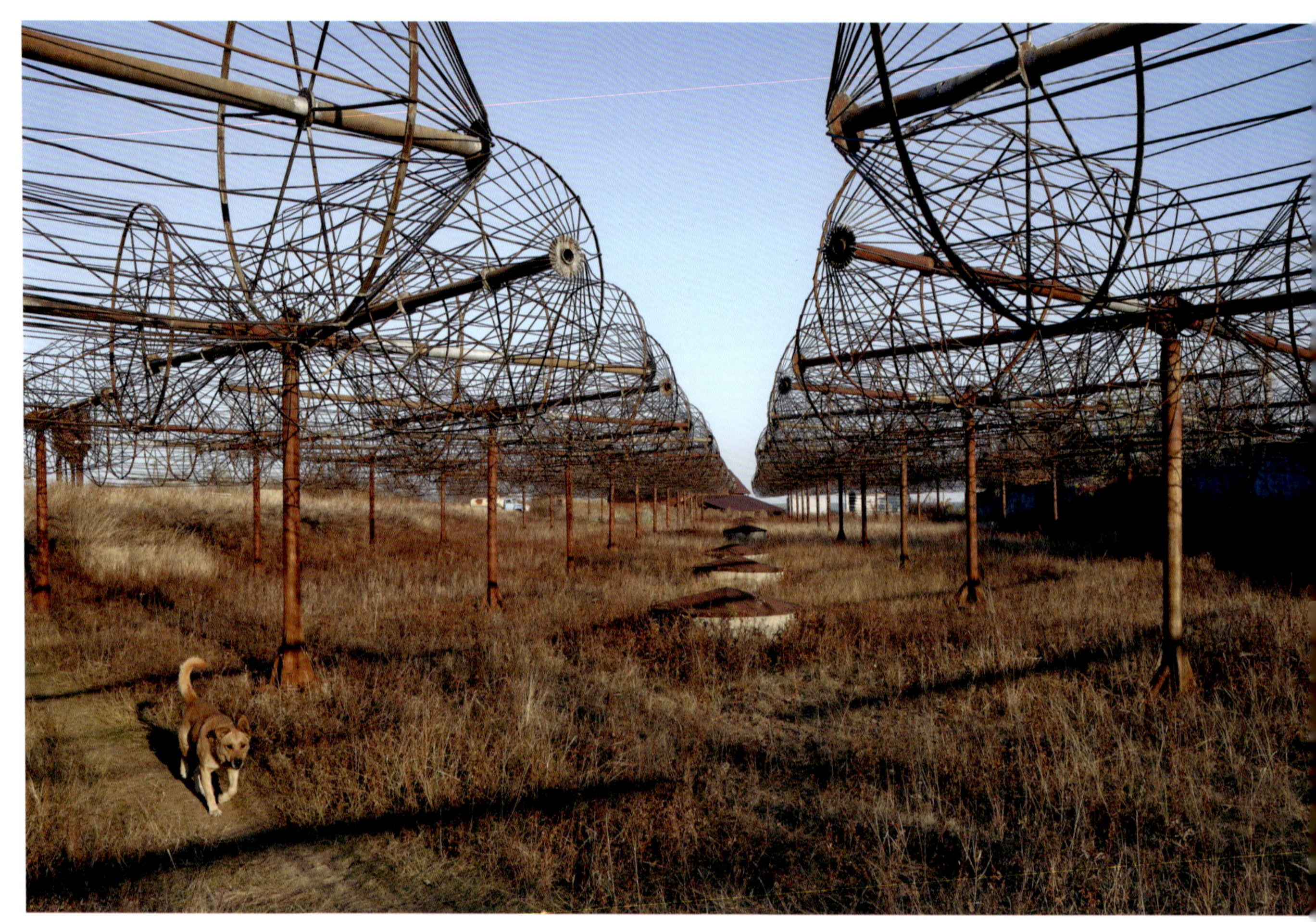

The URAN-1 (Ukrainian Radio Interferometer of the National Academy of Sciences of Ukraine) station was built in 1975. Alongside three other stations, it forms part of a low-frequency array of radio telescopes spread across Ukraine.

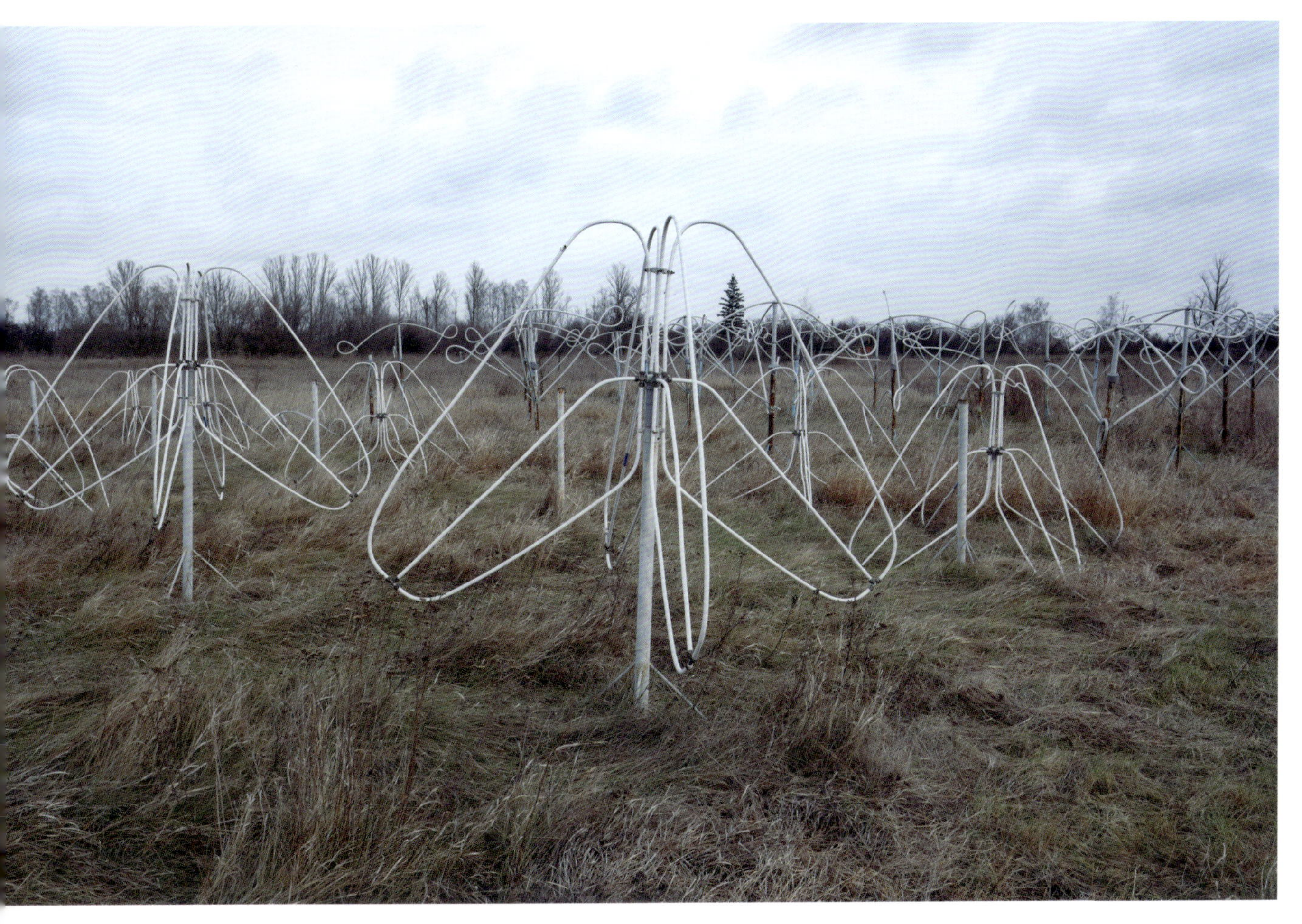

Antennas belonging to GURT (Giant Ukrainian Radio Telescope). Currently under development, this new radio telescope is a phased array composed of many identical subarrays.

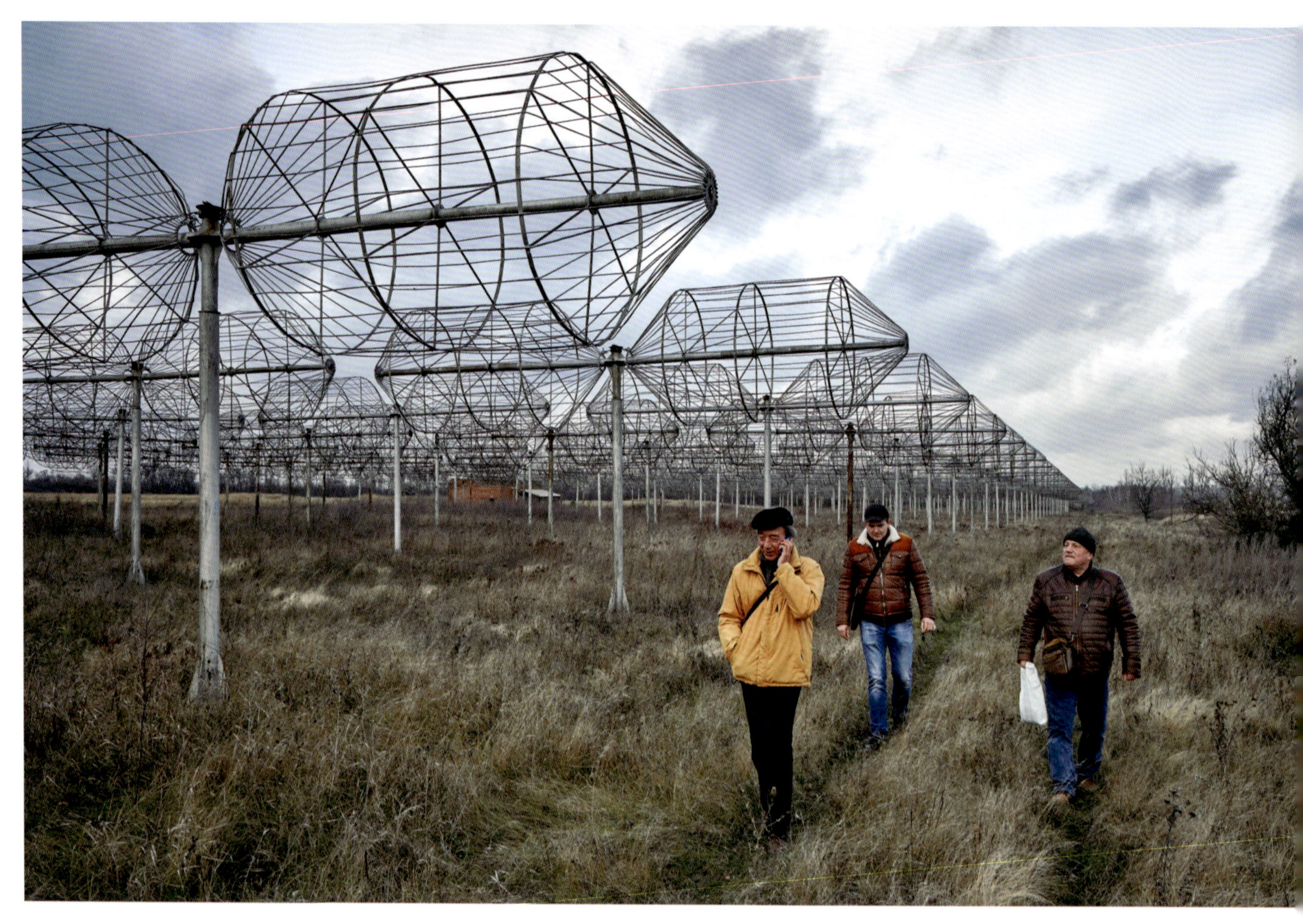

Researchers (left to right) Mykhailo Sidorchuk, Yevhen Vasylkivskyi and Oleksandr Reznichenko walk past antennas of the UTR-2 system. As the site has not been yet cleared by deminers, the researchers are restricted to walking only on cleared paths, such as these tracks left by a tractor, to ensure their safety.

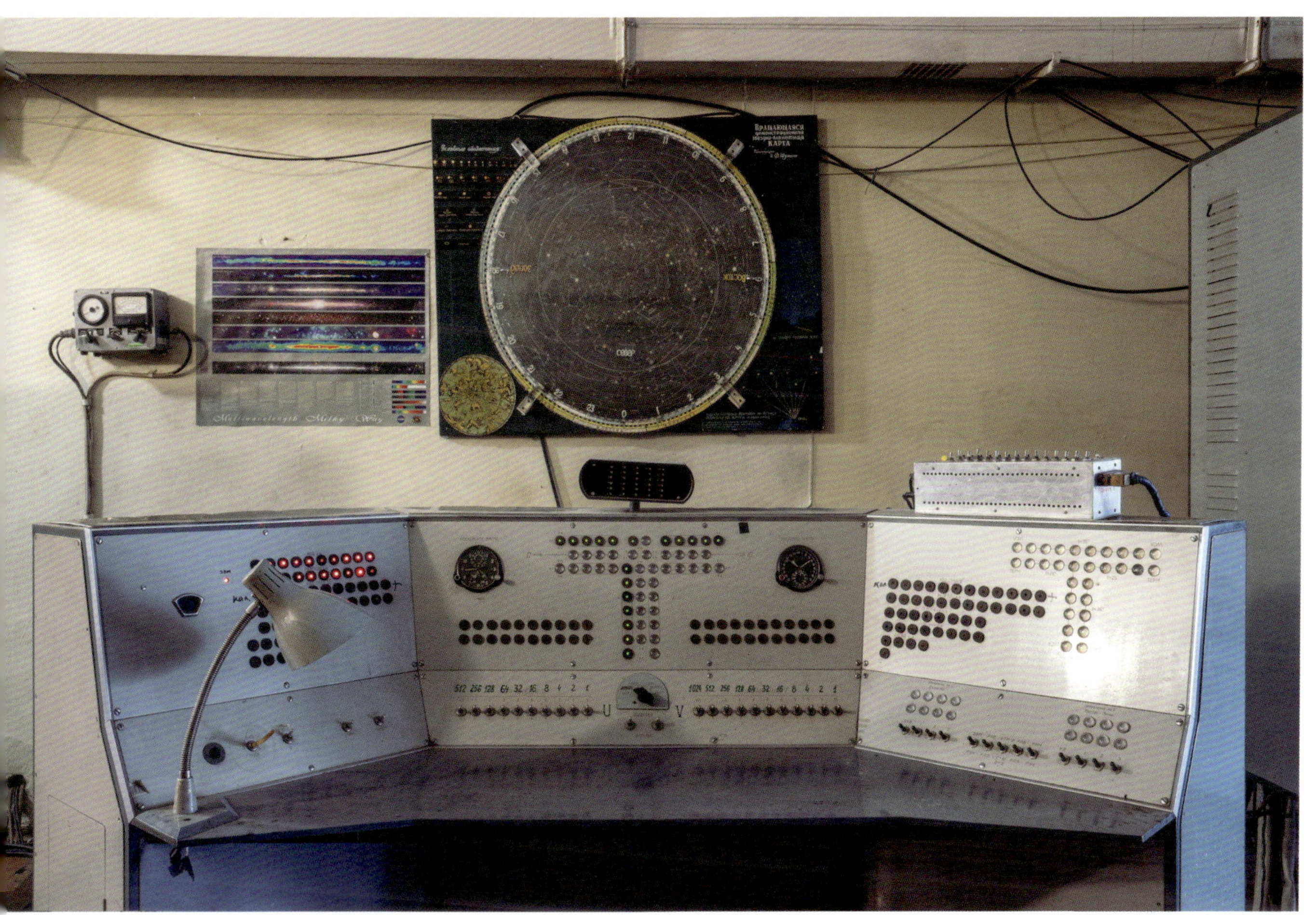

The UTR-2 antenna control panel. This photograph was taken a few weeks before the Russian invasion.

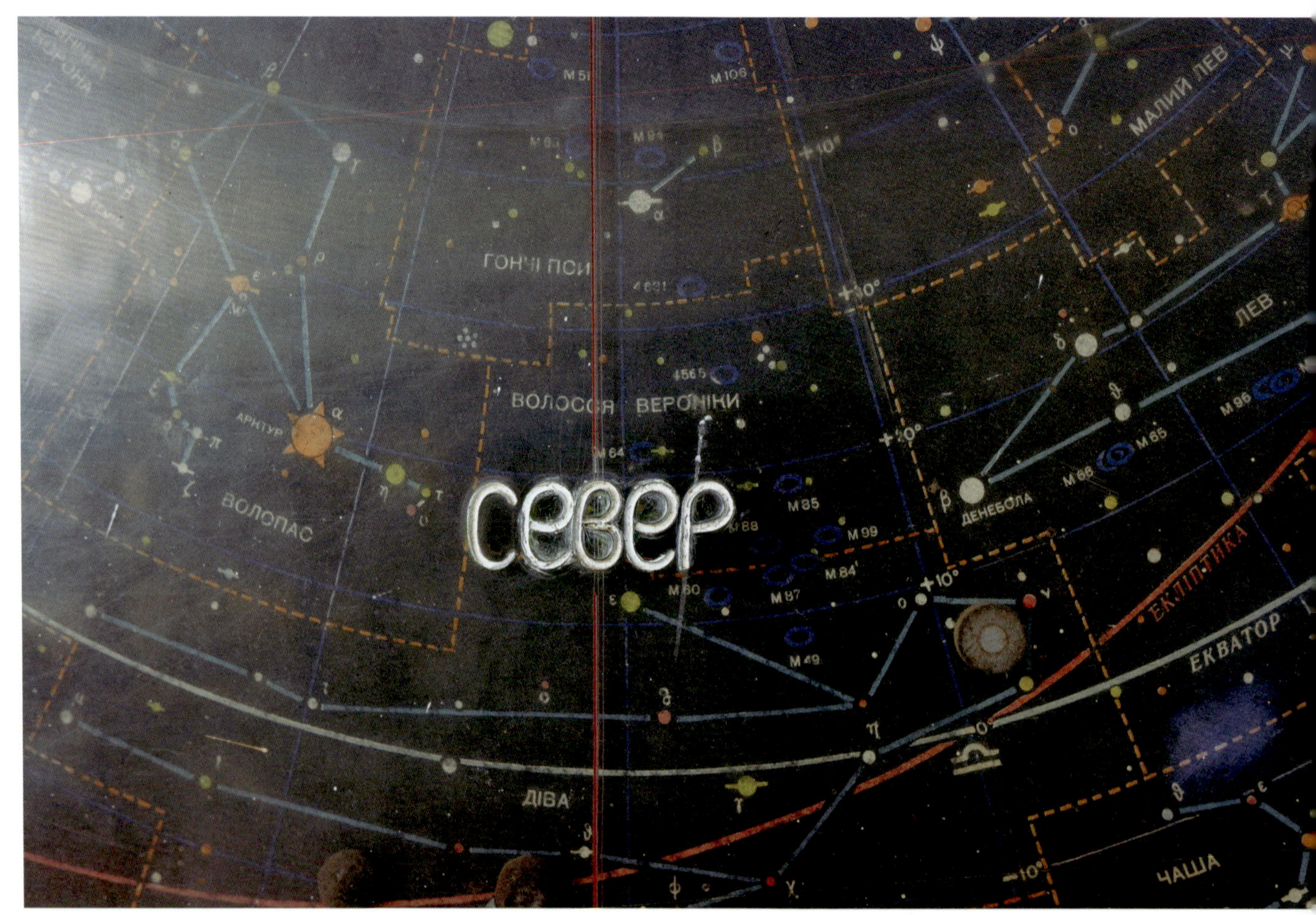

A detail of the control panel sky map, showing the north cardinal marked in white.

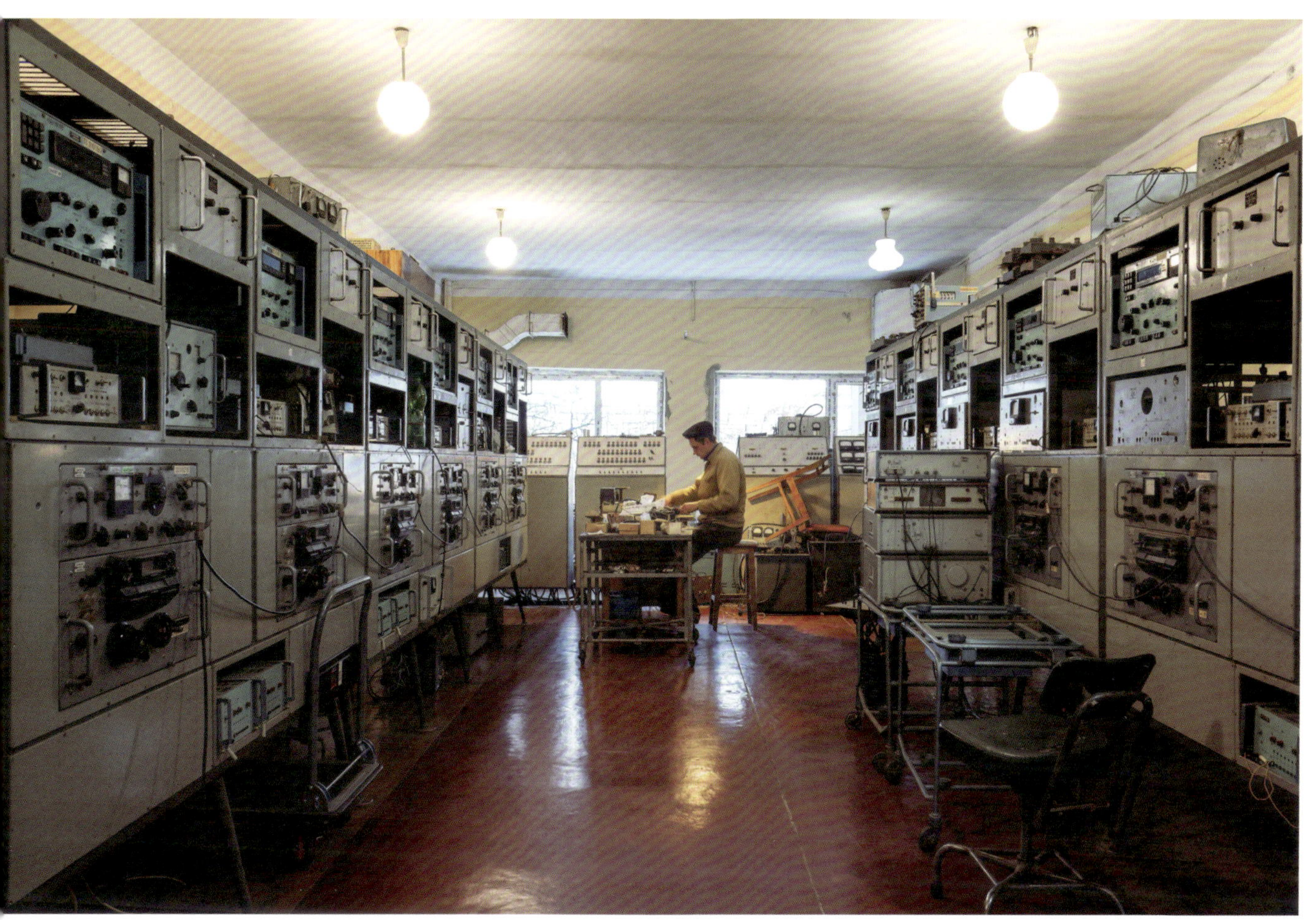

The tube receivers' room, where data from the UTR-2 was collected. This photograph was taken a few weeks before the war.

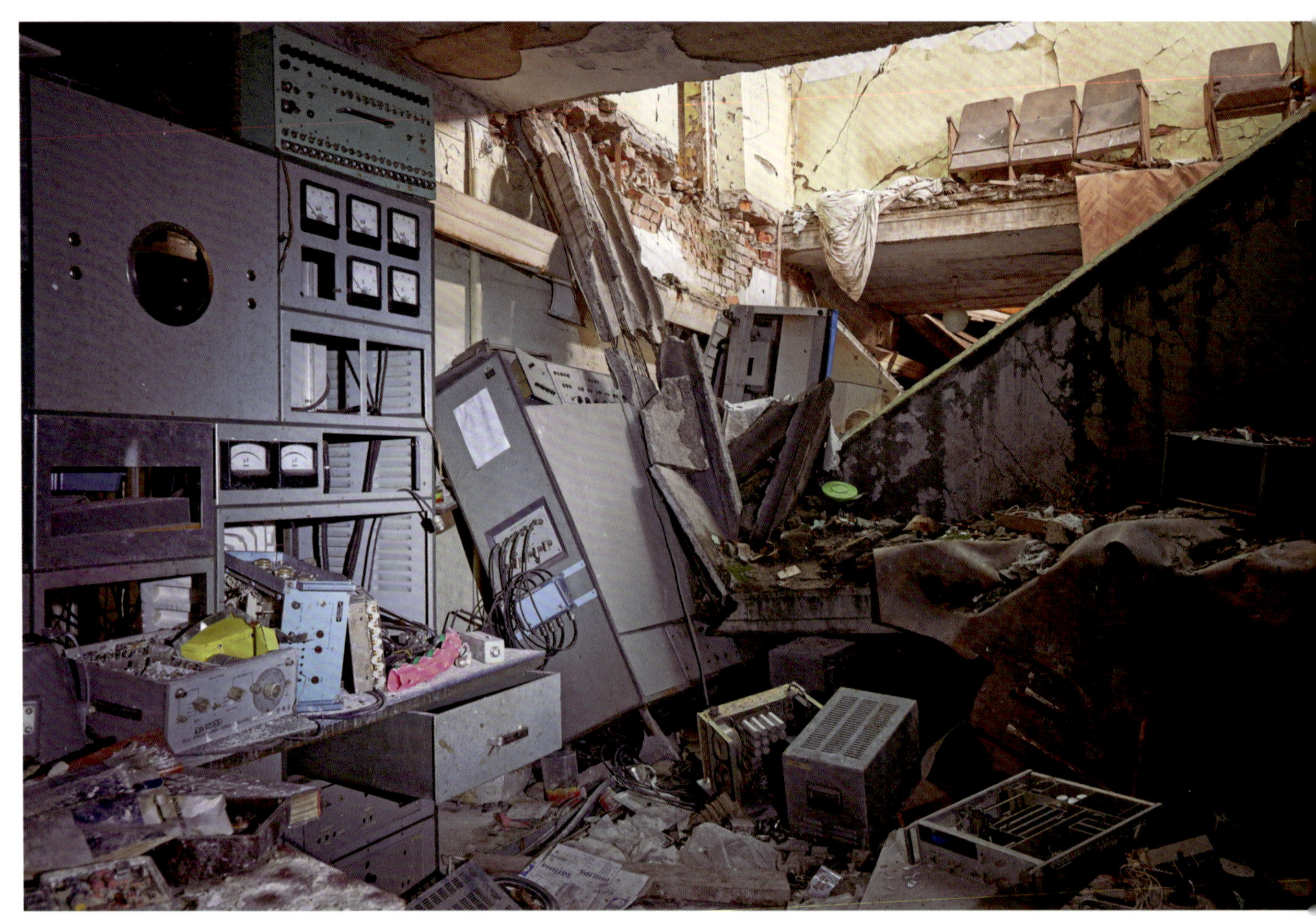

After coming under artillery fire, the building was hit and the monitoring equipment destroyed by falling concrete blocks.

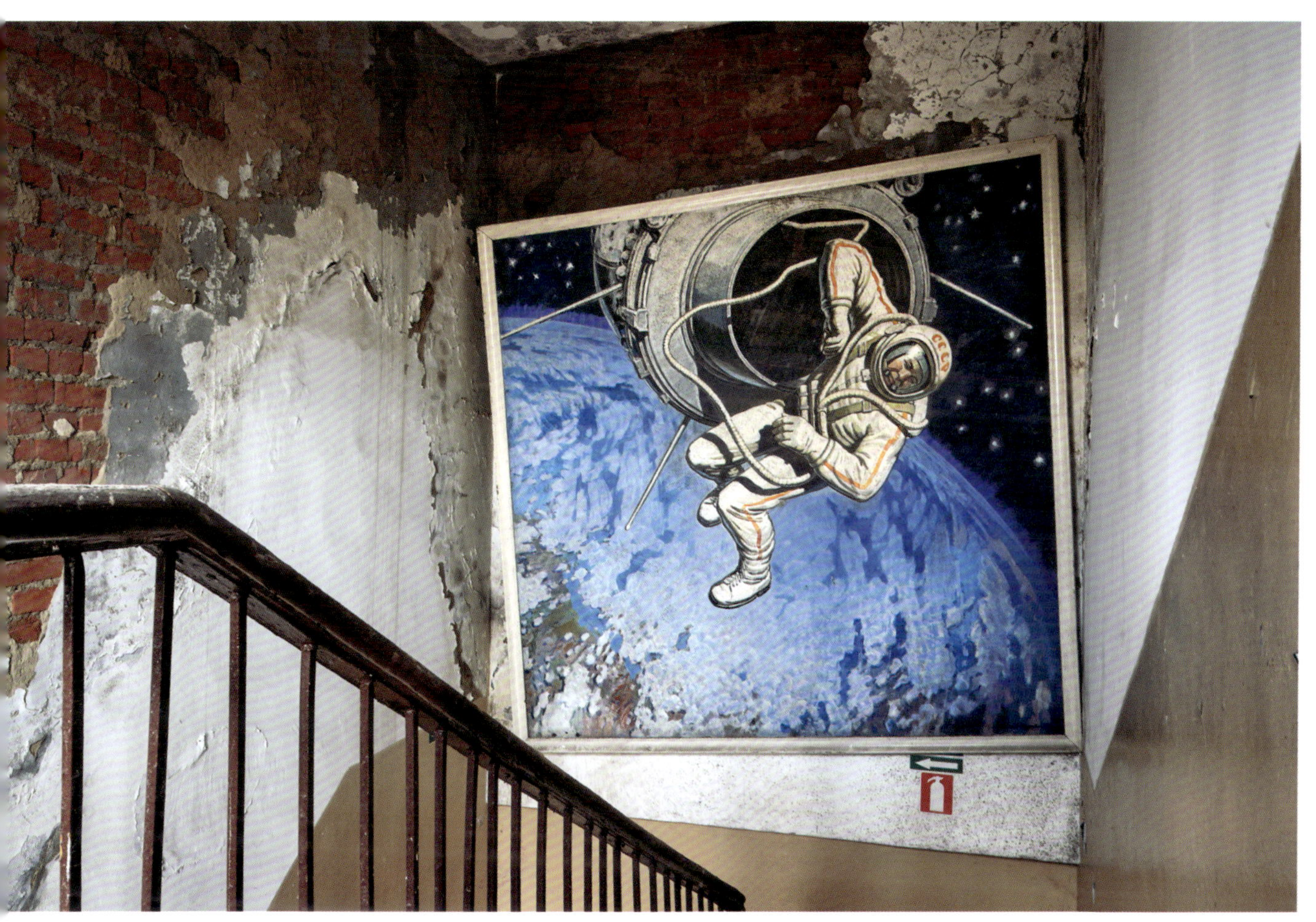

A stairwell in the damaged building. The painting depicts the first spacewalk performed in 1965 by twice Hero of the Soviet Union, cosmonaut Alexei Leonov (1934–2019).

KHARKIV INSTITUTE OF PHYSICS AND TECHNOLOGY

National Academy of Sciences of Ukraine

Kharkiv, UKRAINE

Founded in 1928 on the initiative of Abram Ioffe (1880–1960), the Ukrainian Institute of Physics and Technology (UFTI, as it was first known), with its team of enthusiastic young scientists and state-of-the-art equipment, soon became one of the USSR's leading centres for physics.

In 1932, the cryogenic laboratory led by Lev Shubnikov (1901–1937) was the first in the USSR to achieve helium liquefaction, which major technological breakthrough facilitated further research, culminating in the discovery of type II superconductivity (named the Shubnikov phase) in 1936.

In April 1932, John Cockcroft (1897–1967) and Ernest Walton (1903–1995) became the first to split the atomic nucleus by bombarding lithium atoms with high-energy protons, a feat for which they shared the 1951 Nobel Prize. A group of scientists at the Kharkiv Institute, led by Kyrylo Synelnykov (1901–1966), was able to replicate this experiment just six months later, becoming the first to do so in the USSR. The state-controlled newspaper *Pravda* proclaimed this to be 'The Greatest Achievement of Soviet Scientists.' The 'Snipers of the Atomic Nucleus', as Synelnykov's team were called by the press, laid the foundations of nuclear physics in the Soviet Union. At the same time, the brilliant theorist Lev Landau (1908–1968), later awarded the Nobel Prize in 1962, founded an internationally acclaimed school of theoretical physics in Kharkiv.

Thanks to these significant achievements, Kharkiv became an important hub for physics, attracting eminent Western pioneers such as Niels Bohr, Paul Dirac, Jean Perrin and others, and fostering an informal global society of scientists. This situation ended abruptly with Stalin's purges. In 1937, the NKVD arrested sixteen physicists, eight of whom were put to death, among them 36-year-old Shubnikov. Landau fled Kharkiv to escape persecution, as foreign scientists were forced to leave the USSR and a number of German colleagues were handed over to the Gestapo.

After World War II, the Communist Party intensified research towards military applications, resulting in the work of the institute being highly classified. This included a large-scale nuclear weapons programme to compete with America, making research into physics a state priority. The Kharkiv Institute, designated Laboratory No. 1, played a crucial role in the development of the first Soviet atomic bomb. Thirteen departments equipped with particle accelerators conducted studies of nuclear reactions, and the data collected was forwarded to Laboratory No. 2 in Moscow, later known as the Kurchatov Institute of Atomic Energy. The USSR tested its first atom bomb in 1949 and its first thermonuclear device in 1953.

Today, located in the heart of Kharkiv, this unique scientific complex continues to conduct research into solid-state physics. Recognising its historical significance, researchers hope to convert a part of the complex into a public museum.

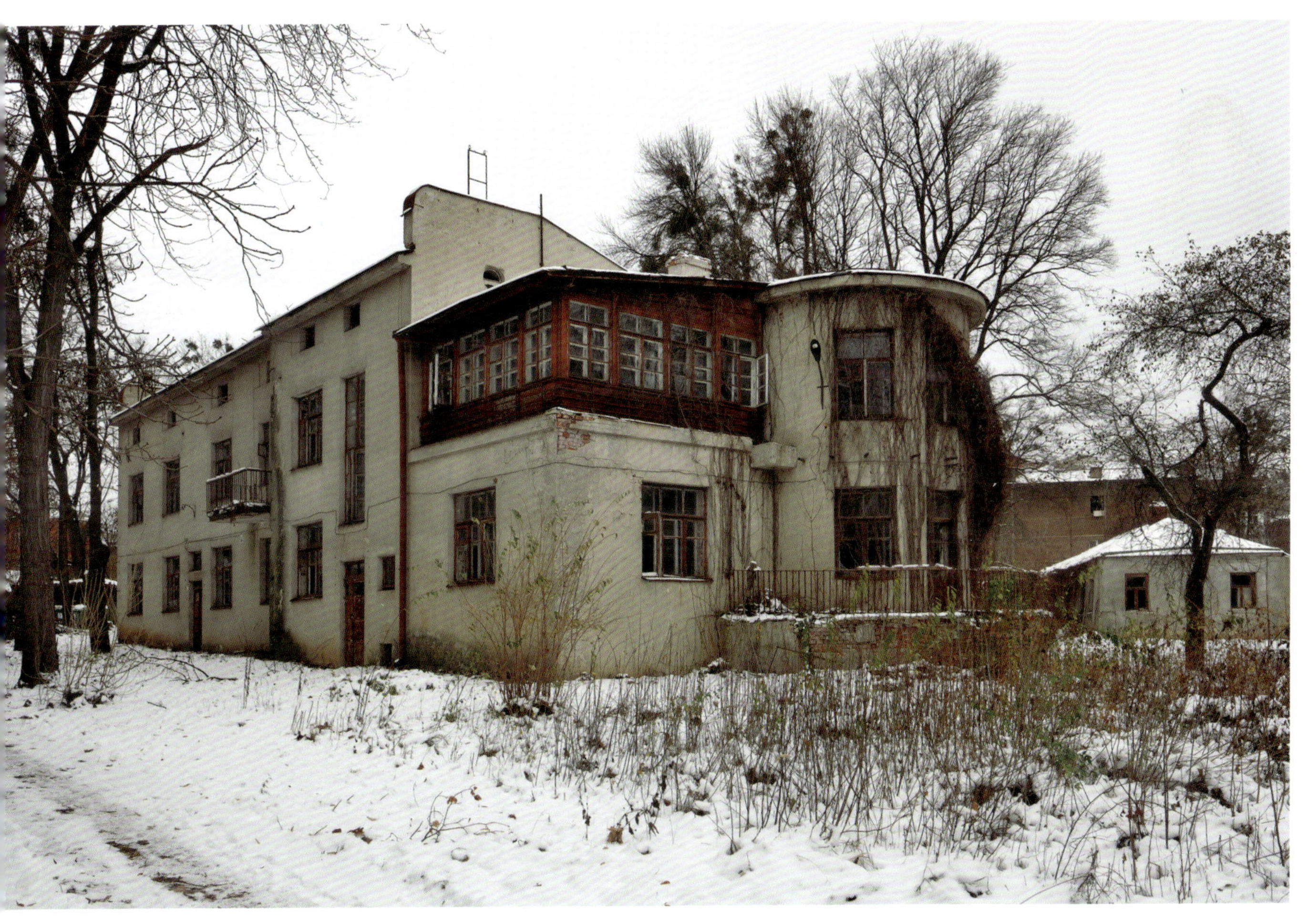

The Theoretical Building was built in the 1930s in the Constructivist architectural style. The fifth director of the institute, Kyrylo Synelnykov (1901–1966), lived here together with his family. The building was used to accommodate foreign scientists and specialists, visiting to attend international conferences.

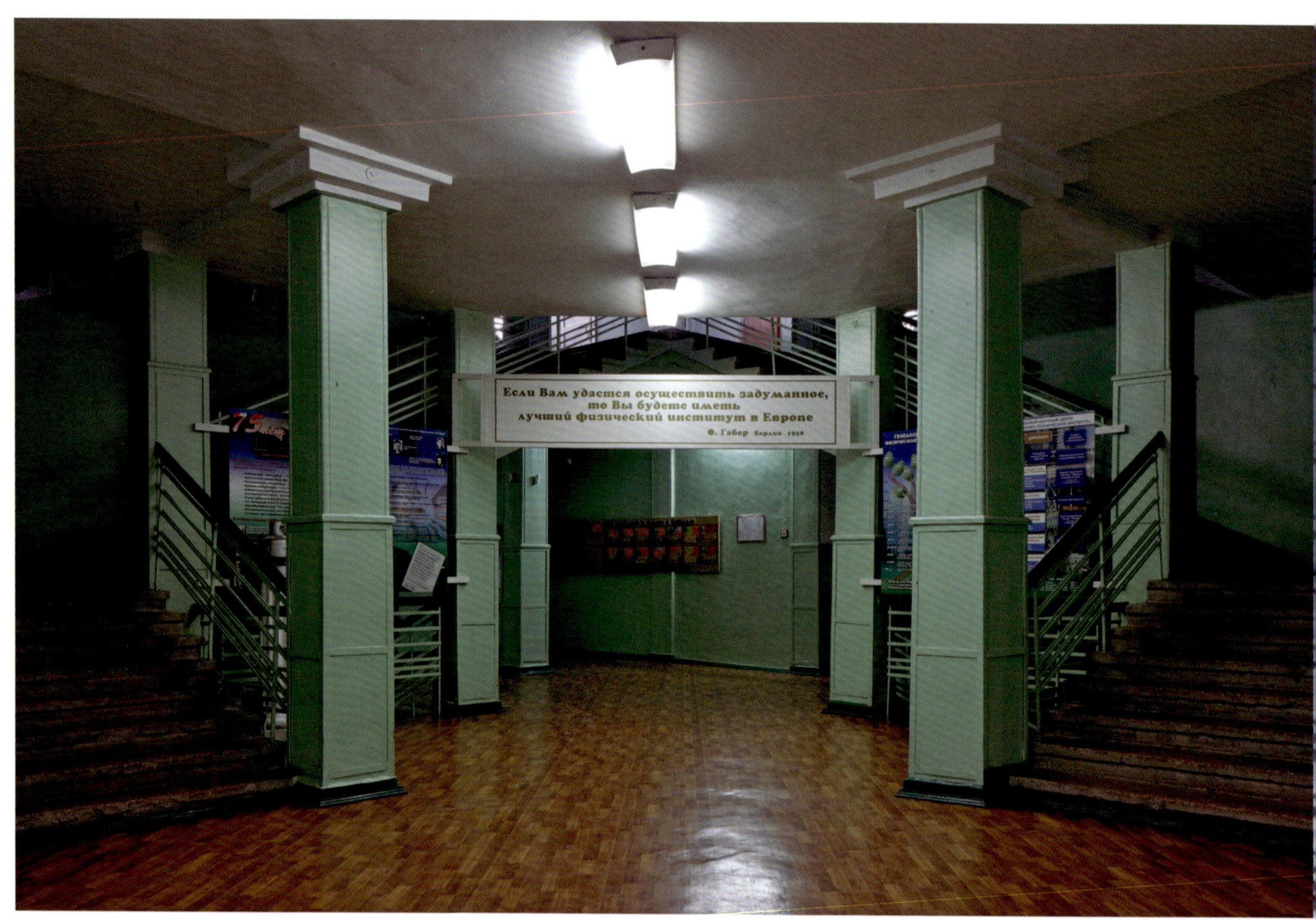

The entrance to the main building. The steel columns were salvaged from the Russian battleship *Empress Maria*, which sunk in Sebastopol Bay in 1916 and was refloated in 1928. A quote from Fritz Haber (1868–1934), the 1918 Nobel Prize winner for chemistry, hangs in the centre of the hall: 'If you succeed in your plans, you will have the best physics institute in Europe'.

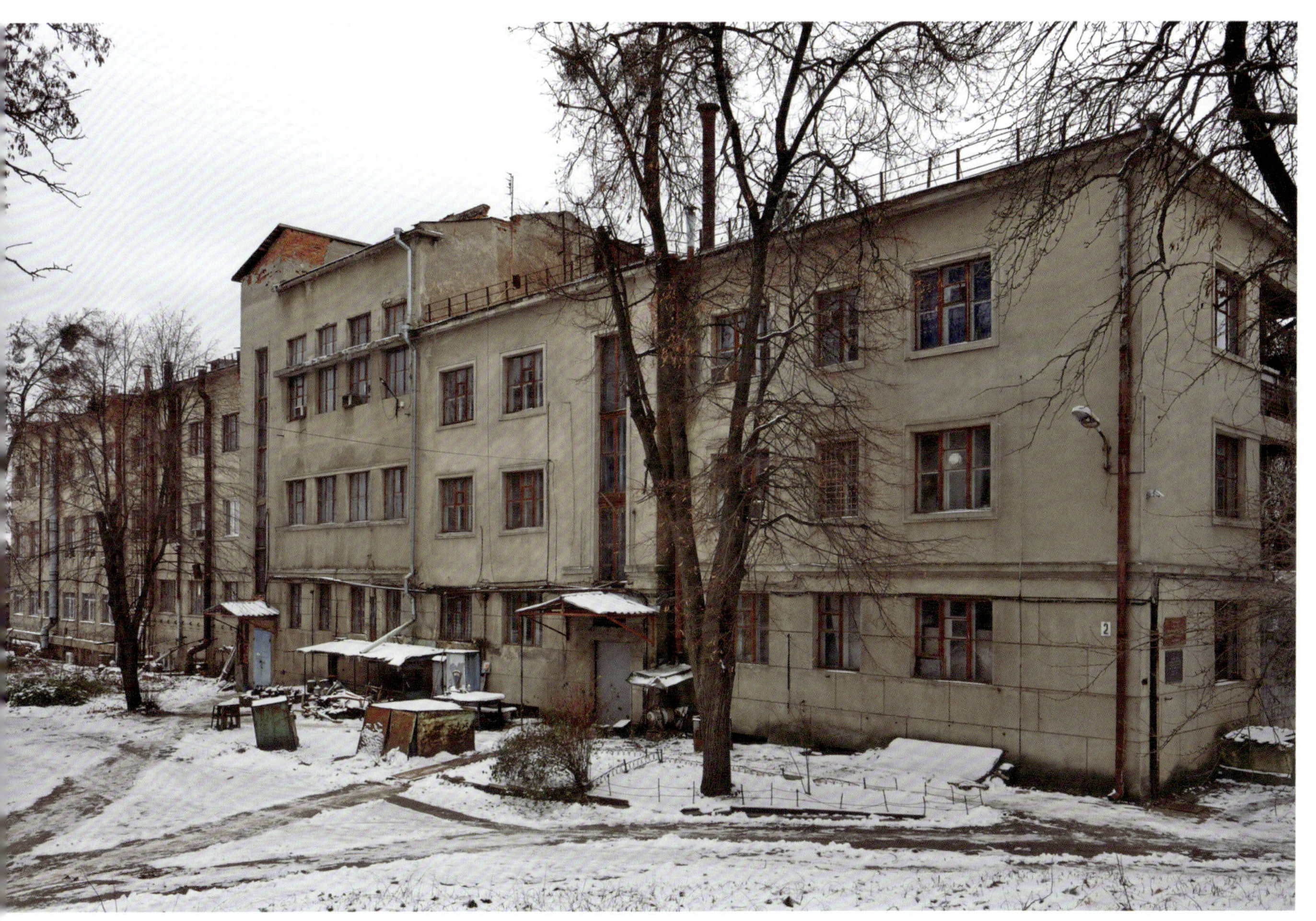

This building housed the institute's Laboratory No. 1 from 1946 until 1960.

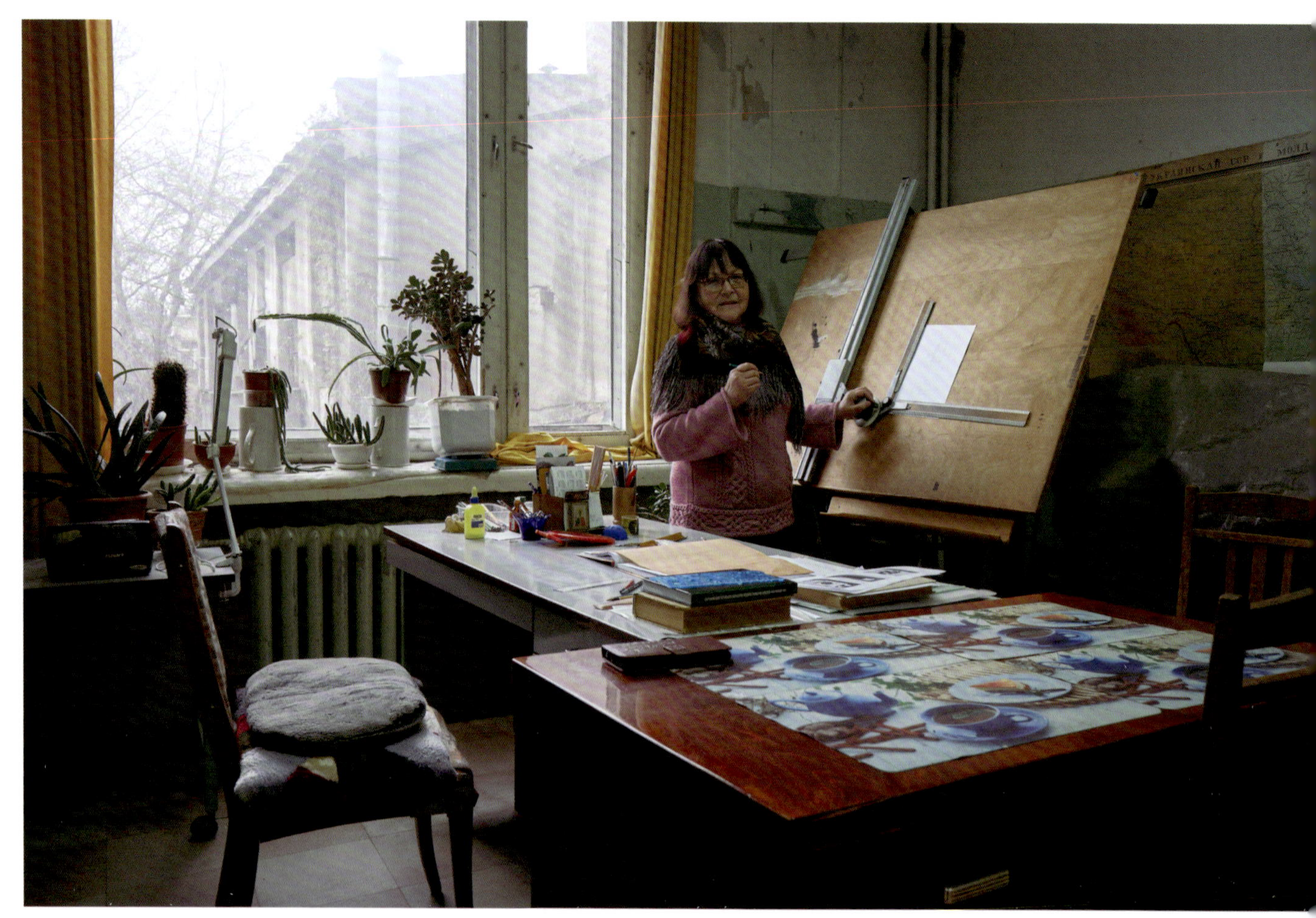

Engineer Olena Roskoshna at work in her office. The central heating was out of service due to bomb damage.

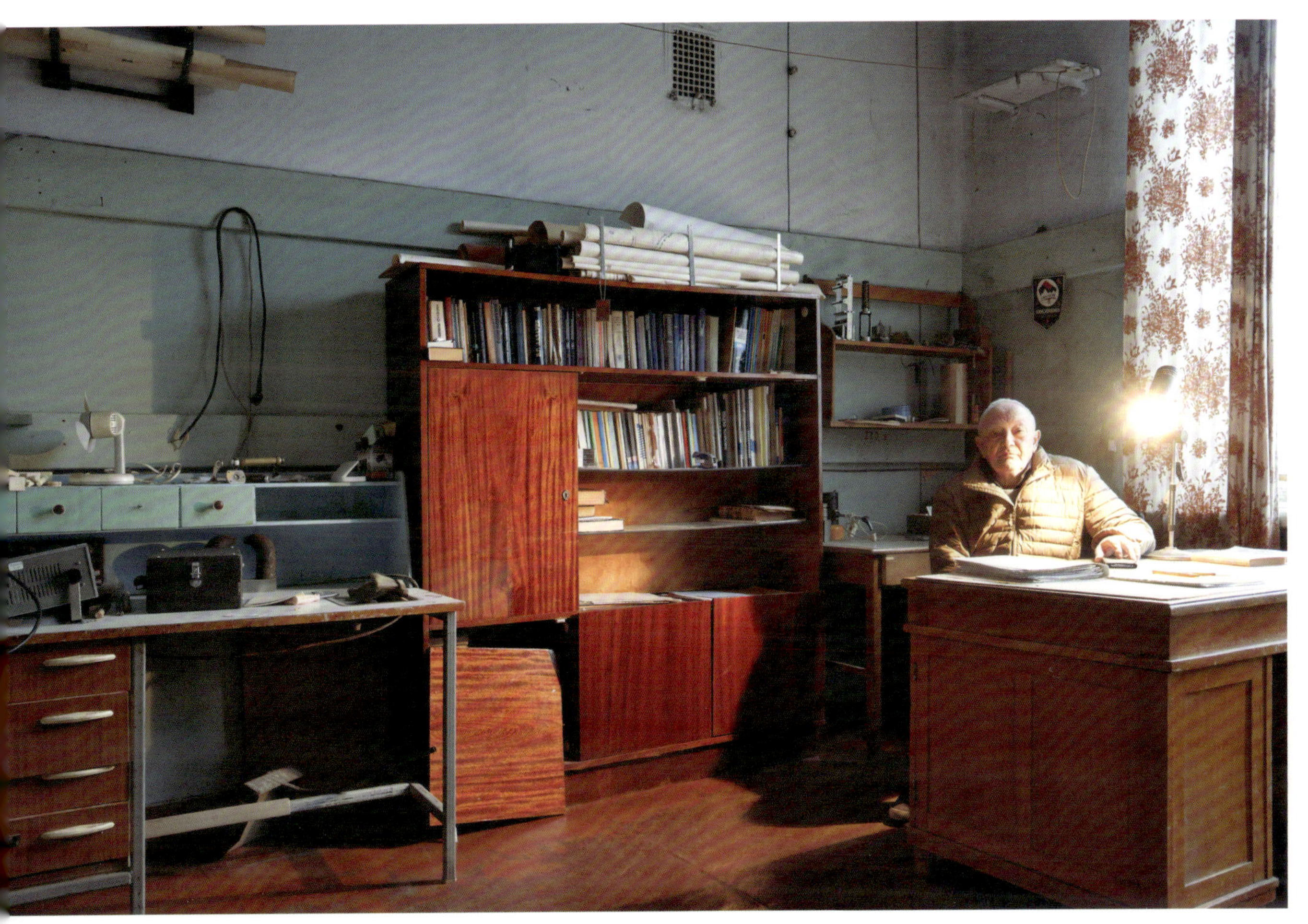

Mykola Tchernyak is a researcher specialising in ferromagnetic materials.

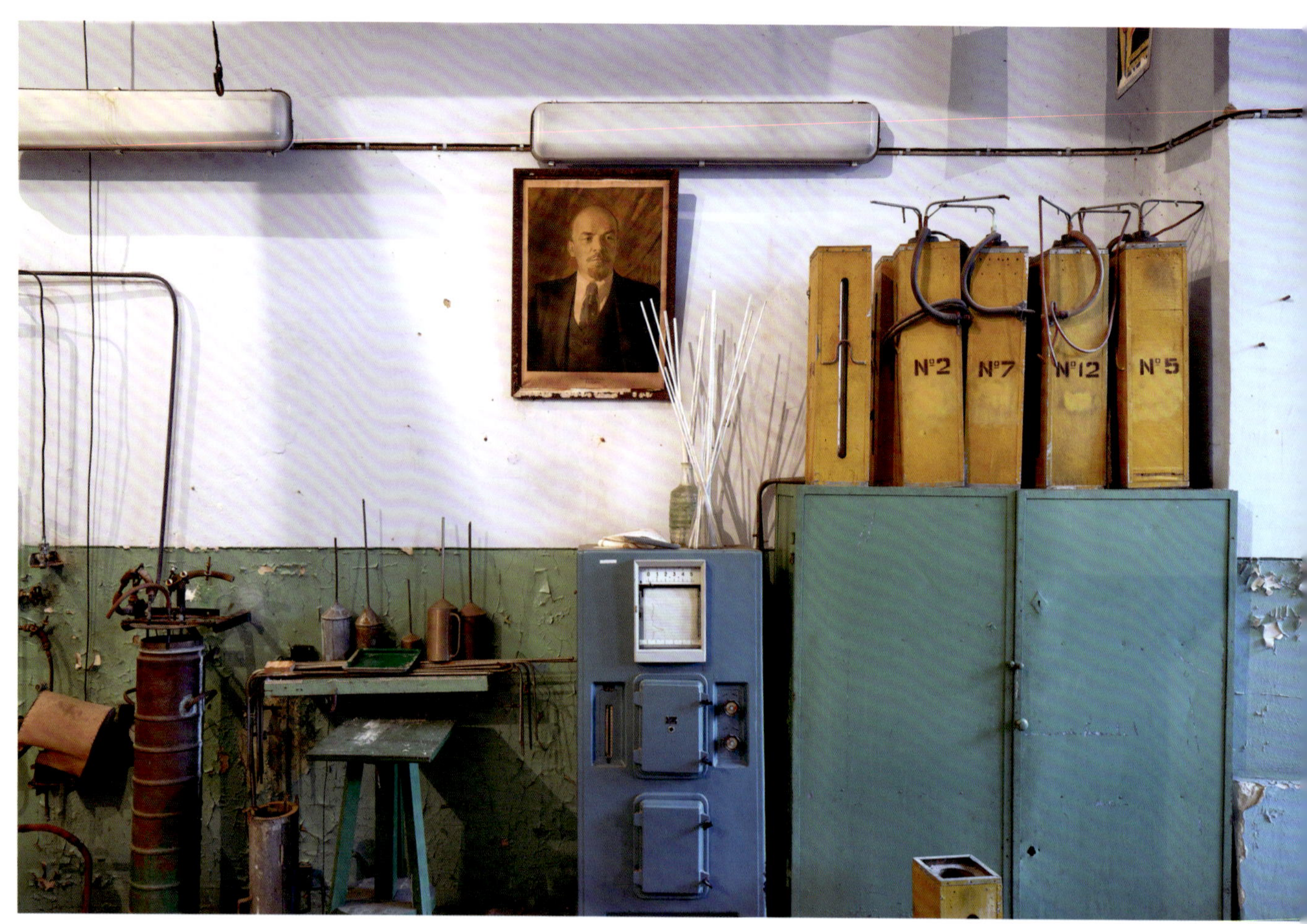

The cryogenic laboratory is being preserved with the intention of eventually converting it into a museum. This requires that the portrait of Lenin (1870–1924), founder of the Soviet state, remains hanging on the wall – a rare situation in Ukraine, after the passing of the decommunisation laws of 2015. The yellow containers were used to store liquid helium.

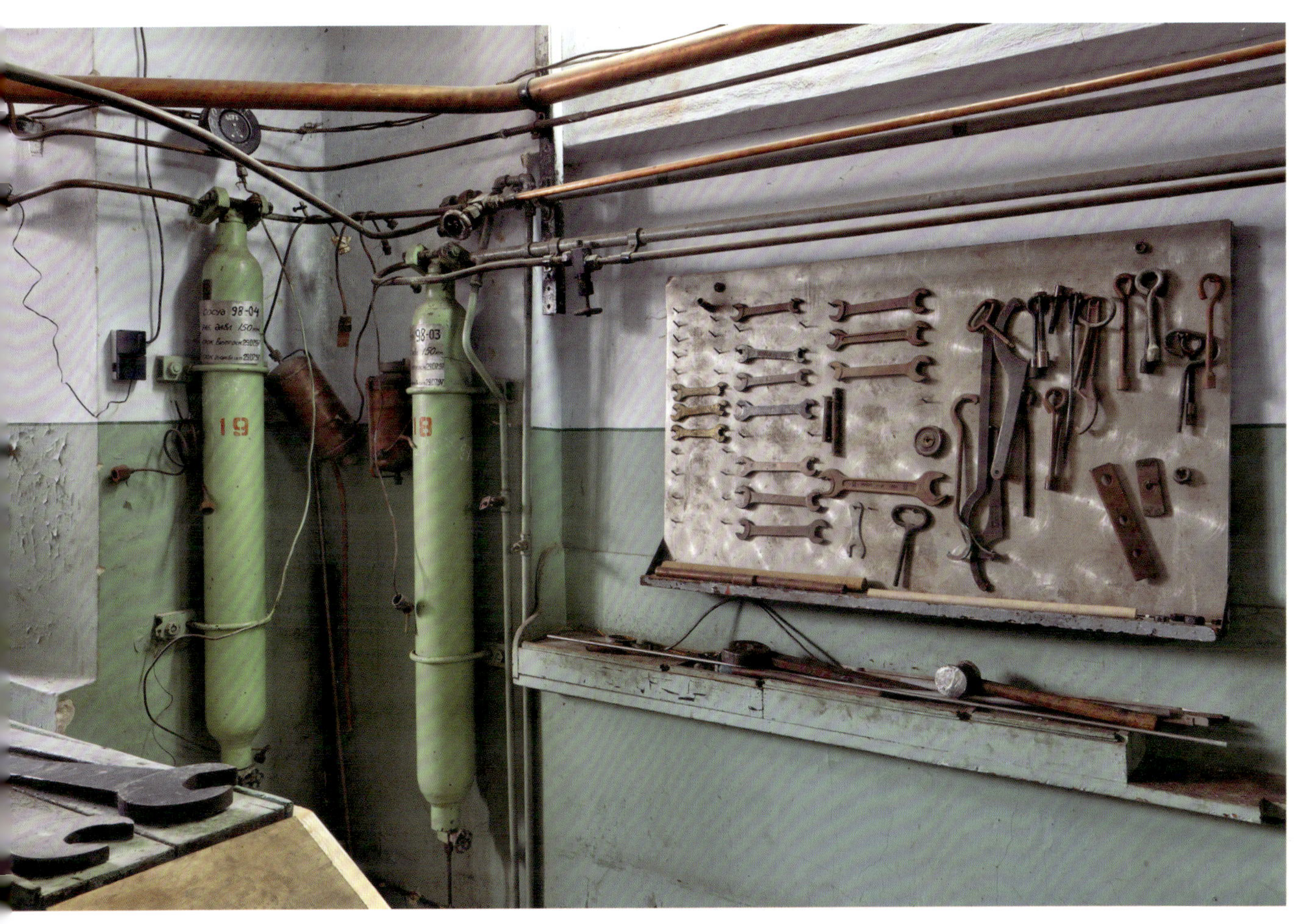

Tools hanging in the cryogenic laboratory. These are used to maintain a Dutch compressor from the 1930s, which is still in working order.

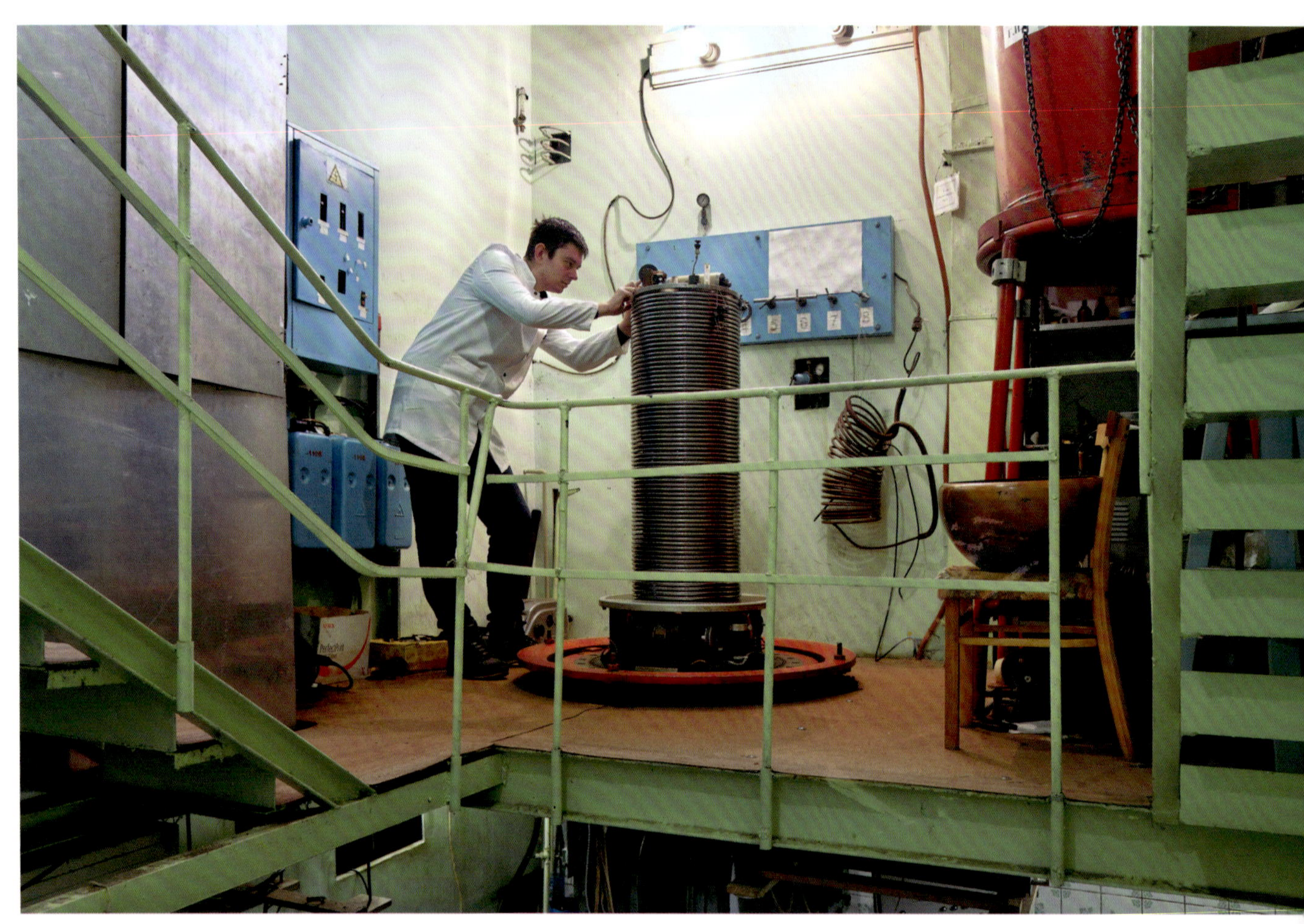

Vladyslav Karnach, junior researcher, works on the column of the ESU-2 particle accelerator.
Right: The cryogenic laboratory.

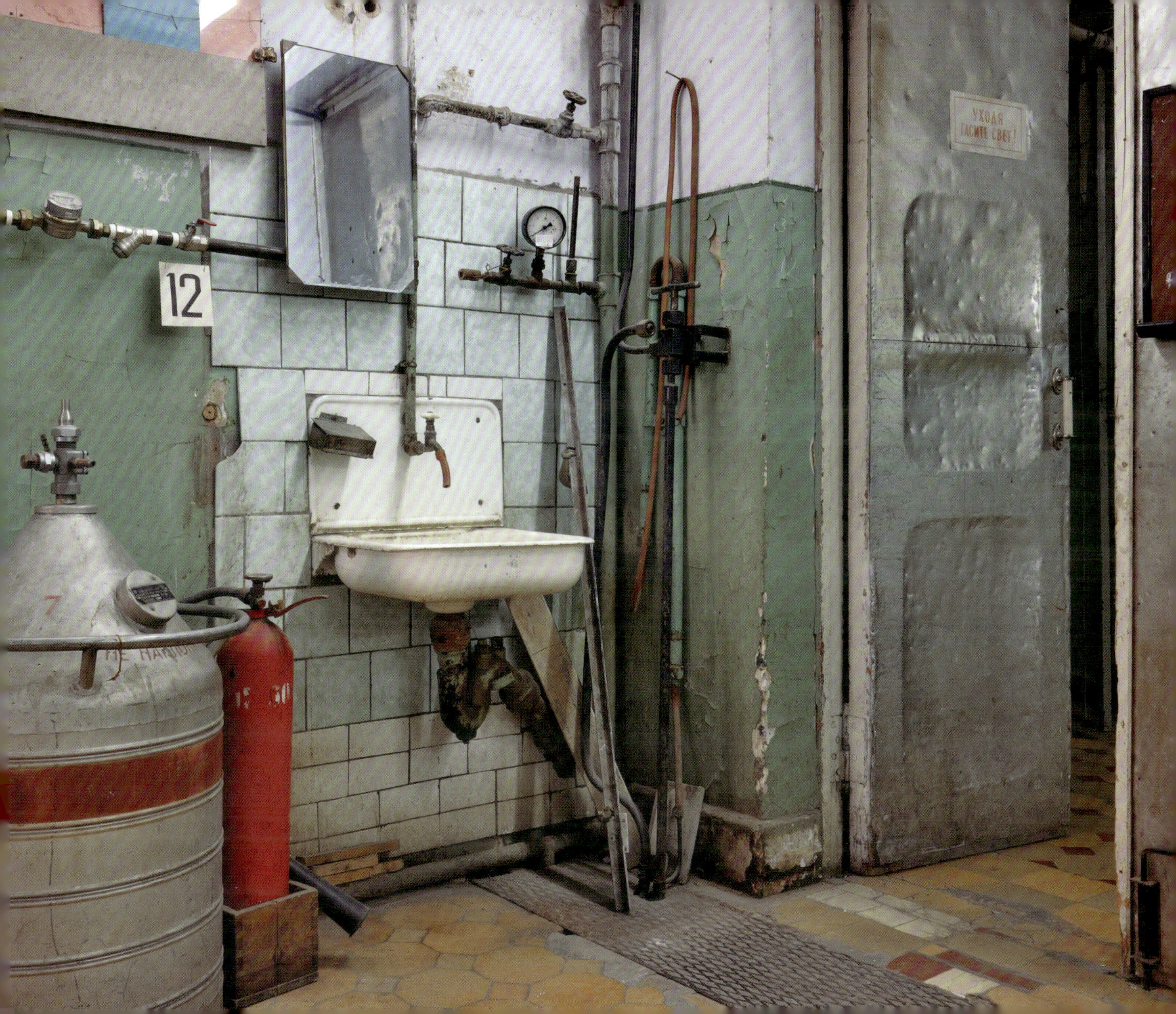
12
7
УХОДЯ
ГАСИТЕ СВЕТ!

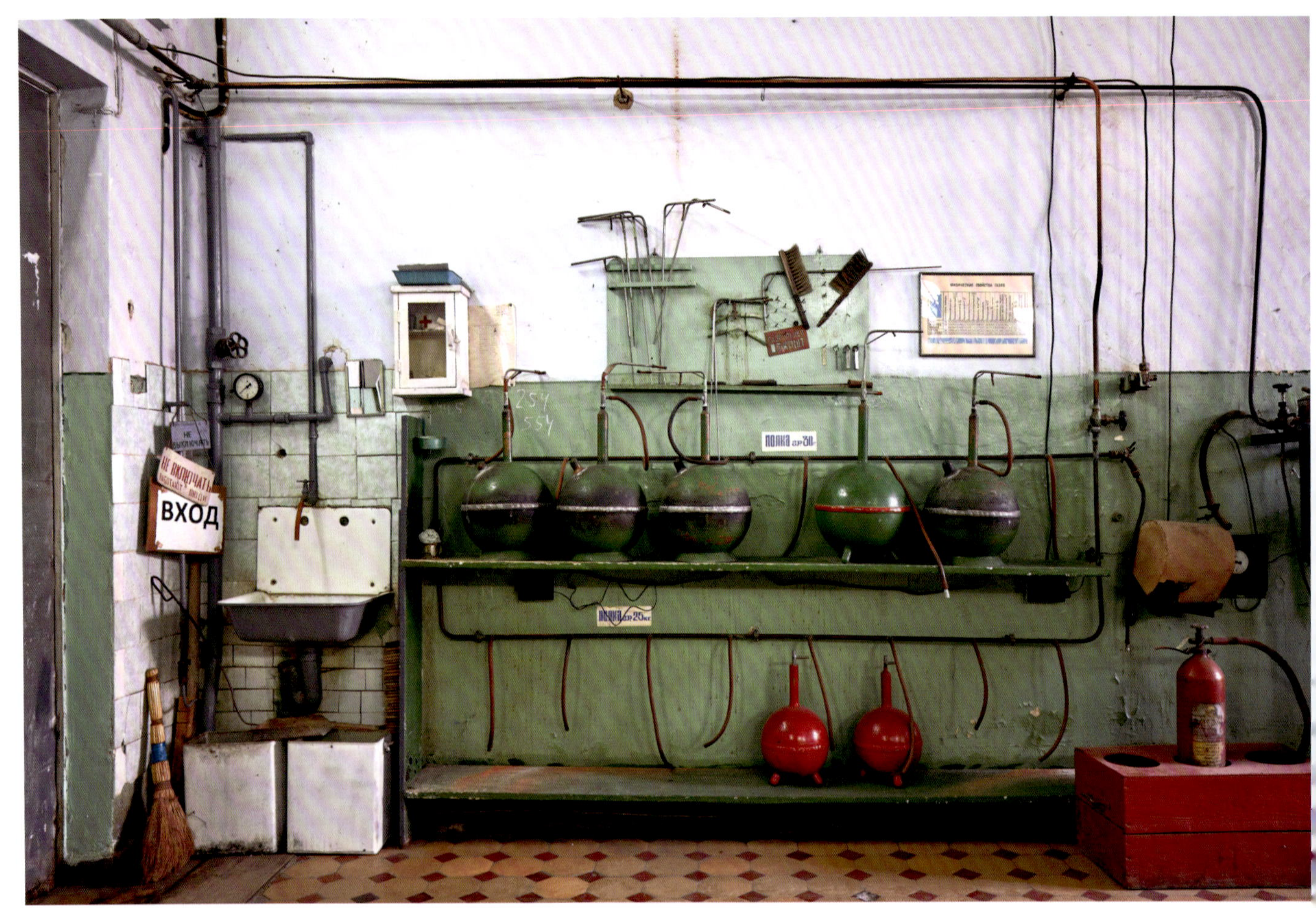

The cryogenic laboratory. The spherical containers were used for the storage of liquid hydrogen.

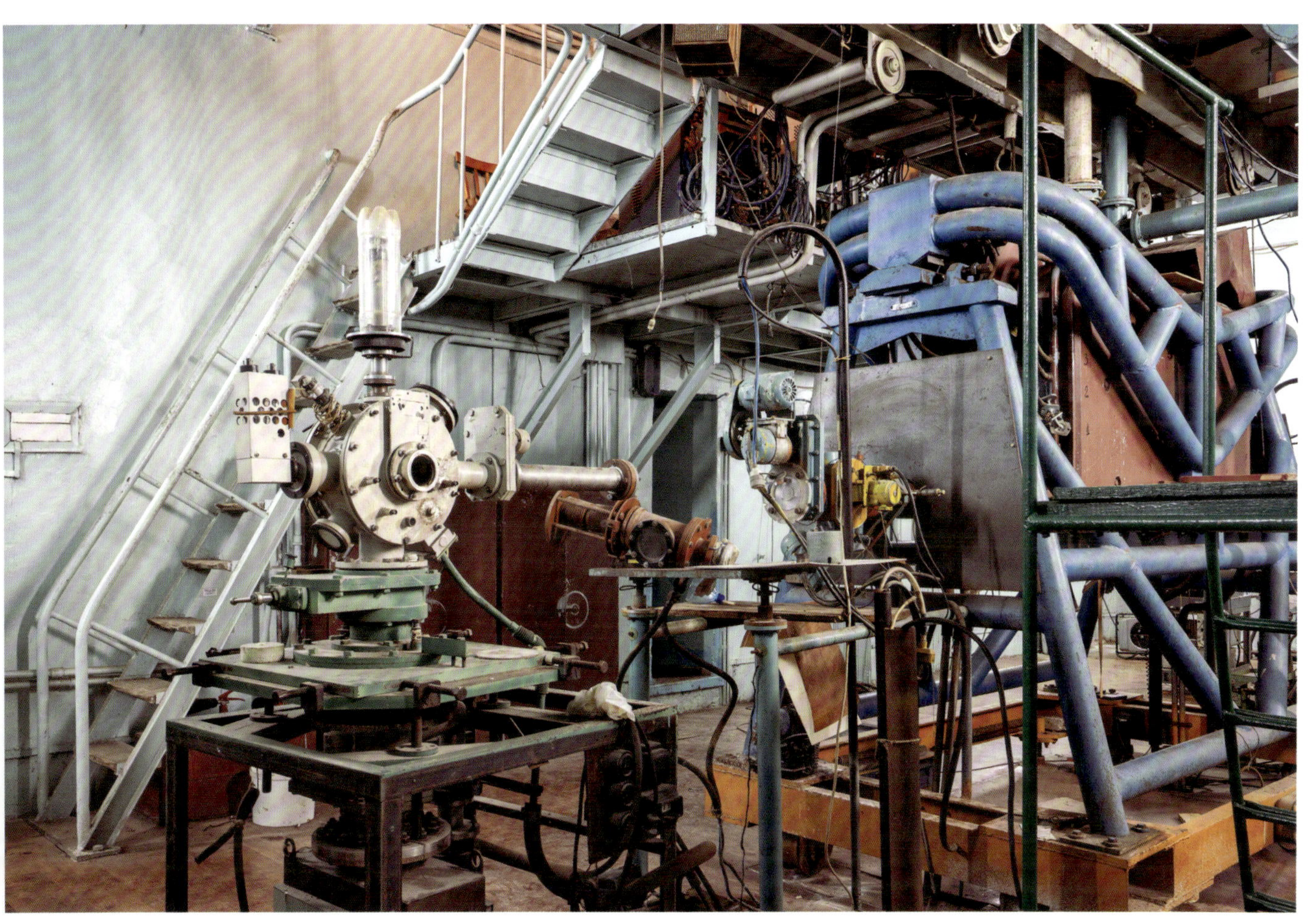

Part of the ESU-5 electrostatic proton accelerator, created by Kyrylo Synelnykov (1901–1966) and Anton Walter (1905–1965) in 1950. This device enabled them to conduct fundamental studies in nuclear physics, as well as exploring the practical applications of the physical, chemical and biological modification of materials using accelerated charged particles.

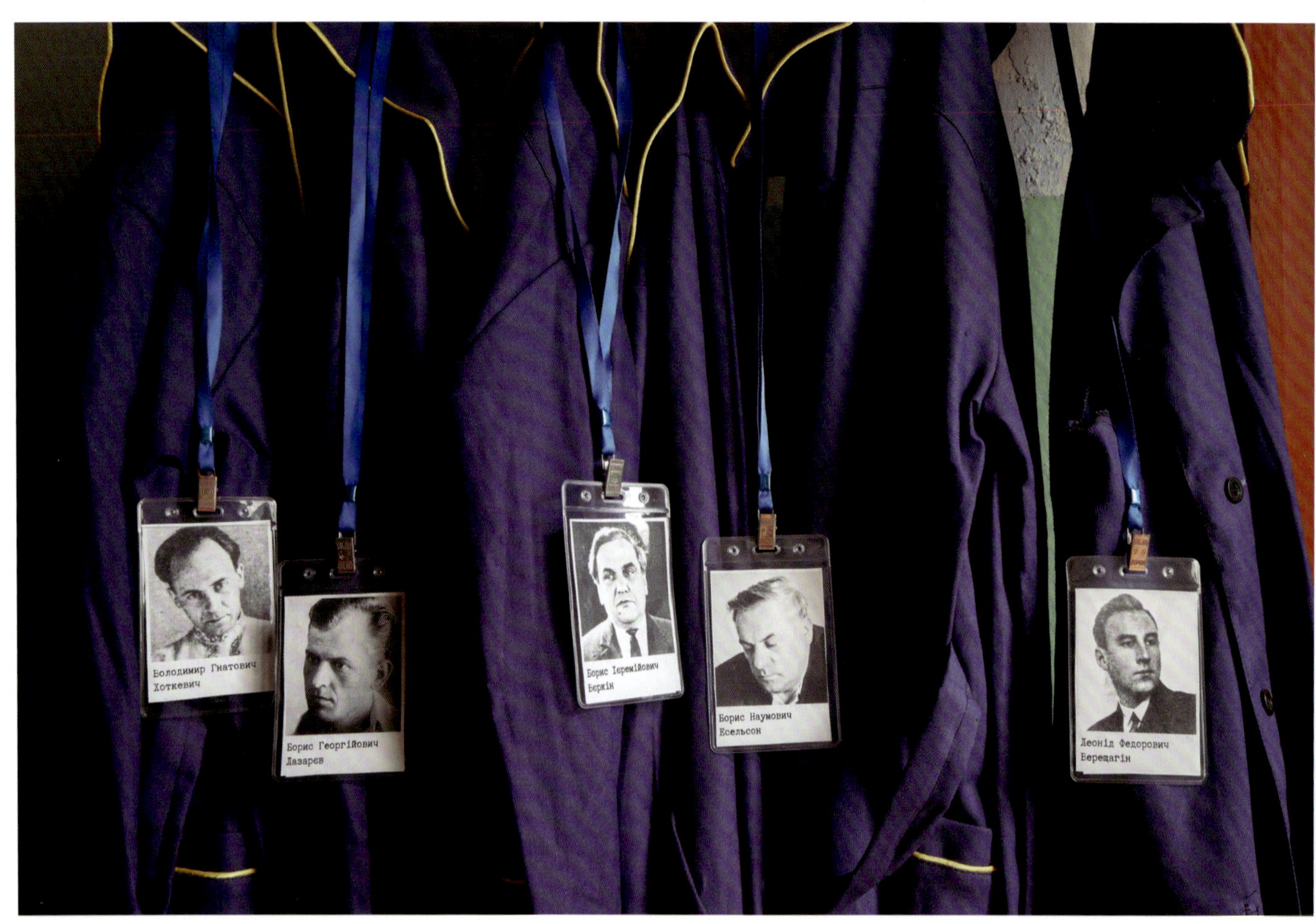

Photographic portraits of some of Kharkiv's leading scientists feature on the reverse of employee entrance passes: (from left to right) Volodymyr Khotkevych (1913–1982); Borys Lazarev (1906–2001); Borys Verkin (1919–1990); Borys Eselson (1917–1980) and Leonid Vereshchagin (1909–1977).

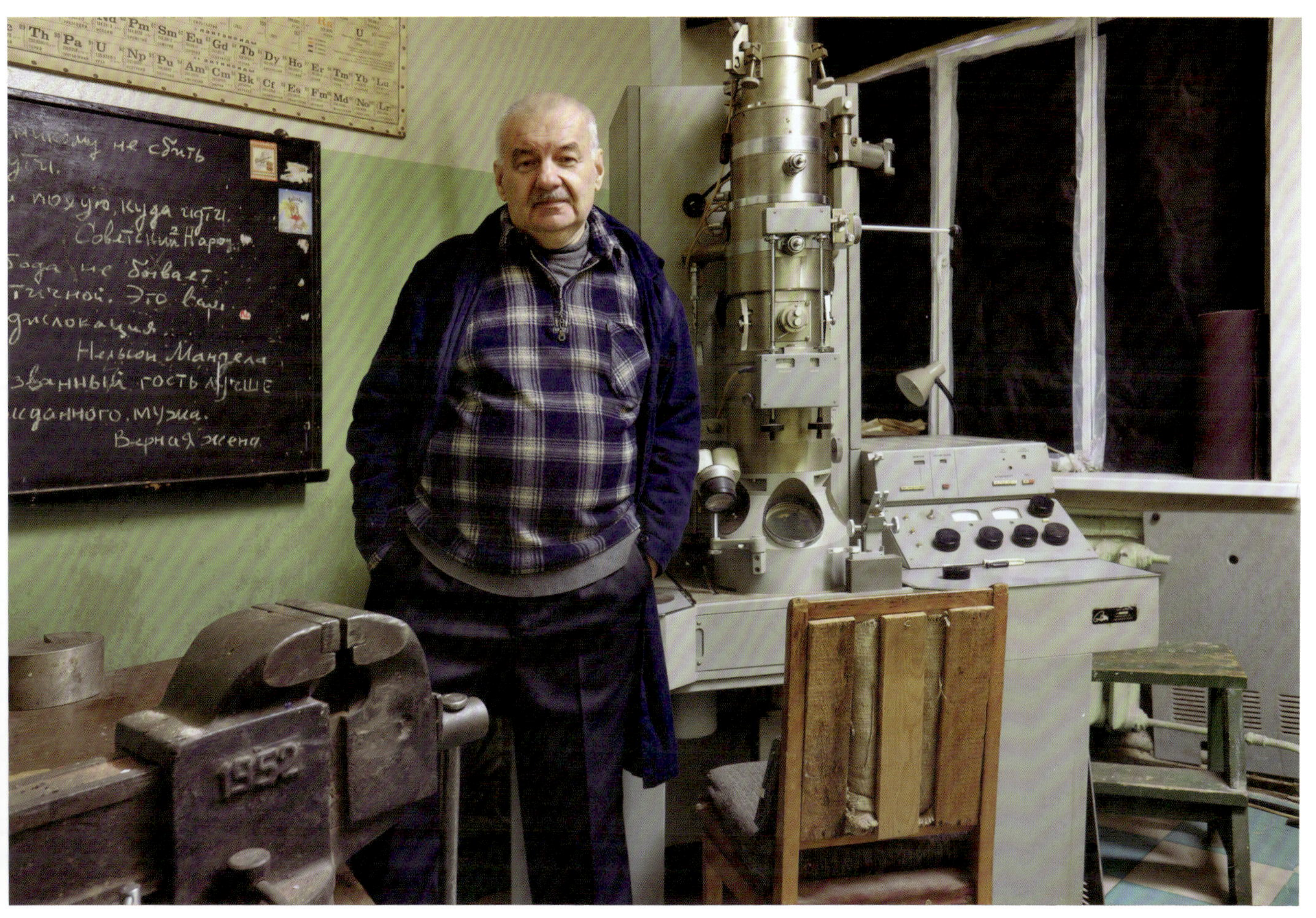

Metals specialist Alexander Mats stands next to a Soviet-era EMV-100 electron microscope, manufactured in Sumy, Ukraine.

INSTITUTE OF PLASMA PHYSICS

National Academy of Sciences of Ukraine

Kharkiv, UKRAINE

In the 1950s, thermonuclear research was launched in earnest in the Soviet Union, United States and Great Britain. Utilising their expertise in nuclear physics, a group of scientists in Kharkiv, led by Kyrylo Synelnykov (1901–1966), began a pioneering research programme aimed at controlling thermonuclear fusion – one of the most ambitious scientific challenges of the era.

Nuclear fusion involves combining light atomic nuclei to make a heavier nucleus, releasing huge amounts of energy. This reaction occurs in plasma, a hot gas of ionised particles also known as the fourth state of matter. To achieve this, matter must be heated to hundreds of millions of degrees, while being kept isolated from the environment within a powerful magnetic field. Ultimately, this could provide an unlimited, sustainable and clean energy source.

In the course of his work Synelnykov organised an intensive training regimen for young researchers in plasma physics. Veteran scientist Volodymyr Tolok (1926–2012), then a student at Kharkiv University, recalled the strict security surrounding the programme: theories were only permitted to be discussed exclusively with Synelnykov, while lecture notes were written in dedicated exercise books with numbered pages, which were then laced shut and sealed with wax.

In 1969, a new site for the Kharkiv Institute of Physics and Technology was built, devoted to theoretical physics, high-energy physics, plasma electronics, plasma physics, nuclear physics, solid-state physics and new acceleration methods. By the end of the 1980s, this major scientific centre employed over 5,000 people. The complex included staff accommodation, a school, a hospital, a clubhouse, a cinema, the Faculty of Physics and a student dormitory. The predominant research undertaken at the site was for defence purposes and consequently highly secret. However, fusion was one of the few areas in which international collaboration was initiated at the highest political level, resulting in the establishment of a USSR-USA Joint Fusion Power Coordination Committee (1973). At the plasma physics division, Tolok and his team constructed a large number of experimental facilities including, in 1970, the world's first torsatron (a type of stellarator which is a device for confining plasma), named Saturn-1. This success led to the development of a series of advanced stellarators named Uragan (Hurricane). Since 2017, the institute has been a member of the EUROfusion consortium (which aims to realise fusion electricity by 2050), contributing data from its stellarators and quasi-stationary plasma accelerators.

Located close to the Russian border, the centre was hit by over 100 projectiles at the onset of the Russian invasion in 2022, which fortunately caused no damage to any of the apparatus. During this very difficult period, many scientists and engineers have left Kharkiv, seeking work at other fusion facilities abroad.

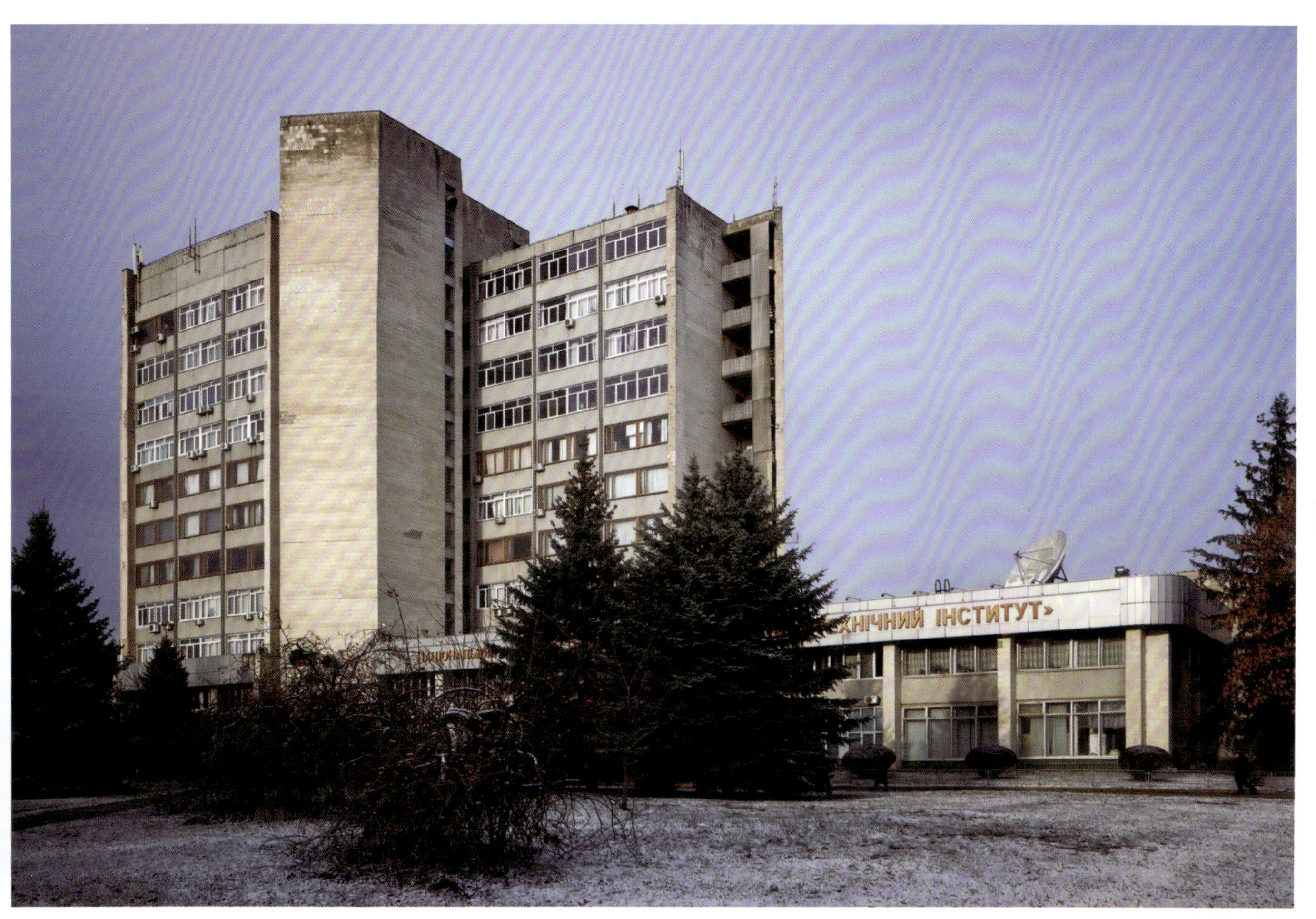

The main building of the National Science Centre Kharkiv Institute of Physics and Technology (NSC KIPT), which includes the Institute of Plasma Physics.

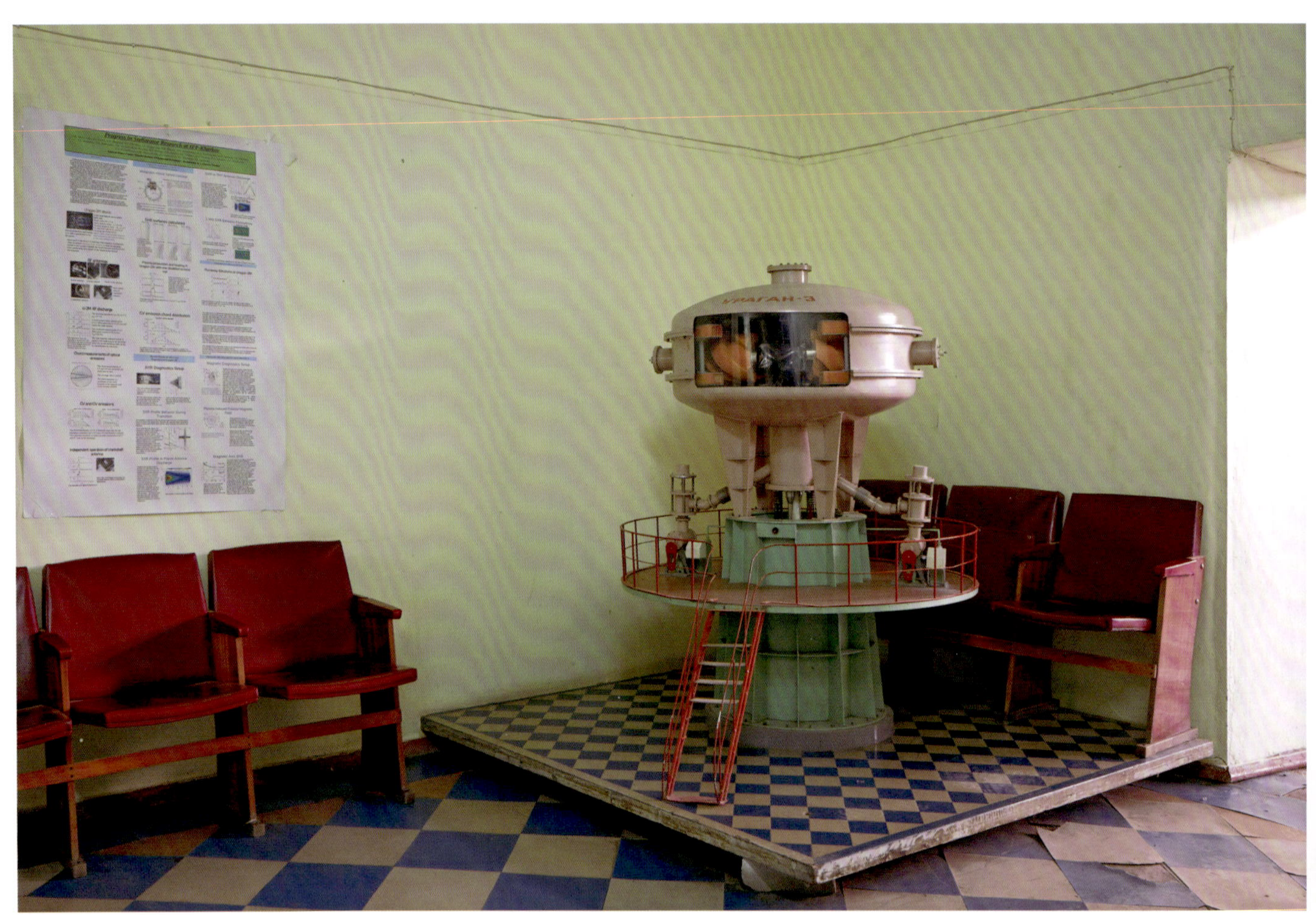

The reception area houses a scale model of the Uragan-3 torsatron stellarator with a cut-away to show its interior workings.

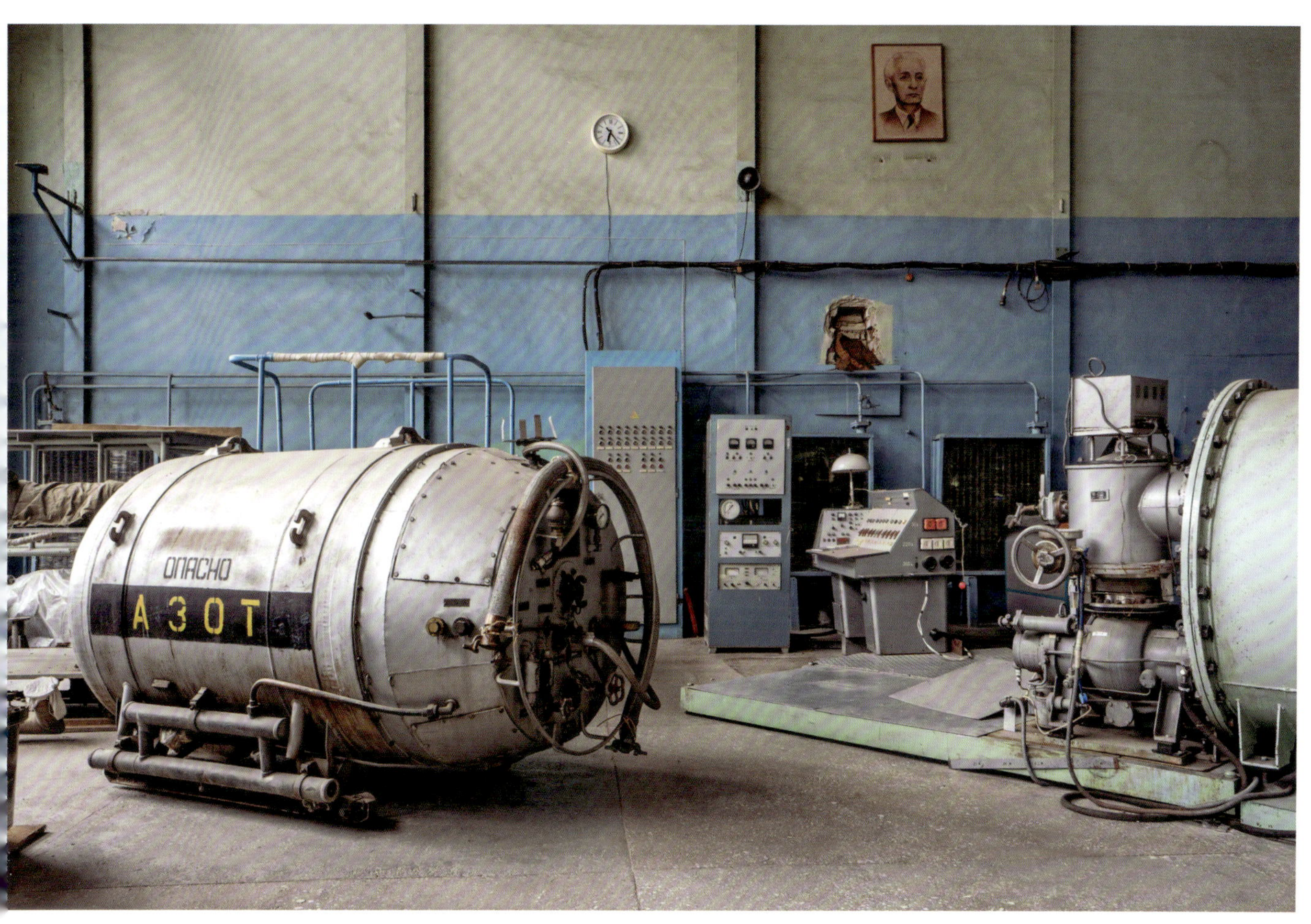

These cryogenic tanks are used by the Uragan-3M stellarator. A portrait of Kyrylo Synelnykov (1901–1966), director of the Kharkiv Institute of Physics and Technology from 1944 to 1965, hangs from the wall.

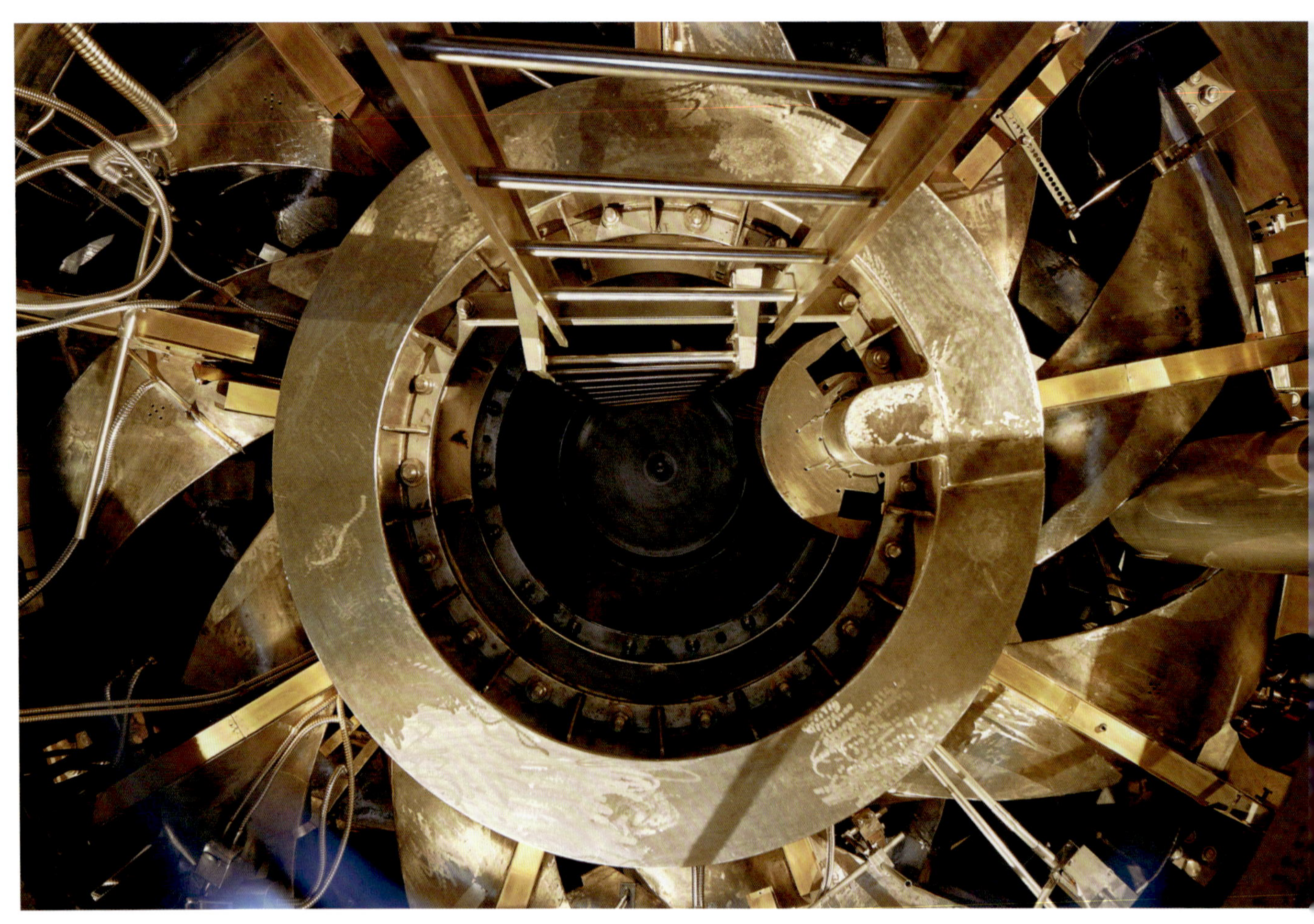

The vacuum chamber of the Uragan-3M has a volume of 70 cubic metres in which the plasma is confined and heated. It also houses the entire magnetic system.

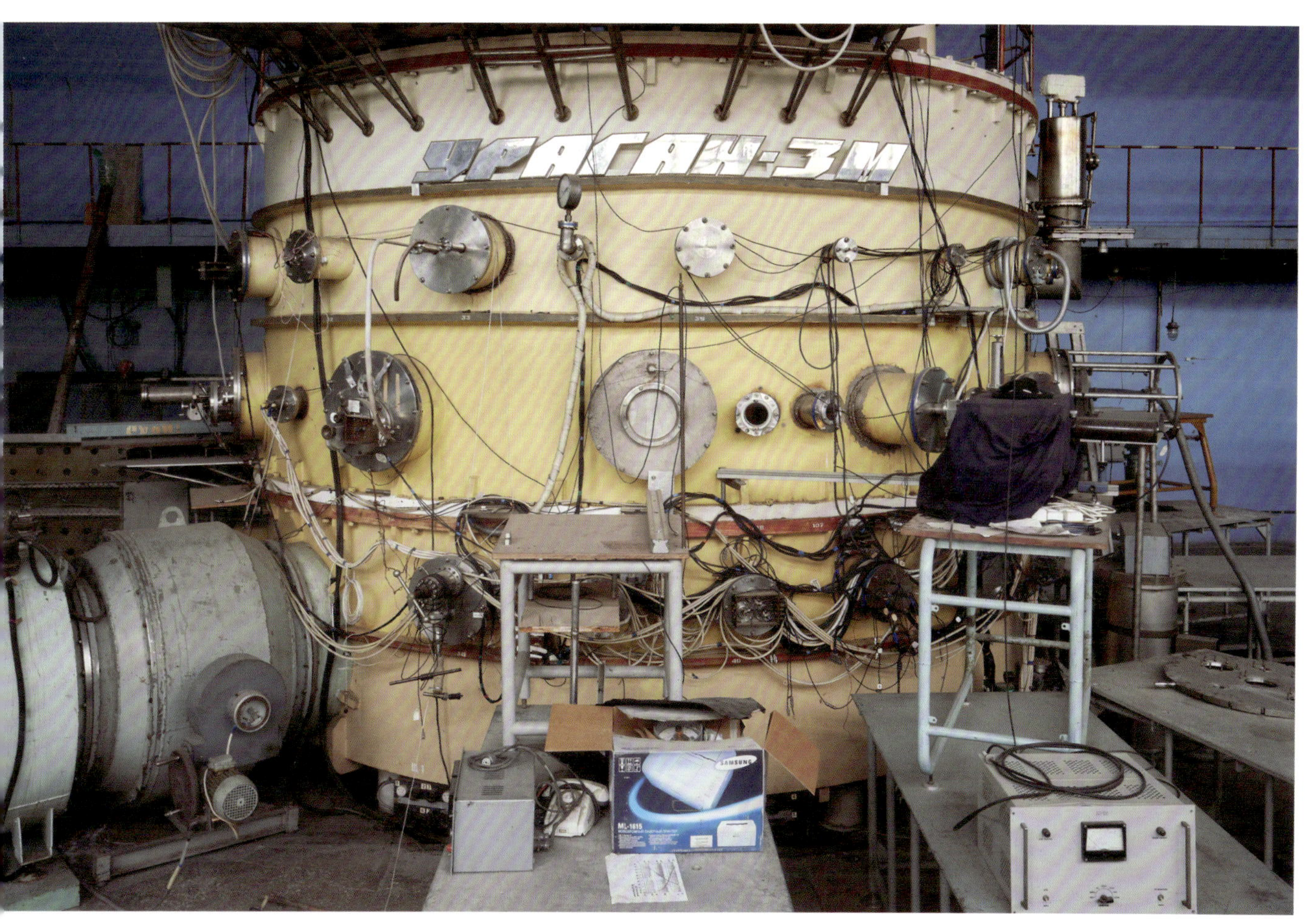

The exterior of the Uragan-3M with its cyrillic metal nameplate. When it began operating in 1982, Uragan-3 was one of the world's largest stellarators. In 1988, with the installation of more advanced helical coils, it was upgraded to the Uragan-3M.

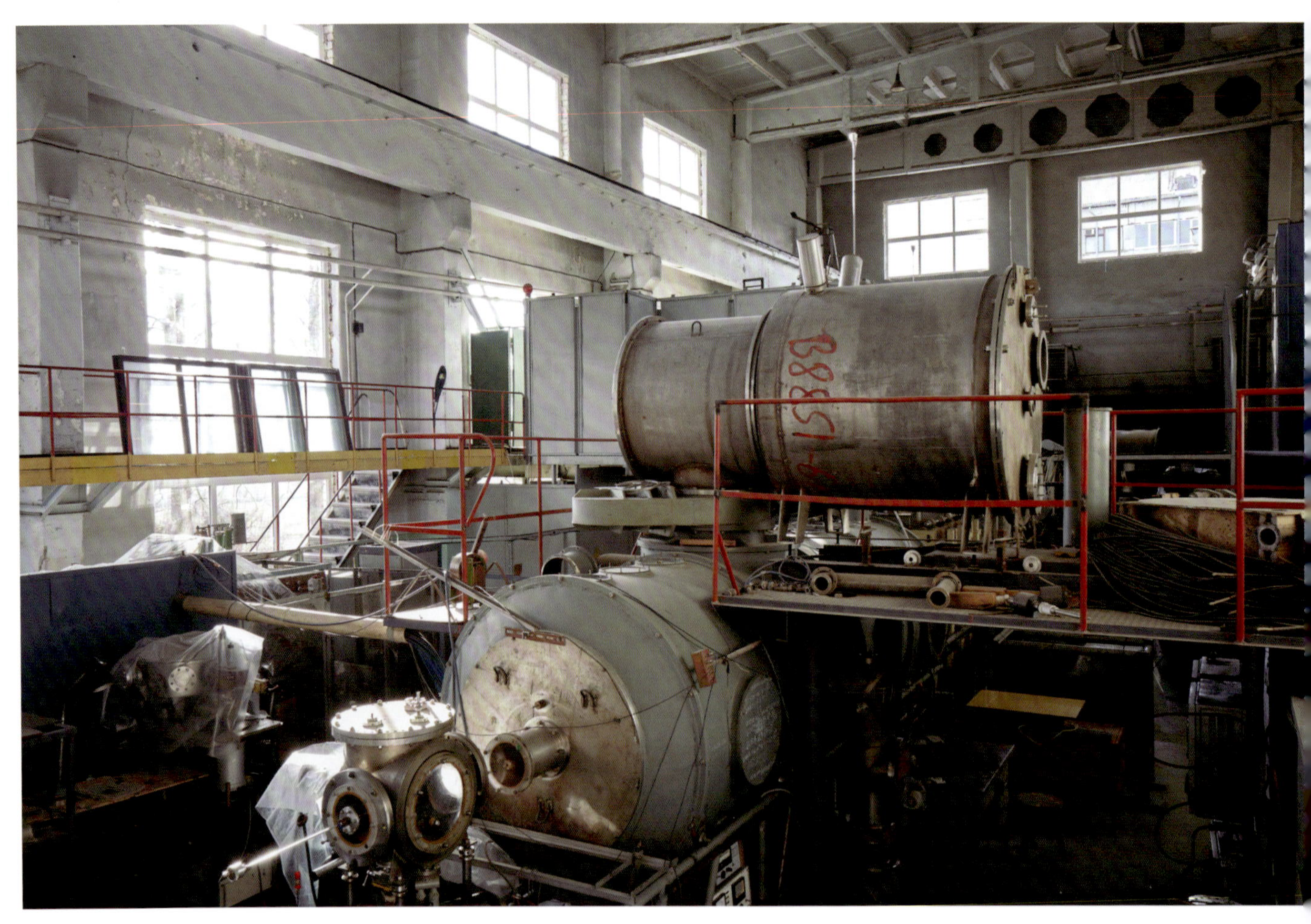

The quasi-stationary plasma accelerator, QSPA Kh-50, simulates effects of intense, transient heat loads on the behaviour of materials intended for use in fusion reactors. This allows researchers to investigate the erosion mechanisms (melting, cracking and particle emission) of plasma-facing materials such as tungsten and carbon composites under these intense conditions.

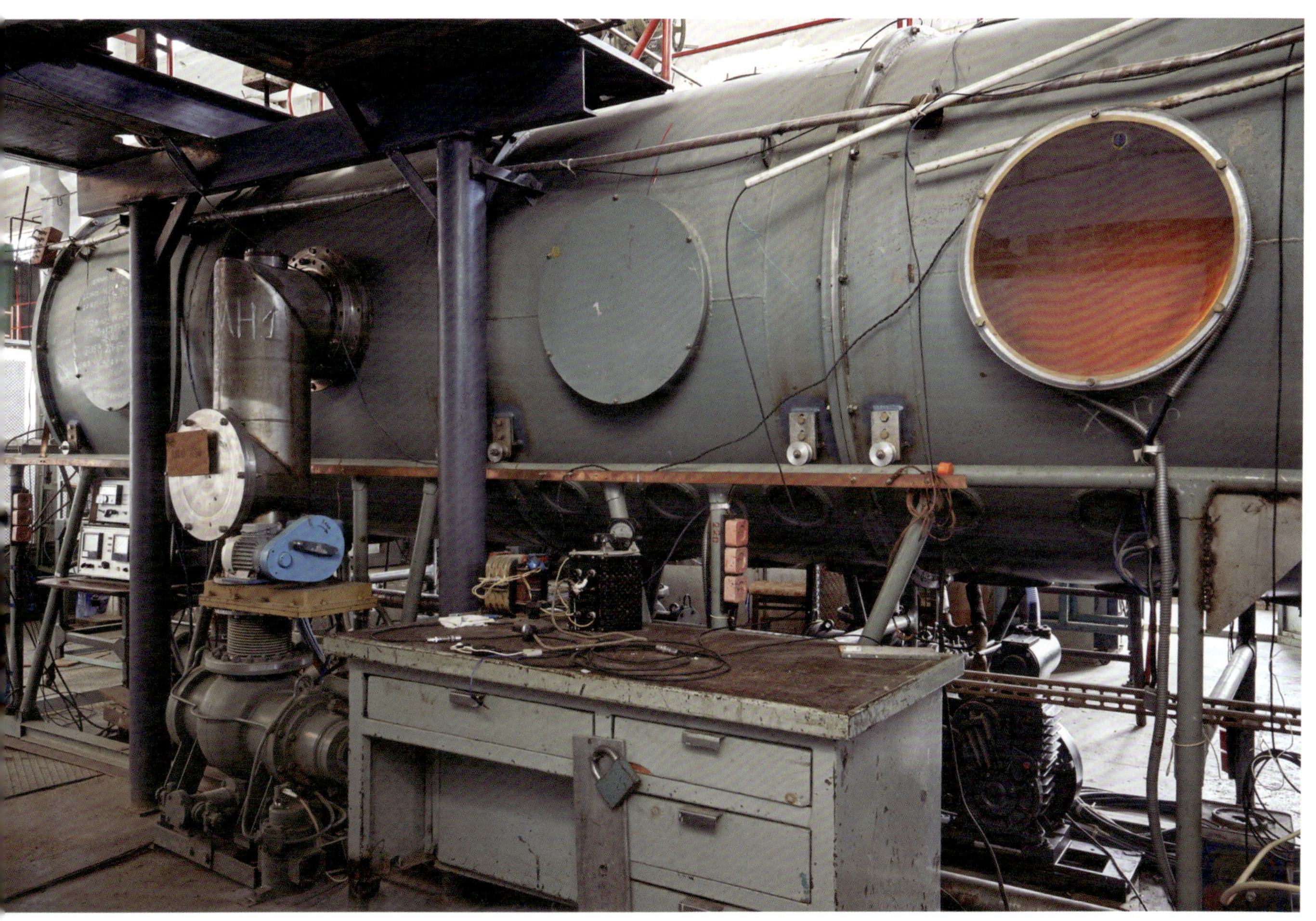

The QSPA Kh-50, began operating in 1990. It is the largest and most powerful quasi-stationary plasma accelerator in the world.

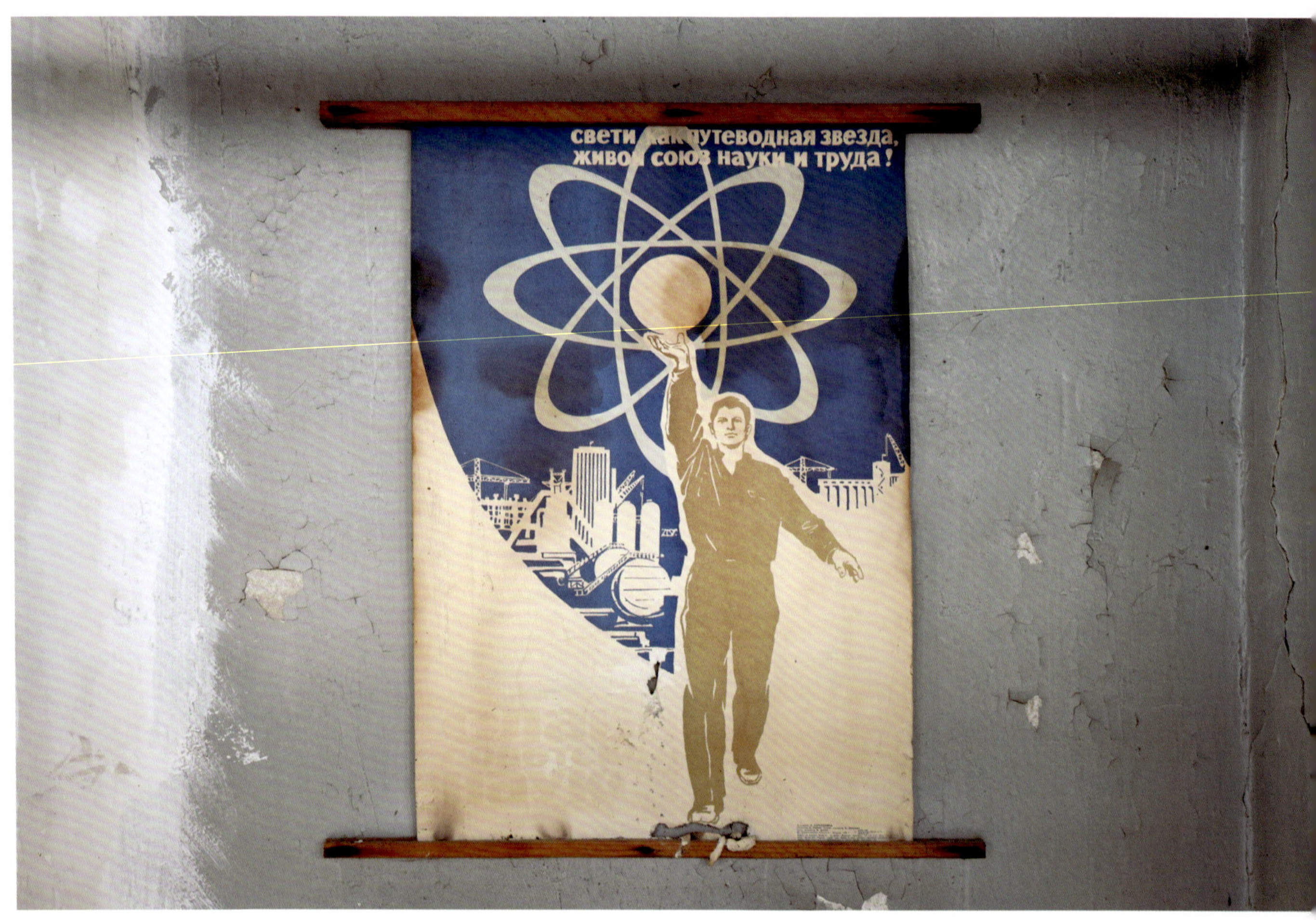

A faded Soviet-era poster, with its red-colour communist symbols and slogans (such as the hammer and sickle) almost completely vanished. The Russian text reads: 'Shine like a guiding star, living union of science and labour! Glory to Soviet Science!'
Right: Posters from the late 1980s celebrate the reforms of Glasnost and Perestroika.

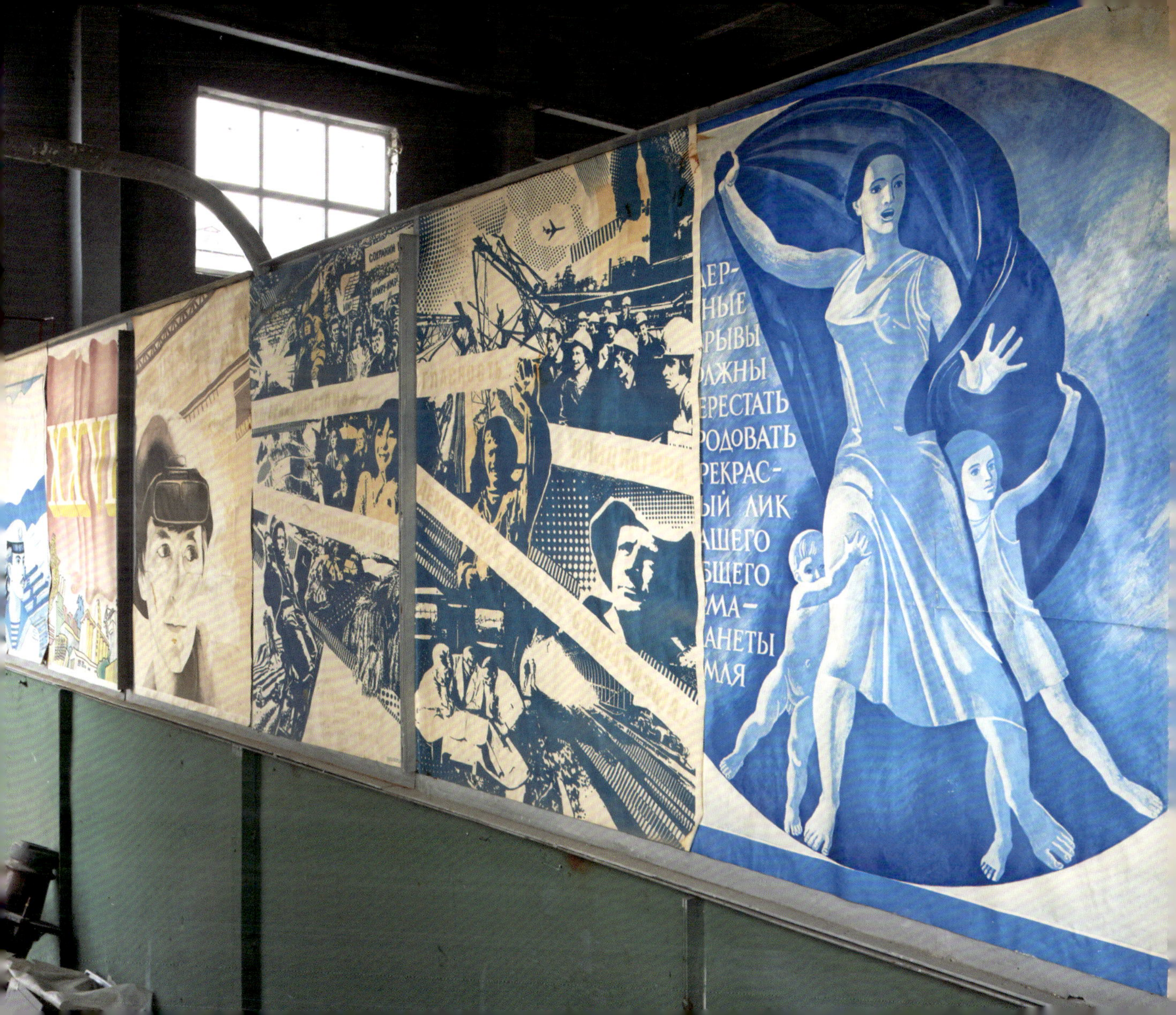

дер-
ные
рывы
лжны
ерестать
родовать
рекрас-
ый лик
ашего
бщего
ма—
анеты
мля

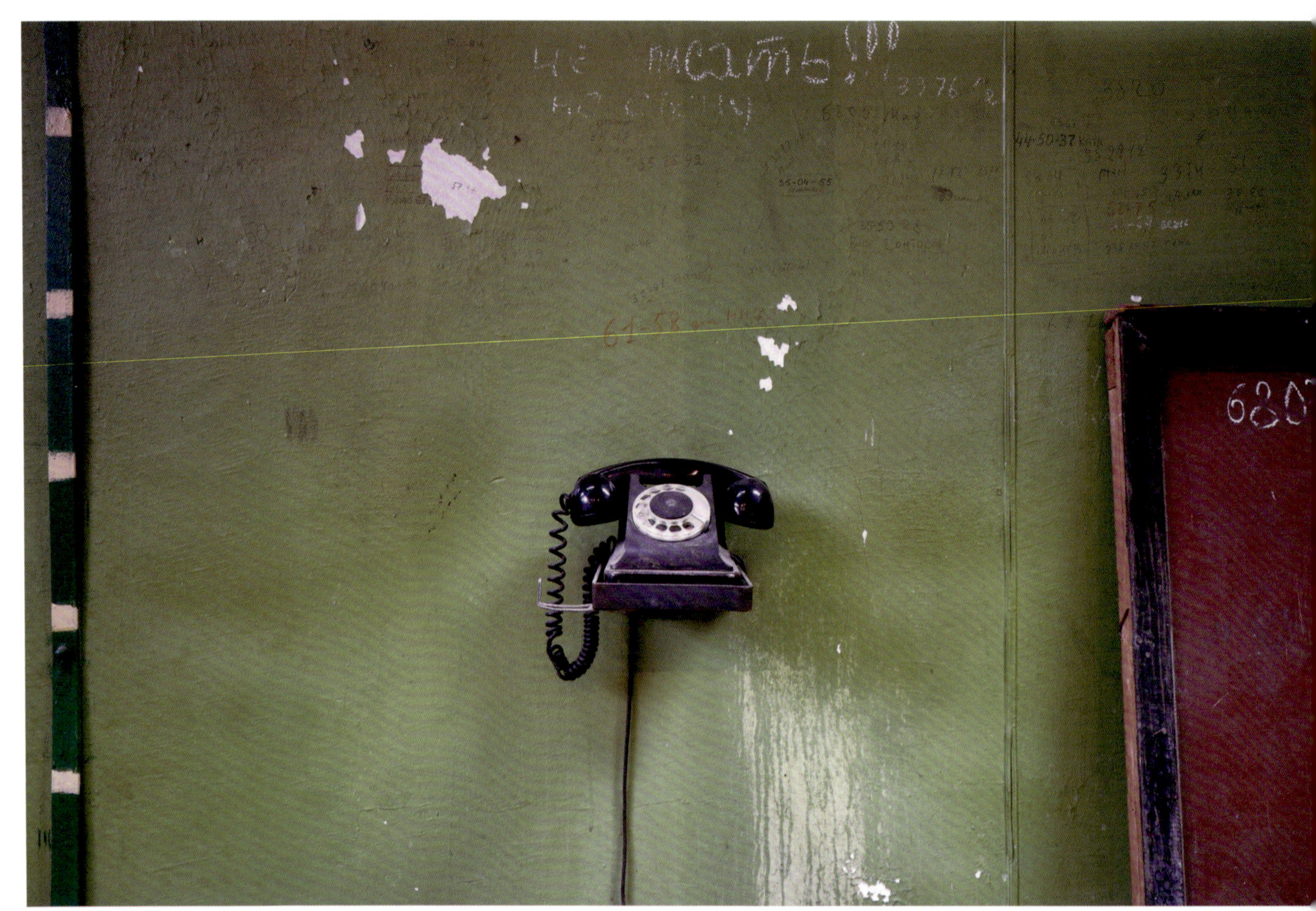

A Soviet-era telephone sits on its dedicated shelf. A command, hand-written on the wall, instructs users: 'Do not write phone numbers on the wall!'

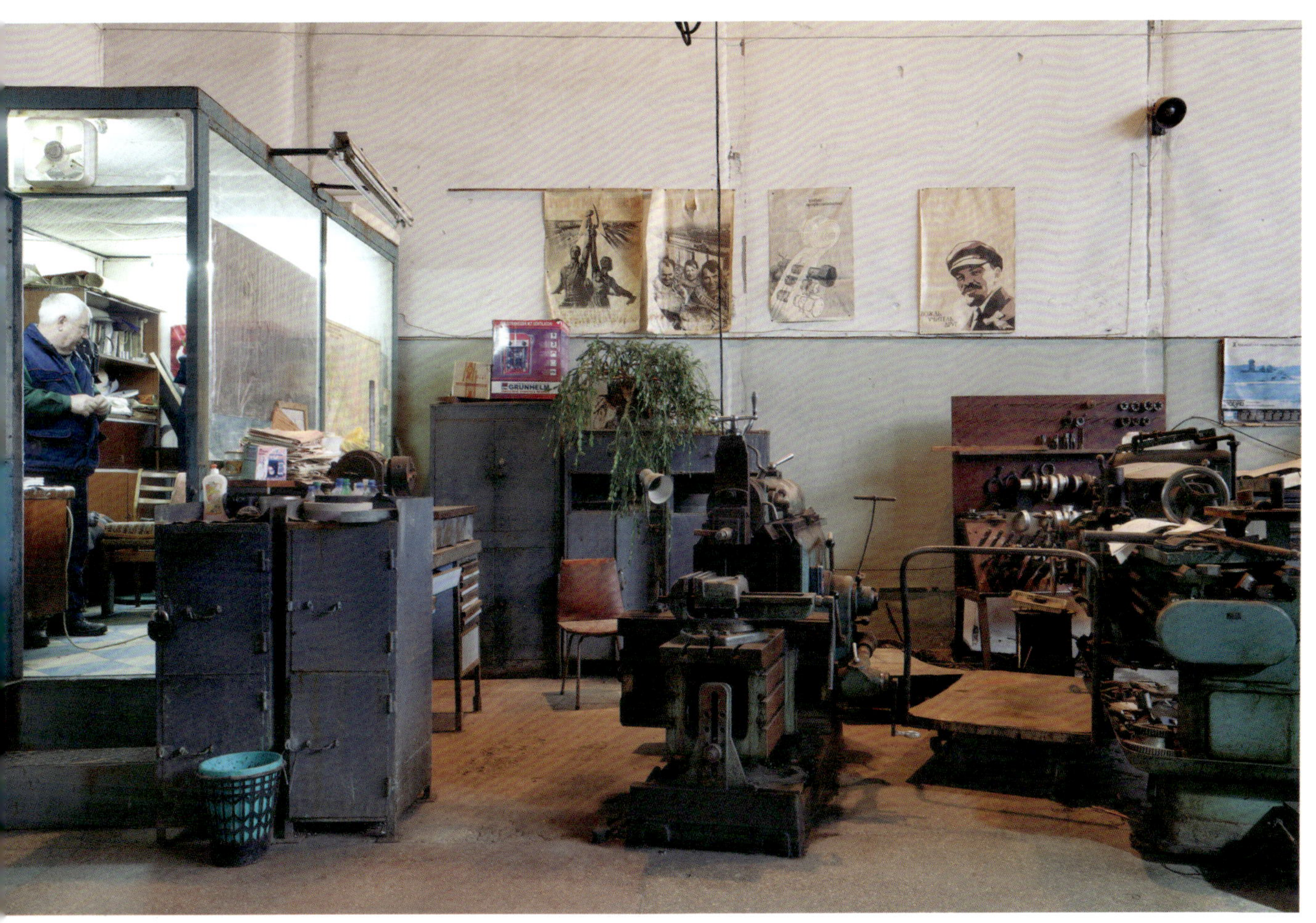

The mechanical workshop. A few faded Soviet-era posters remain pinned to the wall.

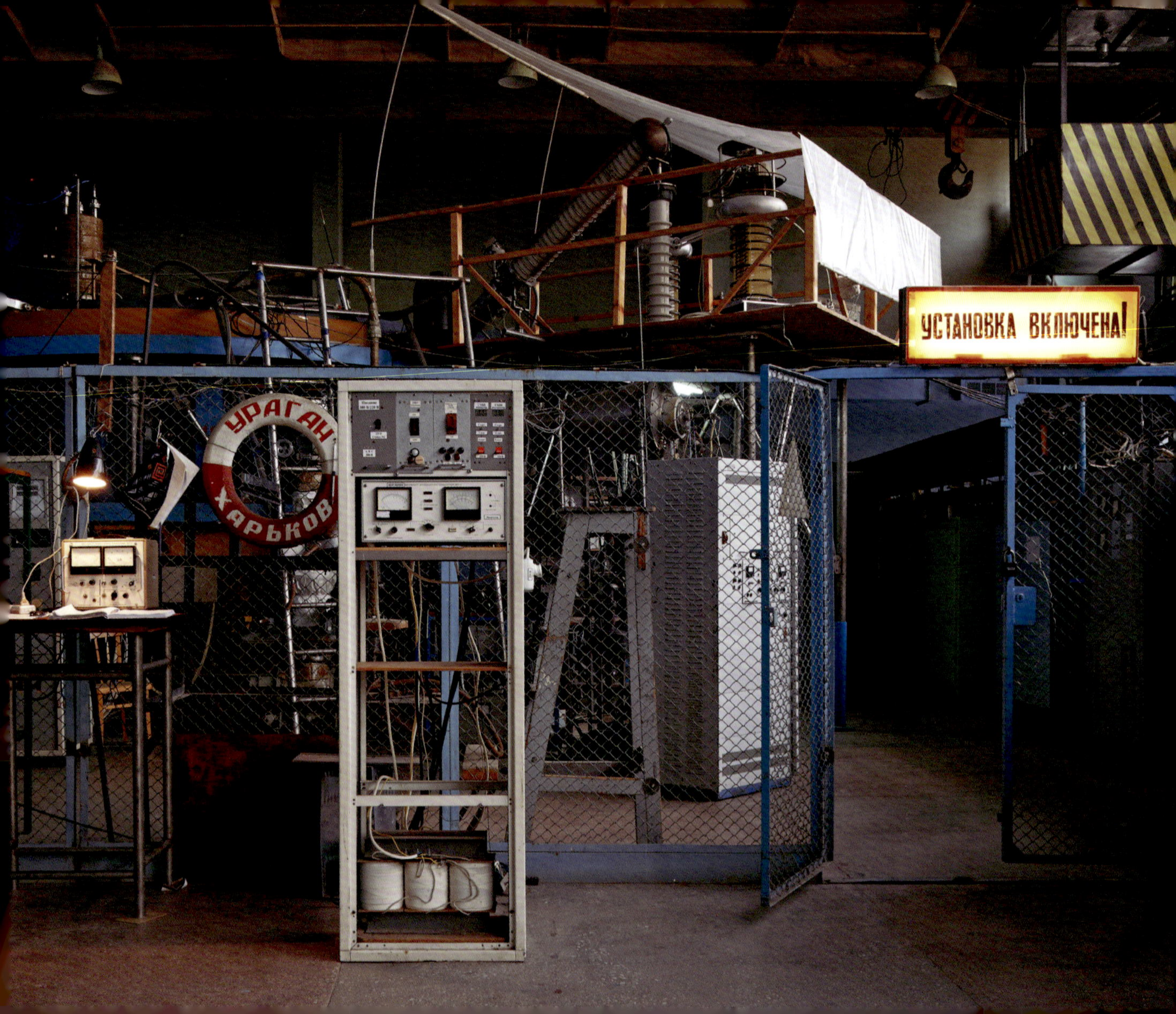
УСТАНОВКА ВКЛЮЧЕНА!
УРАГАН
ХАРЬКОВ

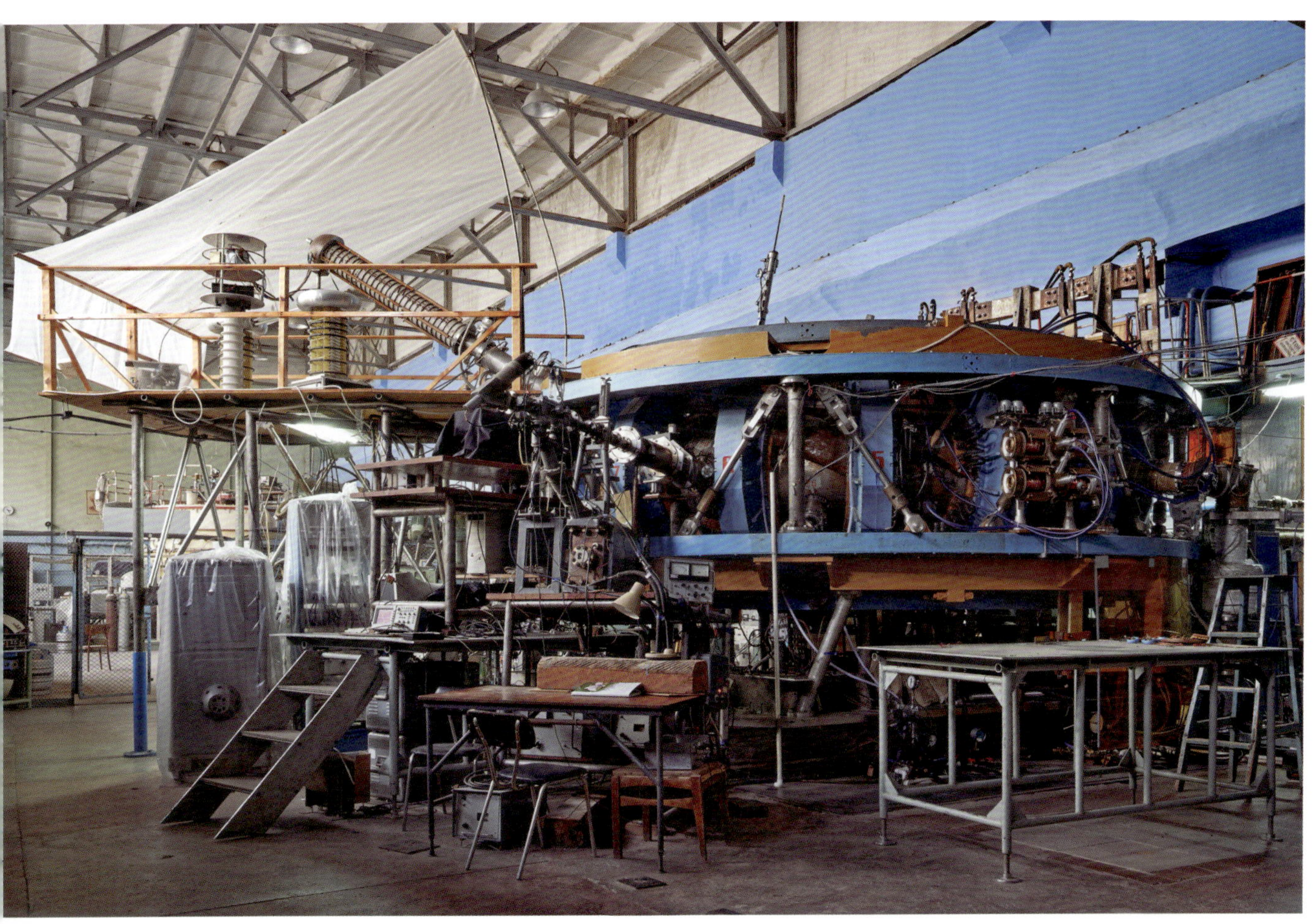

The exterior of the Uragan-2M stellarator.
Left: The entrance to the Uragan-2M. The illuminated sign above the doors reads 'The equipment is on!' The lifebuoy reads
'Uragan – Kharkiv' and hangs next to the stellarator for humorous effect.

INSTITUTE OF MATERIALS SCIENCE

Academy of Sciences of Uzbekistan

Parkent, UZBEKISTAN

Nestled in the foothills of the Tien Shan mountains, 50 kilometres from the capital Tashkent, the Big Solar Furnace is one of the world's largest solar research facilities. Built in 1981, this monumental installation harnesses the power of the Sun for cutting-edge science.

Uzbekistan has a long history of research into solar energy, which began in 1925 with the use of actinometry (the measurement of radiant energy using chemical reactions) at the Uzbek Hydro-meteorological Institute. In 1934 a helio-laboratory was established in Tashkent, focusing on agricultural and industrial uses, eventually paving the way for the creation of the solar furnace.

There are only two furnaces of this type in the world. The first was built in France and began operating in 1969. The decision to construct a Soviet counterpart was made in the 1970s, after a suitable location had been selected. Receiving between 280 and 320 days of sunshine per year and being situated at an altitude of 1,050 metres above sea level where the thinner air increases furnace efficiency, the facility was also built on a rocky outcrop for protection against earthquakes.

Construction took place from 1981 to 1986, and the facility began operations in 1987. The scientific helio-complex comprises the main building, the heliostat field, the concentrator and the technological tower. The main concentrator is made up of 10,700 individual mirrors arranged on a vast parabolic dish. Sunlight is first reflected onto the concentrator by 62 large, automatically controlled heliostats, which track the Sun's movement. The concentrator then focuses the solar energy onto to a single point where the target object is placed. Here, the temperature is capable of reaching 3,000 °C almost instantly.

The function of the furnace is one of research into high-temperature physics and chemistry, and the development of new advanced high-entropy materials. One application of this technology is hard sharpening, whereby a material is toughened by very rapid heating and cooling – a process unachievable by any other method.

A further advantage of solar radiation is that it does not cause pollution through combustion when generating heat. This allows materials of a very high purity to be obtained, such as refractory alloys, heat-resistant and high-voltage electrical ceramics, artificial gems (ruby, garnet, spinel, sapphire, etc.) and other substances. These innovations are in high demand in the varied industries of optics, nuclear, oil and gas power, etc.

During the Soviet period the furnace was used to test the efficacy of the Buran spaceplane's thermal shielding. Today the facility is used for civilian research and specialist industrial orders.

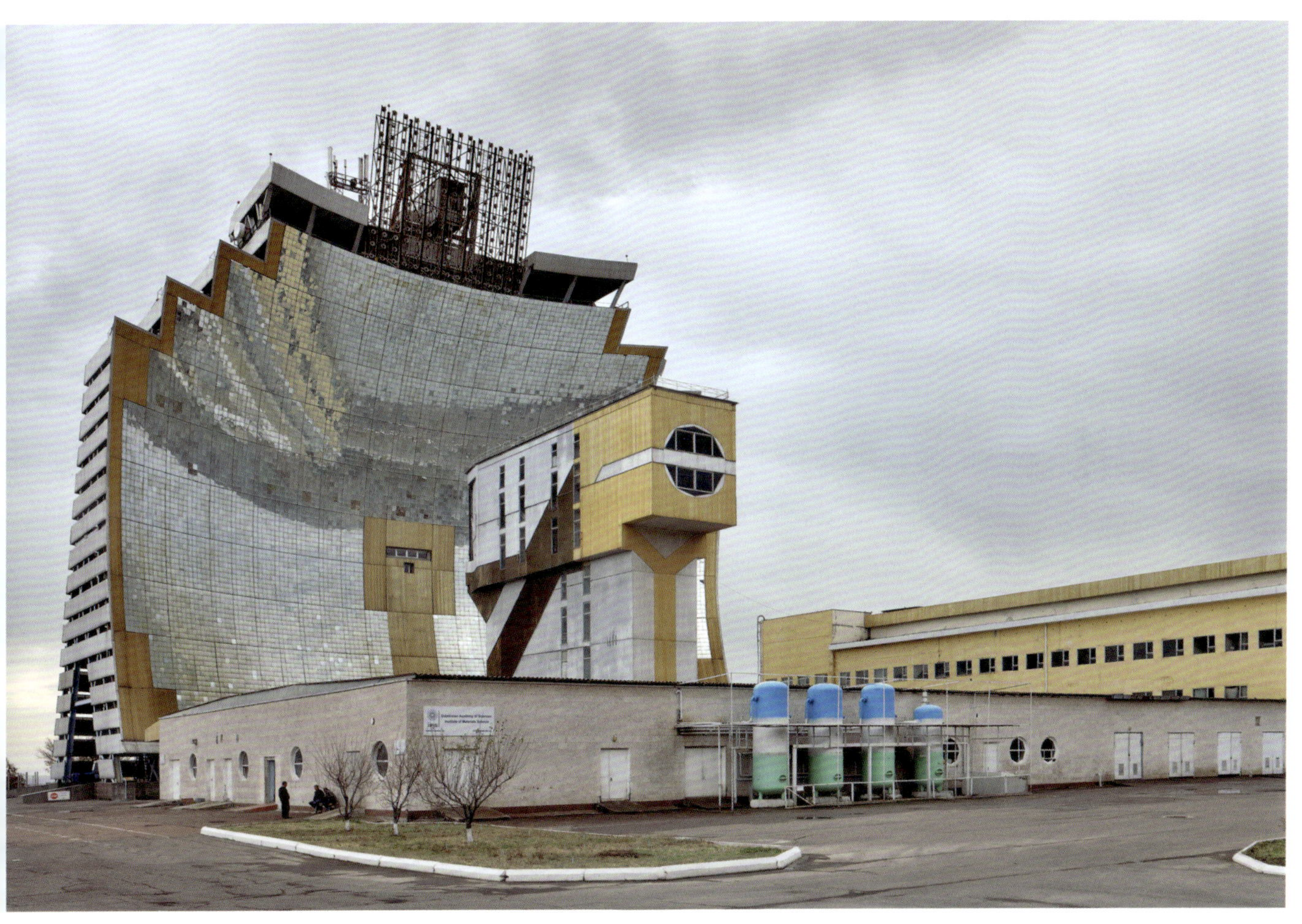

The solar energy concentrator uses 10,700 mirrors to focus light reflected from an array of heliostats onto a single focal point.

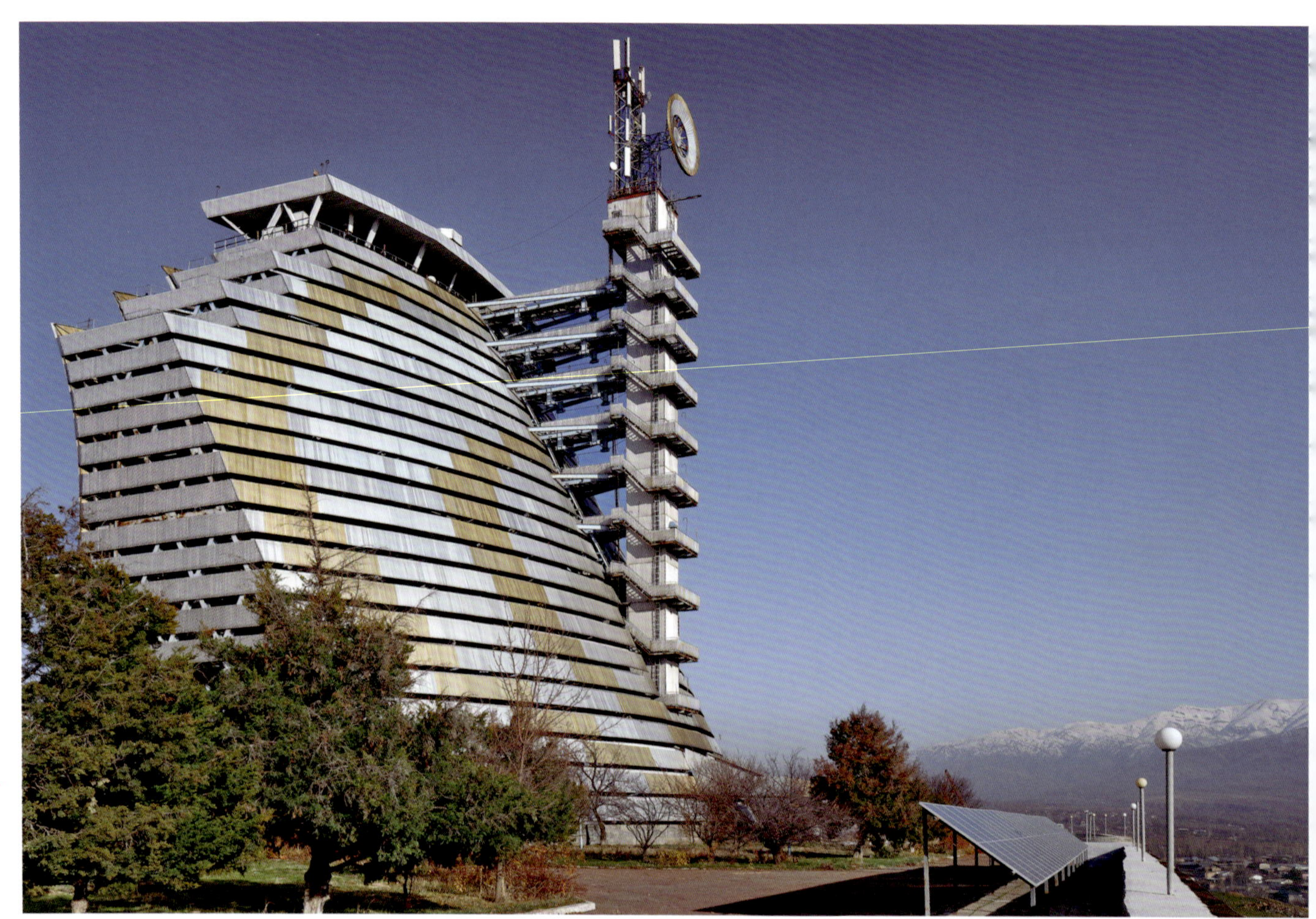

The concentrator is 54 metres high and 47 metres wide.

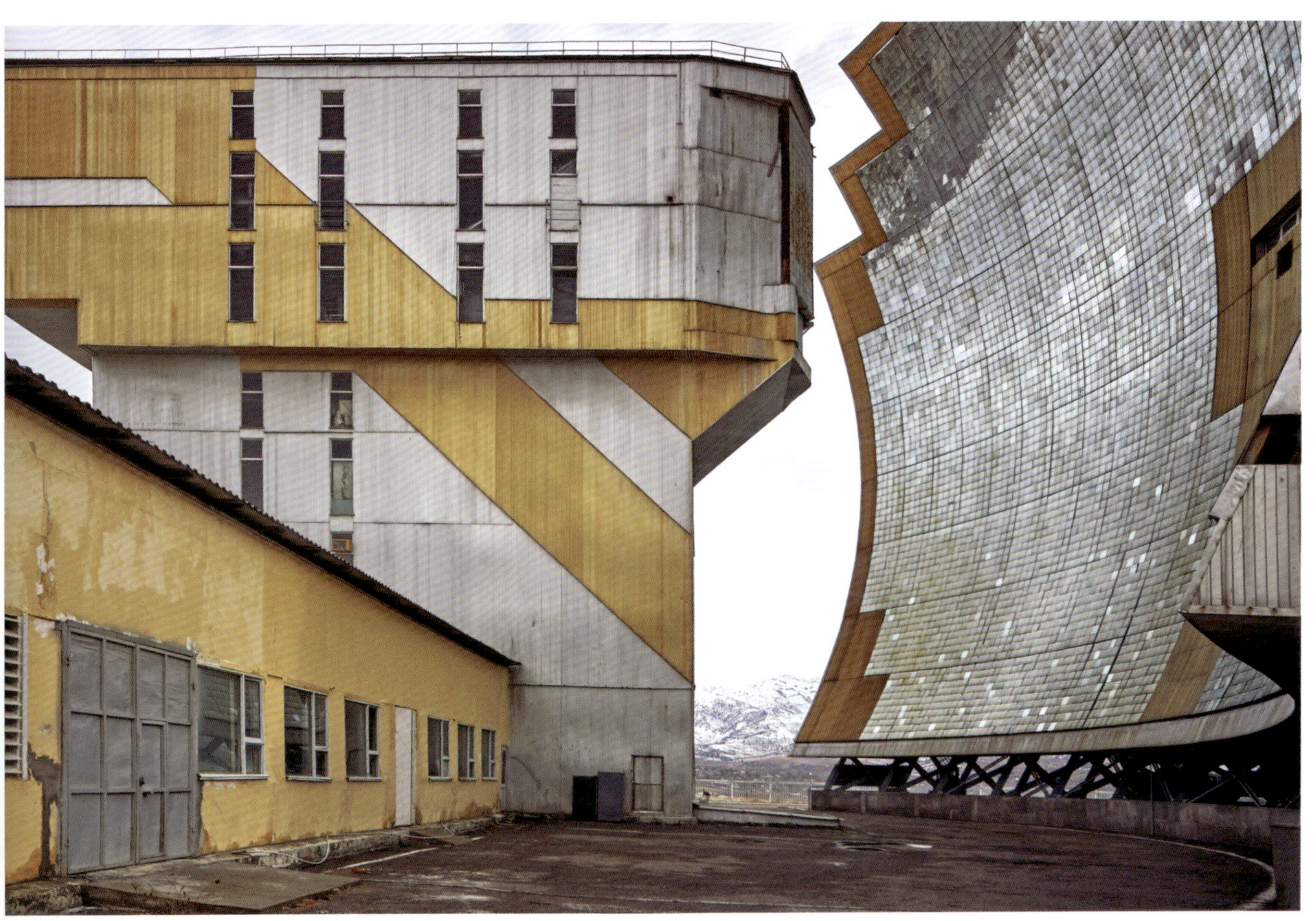

The technology tower containing the furnace is situated 18 metres away, at the focal length of the paraboloid concentrator.

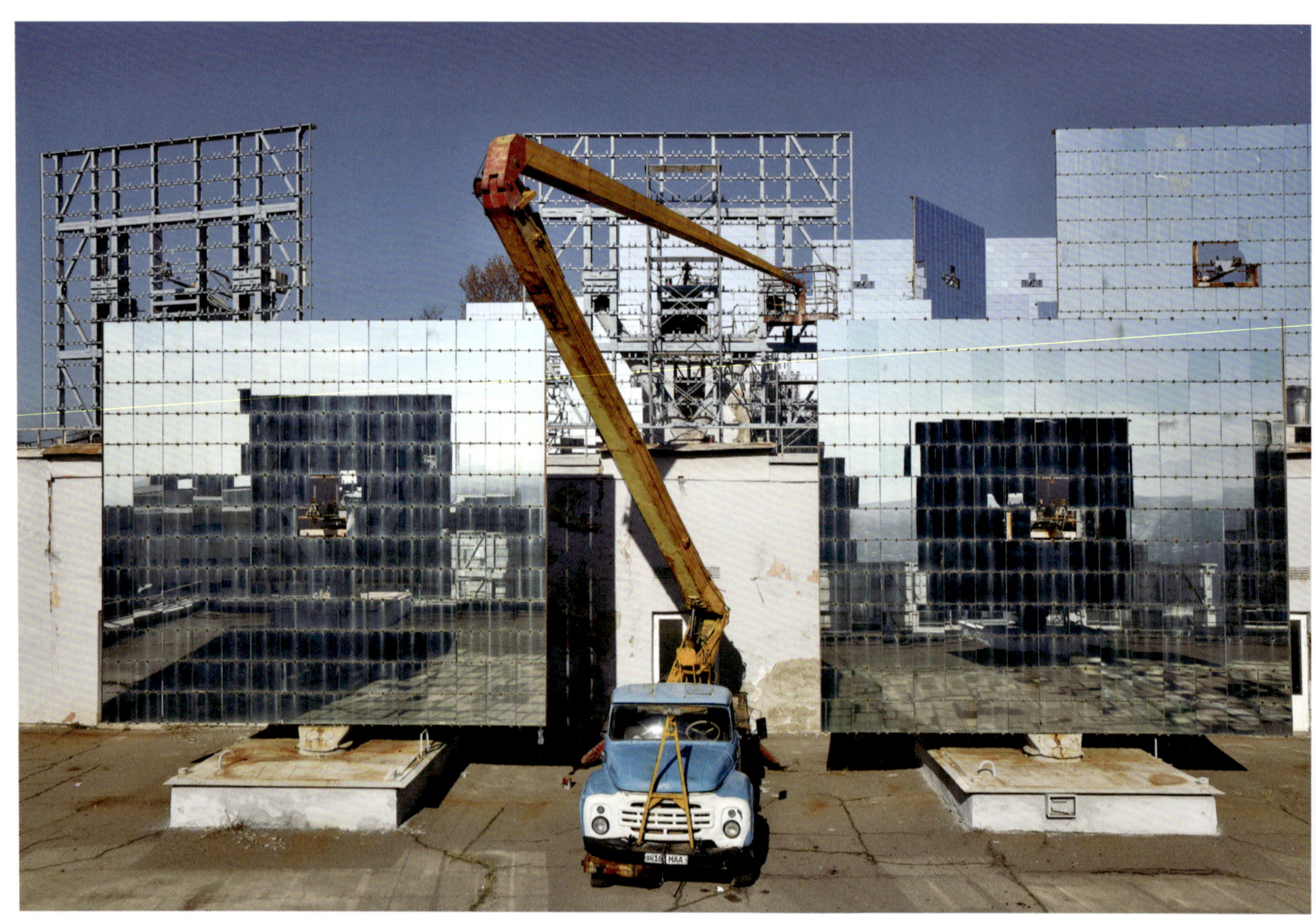

The heliostat field, which directs sunlight onto the concentrator, consists of 62 blocks. Each one measures 7.5 × 6.5 metres and is comprised of 195 individual mirrors, measuring 0.5 × 0.5 metres each. The system requires constant maintenance, with mirrors frequently needing replacement.

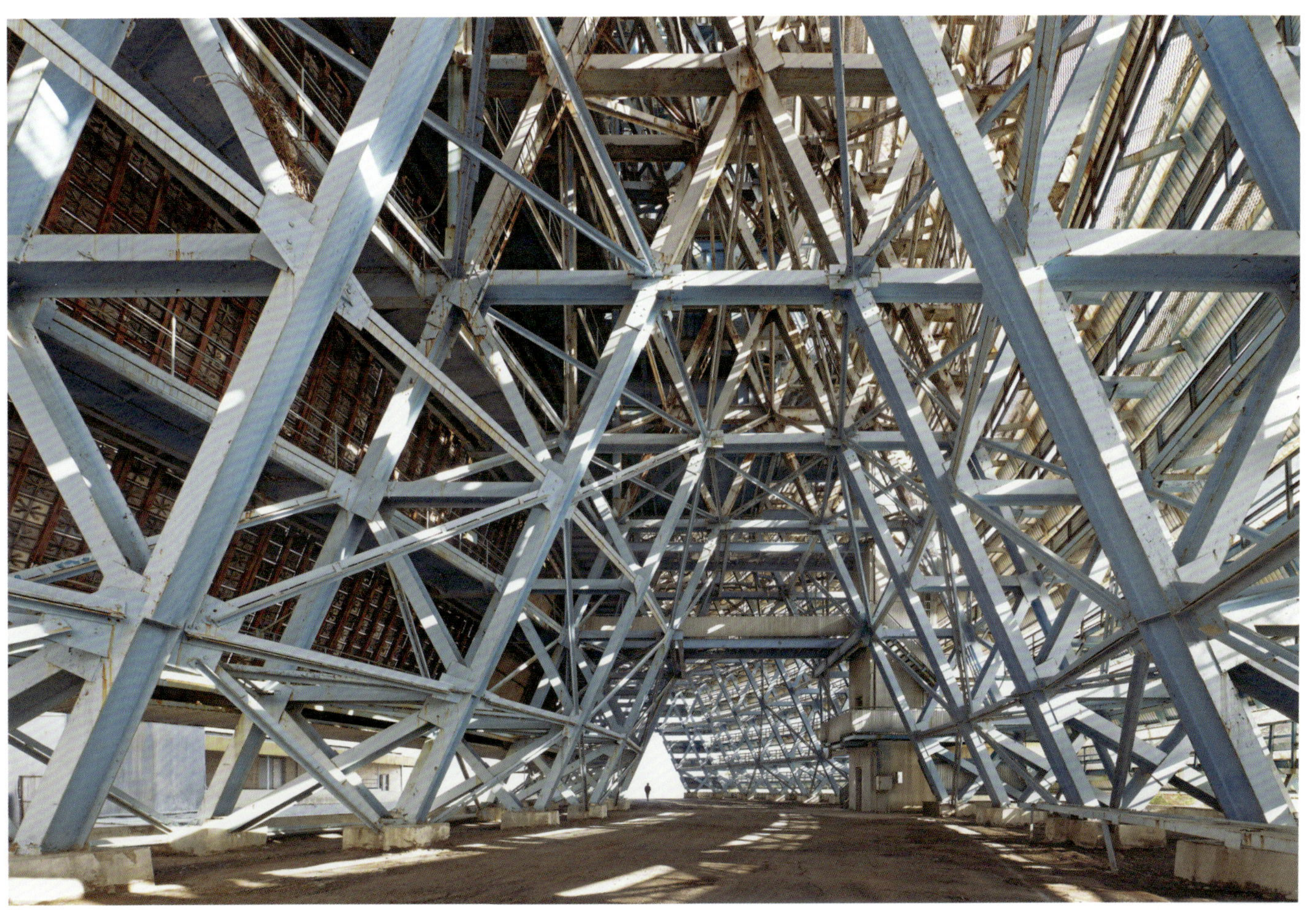

The metal structure of the paraboloid-shaped concentrator.

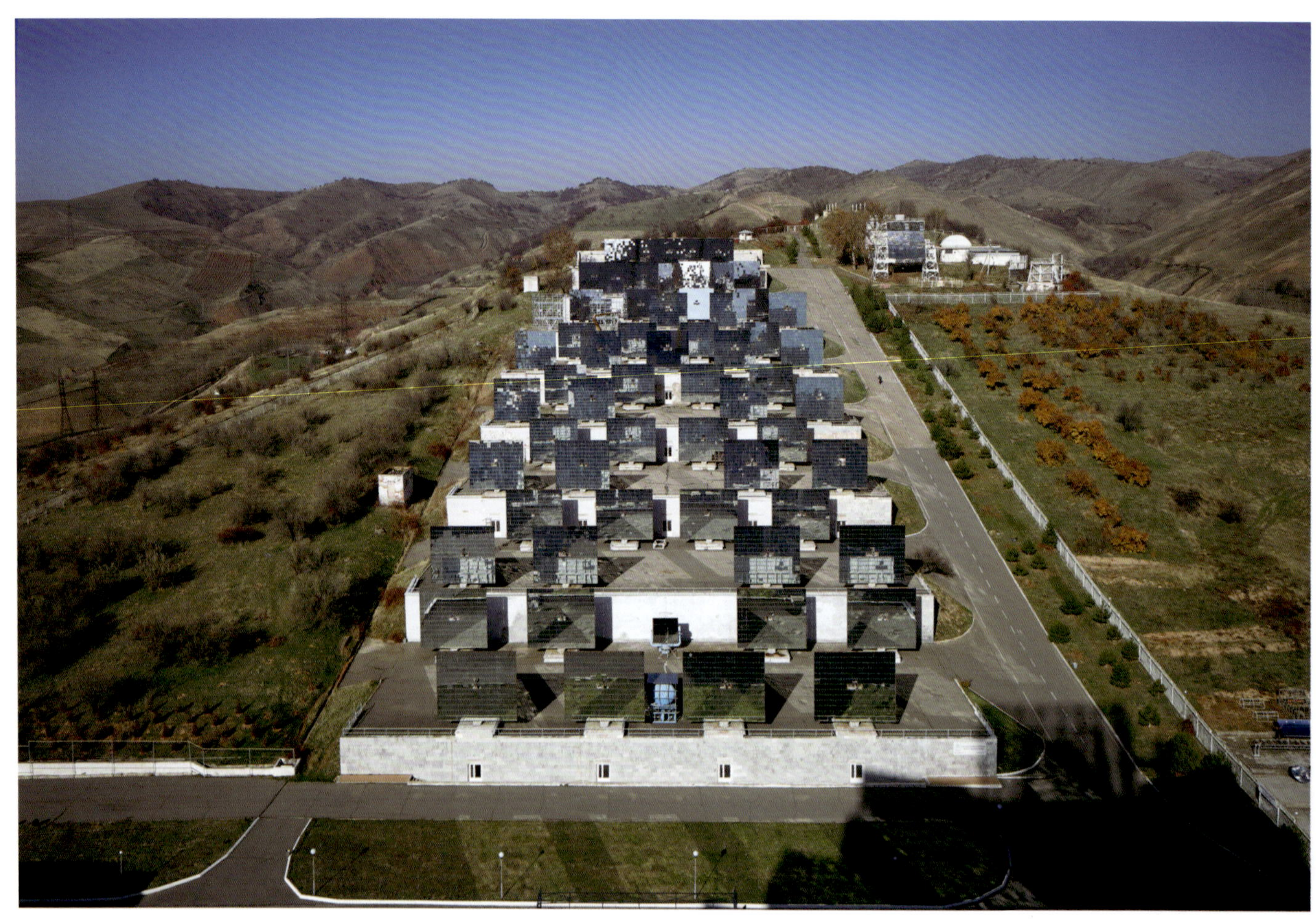

In order to reduce the issue of mutual shading, the heliostats set across a slope on eight tiered terraces, in a staggered, chequerboard formation. Sensors and an automatic control system track the Sun, adjusting the position of each heliostat in unison, to reflect sunlight precisely onto the concentrator.

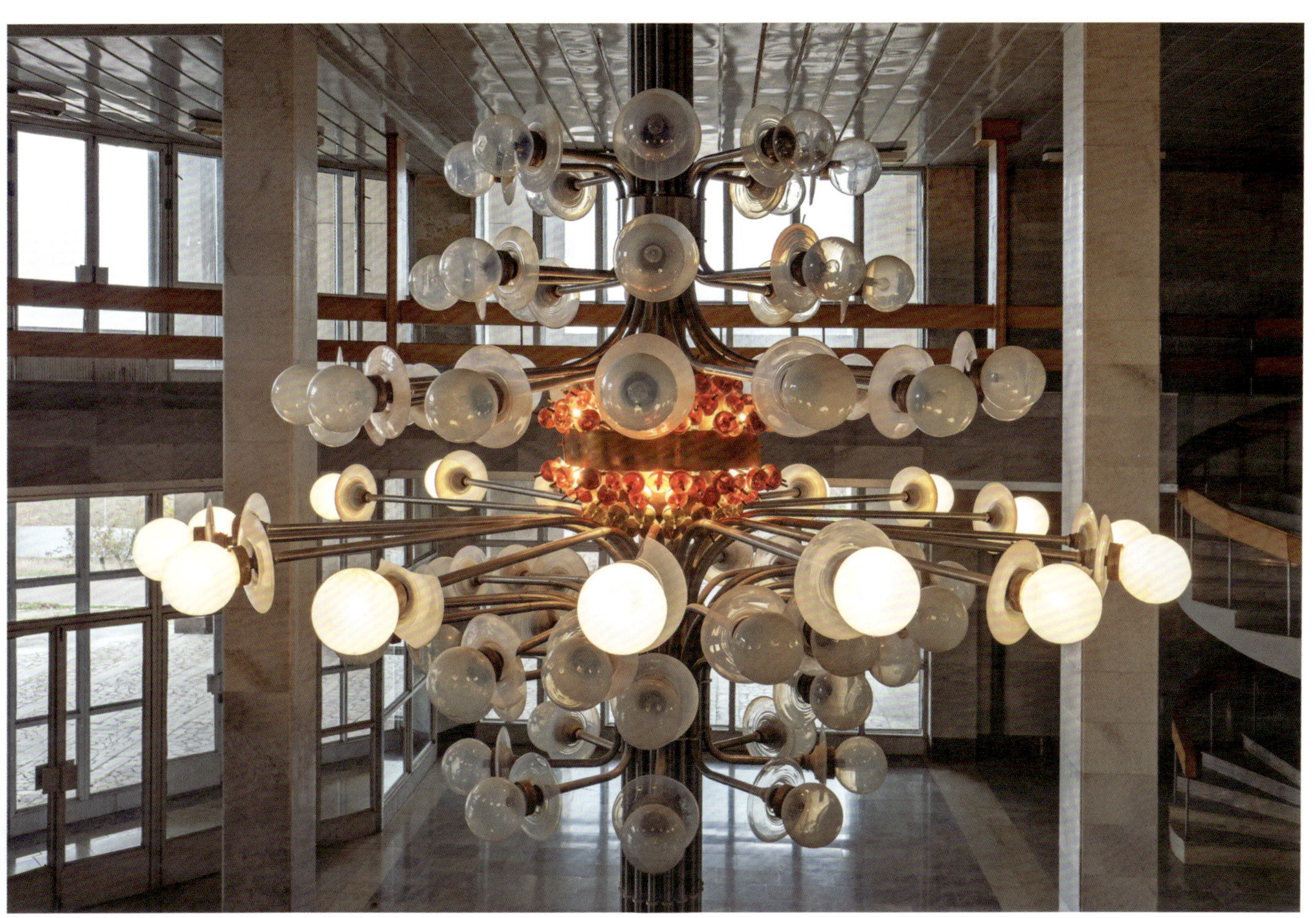

Created by Lithuanian stained-glass artist Irena Lipene (1939–2016), the 'Moon' chandelier is situated in the institute foyer.
Overleaf: The concentrator.

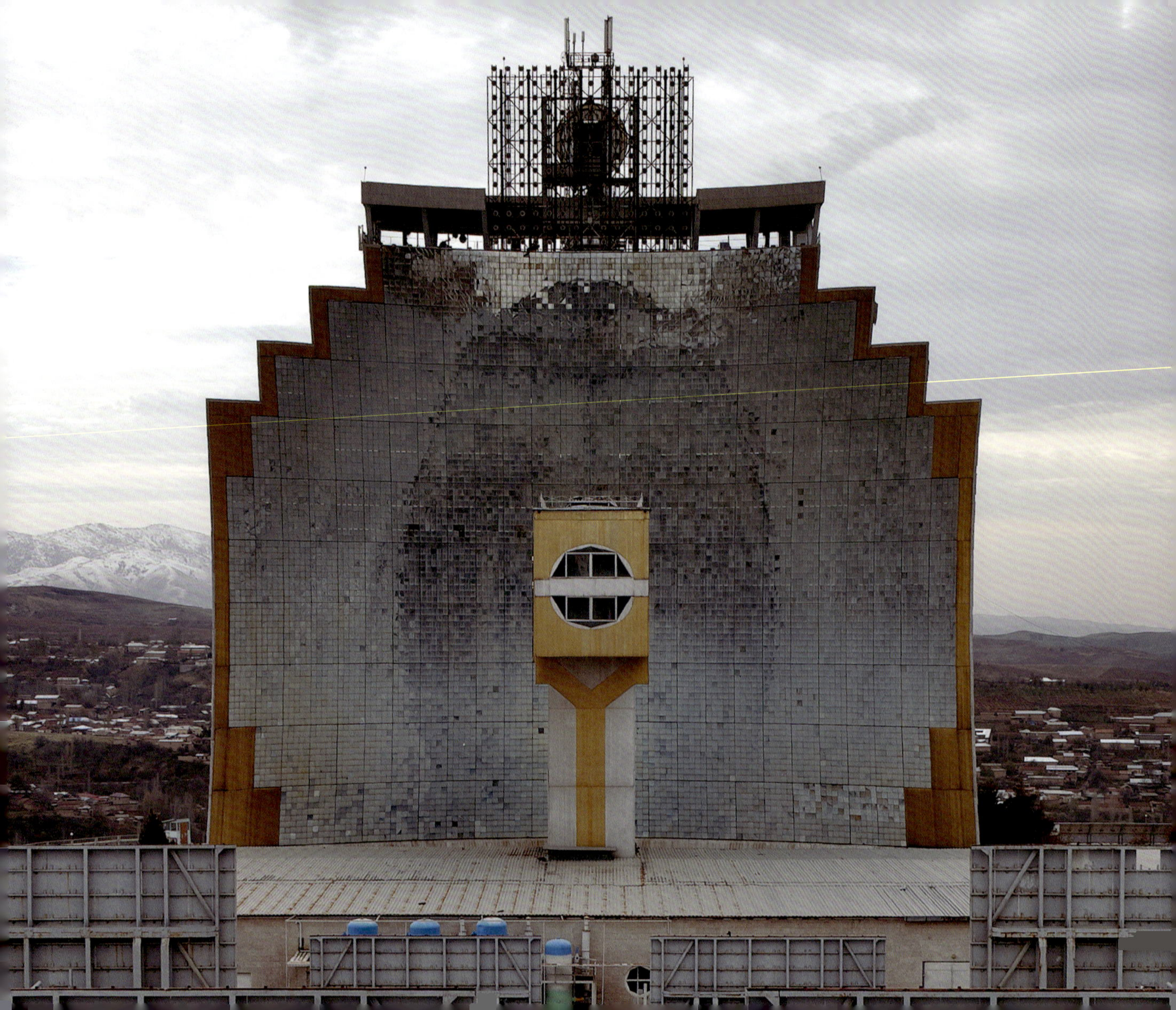

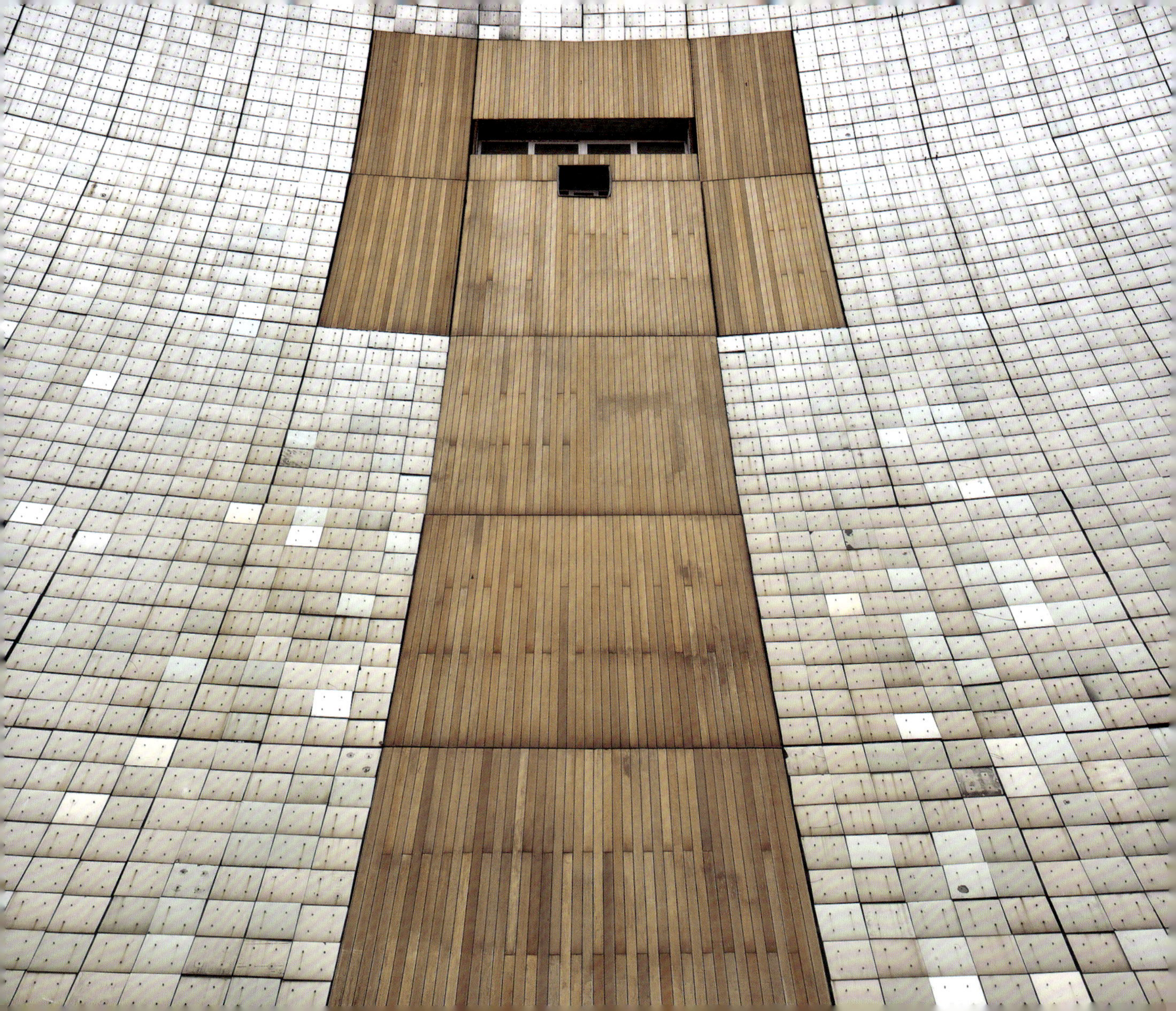

AFTERWORD
Eric Lusito

The geographical isolation, the silence, large halls with few people. A hushed and austere atmosphere, very different from the hustle and bustle of a factory. Several times, as I entered these research institutes, I had the impression of stepping into a temple, guided by enthusiastic priests who led me towards their technological oracles, capable of revealing the secrets of the universe to the initiated. Oracles were institutions of the ancient world, sacred sites and intermediaries between gods and mortals. In Greece, an 'enthusiast' was someone who received the gift of divination. The term 'enthusiasm' is also used to describe the state of exaltation experienced by an artist in the throes of inspiration.

'There are always flowers for those who want to see them,' wrote the French painter Henri Matisse. This scientific world sparked my imagination. Initially, it reminded me of the comic books from my childhood, such as those by Hergé and Edgar P. Jacobs. Science played an important role in their work, and both Belgian cartoonists were renowned for their attention to detail and realism. Jacobs was notably influenced by the English writer H.G. Wells, known as the 'father of science fiction'. While we cannot travel with a time machine, a photograph can effectively reflect the past: an image from a high-voltage laboratory reveals that it was established in 1930 and has changed little in a century. Still in operation, more vibrant than a museum or abandoned site, it remains an authentic testament to the dedication of the people who have worked there over time.

A scientist once explained to me that a big physics facility resembles the course of human life. After birth comes a learning period of 10 to 20 years, followed by a long period of maturity, when the facility is at its best. This is inevitably followed by a decline in its scientific value – the normal process of the technological cycle. Researchers showed me their new equipment, but I felt no inspiration in a room full of modern computers. I was drawn to analogue instruments, even though some of them were obsolete. We live in an increasingly virtual world, but these machines have a tangible presence. Their functional and aesthetic characters bestow on them a special aura, rendering them remarkable objects. Like the instinctive itch one has to play the keys of a piano, these buttons, dials and levers stir an innate desire to experiment. Fortunately, I was permitted only to take photographs.

The scientists I met cherish these facilities that have been a part of their lives for decades, but not in a nostalgic way. They do everything they can to maintain and upgrade them, looking towards the future, despite the difficulties they encounter. From the grip of the Soviet totalitarian regime to its collapse, and the aftermath that still reverberates today, their motivation to pursue their research – even during a time of war – is truly heroic. Through difficult times Ukrainian science endures. The bombing of cities has caused significant damage to more than a third of buildings belonging to scientific institutions. Despite this devastation Ukrainian scientists stand resolute. We may not realise it, but their future achievements will benefit us all.

You can help Ukrainian science using these links:

Donations to the National Research Foundation of Ukraine:
https://nrfu.org.ua/en/fundraising_en/
To support the Ukrainian academic community:
https://scienceforukraine.eu
To send equipment, the ILO Ukraine initiative provides logistical support: https://rilogistica.eu/guidelines-ilo/
To help a particular institute in Kharkiv, please contact Dr Sergii Pugach, National Science Centre Kharkiv Institute of Physics and Technology (projectoffice@kipt.kharkov.ua).

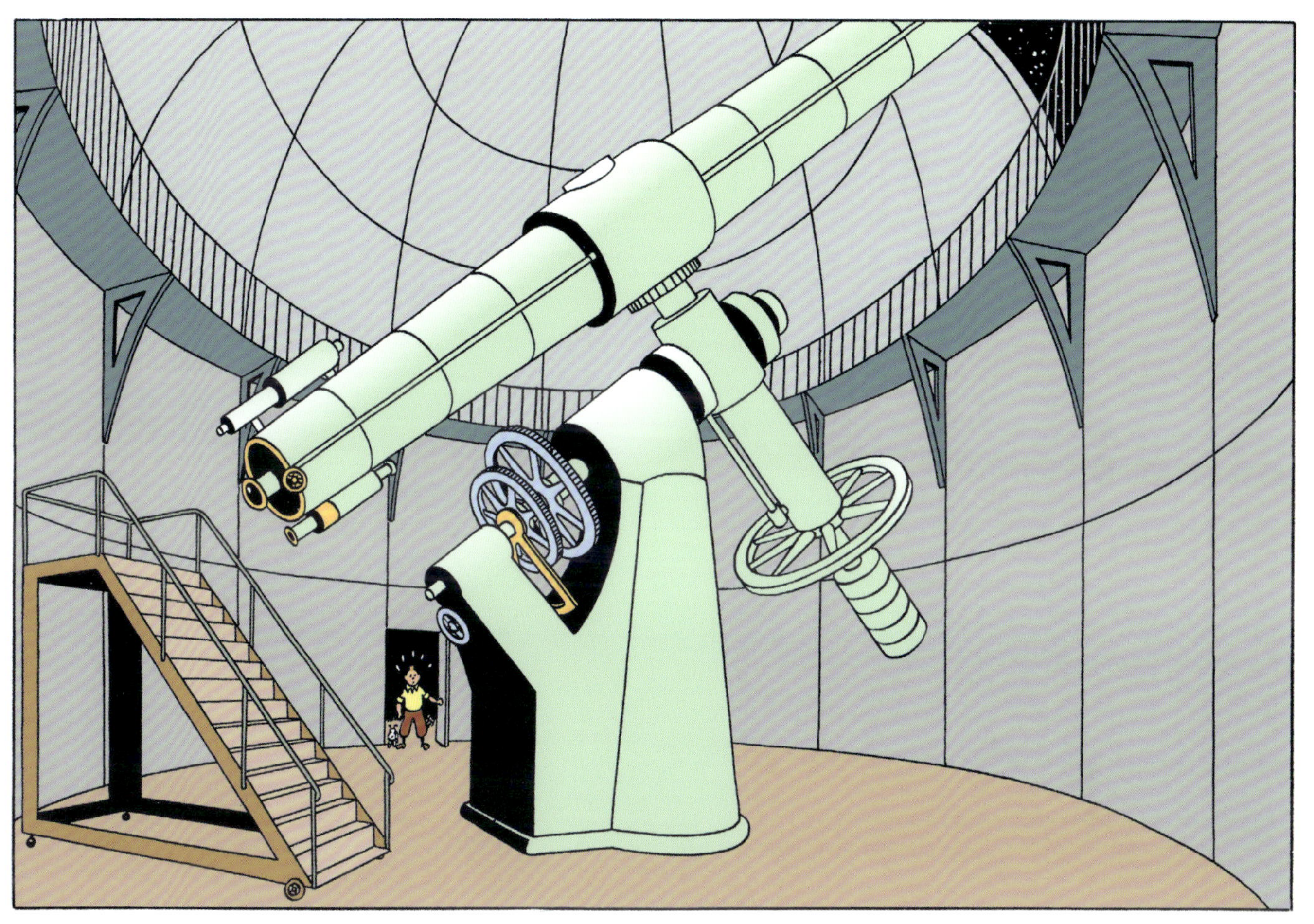

From *The Adventures of Tintin, The Shooting Star*, 1942

Eric Lusito is a French photographer who has been travelling in the former Soviet bloc since the 2000s. In Kharkiv in 2021, he met a scientist who agreed to show him his laboratory. The facility reminded him of the comic books of his childhood, inspiring him to begin this project, exploring this rarely documented world of science.

Paul Josephson, professor emeritus in history, Colby College, has studied big science and technology across the globe for over four decades. In former Soviet spaces he has stepped into research institutes from the Kola Peninsula and the Arctic Circle to the Ural Mountains and Siberia, and from Ukraine to Bulgaria, Hungary, the Czech Republic and the Baltic states.

Published in 2026

FUEL Design & Publishing
33 Fournier Street
London E1 6QE

fuel-design.com
@fuelpublishing

Designed and edited by Murray & Sorrell FUEL
Photographs and text © Eric Lusito
Introduction © Paul Josephson
Copy edited by FUEL and Fergal Stapleton
Page 207 © Hergé, Tintinimaginatio

Distribution by Thames & Hudson / D. A. P.
ISBN: 978-1-0682946-0-0
Printed in China

EU Authorised Representative: Interart S.A.R.L.
19 rue Charles Auray, 93500 Pantin, Paris, France
www.interart.fr

The historical and scientific information provided in the texts is only intended to give the photographs context. In the editing process some details may have been simplified or omitted due to limited space.

Endpapers:
1: Nebula near Cygnus. Astrophysical Institute, Kazakhstan.
2: Nebula M16. Astrophysical Institute, Kazakhstan.
3: Halley's Comet photographed in 1986. Astrophysical Institute, Kazakhstan.
4: Electron diffraction analysis of a crystal. Kharkiv Institute of Physics and Technology, Ukraine.
5: The dark nebula region near Cygnus. Astrophysical Institute, Kazakhstan.
6: Glass plate from the First Byurakan Survey, on which the energy spectra of stars were photographed. Byurakan Astrophysical Observatory, Armenia.

Eric Lusito wishes to express his gratitude to the scientists who opened their laboratories, and to thank everyone who has helped him in one way or another over the years.

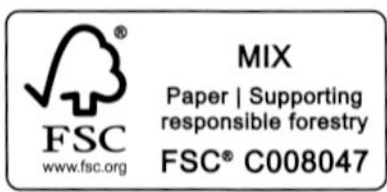

Printed with non mineral ink on FSC®(Forest Stewardship Council) certified paper, EUDR (EU Deforestation Regulation) compliant, from responsibly managed forests and recycled materials, ensuring sustainable forestry practices and environmental protection.

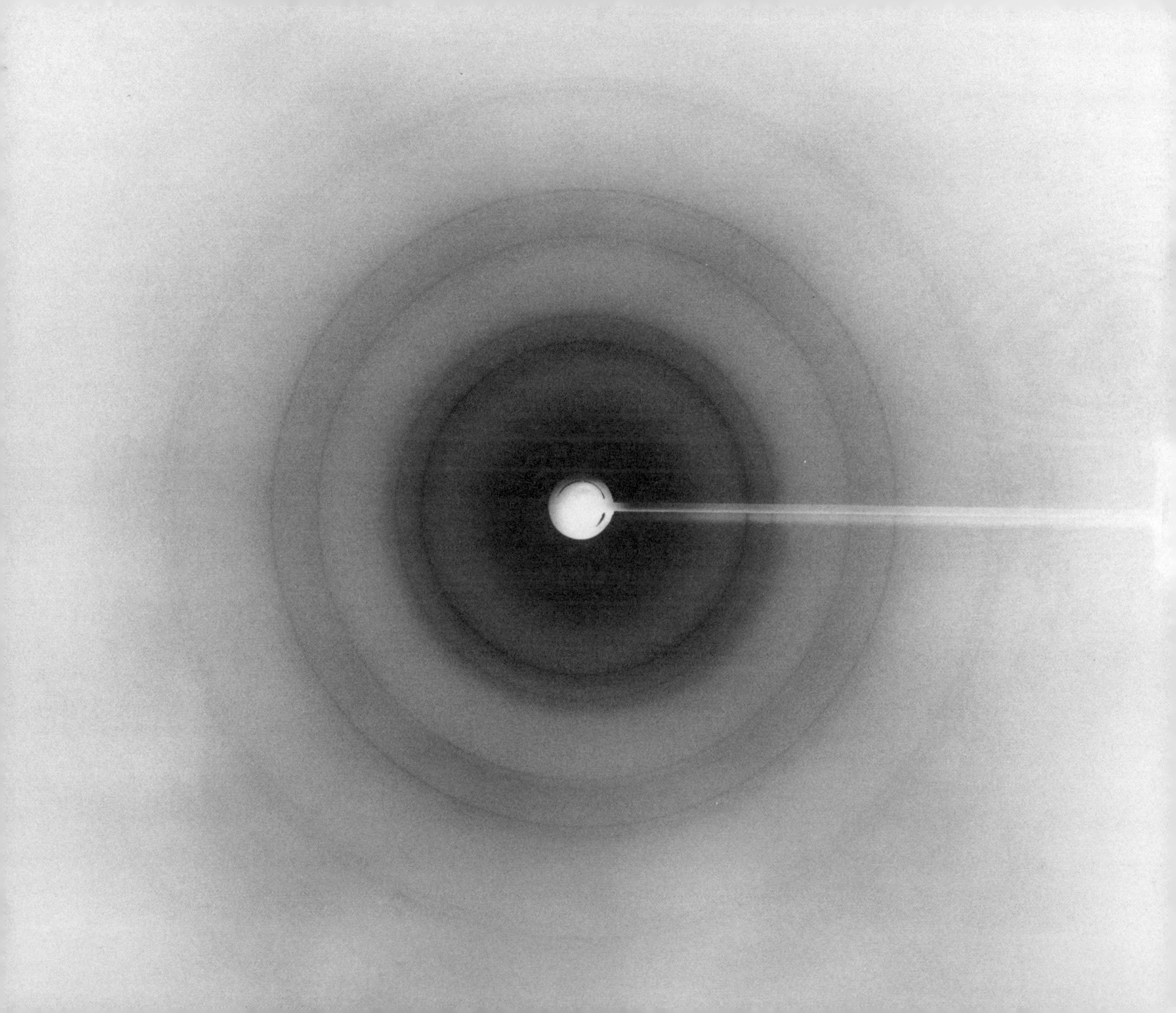

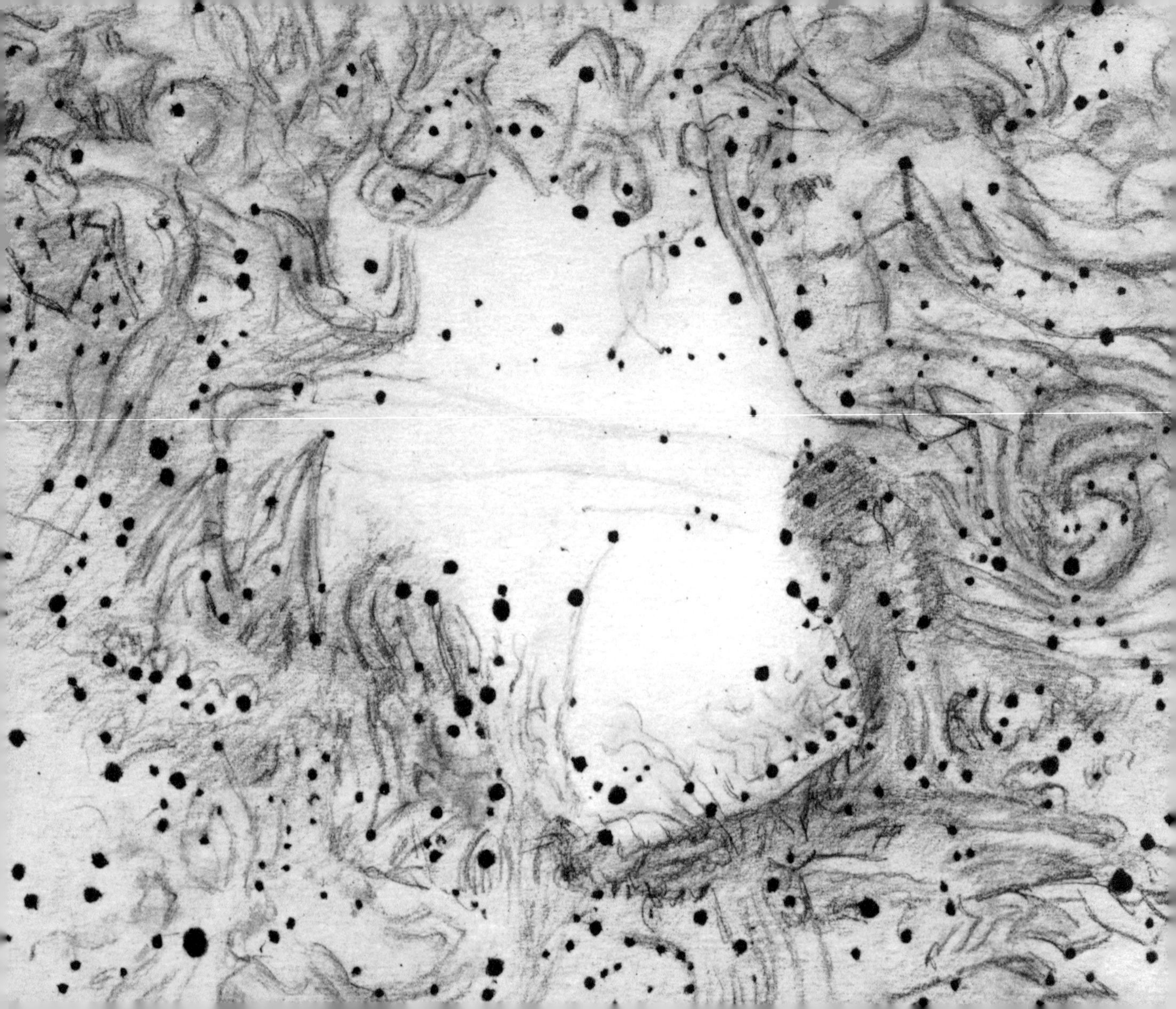